FRONTIERS IN SOCIAL INNOVATION

FRONTIERS IN SOCIAL INNOVATION

EDITED BY
NEIL MALHOTRA

EDITH M. CORNELL
PROFESSOR OF
POLITICAL ECONOMY
STANFORD GRADUATE
SCHOOL OF BUSINESS

Harvard Business Review Press
Boston, Massachusetts

Library of Congress Cataloging-in-Publication Data

Names: Malhotra, Neil Ankur, editor.
  Title: Frontiers in social innovation / edited by Neil Malhotra.
  Description: Boston, Massachusetts : Harvard Business Review Press, [2021] |
  Identifiers: LCCN 2021034680 (print) | LCCN 2021034681 (ebook) |
    ISBN 9781647821418 (hardcover) | ISBN 9781647821425 (ebook)
  Subjects: LCSH: Social entrepreneurship. | Social change. | Industries—
  Social aspects. | Social responsibility of business.
  Classification: LCC HD60 .F77 2021 (print) | LCC HD60 (ebook) |
    DDC 338/.04—dc23
  LC record available at https://lccn.loc.gov/2021034680
  LC ebook record available at https://lccn.loc.gov/2021034681

ISBN: 978-1-64782-141-8
eISBN: 978-1-64782-142-5

Contents

Introduction

Social Innovation in the Twenty-First Century

Neil Malhotra

Social innovation is the process of developing and deploying effective solutions to challenging and systemic social and environmental issues in support of social progress. It is not the prerogative or privilege of any organizational form or legal structure.

Solutions often require the active collaboration of stakeholders across government, business, and the nonprofit world. A diverse group of people—ranging from students to seasoned executives—have become increasingly interested in social innovation as a means of leveraging organizations to solve social problems. This volume—which brings together leading academics, practitioners, thinkers, and leaders—discusses several important topics at the cutting edge of the field of social innovation.

Twenty years ago, social innovation was dominated by nonprofits and primarily funded through philanthropy or government aid. People interested in becoming social innovators tended to narrowly focus on building skills in nonprofit management. But the last few decades have witnessed a dramatic transformation in social innovation in that mission-driven for-profit companies as well as newer organizational forms (such as benefit corporations and companies certified as B Corporations) have emerged as powerful drivers of social change. In tandem with the diversity of organizational forms, government money and philanthropic capital are no longer the only sources of funding. Impact investing funds, as well as traditional sources of money, such as venture capital, have helped fuel the social innovation engine. At the same time, nonprofits have begun to explore more-creative business models that take advantage of earned revenue rather than having to constantly raise money.

Three Key Concepts in Social Innovation

While the organizational forms that constitute social innovation are increasingly diverse, the field has also become more disciplined, centering on three core concepts. First, many funders require that social enterprises have a *theory of change*, or a conceptual pathway for how the social intervention will actually produce the social change it purports to make. A theory of change is quite simply a set of causal hypotheses that trace inputs to activities to outputs, and ultimately to outcomes and impact. One crucial benefit of a theory of change is that it clarifies that outputs, outcomes, and impact are not all the same—even though many social enterprises have conflated them for years. For example, an educational technology startup must explain how its outputs (e.g., number of students using a gamified math app) translate into outcomes (improved standardized test scores) and ultimately impact (greater educational attainment and better life outcomes for students). It is not enough simply to point to a large number of users; that could reflect an addictive app with little educational value. Though the components of a theory of change are just hypotheses, the framework helps social entrepreneurs think through the causal logic of their proposed solutions. A more thorough exploration of the theory of change methodology can be found in Gloria Lee's chapter 8.

BIOGRAPHY

NEIL MALHOTRA is the Edith M. Cornell Professor of Political Economy at the Stanford Graduate School of Business, where he serves as the Louise and Claude N. Rosenberg Jr. Director of the Center for Social Innovation. He has published over seventy-five academic articles in leading journals on numerous topics, including the role of business in society. He is the author of the forthcoming book *Leading with Values: Strategies for Making Ethical Decisions in Business and Life.*

Second, social innovators have to bring data to the theoretical hypotheses embedded in the theory of change. This is where the concept of *impact measurement* comes in. Social scientists have identified the gold standard approach for evaluating social interventions—the randomized controlled trial (RCT). In practice, RCTs can be difficult to implement quickly. Hence, many social entrepreneurs rely on less-rigorous but more-efficient "lean data" approaches (e.g., surveys, interviews, and focus groups) that allow rapid iteration and improvements. In chapter 4, Paul Brest and Colleen Honigsberg discuss in detail different ways of measuring and accounting for social impact. In chapter 15, Stephen Comello, Julia Reichelstein, and Stefan Reichelstein explain the challenges involved in measuring environmental impact and carbon offsets.

Furthermore, RCTs often cannot test all the proposed theoretical mechanisms outlined in a theory of change. Nor can they evaluate general equilibrium effects of how an intervention may create markets (see Matt Bannick's chapter 6 on how social enterprises can have market-creating spillovers). Nonetheless, it's becoming more important for social enterprises to measure impact—particularly given that impact investing funds seek to report these metrics—rather than just assert its existence.

Third, a concept that is transforming social innovation is the *design thinking* approach (see Stuart Coulson's chapter 11 for a deeper dive into the topic). There has been pushback against paternalistic entrepreneurs swooping into a disadvantaged population to "fix the problem." Instead, design thinking shifts the approach to empathetic listening, designing for users, and prototyping and iterating rapidly based on user feedback.

These are exciting and positive developments in social innovation, which have helped the field to advance dramatically over the last few decades, with practitioners now sharing a common language and set of models.

Challenges and Open Questions

But even as the field of social innovation has become more disciplined, important questions have remained and new ones have emerged that social enterprises, impact investors, philanthropists and foundations, and nonprofit and government leaders will be forced to grapple with. Many chapters in this volume confront these thorny questions head-on.

Ultimately, it will be up to the next generation of leaders—including readers of this volume—to address these issues.

The first major question is: What is the difference between investing and impact investing? Traditionally, investing has focused on maximizing risk-adjusted returns. Impact investing posits a third factor in the objective function in addition to risk and return: impact. Note that this conflicts with "win-win" conceptions of impact investing that assume away trade-offs (i.e., "The best way to maximize long-term profits is to take into account social performance."). If you believe in this world of no trade-offs, then there is no difference between investing and impact investing. The only value of the concept of impact investing is that we need to consider scenarios where we gain impact at the expense of risk-adjusted return. A related concept is *additionality* (see chapters 6 and 15), which asks us to engage in a counterfactual analysis: Was this enterprise funded because of the impact investment, or would traditional market capital have found its way to the enterprise anyway?

This is not just a matter of language, as this distinction has important implications for what sources of capital can be directed toward social innovation. The Employment Retirement Income Security Act of 1974 (ERISA) mandates that trustees for private pension plans have a fiduciary duty to maximize risk-adjusted returns. In 2020, Secretary of Labor Eugene Scalia issued a rule that forbids ERISA plan fiduciaries from participating in impact investments if they compromise risk-adjusted returns. It is expected that the Biden administration will revert to Obama-era rules that allow plan fiduciaries to take impact into account as a tiebreaker between investments that offer equivalent risk-adjusted returns. Presumably, this would give pension fund managers broader discretion in incorporating impact into investment decisions.

A related open question for impact investors is whether impact investment should simply be subject to environmental, social, and governance (ESG) constraints (i.e., a "do no harm" approach) or seek investments that make active, positive social change.

Perhaps one way to resolve the tension between investing and impact investing is to look at it from the social entrepreneur's point of view rather than the financier's. Some social entrepreneurs may prefer to work with impact investing funds with good reputations because such investors may support and encourage entrepreneurs to stay true to social missions rather than compromise impact for profits.

Related to the question of distinguishing investing from impact investing is how impact is measured. If impact investors are to take into account risk, return, *and* impact, then they need to have systematic and reliable ways of measuring impact (as discussed earlier). There are no standard operating procedures, opening the door to post hoc rationalization and "impact washing." This brings us to the second important question and challenge for practitioners of social innovation: How do we properly measure impact?

The third big question is: How will the field respond to Anand Giridharadas's polemic book *Winners Take All: The Elite Charade of Changing the World*? This influential book is a direct criticism of many facets of social innovation: philanthropy, nonprofits, impact investors, and social entrepreneurs. Giridharadas's main argument is that the global elite have used the vehicles of social innovation to impede true structural reform needed to achieve social progress. Giridharadas claims that policy changes to the rules of the game are the only real mechanisms for achieving social progress.

While we could spend the rest of these pages just debating his thesis, we won't—though it will come up. As I see it, there is a main flaw in Giridharadas's argument: he's positioned it as an either/or proposition, not recognizing that social innovation can be a complement to—rather than a substitute for—policy reform. Furthermore, given policy gridlock in many advanced democracies—and the urgency of social problems such as climate change—social innovators need to step in where government has failed. Nonetheless, social innovators should not defensively dismiss Giridharadas's critique. How are they ensuring that social innovations are a bridge to more-meaningful policy reform rather than a half-hearted replacement? The next generation of social innovation leaders will have to directly engage with this (and the other previously mentioned vexing questions).

Organization of the Book

This volume serves as both a handbook of long-standing existing knowledge and a discussion of issues on the frontier of social innovation. As such, it is intended for a diverse audience, both newcomers and veterans to the space. The key lessons and insights are valuable for students embarking on their careers, as well as seasoned executives wondering how to incorporate social innovation into their traditional for-profit business models. The volume touches on all aspects of the social innovation universe: philanthropy, nonprofits, social entrepreneurship, impact investing, public-private partnerships, and corporate social responsibility.

Although you can—and I will argue you should—read this entire book, some parts may be more valuable to you than others, depending on your context. I encourage you to seek the parts that are most valuable to you. The book has been divided into four parts, with each part organized around a theme. The parts progress logically, from high-level foundational material, to frameworks, to tactics, and finally to case examples that shine a light on all the aspects of social innovation discussed up to that point.

Part One: Foundations presents three high-level chapters and will lay important groundwork. Laura Arrillaga-Andreesen (chapter 1) and Kim Starkey (chapter 2) discuss qualities of successful social innovation leaders. William F. Meehan III (chapter 3) challenges extant models of philanthropy, engaging with many of Giridharadas's arguments but also seeing a path forward.

Part Two: Metrics and Models features analytical frameworks for understanding key social innovation concepts. In chapter 4, Paul Brest and Colleen Honigsberg discuss challenges and opportunities for the measurement and reporting of ESG metrics. In chapter 5, Bernadette Clavier discusses the challenges of the existing impact investing model for making social change and offers some potential solutions. In chapter 6, Matt Bannick explores how social innovators can catalyze the creation of new markets. In chapter 7, Steve Davis discusses an understudied but important question: How can social enterprises scale their impact, and what are the unique scaling challenges they face compared to traditional enterprises? Finally, in chapter 8, Gloria Lee provides a summary framework (the "impact triangle") that captures several of the concepts in part two.

Part Three: Learning and Incubating contains three chapters that describe educational models for fostering and incubating social innovation. Although you should always be wary of directly exporting an educational model to your institutional setting, the chapters contain many great ideas that can easily be built on and adapted. In chapter 9, Bernadette Clavier explores how educational institutions can cultivate leadership skills essential for social innovation. In chapter 10, Kim Starkey discusses strategies for incubating early-stage social ventures in the classroom setting. Finally, in chapter 11, Stuart Coulson describes the famous Design for Extreme Affordability course, which popularized the concept of "design thinking" and its application to social innovation.

Finally, Part Four: Applications connects the broad conceptual frameworks to three key social sectors in need of massive change: higher education (chapter 12, by Rob Urstein), health care (chapter 13, by Steve Davis and chapter 14, by Sara Singer, Sevda Memet, Suruchi Kothari, and Gordon Bloom), and the environment (chapter 15, by Stephen Comello, Julia Reichelstein, and Stefan Reichelstein). The health-care chapters specifically discuss how social innovation has addressed societal challenges stemming from the Covid-19 pandemic.

We are excited to begin this journey with you. Upon completion of this volume, you should have both a strong grasp of long-standing frameworks and concepts of social innovation, as well as an understanding of the future challenges on the horizon and the opportunities available to make a real and meaningful difference, improving lives, organizations, and the world.

PART ONE

FOUNDATIONS

1

Renewing Social Entrepreneurship

How Next-Generation Change Makers Meet the Challenges of Today

Laura Arrillaga-Andreessen

[F]or now, keep your mouth shut and your ears and eyes open.

—Gopal Krishna Gokhale to Mahatma Gandhi (1915)

Some entrepreneurs today follow Gokhale's advice to Gandhi and approach social change with empathy and a deep engagement with the people they seek to help. This approach is an enduring and powerful force in the hands of the next generation of social entrepreneurs—from the youngest cohort of Generation X (Gen X) to Gen Y (or millennials, born in the 1980s and early 1990s) and Gen Z (born after 1997). Tapping into a unique and interconnected set of resources, these generations are taking traditional models of social entrepreneurship and renewing them in transformational ways. In this chapter, I examine how three of my former Stanford Graduate School of Business (GSB) students are tackling the social inequities around them. While their contexts are different, three fundamental and shared pillars underpin much of their work and that of other next-generation social entrepreneurs: (1) they are motivated by their passionate commitment to social justice; (2) their environment is built on the digital technologies they grew up with; and

(3) their process is driven and informed by an empathetic approach—the foundation of human-centered design.

Motivated by Social Justice

A unifying force for next-generation social entrepreneurs is the desire to promote social justice, and the deep integration of this desire in their daily lives. This has resulted partly from the disintegration of the boundaries that have historically divided people—technology, geography, and value systems—giving these entrepreneurs a window into today's problems. For many of my generation[1] and those who came before us, geography, income, and indeed the inclination for some to avoid or refuse to see the social ills closest to us placed limits on the scope of our experience. That made it hard for us to build empathy for geographically distant communities or even communities physically closer and experiencing equally troubling levels of systemic racism, poverty, or violence. To younger generations, social injustices do not exist only in some remote location or in a community far removed from their own. They see them right in front of their eyes through the touch of their fingertips on their keyboards. They are also more keenly aware of, and interested in, the issues facing low-income communities nearest to them. For them, investing in social change is not a zero-sum game.

Of course, some people might correctly point out that we are living amid intense political, social, and economic divisiveness. However, that very polarization has served to elevate social justice as a value. In fact, these newer generations place a higher emphasis on social justice, equality, and inclusivity than any cohort we've encountered in the past—

BIOGRAPHY

LAURA ARRILLAGA-ANDREESSEN is founder, chairman emeritus, and former chairman of the Silicon Valley Social Venture Fund (SV2), founder and board chairman of the Stanford Center on Philanthropy and Civil Society (PACS), and founder and president of the Laura Arrillaga-Andreessen Foundation (LAAF). She is a lecturer in business strategy at the Stanford Graduate School of Business and author of the *New York Times* best-selling book *Giving 2.0: Transform Your Giving and Our World*.

EXECUTIVE SUMMARY

This chapter uses three case studies to explore how Generation Y (Gen Y) and Generation Z (Gen Z) social entrepreneurs are tackling complex social challenges. Next-generation change makers have three fundamental characteristics: (1) the desire to promote social justice; (2) the ability to leverage digital technology; and (3) empathy and an understanding of human-centered design.

though many older generations are also striving to live these values. Over the years in which the Case Foundation has been running the Millennial Impact Project, it has consistently found that, regardless of personal background or experience, this generation holds civil rights and racial discrimination among its top concerns.[2] In a recent survey of DoSomething.org members, Covid-19 and racial justice came out as the top factors influencing the way those eighteen to twenty-four years old said they would vote in the 2020 election.[3] One study found that for 65 percent of Gen Z'ers, social change activities were seen as central to their identity.[4]

Social justice has also become a more prominent feature of the culture in the institutions educating this generation of change makers. In addition to rapid growth in the number of international students on campus, universities have been pushing—albeit not always successfully—to become more inclusive places that provide education to all ethnic, racial, religious, and socioeconomic groups. Meanwhile, an even greater shift toward progressive liberal thinking in higher education has elevated discussions of racism, inequity, and civil rights. In my teaching, I see the impact of all this in the social consciousness, purpose, and conviction not just in members of student identity groups but in all my students. What I see is a generation wanting to speak out and whose voices are being listened to in a way that they weren't in the past. Today's students are moving beyond reading the white Anglophone and European canon. In addition to reading authors such as Charles Dickens, Jane Austen, William Faulkner, and F. Scott Fitzgerald, they are reading feminist writer Chimamanda Ngozi Adichie, Ocean Vuong, Ta-Nehisi Coates, Bernadine Evaristo, and others with beautiful intersectional identities.

Digital Technology

The way today's young people think and act has been shaped by the connective tissue of digital technology. Social media and other online digital channels have exposed them to suffering, injustice, and inequality in a way that previous generations were not. As digital natives, this generation of change makers has been able to interact with people from all over the world, including underprivileged communities, and they want to do something to address the suffering, injustice, and inequity they see.

Digital technology has given young social entrepreneurs a window into the world's problems and a powerful tool to help solve them. For example, among respondents to the 2019 Porter Novelli/Cone Gen Z Purpose Study, 80 percent of Gen Z respondents said they believed they could have an impact on issues by using social media.[5] Online, this generation can now engage directly with everyone from smallholder farmers in Bangladesh to schoolteachers in Afghanistan and contribute to making a difference in their lives. Back in 2005, Kiva.org showed how technology could make this possible. Kiva (cofounded by Jessica Jackley, one of my former Stanford GSB students) pioneered online peer-to-peer loans between individual donors and people in developing countries. Critically, Kiva also enabled lenders to receive direct feedback on their loans, via photos of the borrowers and from their stories about what the loan helped them achieve.

As Kiva and the others that followed have demonstrated, digital technology is the lifeblood for this generation of social entrepreneurs. It not only provides visibility and transparency but also makes possible the design of social change models that simply would not have been feasible in a predigital age. Digital technology also offers the new generation of social entrepreneurs channels through which to fundraise at scale and to spread the word about the social issues they care about and what they are doing to address them.

Using an Empathetic Approach

For the longest time, decisions about the direction of social change lay largely in the hands of experts or technocratic elites. Whether the issue was health care, education, or homelessness, social change was about bringing in specialists who, with the best of intentions, created organizations and programs based on their professional knowledge, years of study and research, and the academic studies produced by peers in their field.

The research-based approach is certainly not to be dismissed. In fact, in recent years, mistrust of science (including the social sciences) and the diminished respect for experts has not helped the world, contributing to political upheavals and exacerbating a pandemic that the world is still struggling to control. However, in the domain of social change, the focus on top-down, paternalistic approaches often comes at the expense of the very individuals and communities social entrepreneurs aspire to help.

The good news is that, underpinned by ethnographic approaches long utilized by certain academics in multiple fields,[6] these next-generation social entrepreneurs are moving toward an approach that is often described as a human-centered design model.[7] This model does not rely on long-held assumptions or standard narratives about what we think people need. Instead, entrepreneurs are led by empathy, gained by listening to and engaging with the individuals and communities they aspire to serve and learning directly from them what they need and want.

For the entrepreneurs in these three case studies, human-centered design provides the guiding framework for their organizations (see also in this volume Stuart Coulson's chapter 11 on the topic). Listening is the first step to identifying and defining the problem, and it is central throughout the process. Brainstorming and idea generation follow—with social entrepreneurs participating alongside those who will use or benefit from their products, programs, or services. Collaborative designing, prototyping, and testing come next. Finally, rapid feedback loops are created through surveys, interviews, focus groups, and conversations with users. This iterative process enables social entrepreneurs to improve their products, programs, or services and course correct or adapt them to minimize or eradicate potential errors or misunderstandings. Most importantly, it also centers the voices and experiences of the individuals they strive to serve at all stages of organizational, service, and product development. By engaging directly with and listening to these individuals, these next-generation social entrepreneurs prioritize empathy at every step.

More than any previous generation, today's newer-generation change makers have grasped and elevated the importance of this human-centered design approach. They know that in designing products and services for the benefit of society, they need to understand the aspirations of the people who will ultimately use those products or services, as well as what obstacles affect those people's lives. Of course, it can take years or decades for the ultimate impact of any investment in social change to become clear. But one thing we can measure immediately is whether the voice of the people we aspire to serve has been heard and integrated into program models. Developing empathy and human-centered feedback loops is fundamental to success for this next wave of social entrepreneurship.

Today's generation understands the importance of learning from what they've experienced personally and what they've heard from people they aspire to serve. This is a generation that sees its work to fix social problems in the context of social justice and treats technology in the same way previous generations treated electricity, banking, or the printing press: as an essential tool and an enabler of innovation, education, and communication; of new business models and sources of finance; and—ultimately—of social impact. In the following case studies, I'll show how three of my past Stanford GSB students have put all this into practice.

Filling the Gaps by Connecting the Dots: Christina Guilbeau, Hopebound

One of the wonders of the natural world is symbiosis, the process through which mutually beneficial relationships enable plants and animals to provide each other with elements essential for both to survive and grow. After listening to the communities around her, twenty-nine-year-old social entrepreneur Christina Guilbeau applied this principle to her model of social change. Through Hopebound, the organization she launched in 2019, she is using the power of technology to connect mental health clinician interns with young people who are struggling with mental health problems.

Hopebound partners with schools and community organizations to enable mental health clinician interns who need to obtain required supervised practicum hours to deliver virtual one-on-one mental health support to adolescents who would otherwise be unable to access therapy services. In Hopebound, the three pillars guiding this generation's work can be clearly seen: Guilbeau has tapped into empathy, using her deep understanding of the communities the organization serves to inform the design of a human-centered model of social change. She is advancing social justice by increasing access to mental health services to populations who, for both geographic and economic reasons, otherwise would not likely have such access. To do so, she is harnessing the matchmaking power of technology.

In creating Hopebound, Guilbeau has also reinvented traditional service delivery relationships, in which needy communities receive support that is funded with charitable dollars and delivered by nonprofits or other social sector organizations. Instead, she has created a symbiotic ecosystem in which the service providers also benefit. "My primary mission is to make mental health support more accessible to adolescents, but my secondary mission is to make the pre-licensure process as efficient and high-quality as possible," she says.[8] In bringing these two communities together, Guilbeau has therefore created a model in which everybody wins.

A Problem Rooted in Economic Injustice

At age eleven, Guilbeau first came to understand social injustice. She and her brother were volunteering in an after-school program in their neighboring town, Red Bank, New Jersey. They were surprised to see how education levels there compared to those of their own hometown, Fair Haven. "The children in the after-school program didn't have the resources and weren't being educated in the same way as us," she recalls. Guilbeau realized that this was a problem rooted in economic inequity. "The injustice lay in the fact that just because people were born in a different zip code the trajectory of their lives was changed," she says.

Then, while at Stanford, Guilbeau came face-to-face with the realities of young people's mental health challenges. A former student with whom she'd maintained contact from the days when she had taught sixth- and seventh-grade math students in Baton Rouge through the Teach for America program had always struggled with her mental health. However, during the summer between Guilbeau's first and second years of business school, her student's problems reached the breaking point. "She was struggling," says Guilbeau. "I realized I had no resources to point her to. And I realized my limited ability to simply listen was not going to be enough."

Sadly, the experience of Guilbeau's student is all too common. Scarce resources mean many young people are not able to access mental health support. Mental Health America found that almost 60 percent of America's youth with major depression receive no mental health treatment, and even in the states where such treatment for young people is most widespread, more than one in three are still not receiving the mental health services they need.[9] In 2021, Mental Health America reported that, in the previous year alone, almost 14 percent of Americans between the ages of twelve and seventeen reported suffering at least one major depressive episode (MDE). Mental Health America also found that the number of young people experiencing MDEs rose by 206,000 from the previous year.[10]

After seeing what her student had been going through, Guilbeau started doing some research on youth mental health. What she learned shocked her. For example, suicide is the second-leading cause of death among young people fifteen to nineteen.[11] Half of all lifelong cases of mental illness start by age fourteen.[12] "The research confirmed that this was a demographic group that was not receiving the care they needed," Guilbeau says.[13]

Wanting to help change this, Guilbeau began exploring virtual therapy sessions as a possible solution. "A lot of studies show that video-based therapy can be as effective as in-person therapy, as you can pick up body language," she says.[14]

However, it was when Guilbeau found another community in need of help that she connected the dots and formed the basis for the Hopebound model. From friends and family members undergoing graduate training in clinical psychology, social work, and therapy, she learned that it was hard to put in the thousands of hours of counseling needed to become licensed to work in this field. By connecting them with adolescents in need of therapy and hiring licensed supervisors to review their cases, as required by the licensure process, she could also address this problem. "The idea was to link adolescents with students needing to do hours to qualify," she says. "And the last validation was that these therapists in training were effective practitioners—their education is much more recent and every week they get detailed feedback on their cases from licensed clinicians."

After being awarded a Stanford Social Innovation Fellowship in late May 2018, Guilbeau, who was studying for her MBA at the Stanford Graduate School of Business, was able to develop her idea. This fellowship provides not only funding but also mentorship and advice to students who want to start a high-impact for-profit or nonprofit social venture.

The challenge for Guilbeau was in taking the next step. "After I graduated from the Stanford Graduate School of Business, I moved to Atlanta and started working full time on it," she explains. "But what I was most afraid of was doing harm, giving these kids mental health services without thinking through all the implications. It was such a fragile concept that I didn't want to treat anyone as a guinea pig." She also experienced something that, unfortunately, is common among female professionals, "impostor syndrome," with its feelings of inadequacy and questions about whether the project was right for her.

In March 2020, when the Covid-19 pandemic hit the United States, Guilbeau knew she had to act. "I forced myself to get out there and provide these services because now I knew these kids needed it more than ever," she recalls. "I launched the pilot and now I'm serving 50 kids."

A Human-Centered Model of Change

Guilbeau's model follows a human-centered approach to social change that prioritizes the beneficiaries and their needs. It means finding solutions within the existing ecosystem of a social problem and meeting people where they are, in every sense, from financial and educational to physical (or, in Hopebound's case, virtual).

Rather than imposing her ideas about what communities need, Guilbeau has listened to what they *actually* need, designing Hopebound based on the experiences of the adolescents and mental health interns she wants to serve. And unlike much traditional social entrepreneurship—which helps people survive current challenges rather than preventing problems from occurring—Hopebound's model goes further by helping people to not only survive but also achieve a better life.

Transforming a Region by Investing in Leaders: Diego Ontaneda Benavides, Latin American Leadership Academy (LALA)

To some, setting a goal of transforming an entire continent might seem impossibly ambitious. However, Diego Ontaneda Benavides, a thirty-two-year-old Peruvian social entrepreneur, believes he can make an outsized contribution to this mission by focusing his resources on one goal: identifying the talented, purpose-driven leaders of tomorrow and equipping them to achieve their social change goals.

Based in Medellín, Colombia's second-largest city, Latin American Leadership Academy (LALA) is building a systematic pipeline of ethical, entrepreneurial, purpose-driven Latin American leaders from every background. Its human development model is built around social innovation, entrepreneurship, leadership, social and emotional learning, and critical thinking. It includes both short and intense programs (the Leadership Bootcamps) and a gap-year residential program (the Leadership Academy). All LALA young leaders also join a lifelong community of mentors, resources, and opportunities, in which they find the guidance and support they need to chase their biggest dreams.

Long before he conceived of the idea of LALA, which he launched in 2018 with his cofounder, educator David Baptista, Ontaneda was aware not only of the obstacles preventing young people from realizing their dreams but also of what would make it possible for them to succeed. He learned this from personal experience. At age twelve, his parents' business went into bankruptcy—"That burst my bubble," he says.[15]

Fortunately, he was able to secure scholarships at top international schools in Peru and, later, at Williams College in Williamstown, Massachusetts. "I had a lot of luck and resources," he says. "But many people are not able to reach their full potential because there's no safety net. So, one of my biggest motivations behind creating LALA was finding purpose-driven teenagers and empowering them to chase their dreams."

Of course, LALA was not the first boot camp for social entrepreneurs. What makes it different, however, is its focus on including groups of socially driven leaders from the entire socioeconomic spectrum, including the region's most underprivileged communities. In this, explains Ontaneda, LALA is rejecting the traditional model of development that prevails in Latin America, whereby experts bring in programs from New York or Washington, DC, while the role of local communities is limited to implementation.

"I've seen that fail again and again," says Ontaneda. "Instead, we're saying let's find people who've grown up in those communities, who have experienced that injustice, that poor education, that lack of infrastructure, who have more trust from the local community because they are from there, and who might identify more innovative solutions because they understand the problem more deeply."[16]

Filling a Social Justice Gap

In 2011, Ontaneda joined McKinsey & Company as a consultant in the firm's San Francisco office. Initially, he thought he would remain at the firm for ten to fifteen years and make a difference by working at a consultancy with a global reach. He soon realized that the impact he could make through his role in the professional services sector would only be incremental. But while he knew he wanted to do more, he was struggling to identify a single cause that could bring about change at a scale that would satisfy his ambitions.

Then, when working in South Africa at the Johannesburg-based African Leadership Academy (ALA), Ontaneda encountered an entirely different approach to social change. Rather than focusing on a single cause, he realized that by investing in the development of the next generation of ambitious social entrepreneurs, ethical public servants, and conscious business leaders, his individual, direct impact could be multiplied. "There are teenagers all over Latin America from every background who already have an incredible sense of mission and want to solve the big problems they're seeing in their communities," he says. "LALA finds these kids before it's too late, and then the whole model is built around removing barriers for them to reach their full potential and become the transformational leaders we know they can be."[17]

While he loved his work at ALA, Ontaneda wanted to help unleash the potential of young leaders back in his own region. "Latin America has been held back for decades in terms of social and economic development," he says. "And a big part of that is attributable to the poor supply of high-quality ethical leaders, whether that's in the public sector, the private sector, or the social sector."[18]

Research supports his view. In Transparency International's survey of more than twenty-two thousand citizens in twenty countries in Latin America and the Caribbean, almost half (47 percent) said they thought that the police and elected representatives were mostly or entirely corrupt. Similar proportions said the same of local government officials, officials in the office of the president or prime minister, and judges or magistrates.[19] Research has shown that this corruption has a negative impact on economic growth and people's ability to gain secure livelihoods.[20]

Ontaneda had identified the root cause of many of the region's challenges: that whether individuals are corrupt or simply ineffective, poor leadership makes it impossible to fix the other problems in society. He explained, "We see a vicious cycle where the shortage of high-quality leaders leads to bad policy making, ineffective social enterprises, and less-than-conscious businesses. These perpetuate our high income inequality, poor education, and minimal social mobility, which in turn waste our talent year after year, ultimately hurting the future supply of leaders." He also identified a gap. "The region didn't have anything like ALA," he says. "High-purpose teenagers didn't have an institution to find, connect, and develop them."[21]

The Multiplier Effect

In this case, the model is based on indirect impact—that is, the impact created by the graduates of LALA's programs and how those graduates positively touch and transform society.

Take Giullia, who grew up in Belford Roxo, a favela in Rio de Janeiro, and at age fourteen started making candies and selling them in the streets "so her sister wouldn't have to." This meant she was unable to progress academically, despite being exceptionally talented, since all her time was taken up with making and selling her candies. After participating in a LALA Bootcamp in Peru, she gained the confidence and skills to start working on a social enterprise designed to help incarcerated women, a community she understood all too well, having grown up with many incarcerated women in her community. Absorvidas, the social enterprise she founded, empowers incarcerated women by teaching them to produce reusable menstrual pads. Since then, Giullia has perfected her Spanish and has been accepted at Babson College with a full scholarship.

Another LALA graduate is Rocío, who grew up in Cusco, Peru, and founded a project called FUTUPLAN to empower rural and indigenous vulnerable young people through sex education, life planning, and gender-violence awareness workshops. After participating in a LALA Bootcamp, she joined LALA's Committee for Inclusion to explore the intersection of gender, race, and socioeconomic conditions. She is now a King Scholar at Dartmouth College with a full scholarship for low-income students from developing countries who want to alleviate poverty in their home countries. She plans to major in public policy in order to make a difference in Peru's political sphere.

"The multiplier effect of the LALA model," explains Ontaneda, "is that by choosing a person who is trying to create big change in their community, and by focusing on skill sets around things like leadership and entrepreneurship, you get the human empowerment that's enriching and personally transformative—but then there's also a collective macro impact through them—they impact their communities and become role models and beacons of hope for those around them."[22]

Reaping a Digital Dividend

Like Guilbeau, Ontaneda harnessed the power of technology to expand the LALA model, something that has accelerated because of the pandemic. "It forced us to reconsider some of our assumptions," he says. "We'd always assumed that LALA had to be in-person, and we discovered that we could find ways to do our programming virtually and with excellence."

In fact, shifting to a virtual model has enabled LALA to be even more inclusive. This is partly because it means its programs can be offered to even more young social entrepreneurs, since travel is no longer a barrier, and at a lower price, since most of the cost savings of not running in-person programs are passed on to students.

However, the virtual format itself offers advantages over the in-person experience, where mutual understanding is based only on verbal and visual cues. Online, the chat function enables deeper interactions and makes participation easier for more introverted individuals who might not speak up in a face-to-face setting. "In Zoom, the chat window is on fire the whole time," says Ontaneda. "You're reading other people's thoughts and feelings and reactions—so you might find a connection to someone that you wouldn't by just seeing their face. That's been really powerful."

In addition, technology enables program participants to get to know each other in entirely new ways. "They've been organizing sessions where they show each other their houses, their neighborhoods, their families, their pets," says Ontaneda. "That's creating literal windows into other people's lives that help create this empathy, mutual understanding, and connection across distances and differences."[23]

Ontaneda and Baptista are now entering a new technology-enabled frontier: an online ecosystem to accelerate their young leaders' growth and intentionally fast-track their progress toward positions of influence and impact. "We are mapping the most common paths to impactful careers—whether in business, politics, entrepreneurship, activism, or STEM [science, technology, engineering, and mathematics]—and understanding the most common barriers that our alumni face," says Ontaneda. "With this knowledge, we will build learning paths, partnerships, and bridges to social and financial capital. The result will be a pipeline of thousands of ethical, purpose-driven leaders of the highest caliber, and an online ecosystem to catalyze collaborations in a way Latin America has never seen."[24]

Harnessing Technology to Tackle Poverty: Manu Chopra, Chopra Foundation

When technology and innovation unite, it can be the catalyst for the creation of global enterprises capable of generating vast revenues and transforming the way people live. However, as twenty-three-year-old Manu Chopra is demonstrating, when technology and innovation are matched with human-centered design, they can create a powerful driver of social change. In his desire to help defeat extreme poverty, Chopra is providing villagers in India with dignified ways of earning a living by enabling them to use smartphones to build computational models for thousands of India's languages. These models are then used by tech companies to build artificial intelligence (AI) algorithms.

The child of refugees from Pakistan, Chopra grew up in an urban slum in India and thus directly understands the nature of poverty. One of his earliest memories was witnessing a "dowry death," a form of violence in which a woman is murdered by her husband or his family because her family refused to pay an additional dowry. "That shaped me a lot," he says. "I cannot sit still when things like this are happening."[25] Through his parents' hard work, he was able to receive an education at top schools, which eventually took him to Stanford at age sixteen. "I saw a level of mobility that most people don't experience," he says.

Seeing poverty and abuse firsthand and experiencing the transformative power of education and social mobility, Chopra was driven to use his powers of innovation to promote social justice. While in high school, for example, he invented an antimolestation device for women at a time when rape cases in India were on the rise. Later, at Stanford, he was one of a team that created CS + Social Good, a student-led group that runs fellowships, courses, speaker series, and other events focused on using technology as a tool to help solve big global challenges and to maximize positive social impact.

Chopra is nothing if not ambitious. He is now building a sustainable city in Kerala, in southern India, and he has launched one of India's largest universal basic income experiments in more than fifty villages across the country.

However, a key focus for Chopra has been to tackle the extreme poverty that still plagues his home country, so upon returning to India after graduation, with the help of a grant from the Bill & Melinda Gates Foundation, he spent six months traveling across the country, visiting more than a thousand villages—some of India's poorest. While doing so, he followed the advice that Gopal Krishna Gokhale gave to Mahatma Gandhi and I cited at the start of this chapter: he kept his eyes and ears open but his mouth shut.

Like others of his generation, Chopra was putting empathy to work, and what he learned while visiting the villages and by listening to the people he met was that not one of them wanted charity. They wanted fair treatment, to be free from discrimination, and to have access to the same social and economic opportunities as others. In short, they wanted social justice. "I realized that poor Indians are incredibly aspirational," he says. "All they want is an opportunity for a job. They're not interested in handouts. So, then the question was: What jobs can you give people?"[26]

The question is one many have tried to answer. Conventional wisdom is that poor people need education and training. However, with 800 million Indians either unemployed or underemployed, sheer numbers mean this is not a solution, at least in the short term. "There is no way you can train 800 million people," says Chopra. "You can't build enough schools and most people don't have computers. My question was: What skills do they already have that they can get paid for?"[27]

Chopra realized that the answer lay in the languages and dialects they speak—more than 19,500 of them, according to an analysis of census data.[28] Chopra knew that technology companies were rushing to develop AI-driven and crowdsourcing platforms across the Indian market. To do so, they needed to develop databases in local languages, and it takes a million spoken hours to build a database in a given language. "I saw a fundamental gap," says Chopra. "There were hundreds of millions of people who spoke these languages who had no money, and there were all these American and Indian companies saying we need data."[29]

Through his Chopra Foundation, villagers are provided with free Android smartphones, along with solar chargers, so they can build computational language models for their dialects, digitize local government documents, and perform other kinds of digital work—all of which means they can generate the income they need to build better lives. Since 2020, says Chopra, the programs—which also prioritize women, tribal people, and those from low-caste communities—have moved more than 100,000 rural Indians out of poverty. "If you think about a ladder of social mobility, in India the bottom rungs are missing," he says. "The idea of this work was to fill in the bottom rung of the ladder."[30]

Chopra's way of advancing social justice is to bring about a transformation in the lives of the people he works with, enabling them to move from merely surviving to thriving and striving by giving them a stepping-stone to the next economic opportunity. While earning money, villagers are also building skills, since for many this is their first encounter with a smartphone, a key tool in today's economy. It's a model that's opening a door to poor communities and letting them step in to participate in the economy in a way that would not otherwise be possible.

Moreover, in doing so, the impact of the Chopra Foundation programs extends far beyond the immediate recipients of the digital work. "They can make around $2,000 a month, which is significantly more than they had before, and they start using that to help other people," Chopra says. "In India, one person's problem is everyone's problem, so you create this circle of compassion." He sees this effect when villagers, recognizing the potential for self-improvement in the digital work, make it a shared project. "After the first week, everyone becomes closer and helps each other with pronunciation," he says. "There are villages that are half Muslim, half Hindu—this brings people together."[31]

A New Generation Steps Forward

While the initiatives of each of these social entrepreneurs rely on approaches that are distinct, all three illustrate how empathy, social justice, and technology shape the causes they focus on, the nature of their social innovations, and how they execute their ideas. These interconnected pillars are critical to enabling them to use a human-centered design approach to bring about meaningful change, thus renewing how social entrepreneurship is practiced.

For example, by traveling across India, listening to villagers, and learning about the skills they could tap into to earn money and change their own lives, Chopra has used empathy to inform his strategy for combating extreme poverty, treating the people he wants to help as strategic partners rather than passive beneficiaries. In helping adolescents access therapy services while also making it easier for mental health clinician interns to become licensed, Guilbeau is harnessing the connective power of digital technology. And, in focusing on developing the Latin American leaders of the future, Ontaneda is using empathy and digital technology to empower a new cohort of change makers to advance social justice in Latin America at scale.

To achieve this kind of ripple effect, in 1998 I developed and launched the Silicon Valley Social Venture Fund (SV2). I wanted to unleash the resources of other change makers by helping them connect and support each other while exploring social issues and learning how to give more effectively through experiential education in grant-making, high-engagement relationships with SV2's grantee partners, and collaborations with their fellow philanthropists.

In developing SV2, I was also informed by an empathy-led approach. I started by interviewing more than a hundred individuals. Through these conversations, I realized that they, like me, wanted to give more strategically, to pool their resources for greater impact, and to learn through doing. At the time, no organization existed to bring together these individuals to share passions, exchange ideas, and learn how to practice strategic philanthropy by actually practicing it. Now, twenty-three years into SV2's life cycle, we are reinventing our model to prioritize empathy, social justice, and the power of technology through virtual education for our investors, collaboration with our grantee partners, and community building with all our stakeholders.

These kinds of approaches are being embraced by the next generation early on in their careers. They are starting their journeys in their early to midtwenties rather than waiting until retirement as so many have in the past. For these generations, this work is not something to do when they have spare time or money. They are immersing themselves in society to understand the gaps that need to be filled and how they can fill those gaps by using empathy, technology, networks, and experiences. Importantly, young social entrepreneurs have recognized that, if they focus on listening to the communities they aspire to help, they can achieve their goals with the resources they have at their disposal today.

By grounding their strategies in empathy and human-centered design, a commitment to social justice, and the power of digital technologies, next-generation social entrepreneurs are democratizing social change—how it is created, who gets to participate, and which voices inform the models that are implemented. As someone who believes fervently in the need for this kind of democratization, I find the approaches of Guilbeau, Ontaneda, Chopra, and others like them tremendously exciting. From the Covid-19 pandemic to climate change, the problems we face today are global, rife with complexities, and often seemingly impossible to fix. But as I look at the way this generation approaches impact, I am filled with unbridled optimism that the next wave of social entrepreneurs will be increasingly young, diverse, empathetic, passionate, innovative, and able to scale up their ideas in new ways—and as a result may do more to solve today's problems than any generation before them.

FOR FURTHER READING

For readers interested in exploring leadership in social innovation more deeply, I recommend four books. My book *Giving 2.0: Transform Your Giving and Our World* (Jossey-Bass, 2011) redefines what a philanthropist is and offers innovative and powerful methods for individuals to give their time, money, networks, and expertise. *Designing Your Life: How to Build a Well-Lived, Joyful Life* (Alfred A. Knopf, 2016), by Bill Burnett and Dave Evans, demonstrates how the practice of design thinking shapes and builds meaningful and fulfilling professional and personal lives. *Social Startup Success: How the Best Nonprofits Launch, Scale Up, and Make a Difference* (Da Capo Lifelong Books, 2018), by Kathleen K. Janus, uses real-life examples to help guide social entrepreneurs in building initiatives to scale and achieve sustainability. Finally, *Getting Beyond Better: How Social Entrepreneurship Works* (Harvard Business Review Press, 2015), by Roger L. Martin and Sally R. Osberg, provides a theoretical framework for social entrepreneurship and demonstrates how social entrepreneurs innovate and build solutions to maximize impact.

Notes

1. I am part of the elder half of Gen X (born between the mid-1960s and the early 1980s), although I have the spirit of a Gen Y'er.
2. The Case Foundation, "The Millennial Impact Report: 10 Years Looking Back," 2018, http://www.themillennialimpact.com/sites/default/files/images/2018/MIR-10-Years-Looking-Back.pdf.
3. DoSomething.org, "The Pulse of Gen Z in the Time of COVID-19," Medium, April 26, 2020, https://medium.com/dosomethingstrategic/gen-zs-thoughts-on-covid-19-2067b0f36af1.
4. Zapier Editorial Team, "Misunderstood Generations: What Millennials and Gen Z Actually Think about Work," Zapier Editorial Team, January 27, 2020, https://zapier.com/blog/digital-natives-report/.
5. Cone, a Porter Novelli company, "2019 Porter Novelli/Cone Gen Z Purpose Study," 2019, https://www.conecomm.com/research-blog/cone-gen-z-purpose-study.

6. See, for example, Abhijit Banerjee and Esther Duflo, *Poor Economics: A Radical Rethinking of the Way to Fight Global Poverty* (New York: Public Affairs, 2011).

7. Paul Brest, Nadia Roumani, and Jason Bade, *Problem Solving, Human-Centered Design, and Strategic Processes* (Stanford, CA: Stanford Center on Philanthropy and Civil Society, 2015).

8. Christina Guilbeau, Hopebound, interview, October 26, 2020. All quotations from Guilbeau are from this source unless stated otherwise.

9. Mental Health America, "Youth Data 2021," 2021, https://www.mhanational.org/issues/2021/mental-health-america-youth-data.

10. Ibid.

11. Ibid.

12. World Health Organization, "Improving the Mental and Brain Health of Children and Adolescents," https://www.who.int/activities/Improving-the-mental-and-brain-health-of-children-and-adolescents.

13. Christina Guilbeau, Hopebound, interview, November 2, 2020.

14. Ibid.

15. Diego Ontaneda Benavides, Latin American Leadership Academy (LALA), interview, October 26, 2020. All quotations from Ontaneda are from this source unless stated otherwise.

16. Ibid., January 27, 2021.

17. Ibid., November 3, 2020.

18. Ibid.

19. Transparency International, "People and Corruption: Latin America and the Caribbean," Global Corruption Barometer, 2017, https://images.transparencycdn.org/images/2017_GCB_AME_EN.pdf.

20. Ibid., 11.

21. Diego Ontaneda Benavides, interview, November 3, 2020.

22. Ibid.

23. Ibid., January 27, 2021.

24. Ibid.

25. Manu Chopra, Chopra Foundation, interview, October 28, 2020. All quotations from Chopra are from this source unless stated otherwise.

26. Ibid., November 4, 2020.

27. Ibid.

28. Office of the Registrar General, Census of India 2011, *Language* (New Delhi: Office of the Registrar General, Census of India 2011, 2018), https://censusindia.gov.in/2011Census/C-16_25062018_NEW.pdf.

29. Manu Chopra, November 4, 2020.

30. Ibid.

31. Ibid.

2

High-Performance Leadership

Skills and Qualities That Drive Impact at Scale

Kim Starkey

"**S**imply put, it is substantially more difficult to build a great social-sector organization than to build a great business corporation of similar scale. And that is why the best-run, most-impactful nonprofits stand as some of the most impressive enterprises in the world."[1] So wrote renowned management expert Jim Collins in the foreword to *Engine of Impact: Essentials of Strategic Leadership in the Nonprofit Sector*, a book that I coauthored with Bill Meehan.

Leading social sector organizations *is* difficult—exceedingly so. Over many years of working in the social sector, I have come to understand that it is characterized by a number of inherent and relatively unique structural challenges that can create barriers to innovation and the achievement of impact at scale. These challenges range from underfunded, highly stressful working environments to the long time horizon for achieving impact.

I have also observed that those all-too-rare organizations that overcome these obstacles and achieve outsized impact invariably have one thing in common: a high-performing leader at the helm. Analyzing the skills and practices that make their leadership exemplary enables all of us to become better leaders and thereby strengthen the sector in this era of urgent need. It can also enable funders to make better decisions regarding which organizations to support.

I will devote this chapter to sharing insights and inspiring lessons drawn from my research and from extensive working relationships with extraordinary social sector leaders. Some of these leaders are household names, whereas others are quiet, unsung heroes. All share a jaw-dropping commitment to their organization and its mission, coupled with deep leadership expertise, wisdom, and insight acquired over decades of working to generate massive impact at scale.

My perspectives are informed by my research and teaching at the Stanford Graduate School of Business and by my role as president and CEO of King Philanthropies, a grant-making foundation whose mission is "to make a meaningful difference in the lives of the world's poorest people by multiplying the impact of high performing leaders and organizations."[2] Our rigorous selection criteria, which apply a lens that focuses on leadership, have enabled us to create a portfolio of organizations that—despite working in different spaces, geographies, and cultures and with very different kinds of interventions—have a great deal in common in their leadership practices.

I will begin the chapter by discussing two skill sets that every social sector leader needs to master. First, these leaders must be astute practitioners of *strategic thinking*, which involves a commitment to—and a capacity for—fact-based problem-solving. Second, they must excel at strategic management, which involves a laser-like focus on execution. Together, strategic thinking and strategic management form the basis of strategic leadership. Bill Meehan and I first presented this framework in *Engine of Impact*. Here, I will summarize that framework and its various elements, illustrating it with powerful fresh case examples from my recent work funding a portfolio of high-performing leaders and organizations at King Philanthropies.

BIOGRAPHY

KIM STARKEY is president and CEO of King Philanthropies and lecturer in management at the Stanford Graduate School of Business. She is coauthor, with Bill Meehan, of *Engine of Impact: Essentials of Strategic Leadership in the Nonprofit Sector*.

EXECUTIVE SUMMARY

The all-too-rare organizations that achieve outsized impact in the social sector invariably have one thing in common: high-performing leaders at the helm. Critically, these leaders are made, not born. This chapter will help readers understand the most important skills and qualities that high-performing leaders cultivate (and have in common—despite working in diverse geographies and sectors). Intentionally and proactively developing these skills and qualities will equip current and future leaders to overcome structural challenges in the social sector that can create barriers to innovation and obstruct efforts to achieve lasting impact at scale.

Next, I will discuss a set of personal qualities that I have come to view as the "secret sauce" of high-performing leadership in the social sector. In *Engine of Impact*, we began to explore these qualities in a chapter titled "Insight and Courage." In addition to their ability to strategically design effective programs and manage around organizational challenges, great social sector leaders are able to see what others don't and go where others won't. It is this capacity for insight and courage that equips leaders to overcome structural challenges that would otherwise obstruct innovation and the achievement of impact at scale.

Time and again, in my work with high-performing leaders at King Philanthropies, I have seen certain qualities that define insight and courage as the key ingredients in successful leadership. These qualities mark the difference between good enough and truly excellent leadership. Ultimately, I have found that the most effective leaders are made, not born; they forge and hone their leadership skills during years of deep training and on-the-ground testing.

Strategic Thinking

In *Engine of Impact*, Bill Meehan and I compared strategic leadership in the nonprofit sector to a high-performance engine with multiple components. The comparison was not meant to be exact but rather to convey the basic truth that nonprofit leaders must engage all components of the "engine" if they intend to make a significant and enduring impact. The components of strategic thinking include mission, strategy, and impact evaluation; honing these is akin to tuning an engine—the engine of impact. (Insight and courage are additional components of strategic thinking, which I discuss later in this chapter.) Strategic management, meanwhile, encompasses funding, organization, and board governance; harnessing these provides the fuel that propels the engine forward. In this and the following section, I will discuss each of these components in turn.

Mission

When it comes to social sector organizations, everything starts with mission. Because nonprofits are by definition mission driven, it is essential that they have a mission that is clear and tightly focused. This mission must be conveyed in a concise statement that is easy to remember and understand, and that can serve as a guide to all major decisions the organization makes. By contrast, the leaders of a typical corporation can assert that its purpose is to "maximize shareholder value." From that core purpose, any stakeholder can infer how the corporation's performance will be measured and how its leaders will frame strategic decisions and trade-offs.[3] Lacking this inherent clarity of purpose and fully aligned stakeholders, nonprofits need a clear and focused mission statement to guide decision-making and weigh inevitable trade-offs.

Consider the example of Last Mile Health (LMH), which we at King Philanthropies have funded since 2018. It was cofounded in 2007 by Raj Panjabi, assistant professor of medicine at Harvard Medical School, together with a group of Liberian civil war survivors and American health workers who wanted to bring primary health-care services to remote communities in Liberia. Despite their best intentions, considerable skills, and the great need for their services, they found it hard to find a focused mission. As Panjabi told me in a 2016 interview:

> During our first five years, we faced our fair share of failures. It took our team time to hone our impact model. Our early mission statement was "Advance health care and the fundamental rights of the poor," which was far too broad and unfocused. We eventually refined our mission considerably, evolving it to a statement that is much more targeted: "Save lives in the world's most remote communities." This led Last Mile Health to our focus

on building networks of community health workers, which are a most critical lever in saving lives in the world's most remote communities.[4]

Strategy

Mission is achieved through strategy—which is simply a planned set of actions that are designed to achieve a given objective. In *Engine of Impact*'s chapter on strategy, we provide useful tools, frameworks, and examples as a guide for ensuring that an organization's overall strategy is sound, including Oster's six forces model, which enables analysis of a nonprofit's strategic position within the landscape in which it "competes."[5]

Both mission and strategy should embody and reflect a nonprofit's core competency, but this is overlooked far too frequently in the social sector. In a seminal 1990 *Harvard Business Review* article, C. K. Prahalad and Gary Hamel put forward the insightful, powerful, and simple argument that an organization's strategy must be built on its distinctive skills. In practice, this means that nonprofit leaders must regularly ask, "Does our organization have the core competency (or skill) required to achieve its mission?"[6]

Once LMH established a focused mission, Panjabi and his colleagues worked hard to adhere to it. To be sure, the courage of their conviction was sometimes tested. When the Ebola virus broke out in Liberia in 2014, for example, they found themselves facing existential questions about how to respond meaningfully to the crisis while also staying true to their mission and core competencies. This challenge came to a head when LMH was offered the opportunity to pursue a multimillion-dollar grant to build treatment centers to help stop the outbreak. It was a vital undertaking that would help many people. But, said Panjabi, "[H]ad we said yes, we could have hurt instead of helped, because building treatment centers for Ebola was not a core competency of our organization. If we had taken this on, we would have been managing projects that others could have done much better. Instead, we stayed disciplined and committed to our core competencies."[7] Last Mile Health thus resisted the temptation of substantial funding that would have led to mission creep and instead focused on building a network of community health workers who could help identify patients at risk for Ebola while continuing to provide access to primary health services. In this way, it continued to leverage its core competencies while still helping to halt the spread of the deadly virus.

Landesa, another King Philanthropies grantee, faced a similar situation in the late 1990s. Its mission clearly states that it "champions and works to secure land rights for millions of the world's poorest, mostly rural, women and men to provide opportunity and promote social justice."[8] But, in 1998, it had the opportunity to undertake a major urban land rights project in the former Soviet Union, where it was already working under a grant that would soon expire. Accepting the project would have provided a reliable new funding source and allowed the organization to keep using its hard-earned expertise in Russian land law. The problem was that the project did not focus on the "mostly rural" population that Landesa had explicitly been established to serve and with which it had deep expertise. "In the end, we turned down the urban opportunity because we felt that it was outside of our mission," said Tim Hanstad, who was then Landesa's executive director, "And we felt very strongly that on principle we shouldn't chase after funding that was not mission-focused."[9]

Impact Evaluation

High-performing social sector leaders understand that it is essential to measure the impact of their chosen intervention; only in this way can they know whether they are indeed successfully pursuing their organization's mission with a strategy that works. Although there are numerous methods for conducting rigorous impact evaluation, many otherwise strong social sector leaders fail to pursue them.

Pratham CEO Rukmini Banerji is one social sector leader who does not make this mistake. Pratham, a King Philanthropies grantee—which was founded in 1994 in Mumbai, India, with the mission "Every Child in School and Learning Well"—develops all its programs on the basis of innovation and rigorous evaluation. As a result, it has successfully reconfigured teaching methodologies, challenged traditional learning mechanisms, and delivered substantive and measurable results that directly benefit children in twenty-one of India's twenty-nine states. Its model currently helps shape the education of more than sixty million schoolchildren across India. For more than fifteen years, Pratham has worked with the Abdul Latif Jameel Poverty Action Lab (J-PAL) to design and execute randomized controlled trials (RCTs) to determine whether its high-quality, low-cost, replicable interventions are achieving their intended outcomes. The data provided by J-PAL studies has helped Pratham refine programs to improve outcomes, and this evidence base has fueled Pratham's ability to scale and influence the Indian government's approach to educational programming and social policy.

Strategic Management

Having a clear and powerful mission, a rigorously developed strategy, and a commitment to impact evaluation is necessary—but not sufficient. To achieve not just impact but sustained impact at scale, social sector leaders must also excel at strategic management. They must ensure adequate funding for their organization, structure it well and manage its talent wisely, and optimize their approach to board governance.

Funding

Funding provides essential fuel to any nonprofit and is critical to the smooth functioning of its engine of impact. Ironically, leaders and board members of nonprofits often put more time and effort into financial matters than their counterparts in business do. Indeed, many spend half their working hours—or more—on fundraising efforts. While many nonprofit leaders have a hard time with fundraising, some charismatic individuals excel at it. Success with fundraising often lies in the recognition that nonprofits have to spend money to raise money, which typically means hiring experienced fundraising and development staff. In any event, every outstanding nonprofit leader must be committed to fundraising, generally through earned income, donations, or a combination thereof.

Earned income is not an option for all nonprofits, but for those able to monetize some aspect of their operations—such as program content, goods produced by participants, or data—it can be an excellent source of funding. In addition, it can often directly serve the mission of an organization. BRAC, a global nongovernmental organization that is another high-performing grantee of King Philanthropies, funds much of its antipoverty work in Bangladesh through earned revenue. In 2018, 79 percent of its income came from its microfinance activities and social enterprises.[10] Both these efforts are key parts of its impact model, helping people become self-sufficient even as they generate revenue for the organization—with mission-aligned impact always in the driver's seat.

Importantly, some BRAC enterprises cover their own costs, while others generate net income to support other BRAC projects; 15 percent of profits from its microfinance arm, for example, are contributed to its core budget.[11] Another King Philanthropies grantee, One Acre Fund, has a similar funding structure. Earned revenue from farmers makes up nearly three-quarters of its total income, and this reliance on paying clients ensures that the organization remains keenly attuned to their needs.

CAMFED, a King Philanthropies grantee that provides educational opportunities to girls in Africa, stands out for the creative way that its founders—Ann Cotton, Lucy Lake, and Angeline Murimirwa—approach funding their organization. They have fostered a loyal and successful alumnae network that has effectively created a virtuous cycle of philanthropy to support its mission. On average, every girl who receives a CAMFED bursary goes on to financially support (and mentor) three other girls. At King Philanthropies, we look for organizations with models that are financially sustainable over time, and CAMFED exemplifies one that I call "pay-it-forward scaling."[12] The success of CAMFED demonstrates what I hope will become a future trend: What if we assessed nonprofits not only by their impact on beneficiaries but also by the extent to which those beneficiaries later become donors and leaders who multiply an organization's impact through direct engagement?

Organization and Talent

Money is important to the success of a social sector organization, but people are even more important. That is why outstanding social sector leaders understand that talent is absolutely critical to the organization's success and implement tightly managed talent processes that will attract and retain the best people. As Jim Collins wrote in his book *Good to Great and the Social Sectors*, "Those who build great organizations make sure they have the right people on the bus, the wrong people off the bus, and the right people in the key seats before they figure out where to drive the bus. They always think first about 'who' and then about what."[13]

Pratham is an organization that gets the right people on the bus and keeps them there. It also excels at looking inside the bus to see if it might seat its people in different ways. Each year, Pratham produces the Annual Status of Education Report (ASER), an essential document that provides reliable estimates of children's learning outcomes in every Indian state and rural district. Its findings are used to propel action and create demand for better education services at the ground level. Producing

ASER is a massive undertaking that entails surveying 600,000 children each year in 300,000 sampled households.

The ASER Centre, based in New Delhi, oversees thirty thousand volunteers who go door-to-door each year to conduct the survey—an approach that supports Pratham's low-cost delivery model. Some of these volunteers are Pratham staff who work in other areas of the organization. As Banerji, the CEO, explained to me in a 2016 interview, one goal of starting ASER was to build capacity among Pratham staff "with respect to the nuts and bolts of measurement, evidence, and analysis." She elaborated:

> We realized that a time-based project like ASER teaches people a lot in a very short time. . . . ASER is an excellent short boot camp in which you either perform well or perish. The survey is run like a course in which participants acquire skills that are applicable in other parts of Pratham as well. In fact, the skill acquisition is so strong that . . . within Pratham the next generation of leaders often come from ASER.[14]

Friends of the Children, a nonprofit that has received funding from King Philanthropies through our Founders' Projects grants, is another organization that gets its talent equation right. Friends of the Children empowers youth across the United States who face tremendous obstacles. In contrast to Pratham, it has adopted a model that favors paid professional staff over volunteers as a means for responding to the unique circumstances facing its beneficiaries (troubled youths who need a consistent long-term "friend" in their lives versus volunteers, who tend to come and go). The juxtaposition of these two models demonstrates that there is no strict formula but rather a need to develop a talent model to respond to unique programmatic needs and opportunities.

Also fundamental to the success of Friends of the Children is its recognition that a diverse workforce, an equitable workplace, and an inclusive culture enable a nonprofit to have maximum impact. According to CEO Terri Sorensen, 88 percent of the youths in its program identify as people of color (with 60 percent identifying as Black or African American, or as multiracial), and 68 percent of its program staff identify as people of color. Several years ago, the organization made a deliberate decision to increase the racial and ethnic diversity of its board. "It was incredibly important that we bring more diverse voices to the table who represent the youth we serve," Sorensen told me.[15] In 2020, following the tragic murders of George Floyd, Breonna Taylor, and Ahmaud Arbery, Friends of the Children created a racial equity working group that includes nearly half its board members. It also created a staff-led racial equity working group and a new position (director of equity, diversity, and inclusion) to help make decisions, align chapters, and communicate with stakeholders on racial equity issues.

High-performing social sector leaders recognize that having the right talent onboard is necessary but not sufficient; *how* people are organized matters immensely. There is an emerging organizational model called "team of teams" that is demonstrating early success (see also Bill Meehan's discussion of the concept in chapter 3 of this volume). Meehan and I discussed the team-of-teams model in *Engine of Impact* and in a subsequent article in *Forbes*;[16] we believe that it has the potential to reinvent the way that nonprofits and foundations build and develop their organizations. This model emphasizes decentralized autonomy, meritocracy, and a sense of partnership. Teams come together around specific goals, with a single coordinating executive team at the center, and the composition of each team shifts as needed over time. The team-of-teams model reflects fundamental changes in the world—driven in part by technology, globalization, and workflows that are increasingly project based—on which nonprofits hope to have an impact.

One Acre Fund has had early success in piloting the team-of-teams model. Andrew Youn, its talented founder and CEO, reflected:

> How we approach people is the most important thing behind our success so far. We create very high-autonomy teams. . . . We find the nerds who are really passionate, who are able to reason through new problems, and who have a lot of growth potential. They have the humility to want to grow. And then we put them on teams and give them as much autonomy as possible. I really want them to feel like they're basically running their own NGO.[17]

One advantage of the team-of-teams model is that it provides terrific opportunities for professional development. Youn explained:

> Team-of-teams is most effective when it is very much embedded with the hiring strategy. For example, if we are hiring a bunch of people externally, it can be hard to keep cohesion, but

if we're bringing people and helping them rise from the bottom and develop, then we inherently have the values, culture, vision, and cohesion that are very important to making the strategy effective.[18]

Board Governance

Strong board governance, though rare in practice, is essential for any nonprofit to truly excel. Invariably, a great nonprofit leader is guided by a great board. There tends to be a self-reinforcing process in which an organization's leaders and its board strengthen each other and fuel high performance. In fact, in many of the best nonprofits, there is a healthy tension in which *both* the CEO and the board believe that they are "in charge."

Engine of Impact contains an entire chapter with tips for good governance. Here, however, I hone in on my observation that strong nonprofit leaders know how to manage their boards and, most importantly, are able to extract maximum helpful guidance from them. The strongest nonprofit leaders work proactively to cultivate a board that is engaged, provocative, critical, and willing to ask hard questions. They shun the typical "rubber stamping yes board" and summon the courage to compose their board with people with hardheaded expertise who discuss, wrestle with, and provide guidance on the most important choices facing the organization—including bringing a willingness to push back and say "no" to plans that would cause mission creep or detour the organization from its core competencies. At King Philanthropies, I consider our best board meetings those that aren't necessarily smooth but rather the ones in which the board engages in lively discussion of the most important strategic questions facing our organization, often beginning with disagreements and concluding with alignment that takes us to the next level. Similarly, J-PAL's executive director, Iqbal Dhaliwal, reflects that J-PAL's board members "challenge each other's assumptions. Healthy respect for each other's skills is balanced by a very open environment of questioning, very similar to an academic seminar."[19]

Personal Qualities

High-performing leaders work to cultivate a set of personal qualities that enable them to vault over key obstacles endemic to the sector. These obstacles include an overreliance on inspiring language and lofty visions, rather than concrete plans; a tendency to anchor on "proven" methods and strategies at the expense of continuous improvement; a high, and often unsustainable, level of stress; and the sheer length of time necessary to achieve lasting change. In this section, I will explore four qualities that leaders can develop to overcome these pervasive challenges. The first two, disciplined goal setting and continuous adjustment, help leaders build a high capacity for *insight*. The latter two, a well-developed stress muscle and perseverance over long time horizons, help leaders attain a high level of *courage*.

In part through research I have conducted with my colleague Maya DiRado Andrews, an Olympic gold medalist in swimming, I have deepened my understanding of these qualities.[20] Andrews and I have found that great organizational leaders exhibit many of the same qualities that top athletes use to summon peak performance in their field.

Disciplined Goal Setting

The social sector is characterized by inspiring language and lofty visions. "We are going to end global poverty" is the sort of statement we hear far too often from social sector leaders speaking about their organizations—which typically have the capability to make, at best, a small difference in a few villages in a single region of one country. Social sector leaders default to such language because it ostensibly has the power to inspire and motivate. In the short run, this may be true, but in the long run, trumpeting overly ambitious goals is counterproductive because it can breed disillusionment and frustration if those goals are not achieved. Indeed, a pie-in-the-sky vision can create barriers to innovation and impact if not accompanied by the ability to set the right goals in the right way.

That explains why the highest-performing social sector leaders tend to view goal setting as a science—one that requires discipline and precision. However, while goal setting is pervasive in our culture, goal achievement is rare; just look at New Year's resolutions, which fewer than 2 percent of those who set them manage to fulfill. That's because, like "end global poverty," these resolutions tend to be vague and amorphous, lacking specificity, urgency, and context: Lose weight! Exercise more! Be a better person! The right goal, by contrast, is one that focuses on improvement over time—on achieving what athletes call their "personal best"—rather than comparison with other people or organizations.

High-performing athletes cite two common themes in their specific approaches to goal setting. First, they rely on the incredible power of incremental goals—the power of focusing proactively and explicitly on short-term (even *daily*) objectives. Second, they ensure they will achieve these goals by setting reasonable expectations—an especially critical point for beginners or novices. So, while the ultimate goal may be an Olympic gold medal or an end to poverty in a particular place, the incremental goals are clear, measurable, and down-to-earth. High-performing people, be they athletes or social sector leaders, set goals that are:

- **Specific.** The more specific the goal, the more effective it will be as a mechanism to improve performance. A useful goal is binary in outcome, with no room for ambiguity—either it was achieved or it wasn't.

- **Feedback driven.** Feedback is crucial to the goal-setting process. A goal that is theoretically measurable is better than a goal that is impossible to measure. An easily measurable goal that works with immediate or near-immediate feedback is even better. Cultivating a voracious appetite for feedback helps ensure that all existing feedback mechanisms are utilized and that better, more accurate mechanisms are developed when needed.

- **Self-referential.** A self-referential goal is one that depends on your own actions or those of your organization, and not on comparisons with others. "Control the controllables" is a common refrain in sports that also applies to nonathletic contexts. Indeed, the underlying concept forms the essence of the "serenity prayer" used in twelve-step programs.[21] Controlling things that you can control is essential to effective goal setting.

- **Chunkable.** Even the best, most specific goals need to be broken down into digestible chunks. The more complex the task, the more important "proximal," or near-term, goals become to maintaining motivation. In dynamic situations (read: almost everything in life), performance errors are often caused by an inadequate breakdown of a complex task into intermediate or short-term goals.

BRAC's founder, the late Sir Fazle Hasan Abed, used rigorous goal setting to transform BRAC into one of the largest, most effective non-profits in the world. Born into a comfortable family in what is now Bangladesh, Abed held a plum job as head of finance for Shell Oil in 1970—the year that the deadliest tropical cyclone ever recorded hit his country and killed nearly half a million people. Struck by the suffering he saw, Abed loaded supplies onto a boat and went to help people on the country's worst-hit offshore islands. What he saw forever changed his life, as he said in a 2014 interview conducted at Harvard Business School: "The scene was just horrendous—bodies strewn everywhere—humans, animals, everything. That shocked me to an extent that I felt that the kind of life I led hardly had any meaning in a kind of context in which these people lived—the fragility of life of poor people."[22] Abed immediately started organizing to help cyclone survivors. Just a short time later, the Bangladesh Liberation War broke out; hundreds of thousands of people died, and ten million refugees fled to India. When the war ended in December 1971, the refugees began returning to a newly independent Bangladesh that was in a shambles. Once again, Abed set out to help. Having already quit his job at Shell, he sold a small flat he owned in London and created BRAC. His goal was always large. "Everything we did in Bangladesh we did with one focus: getting poor people out of poverty because we feel that poverty is dehumanizing," Abed told *The Guardian* in 2015.[23]

But Abed and his colleagues always broke down the large goal of liberating people from poverty into specific, measurable chunks. In the aftermath of the war, for example, he targeted two hundred villages in one region and set a very clear, self-referential goal that he hoped donors would support. "I told them, the first year, we'll just build homes, keep the children alive, if we can, by distributing high-protein food, and help the farmers till their land," Abed recalled. In just nine months, BRAC built sixteen thousand homes. It then went on to help people in this same region with agriculture, water, sanitation, hygiene, and more, adopting an integrated approach to poverty alleviation that was always driven by feedback and measurement. When Abed retired from BRAC in 2019, executive director Asif Saleh wrote a tribute that noted his ability to set and achieve goals:

> "Small is beautiful, large is essential"—that was a mantra, that became part of BRAC DNA. He set targets that required a lot

of courage and . . . he delivered on all of them! From going to every single household in Bangladesh to teach mothers how to make oral rehydration saline, to covering half the country with latrines, to ensuring social protection for millions of ultra-poor, he was very clear in setting lofty targets in solving social problems. But there was also a clarity that he could convey in how to achieve those targets which made it look easier and much simpler than it actually was. He wanted to dream big and pushed everyone out of their comfort zone and such is his enigmatic personality that we all wanted to give our all to achieve those dreams.[24]

Continuous Adjustment

Work in the social sector is relentless. The unmet needs that social sector organizations strive to address are tremendous and never-ending, while essential resources always fall short of meeting those needs. Success is so difficult to attain that when it does happen it can be hard to resist the temptation to sit back, rest on hard-earned laurels, and succumb to complacency. Nonprofit leaders also face the temptation to simply do more of the same because they assume that early success on a "proof of concept" initiative affirms their approach.

But truly extraordinary leaders never stop the process of continuous improvement. Indeed, they adjust fearlessly even after proven successes. They adhere to an ethos of never settling for "success," much like top athletes who look beyond wins and losses and are neither fully satisfied by the chance to wear a championship ring nor deterred by watching their championship dream slip away. To these star performers, a given triumph or defeat is simply one step in a lifelong process of pushing toward their absolute limits. Being "great," in their view, is never enough; for them, greatness lies not in achieving an end state but in the process of striving for more. This orientation leads people who are at the top of their game to keep adjusting their performance and to do so without fear that such changes will hinder their forward progress.

Two extraordinary nonprofits illustrate this mindset. CAMFED, as noted previously, enables educational opportunities that have demonstrably improved learning outcomes for more than four million girls in rural African communities. But leaders and alumnae of the organization were not satisfied with that remarkable level of impact. Recognizing that CAMFED's ability to reach more girls would always be limited by its level of fundraising, alumnae came together to form a network that organically supports the CAMFED approach and spreads CAMFED values. Supported by CAMFED leadership, this initiative further "moves the needle" by turning beneficiaries into future leaders and donors. CAMFED's commitment to continuous improvement has allowed it to pursue the "pay-it-forward scaling" model that I discussed earlier.

Similarly, Esther Duflo and Abhijit Banerjee, leaders of J-PAL and recipients of the 2019 Nobel Prize in Economics, could easily rest on their laurels and do "more of the same" extraordinary poverty alleviation work for which they were awarded the Nobel. Instead, they decided to leverage the prize by creating "J-PAL 2.0," which led them to launch a bold initiative that focuses on climate change. This new initiative, called the King Climate Action Initiative and supported by King Philanthropies, seeks to address the damaging effects of climate change on the world's most vulnerable, who will be the most severely and disproportionately affected. Even though the majority of J-PAL's work to date has been in the nonclimate space, Duflo and Banerjee regard this as a very important growth area given that issues of poverty and climate change are increasingly interlinked.

A Well-Developed "Stress Muscle"

We all know that working in the social sector can be stressful. Many social sector workers spend their days providing emergency assistance to children suffering from acute malnutrition, helping those who have been displaced by fires, or addressing other social crises and natural disasters. Even those whose programmatic work isn't oriented toward addressing crises, such as symphony orchestra members or providers of preventive health-care services, nonetheless face organizational challenges and other obstacles that cause stress.

Research that underscores the high stress levels in the sector has been appearing for years. A 2015 survey of nonprofit leaders in Philadelphia found that nearly 59 percent of the 231 executive directors surveyed felt "stressed," "exhausted," or "anxious and worried."[25] In 2016, *The Atlantic* magazine ran an article ("The Plight of the Overworked Nonprofit Employee") that cited pressure from funders to tighten budgets, cut costs, and generally "perform like businesses," which led many nonprofit leaders to work ever-longer hours—and expect the same of their staffs—but without increased compensation.[26]

The Covid-19 pandemic and subsequent economic challenges only increased the stress levels experienced by nonprofit leaders. As reported in *The Chronicle of Philanthropy*, a spring 2020 survey conducted by La Piana Consulting found that nonprofits had lost significant revenue and faced unexpected expenses, causing more than half of them to expect to make cuts in compensation and staffing. Nonprofit leaders who responded to the survey acknowledged feeling guilt and stress as they struggled to grapple with pandemic conditions and economic contraction.[27]

Even so, not all stress is bad stress. In recent years, researchers have demonstrated what elite athletes and other high-level performers have long known: acute stress is often the prelude to excellence.[28] In the right circumstances, being "keyed up" or "on edge" comes with a burst of energy and a keener ability to focus. Just like the rest of us, high-performing social sector leaders feel pressure and get nervous as they prepare for a big event or address a new crisis. But, unlike many of us, they have developed the ability to harness stress for their benefit. As the stakes get higher, true leaders use the pressure of the moment to summon their peak performance. They do so by treating stress, in effect, as another muscle that they can build up and then use. Findings from physiology and brain science demonstrate the beneficial effects of acute stress, and high-performing social sector leaders seem innately inclined to strengthen their "stress muscle."[29]

Sakena Yacoobi, founder of the Afghan Institute of Learning (AIL), built an organization that—like Yacoobi herself—thrived amid wartime stress. I first met Yacoobi in 2009, when she received the Henry R. Kravis Prize in Nonprofit Leadership, which I oversaw at the time. As she explained when I subsequently interviewed her in 2016, she became accustomed to hard work and pressure from an early age:

> After completing twelfth grade in Afghanistan, I had the opportunity to go to university in the U.S. It was an extraordinary but difficult experience. My English was weak, which made the studies very challenging, and I had to do odd jobs at night to pay for my studies. Consequently, I could never sleep more than four hours per night. Many times I considered giving up. But my father taught me to never give up.[30]

Yacoobi's persistence enabled her to build a comfortable life in the United States as a professor, but in 1992 she left that life behind to help Afghan civil war refugees who had fled to Pakistan and were housed in camps. During this period, the Taliban rose to power and began implementing ruthless policies that, among many other things, almost entirely denied girls and women access to education. In 1995, Yacoobi founded AIL to help educate girls who were deprived of this basic right. "At any moment, the Taliban could come after me," she recalled, "I knew I could be killed, and that they would torture me before they killed me. . . . But I continued, quite simply, because I believe in education. It had changed my own life. And I believe that education has the power to help change the lives of the people of Afghanistan." To avoid being targeted, Yacoobi traveled constantly among AIL sites, first in Pakistan and later in Afghanistan. "No one could know my whereabouts, and fear was always there with me," she said. "I had to summon courage on a daily basis. I did so by allowing my passion for the cause to prevail."

Yacoobi's stress muscle was so well developed that it arguably saved her life one day in 1992 when a group of nineteen gun-toting young men blocked the rutted country road on which she was being driven to an AIL center. Yacoobi's driver asked the men what they wanted and they pointed to her, demanding that she exit the vehicle. Terrified though she was, Yacoobi activated the stress muscle she had built up over the years. She explained:

> I knew that if I didn't do what the young men asked, then my staff workers and driver could very well be killed. So I focused on my staff workers and driver and what they needed me to do. I got out of the car. I did not act like I was afraid, even though I was terrified. That is always very important. Never, ever act like you are afraid. As I stood in front of the men, I held on to the car door so that they wouldn't see me shaking and I wouldn't collapse. I looked them directly in the eye. I took deep breaths, which helped me to muster a strong voice so they wouldn't hear my fear. And then I began to negotiate with them.[31]

The young men, it turned out, wanted an opportunity to study—just like the one enjoyed by girls who attended the nearby AIL center. Much as Yacoobi disagreed with their approach, she decided that she could not deny their request. So, after extricating herself from that terrifying encounter, she worked to obtain funding for a boys' education center. The men who accosted her all went on to graduate from high school, and some even went to college. Yacoobi, for her part, continues to hone her "stress muscle" to this day.

Perseverance across Long Time Horizons

The timescale in the social sector tends to be incredibly long. Indeed, many people join the sector fueled by enthusiasm and are determined to make a difference through their contributions, only to find themselves dismayed by how long it takes to achieve deep and transformative impact. As Bill Gates is said to have observed, "Most people overestimate what they can do in one year but underestimate what they can do in ten." In the social sector, this problem is compounded by the fact that the journey toward impact is generally measured not in days, weeks, or even years but decades.

Consequently, the highest-performing social sector leaders demonstrate incredible perseverance. In an age when many people are drawn to quick fixes and instant gratification, these leaders remind us that the road to excellence is long and that it winds through lengthy stretches of trial and error, of mediocrity and failure. Extraordinary social sector leaders are in it for the long haul. Those who are young recognize the importance of surrounding themselves with experienced and wise colleagues who have learned the value of tenacity.

Roy Prosterman, whose work I first encountered when he received the Henry R. Kravis Prize in Nonprofit Leadership in 2006, began his career in the 1960s as a lawyer for an elite Wall Street firm. Client work took him to Liberia (which then had no functioning currency, road system, or telephone service) and Puerto Rico for extended periods and gave him the opportunity to observe the impact of generational poverty and economic inequity. "This violated my sense of justice and fairness," said Prosterman, "This just should not be."[32] After a few years, Prosterman left private practice to teach at the University of Washington Law School. One day in the mid-1960s, he came across a law review article that posited a radical approach to land reform in Latin America. This spurred him to write a critique in which he suggested a more equitable approach that involved buying land at a fair price and then redistributing it to the landless rural poor. His idea came to the attention of the United States Agency for International Development (USAID), and Prosterman soon found himself doing fieldwork in South Vietnam to understand farmers' plight and aspirations, based on which he formulated a land-to-the-tiller law (which was subsequently adopted) in the middle of the Vietnam War, with a million tenant-farmer families becoming owners of the land they tilled and rice production subsequently increasing by 30 percent.[33]

This experience sparked a determination to do more. Prosterman went on to work with several other governments on land reform and eventually, with Hanstad, founded the nonprofit now called Landesa, with the aim of helping to secure land rights for the rural poor around the world. For many years, he worked out of his modest one-bedroom apartment near the University of Washington together with a small handful of staffers, many of them law students, who huddled at the desks that filled the living room; half the organization's files were kept in the bathtub and the other half on the stove! The organization's annual budget was under $200,000 for many years and did not surpass $1 million until two decades later. But Prosterman persisted, determined to promote social justice and help tenant farmers obtain property rights that would provide them with security and opportunity. Step by step, the organization grew and achieved its goals. By 2019, it had a budget of over $13 million and had helped reduce poverty, hunger, and conflict for more than 180 million families in more than fifty countries.[34] Through dogged tenacity over the course of more than five decades, Prosterman and his Landesa colleagues made a positive and enduring impact on some of the world's most persistent challenges. Since 2017, funding from King Philanthropies has enabled Landesa to strengthen and secure land rights for more than 3 million people in Asia and Africa.

For another inspiring example of perseverance, I look to the Bill & Melinda Gates Foundation and specifically to its cofounder Melinda Gates and its president of gender equality, Anita Zaidi, MD, who led a discussion in which I participated at a 2020 Giving Pledge session on gender equality. Both women have demonstrated remarkable perseverance in their personal leadership journeys and professional careers.

Gates noted in her book *The Moment of Lift: How Empowering Women Changes the World* that as a lifelong Catholic—but one who firmly believes that giving women access to contraceptives improves lives—it was difficult for her to cosponsor and address an international summit on family planning in 2012. She nonetheless forced herself to overcome her reluctance, and the summit helped raise billions of dollars for family planning in low-income countries. After the conference, Gates went out to dinner with friends who told her that family planning was just the first step and urged her to do even more for women. At the time, she did not feel equal to that task. Indeed, she wanted instead to "quit" and let others take up the work—but she didn't. As she explained in her book, "I suspect most of us, at one time or another, say 'I quit.' And we often find that 'quitting' is just a painful step on the way to a deeper commitment."[35]

Instead, Gates became increasingly focused on the importance of investing in women and in 2014 wrote an article for the journal *Science* called "Putting Women and Girls at the Center of Development."[36] By 2020, she had committed $1 billion to gender equality in the United States, well aware that the impact of this investment would be measured in years or decades. "We can expect to see change on behalf of women with measurable objectives and data over 5, 10, 15, 20, 25 years," said Gates.[37]

Meanwhile, to support its gender equality efforts, the Gates Foundation had promoted Zaidi from her position as director of vaccine development to the executive leadership team. Zaidi, a medical doctor, studied at Aga Khan University, Duke, and Harvard, and in 2013 she became the first recipient of the $1 million Caplow Children's Prize for her work with children in a poverty-stricken community in Karachi, Pakistan. Throughout her life, she has persevered by always focusing on the work. "For me it has always been about the work that needs to be done," she said in a 2016 interview, "and then leading from that changing the way we think about a problem."[38] Zaidi pushed herself through challenging periods by remaining relentlessly optimistic and taking the long view. "I always look for the good that can come out of things even when something really bad happens," she said. "There can be opportunity in disaster and sometimes disaster is what it takes to change things."[39]

The social sector is a demanding environment—marked by inherent structural challenges, a chronic shortage of funding, and a never-ending surfeit of need—and it requires much of its leaders. Yet, the qualities of a high-performing social sector leader that I have elucidated here are, with a little luck and a lot of hard work, attainable by all of us. The process of pursuing big goals and achieving life-changing impact will never be easy, but all of us can benefit by learning from the best leaders in the sector and by striving to join their ranks.

FOR FURTHER READING

For a deeper dive into the chapter's content, you can read the book that Bill Meehan and I coauthored in 2017, *Engine of Impact: Strategic Leadership in the Nonprofit Sector* (Stanford Business Books). Many of the example leaders and organizations featured in this chapter are discussed in greater depth on the King Philanthropies website, www.kingphilanthropies.org.

Notes

1. Jim Collins, "Foreword," in William F. Meehan III and Kim Starkey Jonker, *Engine of Impact: Essentials of Strategic Leadership in the Nonprofit Sector* (Stanford, CA: Stanford Business Books, 2017).

2. King Philanthropies website homepage, https://kingphilanthropies.org/.

3. Meehan and Starkey Jonker, *Engine of Impact*, 27.

4. Raj Panjabi, Assistant Professor of Medicine, Harvard Medical School, interview with the author, 2016.

5. Sharon M. Oster, *Strategic Management for Nonprofit Organizations: Theory and Cases* (Oxford: Oxford University Press, 1995).

6. C. K. Prahalad and Gary Hamel, "The Core Competence of the Corporation," *Harvard Business Review*, May–June 1990.

7. Panjabi, interview with the author, 2016.

8. Landesa website, https://www.landesa.org/who-we-are/?gclid =CjwKCAjwjdOIBhA_EiwAHz8xmwwKRhRGvsDW99rUlKCLQKaCe0IKOR7v vD0zLSKuAaB-nXoNuVWU3BoCbGUQAvD_BwE.

9. Kim Starkey Jonker and William F. Meehan III, "Rural Development Institute: Should It Tackle the Problem of the Landless Poor in India?," Case SM159A (Stanford, CA: Stanford Graduate School of Business, 2007).

10. BRAC, *2018 Annual Report* (Dhaka, Bangladesh: BRAC, 2018), 66, https:// www.brac.net/sites/default/files/annual-report/2018/Bangladesh-Annual-Report -2018.pdf.

11. "How BRAC, the World's Biggest Charity, Made Bangladesh Richer," *The Economist*, September 7, 2019, https://www.economist.com/international/2019/09 /05/how-brac-the-worlds-biggest-charity-made-bangladesh-richer.

12. Kim Starkey, "Pay-It-Forward Scaling: A Powerful New Approach Exemplified by CAMFED," *Forbes*, February 6, 2020, https://www.forbes.com/sites /kimjonker/2020/02/06/pay-it-forward-scaling-a-powerful-new-approach -exemplified-by-camfed/?sh=31a76d53b5cf.

13. Jim Collins, *Good to Great and the Social Sectors* (Boulder, CO: James C. Collins, 2005).

14. Rukmini Banerji, CEO, Pratham, interview with the author, 2016.

15. Terri Sorensen, CEO, Friends of the Children, interview with the author, March 1, 2021.

16. William F. Meehan III and Kim Starkey, "Team of Teams: An Emerging Organizational Model," *Forbes*, May 30, 2018, https://www.forbes.com/sites /meehanjonker/2018/05/30/team-of-teams-an-emerging-organizational-model /?sh=6ee986f16e79.

17. Andrew Youn, CEO, One Acre Fund, discussion with the author, May 6, 2019.

18. Ibid.

19. Iqbal Dhaliwal, Executive Director, J-PAL, email message to the author, January 18, 2021.

20. This research was summarized in a series of articles on the topic of "An Olympic Frame of Mind," published in July and August 2021 in Kim Starkey's column in Forbes.com: "An Olympic Frame of Mind: How Leaders Can Hone Their Mindset for Peak Performance," July 23, 2021, https://www.forbes.com/sites /kimjonker/2021/07/23/an-olympic-frame-of-mind-how-leaders-can-hone-their -mindset-for-peak-performance/?sh=2061609a4c50; "Setting the Right Goals in the Right Way," July 30, 2021, https://www.forbes.com/sites/kimjonker/2021/07/30 /setting-the-right-goals-in-the-right-way/?sh=14723e451669; "Persistence, Persever-ance, Peak Performance," August 2, 2021, https://www.forbes.com/sites/kimjonker /2021/08/02/persistence-perseverance-peak-performance/?sh=e02ad1775d69; and "Focus on What You Can Control," August 5, 2021, https://www.forbes.com/sites /kimjonker/2021/08/05/focus-on-what-you-can-control/?sh=6ef30215376e.

21. "Grant me the serenity to accept the things I cannot change, the courage to change the things I can, and the wisdom to know the difference," commonly attributed to Reinhold Niebuhr.

22. Sir Fazle Hasan Abed, interview by Tarun Khanna, April 24, 2014, tran-script and recording, Creating Emerging Markets Oral History Collection, Baker Library Historical Collections, Harvard Business School.

23. Sam Jones, "Brac's Sir Fazle Hasan Abed Wins 2015 World Food Prize for Reducing Poverty," *The Guardian*, July 2, 2015, https://www.theguardian.com /global-development/2015/jul/02/brac-sir-fazle-hasan-abed-wins-2015-world-food -prize-reducing-poverty.

24. Asif Saleh, "Five Key Leadership Attributes That Made Sir Fazle Hasan Abed So Unique," LinkedIn, August 12, 2019, https://www.linkedin.com/pulse/five -key-leadership-attributes-made-sir-fazle-hasan-abed-asif-saleh/.

25. Kenneth Hilario, "Philadelphia's Nonprofit Leaders Feel 'Stressed,' 'Exhausted,' Says Study," *Philadelphia Business Journal*, March 17, 2015, https://www .bizjournals.com/philadelphia/news/2015/03/17/philadelphia-s-nonprofit-leaders -feel-stressed.html.

26. Jonathan Timm, "The Plight of the Overworked Nonprofit Employee," *The Atlantic*, August 24, 2016.

27. Jessamyn Shams-Lau, "Foundation Leaders Can Prevent an Exodus of Nonprofit Staff," *Chronicle of Philanthropy*, April 27, 2020, https://www.philanthropy .com/article/foundation-leaders-can-prevent-an-exodus-of-nonprofit-staff/.

28. See, for example, Alia J. Crum, Peter Salovey, and Shawn Achor, "Rethink-ing Stress: The Role of Mindsets in Determining the Stress Response," *Journal of*

Personality and Social Psychology 104, no. 4 (2013): 716–733, https://pdfs
.semanticscholar.org/a4af/f1e3f1a555e2868a306b70123525dd5f713c.pdf.

29. Ibid.

30. Sakena Yacoobi, interview with the author, 2016.

31. Ibid.

32. "Profiles in Giving: Roy Prosterman, Founder of Seattle-Based Landesa,"
Seattle Business Magazine, https://www.seattlebusinessmag.com/blog/profiles-giving
-roy-prosterman-founder-seattle-based-landesa.

33. Meehan and Starkey Jonker, *Engine of Impact*, 105.

34. Landesa, "What We Do," accessed January 26, 2021, https://www.landesa
.org/what-we-do/.

35. Melinda Gates, *The Moment of Lift: How Empowering Women Changes the
World* (New York: Flatiron Books, 2019), 24.

36. Melinda Gates, "Putting Women and Girls at the Center of Development,"
Science 345, no. 6202 (2014): 1273–1275, https://doi.org/10.1126/science.1258882.

37. "Melinda Gates Pledges $1 Billion to Speed Up Gender Equality," *VOA
News*, October 2, 2019, https://www.voanews.com/usa/melinda-gates-pledges-1
-billion-speed-gender-equality.

38. Sana Syed, "A Conversation with Anita Zaidi—a Discussion of Global Child
Health, Empowering Women and Creating Change for the Better," Medium,
December 5, 2016, https://medium.com/@syedsana/a-conversation-with-anita-zaidi
-a-discussion-of-global-child-health-af47699f070b.

39. Ibid.

3

Rethinking Billionaire Philanthropy

"BillPhils, About Face!"

William F. Meehan III

"For unto whomsoever much is given, of him shall much be required: and to whom men have committed much, of him they will ask the more."

—Luke 12:48

In August 2010, 40 of America's wealthiest people joined together in a commitment to give the majority of their wealth to address some of society's most pressing problems. Created by Bill and Melinda Gates and Warren Buffett, the Giving Pledge came to life following a series of conversations with philanthropists around the world about how they could collectively set a new standard of generosity among the ultra-wealthy.

So reads "About the Pledge" from the Giving Pledge website. It continues, "The Giving Pledge is a simple concept: an open invitation for billionaires, or those who would be if not for their giving, to publicly commit to giving the majority of their wealth to philanthropy."[1]

The Giving Pledge seems an unabashed reason to celebrate the billionaire philanthropists' (hereafter BillPhils) generosity, with the hope that when historians look back on our time, they draw the conclusion that BillPhils were not only generous but also played important roles in addressing some of our most pressing societal issues.

Our BillPhils' personal wealth available for social impact is enormous. *Forbes* reported 614 billionaires in the United States in 2020. Of those, 400 had individual net worth of $2.1 billion or more and combined net worth of about $3.2 trillion as of mid-2020.[2] These constitute the *Forbes* 400. Those who had a mere single billion, putting them below the bottom of the *Forbes* 400, get us to $4 trillion.[3]

Unfortunately, the Giving Pledgers' and other BillPhils' first decade as generous, impactful philanthropists can only be called a sluggish start. A few facts:

Few commitments. Just 74 of the *Forbes* 400 have signed the Giving Pledge, though all are eligible.[4]

Slow progress in honoring commitments. Of the over two hundred who have signed the Giving Pledge, few have transferred anywhere close to the half of their net worth they committed to giving away in their lifetimes. The Bill & Melinda Gates Foundation commissioned a Bridgespan report in 2018 that focused on about two thousand of the very wealthiest American families—those with assets of $500 million or more—and found that they donated about 1.2 percent of their assets to charity in 2017.[5] An Urban Institute study found, more generally, "no class of wealthholders gives away even 0.5 percent of their wealth in a year."[6]

Meanwhile, their wealth is still growing. The personal wealth of every Giving Pledger has increased since they signed. "The rise in wealth

BIOGRAPHY

WILLIAM F. MEEHAN III is the Raccoon Partners Lecturer in Strategic Management at the Stanford University Graduate School of Business and senior partner emeritus at McKinsey & Company. He is coauthor, with Kim Starkey, of *Engine of Impact: Essentials of Strategic Leadership in the Nonprofit Sector*.

EXECUTIVE SUMMARY

Since August 2010, when Bill and Melinda Gates and Warren Buffett announced the Giving Pledge, the philanthropy of the superwealthy has become part of our broader public debate about the huge and still growing socioeconomic gap that exists in our society and the capitalistic political economic system that many believe causes it. I argue for four shifts that billionaire philanthropists should make in their giving: (1) "giving while living"; (2) focusing on the immense social impact achievable through evidence-based interventions instead of embracing a false confidence as a source of much riskier innovation; (3) adopting the team-based organizational model prevalent in all other knowledge-based sectors and leaving the still dominant bureaucratic foundation models to the past; (4) adopting a "servant philanthropy" mindset, resisting the inevitable ego-enlarging pressures that come from giving away large amounts of money.

is far outstripping the amount of giving," said Rob Reich, a Stanford professor and scholar of philanthropy, in June 2018.[7]

Many Giving Pledgers (and other BillPhils) give to their private foundations and donor advised funds (DAFs),[8] neither of which has an obligation to distribute a majority of the corpus during the donor's lifetime. In the United States, foundations are required by law to grant no less than 5 percent of assets annually to nonprofits. Donor-advised funds are an IRS loophole of illogic, dating as far back as the 1930s,[9] that is now too large to close—one *gives up* control to get their deduction but *exercises* control to "advise" where their donation goes. As a result, according to the 2020 *Forbes* 400, little of the BillPhils' giving is going to operating charities. "With hundreds of billions of dollars in *Forbes* 400 members' private charitable foundations, we can verify just a fraction of that sum is actually deployed annually to causes and communities in need," said *Forbes*'s chief content officer, Randall Lane.[10]

Progress will be hard to track. The Giving Pledge is made publicly, although without any legal obligation to fulfill it, and Giving Pledgers and BillPhils in general have very limited requirements to report how much and to what organizations they give. And witness the Chan

Zuckerberg Initiative (CZI) and other Giving Pledgers who have set up an LLC, a legal entity without any philanthropic meaning, or those who use DAFs. Both structures allow their philanthropy to be nearly opaque.

Philanthropists have a long history of demanding transparency from grantees but offering little themselves. As a result, one must rely on one's own observations and occasional fact-based reporting to assess their effectiveness.

Despite their sluggish start, there are reasons to hope that the Bill-Phils, led by the Giving Pledgers, can have great impact once they commit their financial and other resources more fully. The culture of philanthropy and the nonprofit sector generally has been changing dramatically and is poised for a truly transformative era. The center of gravity has shifted from the East Coast and Midwest to the West Coast. In 1975, you could visit virtually every major foundation in a day's walk starting at Grand Central Station in Manhattan and then a quick trip to the Midwest. But since the founding of the David and Lucile Packard Foundation (1964) and the William and Flora Hewlett Foundation (1966), the Gordon and Betty Moore Foundation and Bill & Melinda Gates Foundation (2000), the Emerson Collective (2004), the Omidyar Network (2004), the Chan Zuckerberg Initiative (2015), and others, the center of gravity of philanthropy has become bicoastal. Grant seekers, including development officers from Ivy League universities, can enjoy the mild climate of West Coast winters as they make their now essential trips to Seattle and Silicon Valley.

Foundation leaders, both executives and board members, have historically been a relatively quiet group of professionals largely known only to themselves, and predominantly elite, white, and male. But the leadership of the philanthropic community, now with a broader geographic spread, changing societal demographics and cultural norms, is bringing new energy—in word if not yet fully in deed—to develop an increasingly diverse group of executives and board members.

Witness Darren Walker, CEO of the Ford Foundation since 2013, who is openly gay and outspokenly Black, the son of a single mother, grew up poor in rural Louisiana and described himself as a "member of the first

Head Start class."[11] He is role modeling his commitment to diversity and inclusion in his staff and board and in his grantees. And Walker is a compelling, spirited, articulate but not strident public figure on issues of race, poverty, and social change as well as the role of foundations and philanthropists. One can ask how much he might achieve cajoling the famously political and bureaucratic Ford Foundation organization, but Walker— playing the role of the ultimate "insider-outsider"—is trying to inject "moral courage," diversity, and hopefulness through his iconic leadership of the philanthropic community, bringing social justice to the fore.

With hopes of finding meaning in their lives and work beyond that provided on Wall Street or in consulting for large corporations, many of our nation's top graduates now aspire to careers focused on social impact. In 2007, Stanford University established the Center for Philanthropy and Civil Society (PACS), which publishes the sector's leading journal, *Stanford Social Innovation Review* (SSIR), and the Stanford Graduate School of Business established the Center for Social Innovation (CSI) in 1998. Stanford University also offers countless courses and research programs in poverty, global health, education, diversity, environment, and other areas for social impact. Over six hundred universities now offer courses for their students—and often alumni and friends—as well as research programs in philanthropy, social entrepreneurship, or nonprofit leadership,[12] in addition to areas requiring domain expertise, such as sustainability, economic development, and social justice.

In summary, our BillPhils are poised to seize the opportunity to help address our most pressing problems, though they have not yet done so, and their sluggishness is coming at a significant cost. Let's defer to others a comprehensive review of the challenges we face globally and in the United States today. Suffice it to say that climate change may threaten our species before the end of this century; at a minimum, every year we delay ensures significant economic dislocation in some of our most impoverished and environmentally valuable geographies around the world. Furthermore, baby boomers, who in early adulthood pledged to bring "peace and love" to the world, have presided over dramatic growth in the socioeconomic gap that is now undermining our American social contract: our wealthiest 0.1 percent are worth about the same as all those in the bottom 90 percent combined.[13] The last time we saw such levels of disparity was during the Gilded Age before World War I, which saw Henry Ford, Andrew Carnegie, and John D. Rockefeller create the foundations that are still a prominent presence in the philanthropic sector today. Racism, immigration, and the lack of basic social services such as health care and housing remain open sores in American society.

The dramatic decline in extreme poverty globally since 2000, driven mostly by capitalism in China, India, and developing countries, has been reversed, as the Covid-19 pandemic affected the poor more than the rich. Our great hope for the spread of democracy globally as we approached the twenty-first century has been undermined by autocratic regimes in Eastern Europe, Central Asia, and Latin America, and our great American experiment of a "nation of immigrants" now faces a powerful economic competitor with a far different makeup: 91.6 percent of China is comprised of one ethnic group, the Han.[14]

Finally, specialized artificial intelligence (AI), or machine learning, is already entrenched in our lives, as every click on one of our digital devices provides our personal data to some entities we know and some we don't. We might someday find ourselves waking up to general AI, where a computer's output might be impossible to distinguish from a human's thinking. "The singularity"—when AI's intelligence surpasses humans'—is no doubt something we should already be working to shape and influence.

Observers from outside the philanthropic community are starting to criticize the BillPhils, even questioning why our society has chosen to reward so many with so much for doing so little. Most notable are two books: Anand Giridharadas's *Winners Take All: The Elite Charade of Changing the World*[15] and Rob Reich's *Just Giving: Why Philanthropy Is Failing Democracy and How It Can Do Better.*[16]

A snarky if gimlet-eyed observer, Giridharadas describes several individuals in contemporary philanthropy in support of his view that BillPhils are the same people who have rigged our economic and political system to be skewed hugely in their financial favor. He likewise asserts that whatever their apparent philanthropic generosity, they are doing no more than returning a small portion of their ill-gotten gains and doing so completely on their own terms.

Reich worries that philanthropy is an antidemocratic force in our democratic country. Without a doubt, distributing funds for social needs at the whim of the winners of our "Winners Take All" economy—instead of via a fairly elected legislature—is more oligarchic than democratic.

One prominent BillPhil, Laurene Powell Jobs, number twenty on the *Forbes* 400 list with $20.5 billion, is sympathetic to Giridharadas's and

Reich's concerns, telling the *New York Times*, "It's not right for individuals to accumulate a massive amount of wealth that's equivalent to millions and millions of other people combined. . . . There's nothing fair about that."[17]

To sum up the criticism of Giridharadas, Reich, and others: "If you are so wealthy and smart and well-intentioned, why aren't you solving today's most pressing social problems? And, being more generous? And committing to change the socioeconomic system that represses many and has significantly advantaged you?"

Billionaire philanthropy as it is now practiced is usually not responsive to these critics' essential concerns. Most importantly, unless and until we adopt a much more progressive tax regime to fund more comprehensive government environmental and social programs—a more social democratic approach to political economics, as is common in Scandinavia—we need our BillPhils' trillions of dollars to achieve maximum impact in addressing our most important social needs.

The purpose of this chapter is to outline why and how BillPhils, if they truly want to maximize their impact, must abandon the principles underlying their current approach to philanthropy and shift to four very different principles, often the opposite of what they are currently pursuing:

> First, shift from establishing perpetual foundations to "Giving While Living."
>
> Second, shift from viewing "philanthropy as risk capital" to primarily funding evidence-based interventions that have impact on large societal challenges now.
>
> Third, shift from slow, bureaucratic, conventional organizational models to the "team of teams" model that is used broadly and successfully by most knowledge-based organizations.
>
> Fourth, avoid the ego-distorting effects of philanthropy and instead instill the values and mindset of "servant philanthropy."

Principle Shift Number One: From Perpetual Foundations to "Giving While Living"

Remember the goal of the Giving Pledge: "The Giving Pledge is a simple concept: an open invitation for billionaires, or those who would be if not for their giving, to publicly commit to giving the majority of their wealth to philanthropy."

That said, the Giving Pledge founders have written, "Because Bill, Melinda, and Warren believe the right approach is to focus the foundation's work in the 21st century, we will spend all of our resources within 20 years after Bill's and Melinda's deaths. In addition, Warren has stipulated that the proceeds from the Berkshire Hathaway shares he still owns upon his death are to be used for philanthropic purposes within 10 years after his estate has been settled."[18] Bill Gates and Melinda French Gates intend to fulfill that commitment despite their divorce. Warren Buffett said that he will continue to give through foundations, even after retiring from the Gates Foundation board.

So, what are other Giving Pledgers and BillPhils doing? Based on what we know so far, many are giving to and planning to maintain perpetual foundations. Perhaps they are following the norm set by their Gilded Age forebears such as Carnegie, Ford, Rockefeller, the heir of Russell Sage, and others. (Julius Rosenwald, an early leader of Sears, Roebuck, did give his fortune away while alive, most notably to African American schools in the rural South.[19] He is likely less well known in part because there is no perpetual foundation bearing his name.)

The issue with perpetual foundations was best described by Henry Hansmann, Oscar M. Ruebhausen Professor Emeritus of Law at Yale Law School, who did much of the best work on the economics of non-profits in the 1990s. As he was quoted in 1998, "A stranger from Mars who looks at private universities would probably say they are institutions whose business is to manage large pools of investment assets and that they run educational institutions on the side . . . to act as buffers for the investment pools."[20]

The Martian would likely view managing assets as the primary business of perpetual foundations, which often give away no more than the federally required minimum of 5 percent annually. As Hansmann also pointed out, "Saving is worthwhile only if you have a better use for the money in the future than you do now."

The role model for today's BillPhils should be Chuck Feeney, who in September 2020, at the age of eighty-nine, finished giving away his total personal fortune of $8 billion. Called by *Forbes* "The Billionaire Who Wanted to Die Broke," both Warren Buffett (who called Feeney "my hero") and Bill Gates give Feeney credit for helping to inspire the Giving Pledge.

Feeney's original wealth came from cofounding and leading Duty Free Shoppers, founded in 1960. At first, he gave anonymously, with a highly discreet group of advisers and staff, including Harvey Dale and Joel Fleishman. Atlantic Philanthropies funded many education initiatives, including many at Feeney's alma mater, Cornell, including the launch of Cornell Tech on Roosevelt Island in New York City, conceived by Michael Bloomberg when he was mayor; multiple initiatives supporting peace in Ireland and South Africa; developing health-care systems in Vietnam; and creating the Global Brain Health Institute at the University of California San Francisco and Trinity College Dublin.[21]

In 1980, Feeney founded General Atlantic (GA), originally to manage Atlantic Philanthropies' funds but over time he encouraged GA to be a $40 billion global growth investment firm. Steve Denning, GA's co-founder and chair emeritus, remembers that Feeney told him in his first job interview in 1980 about the two reasons why he created General Atlantic: "to provide other entrepreneurs the opportunity that he had to build a successful business. But, Chuck added, he was creating GA also to increase his ability to give back to society."[22]

Denning then describes candidly how Feeney explained his motivations for Giving While Living: "Chuck said he 'derives great satisfaction in helping others and seeing the impact first-hand.' Besides, he added with his typical wry humor, 'when giving while dead, you don't feel anything.'"[23]

Let's hope that the Feeney's fellow Giving Pledgers lead more Bill-Phils to adopt his "giving while living" principle. John Arnold, the former hedge fund manager turned innovative philanthropist, adds, "The longer the distance between the person who funded the philanthropy and the work, the greater the risk of it becoming bureaucratic and institutional—that's the death knell for philanthropy."[24] And as Laurene Powell Jobs declared firmly to the *New York Times*, "I inherited my wealth from my husband, who didn't care about the accumulation of wealth. . . . If I live long enough, it ends with me."[25]

Without a doubt, ending destructive climate change is the ultimate cause demanding action sooner versus later. Should we stand by and wait for the US government to pass a carbon tax and create the right green incentives for carbon-intensive businesses, and for the global community to push China and India to significantly lower their use of fossil fuels while still fostering their economic growth?

Instead, should our BillPhils protect their foundations' corpus for perpetuity? Let's leave aside the complex arithmetic of computing how much a foundation can give away annually and still sustain its perpetual status. A $1 trillion corpus would lead to $50 billion in grants annually, but for what benefit? To whom? At the risk of our species, our planet?

The "new assumption" for BillPhils should be what Feeney called "giving while living." The arguments to support perpetual foundations or "when my (grand)children die" don't carry much weight when examined. Perhaps one can cite Jesus Christ, who said, "The poor will always be with us" (Matthew 26:11). Well, yes, but are you arguing for someone to starve and be cold tonight for the comfort of another in a hundred years?

We must see clearly two ingrained assumptions that in fact are the supporting rationale for perpetual foundations. If a living founder forms their private foundation as perpetual, it's about immortality, not impact. If a CEO or executive director and the board members don't question the perpetual nature of their existing foundation, it is about organizational self-perpetuation, not impact, a not uncommon motivation throughout the social sector.

It's one thing for a BillPhil to do what they wish with their wealth. It's another thing for some self-anointed group of people three or five generations after the founder's death to retain 95 percent of the total corpus so some other group of self-anointed people are able to do the same thing generation after generation after generation. Perpetuity is a very long time. Isn't there some moral imperative to feed that hungry person or care for that sick person before they die? Or save the species?

Principle Shift Number Two: From "Philanthropy as Risk Capital" to Predominantly Funding Evidence-Based Interventions That Have an Impact on Large Societal Challenges Now

On October 14, 2019, the Nobel Prize in Economics was awarded jointly to Abhijit Banerjee, Esther Duflo, and Michael Kremer for their experimental approach to alleviating global poverty. Banerjee is the Ford Foundation International Professor of Economics at MIT. Duflo is the Abdul Latif Jameel Professor of Poverty Alleviation and Development Economics at MIT. Banerjee and Duflo, a married couple, are the cofounders and codirectors of the Abdul Latif Jameel Poverty Action Lab (J-PAL). Kremer at that time was the Gates Professor of Developing Societies at Harvard.

Those of us who have been part of the movement to bring facts and analysis to decision-making in philanthropy and nonprofits—including all the authors of the chapters in this book—raised a special toast to these winners of the Nobel Prize in Economics, true pioneers of ideas that drive social impact. To quote the Royal Swedish Academy of Sciences,

> [T]heir experimental research methods now entirely dominate development economics. . . . [T]his year's Laureates have introduced a new approach to obtaining reliable answers about the best ways to fight global poverty. In brief, it involves dividing this issue into smaller, more manageable, questions—for example, the most effective interventions for improving educational outcomes or child health.[26]

The Nobel Prize marks not only that "experimental research methods," such as randomized controlled trials (RCTs), transform development economics, and extreme poverty alleviation, but also acknowledges that evidence-based evaluations—usually some form of cost-benefit analysis—have proven to be useful tools to aid decision makers.

Unfortunately, almost all governments and large, established nongovernmental organizations (NGOs) have been sluggish in adopting the practices developed by these Nobel Prize winners and others in our "evidence-based" movement.

More disappointing is that many BillPhils are not seizing the lead in applying evidence-based practices in their grant-making. The core barrier to our movement to make philanthropic decisions—and nonprofit organizational decisions—based on the most rigorous evidence available lies in muddy incentives. My late, sweet mother's rationale for ignoring her physician's advice to have exploratory surgery to determine what was causing her chronic gallbladder pain illustrates one apparent paradox, "What if they find something?"

The same illogic no doubt underlies the common rumor that some NGOs do not inform their board or funders about their RCTs if they show null results. If a nonprofit isn't sure whether its strategy actually achieves its mission and goals, and funders have yet to demand such evidence, why take the risk of bad results?

Muddy incentives or not, if a BillPhil is focused on true impact, there are significant areas of human need that can be addressed with evidence-based programs that have huge needs for funding. There is no more fundamental social justice problem facing us than poverty. The strong evidence-based intervention is giving cash, the new default for helping the poor. GiveDirectly (GD) has successfully pioneered digital and other forms of cash to alleviate extreme poverty in several African countries. In a decade, GD has distributed more than $300 million to hundreds of thousands of people. It has built in randomized controlled trials as part of its core managerial processes.[27] Furthermore, GD has demonstrated that cash can be a powerful intervention in refugee, postcatastrophe, and now Covid-19 settings in the United States.[28] It turns out that if you give desperate people cash, thus empowered, they spend it in ways that best match their needs.

If cash still isn't your thing, check out J-PAL's website or GiveWell .org, which identify evidence-based interventions and organizations in health care, education, entrepreneurship, and other areas. One could spend billions of dollars well just following what you will learn there.

Instead of funding evidence-based inventions that meet large human needs today, many BillPhils seem to subscribe to the long and still widely claimed canard that the role of philanthropy is to be "risk capital," to be "catalytic, transformative, innovative." Who said this is a first principle of philanthropy? Perhaps it made more sense in decades past, before the evidence-based movement identified so many ways for philanthropists to have much more immediate impact. Even Kevin Starr, the enlightened founder and leader of the Mulago Foundation, argues that since "philanthropy should be catalytic,"[29] making cash distributions, particularly regular payments made as universal basic income, is solely government's role. That is hard to argue in the abstract, but what if our poor's need is immediate and is ignored by their government? But we still live in an era dominated by President Ronald Reagan's lasting cynicism: "Government is not a solution to our problem; government is the problem."[30]

With a potential $4 trillion available from the BillPhils, should we ignore the needs of today's hungry, poor, badly educated, and underskilled because our role as BillPhils is only to be catalytic and risk-taking?

And what is the evidence (ironically) that philanthropists and foundations are good at taking risks, leading social change, or intrinsically innovative? Well, there's a bit but not much. Start by reading my always-optimistic mentor and friend Joel Fleishman's fine book *The Foundation: A Great American Secret; How Private Wealth Is Changing the World*.[31] He cites twelve case examples of foundation-sponsored social change, including the Rockefeller Foundation and the Green Revolution; the Carnegie Corporation of New York and Children's Television Workshop; and the Robert Wood Johnson Foundation and tobacco use. Let's not even debate whether these foundations' role was causal or essential.

One might say, "Well, it's venture philanthropy. We need to make lots of bets for one big success." Unfortunately, foundations aren't transparent in a way that allows anyone to validate, or even debate, such an analogy. And, many BillPhils assert that their success in technology or finance positions them for being large-scale social change agents, a proposition that is hardly self-evident to any, perhaps, but themselves and the nonprofit receiving the check.

Reich, in *Just Giving*, sees a risk when large-scale social change is initiated by plutocrats instead of via our democratic processes. One frightening example was the eugenics movement, quietly acknowledged as American philanthropy's "original sin," spawned and funded by the philanthropies of Will Keith Kellogg, Rockefeller, Carnegie, and Sage in the early twentieth century.[32] Of course, our generations aren't capable of making such a mistake. But who is in charge of ensuring that AI, "the singularity," will be human-centered, in the words of Fei-Fei Li, Stanford's leading AI scientist?[33]

BillPhils must earn the right, beyond sheer wealth and business success, if they seek to be "catalytic, innovative, transformative." Meanwhile, give gobs of your dough to organizations already meeting the needs of today's people, supported by evidence available now on the internet.

Principle Shift Number Three: From Slow, Bureaucratic, Conventional Organizational Models to the "Team of Teams" Model Used Broadly and Successfully by Most Knowledge-Based Organizations

The organizational model still deployed by most private foundations remains archaic and often dysfunctional. The "program officer" model centers decision-making in an individual leading a small group, generally organized by program area (e.g., social justice, higher education, health care).[34] Decision processes take months compared to, say, the few weeks that a private equity firm would take for its well-honed due diligence process to lead to a decision to invest billions of dollars. Foundations make an inordinate number of grants, usually hundreds, even a few thousand, which are often so small as to have little chance of making a difference or even justify the cost of the grant-making decision. These are predominantly single-year grants, generally funding a program, not an organization (a leading source of mission creep), and still often making institutional politics more important than evidence. And, if a potential grantee actually thinks the "program officer" is the decision maker, they will be disappointed as they wait and wait for a final decision that must first go up some opaque line of organizational reporting. The proposal may then languish at the board, where perhaps the grandchild of the late founder is discovered to be strongly biased for or against the grant. So many smart, well-intentioned people are trapped in a slow-moving bureaucracy.

After forty years as a student of and adviser to business, nonprofit, and philanthropic organizations, here's my summary for practitioners. Since the post–World War II era if not before, organizational structures have been functional: finance, sales and marketing, operations. Even the large, complex, multifocused organizations that arose in the 1960s and 1970s were organized into "business units," essentially several functional organizations in one company, perhaps with some shared services. Most traditional foundations are functional, with the "program officer" leading "operations." Despite most larger foundations having more program areas than any strategic focus could justify, they often are organized into several "business units."

Most of us in organizations now spend virtually all our time working in teams. This is particularly the case in knowledge-based organizations such as management consulting, private equity, technology, health care, and even universities, where leading researchers create interdisciplinary teams to cut across traditional academic disciplines. Let's call this the "third era of organizations."

The "third era of organizations" emerged well before it gained a name, "team of teams," supported now by so many technologies, globally responsive 24-7, accessing the best knowledge quickly, inviting multiple perspectives, and facilitating evidence-gathering and decision-making processes simply impossible until the twenty-first century.[35]

Bill Drayton, a friend since 1974, is widely credited with the founding of Ashoka in 1980 and with launching the idea and the practice of "social entrepreneurship." In 2013, he restructured Ashoka globally as a "team of teams." Instead of maintaining a traditional structure in which people work in hierarchies based on a function or a formal business unit, under Drayton's approach an organization operates as a constellation of teams that come together around specific goals.

Drayton says, "At the center of this constellation is a coordinating executive team, but the composition of each project team shifts as needed over time. Teams and team members work together in fluid, constantly changing ways."[36] The model emphasizes decentralized autonomy, meritocracy, and a sense of partnership.

Other leaders later promoted a similar approach. In 2015, retired US Army general Stanley McChrystal and his colleagues published *Teams of Teams: New Rules of Engagement for a Complex World*.[37] This work, which chronicles McChrystal's effort to reorganize the fight against Al Qaeda in Iraq, shows that a decentralized model can be effective even in a traditionally hierarchical institution like the US military.

It's time to launch "team of teams" as the organizational norm for foundations. Please don't argue; your most effective leaders operate this way already, if not by name. If you don't know how, ask that management consulting firm you work with, often to conduct a due diligence of a possible grant or a program area strategy. They will deploy a "team of teams," drawing on different types of resources tailored to the problem you have asked them to solve. Or ask that private equity firm with which you are considering an "impact investment." Their due diligence team will assess the several-billion-dollar financial investment in six to eight weeks, and their "social impact" team will conduct an evaluation similar to that of your siloed program team, also in less than two months.

While collaboration occurs among foundations and philanthropists, it's still not the sectorwide norm it should be. There are encouraging examples—after all, once you have a strong, evidence-based case for a specific intervention or nonprofit, why not broaden the sources of funding?

One prominent example is Blue Meridian Partners (BMP), spawned by the Edna McConnell Clark Foundation and led by its former CEO, Nancy Roob. It focuses on youth development and alleviating family poverty and makes "big bets" with long-term (five to ten years) unrestricted funding tied to meeting impact goals.[38] Bridgespan is their partner in evidence-based due diligence. As of late 2020, BMP had pooled more than $2 billion across five portfolios and engaged eighteen other funders as partners in collaborative approaches to these issues.

Another example is The Audacious Project, associated with TED Conferences (Technology, Entertainment, Design), which publicizes evidence-based projects also vetted by Bridgespan and invites donors to fund them. They have raised $750 million as of late 2020. Their partners include many newer philanthropists, including Steve Ballmer, Ray Dalio, John and Laura Arnold, the ELMA Foundation, and MacKenzie Scott.[39]

Others will follow. The "team of teams" organizational approach is designed to collaborate, inside and outside.

Principle Shift Number Four: From Embracing the Ego-Distorting Effect of Philanthropy to Instilling the Values and Mindset of "Servant Philanthropy"

After her windfall $38 billion settlement when she divorced her long-time husband, Jeff Bezos, in July 2020, MacKenzie Scott made gifts to 116 highly diverse nonprofit organizations totaling $1.7 billion. She wrote, "Last year I pledged to give the majority of my wealth back to the society that helped generate it, to do it thoughtfully, to get started soon, and to keep at it until the safe is empty. . . . There's no question in my mind that anyone's personal wealth is the product of a collective effort, and of social structures which present opportunities to some people, and obstacles to countless others."[40]

Later, in mid-December 2020, the *New York Times* reported that "she had given nearly $4.2 billion to 384 organizations in just the last four months. Many of the groups are focused on basic needs, including food banks and Meals on Wheels, in a trying year for millions of people."[41] Scott demonstrates that one BillPhil can break long-held philanthropic paradigms to achieve impact: donating nearly $6 billion in 2020 (comparable only to the much larger Gates Foundation); being well evaluated (due diligence by Bridgespan, no doubt in a team-of-teams organization); funding dozens of those conventional, essential community charities, such as food banks, YMCAs, and other organizations that are, like much of the nonprofit sector, under siege. In mid-2021, Scott announced another $2.74 billion in gifts via a blog post on Medium.

Self-aware foundation leaders and philanthropists observe, usually in private, how difficult a struggle it is to maintain a sense of humility as potential grantees, their friends, and supporters offer flattery for their brilliance and beauty in every interaction. Witness what in the 1980s Tom Wolfe labeled "plutography"[42]—the enjoyment the wealthy find in seeing well-posed pictures of each other in beautiful settings—finds its apotheosis in recent times in an annual issue of *Vanity Fair* on philanthropy and in the *Forbes* 400, where a single billion dollars in personal wealth will leave you below the bottom of the list. Is it any wonder that for BillPhils humility is not yet in danger of replacing hubris as their core philanthropic value?

But Scott is describing what philanthropy should be: an opportunity, often unearned, to serve others. It mirrors the philosophy of "servant leadership," first described by Robert Greenleaf in his 1970 essay "The Leader as Servant" and then published in book form:[43]

> The servant-leader is servant first, it begins with a natural feeling that one wants to serve, to serve first, as opposed to, wanting power, influence, fame, or wealth.[44]
>
> Don't assume, because you are intelligent, able, and well-motivated, that you are open to communication, that you know how to listen.[45]
>
> Care is taken by the servant-first [leader] to make sure that other people's highest priority needs are being served.[46]
>
> Principles of servant-leadership: Listening. Empathy. Healing. Awareness.[47]

Of today's young BillPhils, Cari Tuna and her husband, Dustin Moskovitz (number three at Facebook, now founder and CEO of Asana.com), best combine servant leadership, evidence-based philanthropy, team-of-teams-based organization, and a commitment to "giving while living." The details of their inspiring story are well worth reading, starting with *Giving in the Light of Reason*, by Marc Gunther,[48] but even the gist is compelling.

The youngest people to sign the Giving Pledge, in 2010, their net worth, still increasing as Moskovitz's latest company, Asana.com, went public in 2020, is over $10 billion. Tuna's first action after starting their initial philanthropy, Good Ventures, was to partner with and give her first grant to GiveWell.org, founded by two former Bridgewater associates, Holden Karnofsky and Elie Hassenfeld, and focused on identifying the organizations with evidenced-based programs as the most cost-effective interventions against extreme poverty. After working more closely, Karnofsky and Alexander Berger (co-CEOs as of 2021) founded the Open Philanthropy Project (OPP), Tuna and Moskovitz's overarching organization for social investment, one of their seven entities, including their private foundation, Good Ventures.

In 2015, based on GiveWell.org's evaluation as one of its top-rated charities, Good Ventures made a pathbreaking initial $25 million gift to GiveDirectly.org, helping to put that organization and cash on the map as the benchmark intervention for extreme poverty. The Open Philanthropy Project's leaders are disciples of "effective altruism," espoused by Princeton philosopher Peter Singer,[49] among others, which advocates using evidence to identify the most effective ways to help those most in need. Recently, OPP and others in the effective altruism movement have been expanding their interests to include the potentially damaging effects of AI on humanity.

"Give while living," "team-of-teams organization," "evidence-based decision-making," and "servant philanthropy"—four new principles for all enlightened billionaire philanthropies. Let the debate gain energy, momentum, and be at the center of philanthropy.

FOR FURTHER READING

For a deeper dive into the ideas explored in this chapter, I recommend four books. *The Billionaire Who Wasn't: How Chuck Feeney Secretly Made and Gave Away a Fortune*, by Conor O'Clery, describes the iconic philanthropist known for "giving while living." *The Foundation: The Great American Secret*, by Joel L. Fleishman, goes through specific case examples such as the Green Revolution and Rockefeller Foundation to demonstrate that the private foundations can lead social change. In *Poor Economics: A Radical Rethinking of the Way to Fight Global Poverty*, Nobel Prize–winning MIT economists Abhijit V. Banerjee and Esther Duflo describe the compelling evidence for which interventions do—and don't—alleviate extreme poverty. Finally, I recommend *Doing Good Better: How Effective Altruism Can Help You Make a Difference*, by William MacAskill. Whatever one's personal values, all philanthropists of our time should understand the effective altruism movement, which argues that we should apply an evidence-based and rational approach to understanding how to benefit others the most.

Notes

I thank Melissa S. Brown of Vancouver, Washington, who was with the IU Lilly Family School of Philanthropy for nearly twenty years and is now an independent research colleague. I would also like to acknowledge my long collaboration with

Kim Starkey, who has deeply influenced my thinking about the social sector, most prominently in our coauthored book *Engine of Impact: Essentials of Strategic Leadership in the Nonprofit Sector* (Stanford, CA: Stanford Business Books, 2017).

1. The Giving Pledge, "About the Pledge," https://givingpledge.org/About.aspx.

2. Forbes, "The *Forbes* 400," September 2020, https://www.forbes.com/forbes-400/.

3. Many of the over two hundred Giving Pledgers didn't make the *Forbes* 400 cut, either because their wealth fell below the cutoff or for some other reason related to how *Forbes* composes the list. In addition, there are billionaires who are on neither the *Forbes* list nor the Giving Pledge list, such as members of the family that owns Fidelity Investments, the family that founded Cargill, Inc., founders of SC Johnson, and others. See, for example, Tom Metcalf, "These Are the World's Richest Families," Bloomberg, August 2020, https://www.bloomberg.com/features/richest-families-in-the-world/?sref=o0pP9h0D. See also Kerry A. Dolan, ed., with Chase Peterson-Withorn and Jennifer Wang, "Billon-Dollar Dynasties: These Are the Richest Families in America," *Forbes*, December 17, 2020, https://www.forbes.com/sites/kerryadolan/2020/12/17/billion-dollar-dynasties-these-are-the-richest-families-in-america/?sh=3e62d46772c7.

4. Count as of November 2020 based on US residents named at The Giving Pledge, https://givingpledge.org/.

5. Susan Wolf Ditkoff, Alison Powell, and Kyle Gardner, with Tom Tierney, *Four Pathways to Greater Giving: What Will It Take to Unlock Dramatically More Philanthropy from America's Wealthiest Families?*, Bridgespan Group, November 23, 2018, 3, https://www.bridgespan.org/insights/library/philanthropy/four-pathways-unlock-greater-philanthropic-giving.

6. C. Eugene Steuerle, Jenny Bourne, Joycelyn Ovalle, Brian Raub, Joseph Newcomb, and Ellen Steele, *Patterns of Giving by the Wealthy* (Washington, DC: Urban Institute, 2018), 16, https://www.urban.org/sites/default/files/publication/99018/patterns_of_giving_by_the_wealthy_2.pdf.

7. Marc Gunther and Drew Lindsay, "Has the Giving Pledge Changed Giving?," *Chronicle of Philanthropy*, June 4, 2019, https://www.philanthropy.com/article/has-the-giving-pledge-changed-giving/.

8. Chuck Collins, Helen Flannery, Omar Ocampo, and Kalena Thomhave, *The Giving Pledge at 10: A Case Study in Top Heavy Philanthropy*, Institute for Policy Studies, August 2020, https://inequality.org/wp-content/uploads/2020/08/GivingPledge-Brief-Aug3.pdf/.

9. National Philanthropic Trust, "What Is a Donor-Advised Fund?," https://www.nptrust.org/what-is-a-donor-advised-fund/.

10. Forbes staff, "Enhanced Forbes 400 Philanthropy Score," *Forbes*, September 9, 2020, https://www.forbes.com/sites/forbespr/2020/09/09/enhanced-forbes-400-philanthropy-score-produced-with-support-from-global-citizen-measures-billionaire-money-donated-directly-to-charitable-organizations/?sh=5ffdb7433f93.

11. Ford Foundation, "Darren Walker, President," https://www.fordfoundation.org/about/people/darren-walker/.

12. Rob Fischer quoted on the web page for "Master of Nonprofit Organizations," Case Western Reserve University, https://case.edu/socialwork/academics/master-nonprofit-organizations.

13. Emmanuel Saez and Gabriel Zucman, "Wealth Inequality in the United States since 1913: Evidence from Capitalized Income Data," working paper 20625, National Bureau of Economic Research, Cambridge, MA, October 2014, http://www.nber.org.papers/w/20625.

14. CIA, "Ethnic Groups, China, Han Chinese 91.6%," *The World Factbook*, https://www.cia.gov/the-world-factbook/countries/china/.

15. Anand Giridharadas, *Winners Take All: The Elite Charade of Changing the World* (New York: Vintage, 2019).

16. Rob Reich, *Just Giving: Why Philanthropy Is Failing Democracy and How It Can Do Better* (Princeton, NJ: Princeton University Press, 2018).

17. David Gelles, "Laurene Powell Jobs Is Putting Her Own Dent in the Universe," *New York Times*, February 27, 2020, https://www.nytimes.com/2020/02/27/business/laurene-powell-jobs-corner-office.html/.

18. Gates Foundation, "Who We Are: Foundation Trust," https://www.gatesfoundation.org/Who-We-Are/General-Information/Financials/Foundation-Trust.

19. National Trust for Historic Preservation, "Rosenwald Schools," https://savingplaces.org/places/rosenwald-schools/.

20. Karen Arensen, "Q&A: A Modest Proposal," *New York Times*, August 2, 1998, https://www.nytimes.com/1998/08/02/education/q-a-modest-proposal.html.

21. Steve Bertoni, "Chuck Feeney: The Billionaire Who Is Trying to Go Broke," *Forbes*, September 18, 2012, https://www.forbes.com/sites/stevenbertoni/2012/09/18/chuck-feeney-the-billionaire-who-is-trying-to-go-broke/?sh=6471be43291c.

22. Steve Denning, "Forbes 400 Summit on Philanthropy Remarks for Lifetime Achievement Award," June 17, 2014. Shared with the author in a personal communication.

23. Ibid.

24. Steve Bertoni, "The Billionaire Who Wanted to Die Broke . . . Is Now Officially Broke," *Forbes*, September 15, 2020, https://www.forbes.com/sites/stevenbertoni/2020/09/15/exclusive-the-billionaire-who-wanted-to-die-brokeis-now-officially-broke/?sh=8f60b253a2aa.

25. Gelles, "Laurene Powell Jobs Is Putting Her Own Dent in the Universe."

26. Royal Swedish Academy of Sciences, "The Prize in Economic Sciences 2019," press release, https://www.nobelprize.org/prizes/economic-sciences/2019/press-release/.

27. GiveDirectly.org, "Experimental Evaluations," https://www.givedirectly.org/research-at-give-directly/.

28. GiveDirectly.org, "Project 100+," https://www.givedirectly.org/covid-19/us/.

29. Kevin Starr (@MulagoStarr), "Trying to go big on cash with philanthropy is a dead end. Philanthropy should be catalytic; governments should do UBIs. Mulago would be happy to point your uncertain Pledgers in useful directions :)."

Twitter, October 8, 2020, 6:25 a.m., https://twitter.com/mulagostarr/status /1314557694875897856.

30. Ronald Reagan, *Inaugural Address*, January 20, 1981, https://www .reaganfoundation.org/media/128614/inaguration.pdf.

31. Joel L. Fleishman, *The Foundation: A Great American Secret; How Private Wealth Is Changing the World* (New York: Public Affairs, 2009).

32. Edwin Black, *War against the Weak: Eugenics and America's Campaign to Create a Master Race* (Washington, DC: Dialog Press, 2012).

33. Wu Tsai Neurosciences Institute, "Human-Centered AI: A Case for Cognitively Inspired Machine Intelligence," Stanford University, https:// neuroscience.stanford.edu/events/title-tbd-fei-fei-li.

34. Joel J. Orosz, *The Insider's Guide to Grantmaking: How Foundations Find, Fund, and Manage Effective Programs* (San Francisco: Jossey-Bass, 2000).

35. William F. Meehan III and Kim Starkey, "Team of Teams: An Emerging Organizational Model," *Forbes*, May 30, 2018, https://www.forbes.com/sites /meehanjonker/2018/05/30/team-of-teams-an-emerging-organizational-model /?sh=46e1e78e6e79.

36. Ibid.

37. Stanley McChrystal, with Tantum Collins, David Silverman, and Chris Fussell, *Team of Teams: New Rules of Engagement for a Complex World* (New York: Penguin, 2015).

38. Blue Meridian Partners, "Our Partners," https://www.bluemeridian.org/our -partners/.

39. The Audacious Project, "About," https://audaciousproject.org/.

40. MacKenzie Scott, "116 Organizations Driving Social Change," Medium, July 28, 2020, https://mackenzie-scott.medium.com/116-organizations-driving -change-67354c6d733d.

41. Nicholas Koulish, "Giving Billions Fast, Mackenzie Scott Upends Philan-thropy," *New York Times*, December 20, 2020, https://www.nytimes.com/2020/12 /20/business/mackenzie-scott-philanthropy.html.

42. See https://www.lexico.com/en/definition/plutography.

43. Robert K. Greenleaf, *Servant Leadership: A Journey into the Nature of Legitimate Power and Greatness* (Mahwah, NJ: Paulist Press, 2002).

44. Peter Senge in Greenleaf, *Servant Leadership*," 352.

45. Ibid., 314.

46. Ibid., 27.

47. Celeste DeChryver Mueller, "Servant Leadership: The Way Forward," *Health Progress* 92, no. 5 (2011): 20–25 at 21, https://www.chausa.org/publications /health-progress/article/september-october-2011/servant-leadership-the-way -forward-.

48. Mark Gunther, "Giving in the Light of Reason," *Stanford Social Innovation Review* 16, no. 3 (Summer 2018), https://ssir.org/articles/entry/giving_in_the_light _of_reason#.

49. Peter Singer, *The Most Good You Can Do: How Effective Altruism Is Changing Ideas about Living Ethically* (Melbourne, Australia: Text Publishing, 2015).

PART TWO

METRICS AND MODELS

4

Measuring Corporate Virtue and Vice

Making ESG Metrics Trustworthy

Paul Brest and Colleen Honigsberg

He knows if you've been bad or good
So be good for goodness sake.

—John Frederick Coots, "Santa Claus Is Comin' to Town" (1934)

An increasing number of corporations aspire to meet demands to improve their environmental, social, and governance (ESG) performance. In 2020, one of every three dollars under professional management in the United States was managed according to "sustainable"—a term broadly synonymous with ESG—investing strategies.[1] The stakeholders interested in ESG measures extend well beyond investors and the companies' own managements. They include employees at the company and in its supply chain, consumers, regulators, and those subject to companies' environmental and social impacts.[2] These stakeholders may wish to assess a company's performance for any number of reasons. For example, they may want to improve performance, reward or punish the company, induce a company to internalize its external environmental and social costs, or predict the company's future financial and ESG performance.[3]

It is a cliché, because it is generally true, that you can't manage what you can't measure. There is a broad consensus about the financial metrics used to evaluate a company's balance sheet and its overall value, and these metrics are largely commensurable across a range of industries and geographies. By contrast, ESG factors are dissimilar, the techniques for measuring them are varied and complex, and many are not readily comparable. For these reasons, among others, it is not surprising that the assessments of the various ESG ratings services are poorly correlated with each other[4] and that the question of whether good ESG ratings predict better returns for investors is perennially controverted.[5]

Despite the huge differences between ESG and financial reporting, we believe that practices developed in financial reporting can contribute to achieving high-quality ESG reporting. In particular, we suggest that a comprehensive framework for ESG reporting must address the following three factors:

1. **A limited set of metrics, primarily concerned with a company's key environmental and social impacts.** Part 1 of this chapter summarizes the current state of the measurement of companies' ESG outcomes—particularly the environmental and social (E&S) factors, sometimes referred to as "planet" and "people"[6]—and the prospects for improvements.[7] It concludes by describing the requirements of a full-fledged social account-

BIOGRAPHIES

PAUL BREST is former dean and professor emeritus at Stanford Law School, a lecturer at the Stanford Graduate School of Business, and codirector of the Effective Philanthropy Learning Initiative at the Stanford Center on Philanthropy and Civil Society. He was president of the William and Flora Hewlett Foundation from 2000 to 2012.

  COLLEEN HONIGSBERG is an associate professor at Stanford Law School, where her work focuses on accounting and governance issues. A former certified public accountant, she left practice to pursue degrees at Columbia Law School and Columbia Business School, which awarded her a JD and PhD, respectively. Her research, which has been featured in major mainstream publications such as the *Economist*, the *Wall Street Journal*, and the *New York Times*, has been leveraged by senators and regulatory agencies to craft policy.

EXECUTIVE SUMMARY

To address the interests of a diverse group of stakeholders, an increasing number of corporations aspire to meet demands to improve their environmental, social, and governance (ESG) performance. We suggest that a comprehensive framework for ESG reporting—drawing on practices developed in financial reporting—must address the following three factors: (1) a limited set of metrics, primarily concerned with a company's key environmental and social impacts; (2) a standard-setting body loosely modeled on the Financial Accounting Standards Board (FASB) to develop and particularize those metrics; and (3) reporting infrastructures that enable companies to collect, report, and verify the relevant metrics accurately.

ing framework. Part 2 samples the existing reporting requirements for some basic environmental and social issues. Our goal is to explore the possibilities for developing a robust framework and scalable system that captures a company's major E&S effects.

2. **A standard-setting body modeled on the Financial Accounting Standards Board (FASB) to develop and particularize those metrics.** In part 3, we suggest that the lessons from financial accounting are instructive in developing an ESG standard-setting body. Financial accounting went through a series of standard-setting bodies before creating the FASB, and the FASB is commonly thought to be more successful than its predecessors because of its greater financial, industry, and political independence.

3. **Reporting infrastructures that allow companies to collect, report, and verify the relevant metrics.** The reporting framework must produce information that is accurate, objective, and verifiable, but the history of financial reporting has demonstrated the difficulty of generating this type of high-quality data without formal processes and procedures. Thus, in part 4, we show that companies need robust internal and external reporting frameworks (i.e., internal control systems and third-party auditors) to generate the underlying data and verify the reported information.

Part 1: Measuring Environmental and Social Impact

What is the current state of ESG reporting, and would what a comprehensive system look like?

Current Status of ESG Reporting

ESG reporting is still in a primitive stage, akin to financial reporting in the early twentieth century.[8] In the article "The Current State of Sustainability Reporting," Jill M. D'Aquila describes the following challenges:[9]

- Competing frameworks and standards designed for different audiences

- Lack of standardization of ESG metrics or performance indicators

- Measurement uncertainty (many types of sustainability information cannot be accurately measured)

- Different definitions of "materiality," complicated by evolving criteria related to sustainability

- Inconsistent reporting methods

- Disclosures in the form of vague, nonspecific "boilerplate language"[10]

- Lack of comparability of disclosures[11]

The history of efforts to improve E&S outcomes by monitoring companies and their suppliers has been full of disappointments.[12] While this has led at least one thoughtful student of the field to look for radically different proxies based on the quality and stability of business relationships,[13] it has also motivated several concerted (but not altogether coordinated) efforts to improve the reporting standards:

- Five major sustainability reporting agencies—CDP (formerly Carbon Disclosure Project), CDSB (Climate Disclosure Standards Board), GRI (Global Reporting Initiative), IIRC (International Integrated Reporting Council), and SASB (Sustainability

Accounting Standards Board)—have announced a "Statement of Intent to Work Together Toward Comprehensive Reporting Requirements."[14]

- The trustees of the International Financial Reporting Standards (IFRS) Foundation have proposed to create a Sustainability Standards Board, which would initially focus on the financially material climate risks incurred by corporations but might build incrementally to encompass other environmental issues and "double materiality"—a company's impact on the wider environment aside from financially material risks.[15]

- A report by the World Economic Forum (WEF), produced in collaboration with the Big Four accounting firms (Deloitte, Ernst & Young, KPMG, and PricewaterhouseCoopers) proposes metrics that "reflect not only financial impacts but 'pre-financial' information that may not be strictly material in the short term, but are material to society and planet and therefore may become material to financial performance over the medium or longer term."[16] The title of the WEF report, "Measuring Stakeholder Capitalism: Towards Common Metrics and Consistent Reporting of Sustainable Value Creation," captures its purpose.

- The International Federation of Accountants (IFAC) has proposed the creation of a new International Sustainability Standards Board that would create "a reporting system that delivers consistent, comparable, reliable, and assurable information relevant to enterprise value creation, sustainable development and evolving stakeholder expectations."[17]

- The Impact-Weighted Accounts Initiative (IWAI) at Harvard Business School is an ambitious effort to establish criteria for measurable E&S factors.[18] Its underlying premise is that the true value of a company is not captured by conventional financial metrics but rather must also account for the external costs imposed and external benefits conferred on major stakeholders.[19]

- A paper by Ben Smith and Brad Cooper reports on investors' strong interest in consistent and reliable impact reports by green bond funds.[20]

Elements of a Comprehensive System for Assessing a Company's Impacts

Informed by these efforts, we outline the desired requirements of a full-fledged social accounting framework and then ask what's feasible for some common environmental and social issues.[21] We do not address the costs of implementing the framework other than to note that, although they would be great, so are the potential benefits of improved E&S behaviors.

1. The framework must go beyond the conventional measure of a company's financial value to broadly measure its *"material effects on the economy, environment, and people"* (quoting the GRI) in terms of external costs and benefits. Different stakeholders may be interested in different effects, but if one examines the main standard-setting systems, there is considerable convergence around environmental standards involving greenhouse gas emissions and conventional pollutants, and around social standards involving child labor, forced labor, workplace safety, discrimination, and diversity. The indicators must include a company's significant *positive and negative effects on all stakeholders*, not just investors.

2. Information must be reported in a *timely* manner.

3. In addition to accounting for a *company's own impacts*, the framework should account for the company's contributions to the impacts of *suppliers*, the *consumers* of its products and services, and perhaps *competitors* as well. (In the particular domain of greenhouse gas emissions, these encompass Scope 1, 2, and 3 emissions, which we will discuss.) Accounting for the impacts of consumers is particularly difficult.[22]

4. The indicators of E&S factors must be *accurate, valid, and reliable*. *Accuracy* concerns how precisely the indicator measures the variable of interest.[23] *Validity* concerns whether the indicator captures the effects one is really interested in; indicators typically serve as proxies for the variables of interest, and the validity of the proxies can vary greatly.[24] *Reliability* concerns whether measurements of the same indicator are consistent across time. For example, is the definition of "serious" workplace accidents the same from one year to the next?

5. The information must be sufficiently *objective and verifiable* for auditors, regulators, institutional investors, and litigants to identify and correct material misreporting.

6. The information must be *accessible* to a wide range of stakeholders, either directly or through trustworthy intermediaries.

7. Although the same reporting methods and metrics must be used consistently across different companies and over time, the standards must be *adaptable* to reflect the evolution of technologies and the standards themselves. To reconcile adaptability with reliability, companies must restate prior years' metrics in terms of the new standard.

8. One must be able to *meaningfully compare the impacts of different companies within and across sectors*. For example, the IAWI initiative uses the concept of "environmental intensity" to reflect a company's negative environmental impact as a percentage of its operating income from sales.[25]

9. Ideally, measurements of indicators must be *monetizable*[26] or at least be reducible to a *common metric* such as quality-adjusted life years (QALYs).[27] Although some stakeholders may only care about one particular indicator, such as greenhouse gas (GHG) emissions, others may care about a company's aggregate benefits and harms. Just as conventional financial reports are intrinsically monetized, monetization of E&S factors provides a common value for comparing a wide variety of financial, environmental, and social effects. Monetization is essential for understanding the inevitable trade-offs among the goals of various stakeholders. It also "is a necessary condition for the development of capital markets driven by sustainability considerations."[28] This is almost surely the most challenging criterion in the list.

10. Standards should ultimately be set by an organization that is, to the extent reasonably possible, *independent* of political and industry pressure.

Part 2: Examples of Environmental and Social Standards

The organizations concerned with ESG measurement fall into three groups. The first group *defines indicators* relevant to environmental and social matters, such as pollution and workplace safety, but does not prescribe particular levels of behavior with respect to them. The Global Reporting Initiative (GRI)[29] is paradigmatic of this approach.

The second group *prescribes acceptable behaviors.* Broadly stated, these organizations fall into one of three subcategories. Some organizations, such as SA8000 and Worldwide Responsible Accredited Production (WRAP), rely on external auditors to *certify* that a company has met particular substantive standards concerning issues such as child labor, forced and compulsory labor, health and safety, freedom of association and the right to collective bargaining, discrimination, disciplinary practices, working hours, and remuneration.[30] Other organizations, notably industry-specific groups such as the Fair Labor Association[31] and companies such as Nike, *sanction or shame firms* in supply chains that violate fair labor standards. Finally, B Lab awards *B Corp certification* to companies that achieve a minimum verified score concerning their impact on their workers, customers, community, and environment.[32] The criteria for B Corp certification are broader than those of the other standard-setting organizations, reflected in its complex system of categorization.[33]

Third, there are ratings services, such as MSCI and Bloomberg, that provide investors with ESG information about particular companies based largely on the company's sustainability disclosures and other voluntarily provided information.

This section focuses on the first two categories, with the aim of understanding the scope and limits of the primary data that forms the basis for their reports.

Greenhouse Gas Emissions and Other Environmental Impacts

We first examine the current approach to environmental metrics, which concern a corporation's impact on ecosystems, or the "planet." The universal recognition that greenhouse gases[34] (GHGs) are major contributors to global warming, which both threatens the planet and puts companies at financial risk, has led to the convergence of outcome indicators.

The Greenhouse Gas Protocol Corporate Accounting and Reporting Standard, the product of a multistakeholder collaboration,[35] provides a uniform methodology for the comprehensive disclosure of an organization's emissions. It places GHG emissions in three different categories, designated as "scopes,"[36] which together "encourage companies to move from reporting [activities and] outputs alone to capturing the impacts of their operations on nature and society across the full value chain, in more tangible, sophisticated ways, including the monetary value of impacts."[37]

Scopes 1 and 2, respectively, encompass direct emissions from a corporation's owned or controlled sources and indirect emissions related to the generation of energy purchased by a corporation.[38] They are mutually exclusive, thus avoiding the double counting of emissions.

Scope 3 emissions are a "consequence of the activities of the company but occur from sources not owned or controlled by the company."[39] They broadly encompass purchased goods and services, business travel, employee commuting, waste disposal, use of sold products, transportation and distribution (upstream and downstream), investments (as distinguished from the company's own business), and leased assets and franchises.[40]

Although the definition of Scope 3 emissions is extremely broad, a company has great discretion to determine which emissions to measure. The recommended criteria for selection include whether the emissions are large relative to the company's Scope 1 and Scope 2 emissions, whether they contribute to the company's GHG risk exposure, whether they are deemed critical by key stakeholders (e.g., customers, suppliers, investors, or civil society), and the company's ability to reduce, or influence the reduction of, those emissions.[41] The GHG protocol rightly notes that "since companies have discretion over which categories they choose to report, Scope 3 may not lend itself well to comparisons across companies." For this reason, we focus on Scopes 1 and 2.

The calculation of all three scopes of emissions requires identifying sources and calculating emissions throughout a company's business activities. To promote standardization, the GHG Protocol includes a set of peer-reviewed tools to enable companies to estimate their emissions of key greenhouse gases (e.g., CO_2, methane, and nitrous oxide) converted into metric tons of CO_2 equivalents.[42] The disclosures are theoretically objective, transparent, and comparable. Their standardization makes it possible for companies and stakeholders to track progress and compare emissions across sectors and also—if there is a price on carbon—to capture the *monetary costs* of emissions generated.[43] For all these reasons, the Protocol's framework provides a paradigm for ESG metrics.

Investors and many other stakeholders are concerned with *predicting* a company's future emissions. While disclosure of a company's current and past emissions provides essential data for this task, the Task Force on Climate-Related Financial Disclosures (TCFD) takes the further step of asking companies to disclose their plans and governance practices with respect to emissions. These process indicators fit within ESG's *Governance* category.

The TCFD is concerned with the effects of climate risks and opportunities on a company's financial value.[44] Risks include not only those stemming from the company's own activities but also those imposed on the company by natural causes and other actors. "Opportunities" include efficiencies and new markets accompanying reduced emissions. The TCFD calls for disclosures in four domains:

- **Governance.** The board's and management's roles in assessing and managing climate risks and opportunities.

- **Strategy.** Addressing climate-related risks and opportunities over the short, medium, and long runs.

- **Risk management.** Processes for identifying, assessing, and managing climate-related risks.

- **Metrics and targets.** The metrics used to assess climate-related risks and opportunities, including GHG emissions; the targets used to manage those risks and opportunities;[45] and performance relative to those targets.

These process indicators are precursors to achieving outcomes that minimize GHG emissions. A company's specification of reduction targets and its reports on progress in meeting them are further steps in this direction. Although these disclosures lack the precision and objectivity of actual emissions, they provide valuable predictive information. Indeed, a company's disclosure of its targets for future years provides stakeholders with an important baseline with which to compare actual emissions in those years.[46]

Greenhouse gas emissions are more straightforward to measure than many other environmental impacts, as the impacts of the emission of greenhouse gases are independent of a company's particular situation or geography: a ton of carbon dioxide emitted in one location is identical to a ton emitted in another. By contrast, many other environmental impacts are context dependent. For example, an essential component of GRI standard 303 on Water and Effluents is the amount of water withdrawn from areas with water stress,[47] which is defined as the "ability, or lack thereof, to meet the human and ecological demand for water." The standard explains that water stress involves "the availability, quality, or accessibility of water" and states that it is "based on subjective elements and is assessed differently depending on societal values, such as the suitability of water for drinking or the requirements to be afforded to ecosystems."[48] While the contextualization of many environmental impacts is inevitable, it introduces an element that compromises the objectivity and comparability of the metrics.

Occupational Health and Safety

Almost all standards include provisions concerning workplace safety. For example, SA8000 states:

> The [company] shall provide a safe and healthy workplace environment and shall take effective steps to prevent potential health and safety incidents and occupational injury or illness arising out of, associated with or occurring in the course of work. It shall minimize or eliminate, so far as is reasonably practicable, the causes of all hazards in the workplace environment, based upon the prevailing safety and health knowledge of the industry sector and of any specific hazards.[49]

GRI standard 403 on Occupational Health and Safety requires these disclosures of *processes*:[50]

- Whether an occupational health and safety management system has been implemented

- The processes used to identify work-related hazards and assess risks and to eliminate hazards and minimize risks

- The processes for worker participation and consultation in the development, implementation, and evaluation of the occupational health and safety management system, and for providing access to and communicating relevant information on occupational health and safety to workers

- Any occupational health and safety training provided to workers, including generic training as well as training on specific work-related hazards, hazardous activities, or hazardous situations

- Prevention and mitigation of occupational health and safety impacts directly linked by business relationships (e.g., suppliers)

- The number and percentage of employees who are covered by an occupational health and safety management system

GRI disclosure 403-9 focuses on *outcomes*—that is, on work-related injuries.[51] It requires a company to report, with respect to its own employees:

- The number and rate of fatalities as a result of work-related injuries

- The number and rate of high-consequence (i.e., serious) work-related injuries other than fatalities

- The number and rate of other work-related injuries

- The work-related hazards that pose a risk of high-consequence injury, including how these hazards have been determined; which of these hazards have caused or contributed to high-consequence injuries during the reporting period; actions taken or under way to eliminate these hazards and minimize risks; any actions taken or under way to eliminate other work-related hazards and minimize risks (This is a combination of processes and outcomes.)

In many respects, the GRI disclosures parallel the reports that US employers are required to make to the Occupational Safety and Health Administration (OSHA).[52]

The GRI requires that companies report the number of fatalities or injuries in relation to hours worked.[53] This formula allows one to compare a company's work-related fatalities and injuries of different severities with those of other companies, whether in the same industry or across industries.

Although not called for by the standards, workplace injuries and deaths can be monetized.[54] Companies in the United States and many other countries are subject to mandatory workers' compensation schemes that provide wage replacement and medical benefits to employees injured in the course of employment.[55] The regulations include schedules that put a price on injuries that involve the loss of vision or hearing or of a body part.[56] Of course, the price will vary among different jurisdictions.

Beyond the schedules of workers' compensation programs, there are two widely used measures of the value of health and life: quality-adjusted life years (QALYs) and disability-adjusted life years (DALYs). Both multiply a person's life expectancy by a number between 1 (perfect health) and 0 (death) to represent different degrees of disability or pain.[57] Both measures are ultimately grounded in the concept of the value of a statistical life (VSL),[58] which assigns a fixed monetary value to every human life in a certain population based on people's willingness to pay (WTP) to avoid health and safety risks.[59]

Workplace injuries and deaths fit many of the core elements of an ESG reporting framework described earlier in this chapter. Among other things, the events are auditable, comparable, and monetizable. Also, in principle, such reporting could be extended to include the company's supply chain, though the difficulties of assurance in this context are formidable.[60]

Child Labor

GRI standard 408[61] is typical of international standards in defining a "child" as "a person under the age of 15 years, or under the age of completion of compulsory schooling, whichever is higher." The standard states that "abolishing child labor is a key principle and objective of major human rights instruments and legislation and is the subject of national legislation in almost all countries." The key rationales for prohibiting child labor, as stated by SA8000, are that "childhood should be dedicated to education and development, not to work; child labor often jeopardizes children's chances of becoming productive adults; and child labor perpetuates poverty and social inequality."[62]

With respect to *outcomes*, SA8000 provides that a company "shall not engage in or support the use of child labor" and "shall not expose children . . . to any situations—in or outside of the workplace—that are hazardous or unsafe to their physical and mental health and development."[63] With respect to *procedures*, it requires that companies communicate their policies to workers and interested parties, have procedures for verifying age, and have written procedures for the remediation of child labor.[64]

The GRI standard is essentially *procedural*. It requires that companies report on "operations and suppliers considered to have significant risk for incidents of child labor" and on measures taken by the company "intended to contribute to the effective abolition of child labor."

As with workplace injuries, incidents of child labor by the company itself or by suppliers are in principle auditable, and the numbers are comparable across companies. Although prohibitions of child labor are rooted in value judgments about the importance of childhood, there have been various efforts to monetize its costs. For example, a 2004 study by the International Labor Office (ILO) provides estimates of "the added productive capacity a future generation of workers would enjoy due to their increased education, and the economic gains anticipated from improved health due to the elimination of the worst forms of child labor."[65] Of course, the costs of child labor vary from one country to another depending on available educational and posteducational opportunities. Nonetheless, it should be feasible to come up with a country-specific, or even region-specific, estimate of the costs per child per year that could be used for social accounting purposes.

Discrimination and Diversity

Accounting for discrimination seems considerably more difficult than accounting for workplace safety and child labor. GRI standard 406 defines discrimination as "the act and the result of treating people unequally by imposing unequal burdens or denying benefits, instead of treating each person fairly on the basis of individual merit," and states:

> An organization is expected to avoid discriminating against any person on any grounds, including avoiding discrimination against workers at work. It is also expected to avoid discriminating against customers with respect to the provision of products and services, or against any other stakeholder, including suppliers or business partners.[66]

Under GRI standard 406, the company must report the "total number of incidents of discrimination during the reporting period," where "an 'incident' refers to a legal action or complaint registered with the company or competent authorities through a formal process, or an instance of non-compliance identified by the company through established procedures." The report must describe the status of the incidents and actions taken with respect to them.

In contrast to workplace injuries, what constitutes "discrimination" varies greatly among countries, and determining whether an employer discriminated often entails a complex and protracted process. GRI standard 406 defines an "incident" as including a formal complaint, regardless of whether it was adjudicated or how it was resolved. But complaints alone are likely a weak proxy for actual discrimination, and this expansive definition of "incident" limits the comparability of the reporting across companies, since different companies have different internal reporting and recordkeeping processes.

A potentially less problematic approach would be to limit the definition of "incident" to those instances where a court or cognizant government agency has concluded that an employer engaged in discrimination. After such a determination, applications of GRI standard 406 would be readily comparable across US companies, many of which are subject to Title VII of the Civil Rights Act of 1964.[67] However, this approach would not capture the many complaints that are resolved through arbitrations or settlements, especially when they are subject to nondisclosure agreements.

Violations of some aspects of discrimination are monetizable—after all, courts and administrative agencies regularly award compensatory damages for actions of discrimination. But given the intangible nature of some harms from discrimination and the vagaries of judicial and other dispute resolution systems, the outcomes of contested discrimination claims seem weakly correlated with the magnitude of the actual injuries.

Another related but broader approach to capturing discriminatory practices can be found in GRI disclosure 405-1, which requires disclosure of the percentage of individuals within the organization's governance bodies and workforce by gender, age group, and "other indicators of diversity where relevant (such as minority or vulnerable groups)."[68] Although these disclosures may provide some surface-level information, they fall far short of providing information about the adequacy of a company's diversity and inclusiveness—an increasing concern of institutional investors and other stakeholders. This requires a deep understanding of the industry and the nature of its governance structure and workforce—something that cannot readily be determined, even by adjudication.

Our hypothesis before undertaking the analysis described in this section was that environmental standards would be more likely than social standards to meet the criteria of effective ESG reporting that we outlined in part 1. However, this generalization turns out to be unfounded. Although Scope 1 and 2 greenhouse gas emissions set a benchmark for precision, not all environmental standards meet that benchmark,[69] while some social standards do.

For those standards that do meet the criteria, the next questions involve how they will be created and updated and how to ensure that the reported information is accurate. In particular, there are questions regarding the quality of the company's internal processes for gathering, analyzing, and reporting relevant data, and the ability of outsiders to verify that the data is materially correct. We now turn to those issues.

Part 3: The Need for a Standard-Setting Body

Any ESG reporting framework must have the capacity to evolve and adapt. Even today's best framework will soon be incomplete, and the field needs a standard-setting body to develop a uniform, comprehensive set of metrics and to provide the necessary updates for those metrics.[70] To the degree reasonably possible, the standard setter must be independent of political and financial pressure, and its standards must be uniform and used pervasively. The history of financial accounting provides some insight into how to establish such a body.

Contemporary financial accounting began in the aftermath of the stock market crash of 1929, when Congress adopted the Securities Act of 1933 and the Securities Exchange Act of 1934. The latter created a new agency, the Securities and Exchange Commission (SEC), with the authority to set financial accounting standards for public companies. Rather than prescribing such standards itself, however, the SEC decided to rely on the private sector to establish Generally Accepted Accounting Principles (GAAP).[71] In the roughly eight decades since that decision, we have seen three different private standard setters for financial reporting, as each morphed into the next following internal disagreements and political pressures.

The first private standard-setting organization was a committee of the American Institute of Accountants known simply as the Committee on Accounting Procedure (CAP), which was in place from 1938 to 1959. It was composed of part-time accounting academics and practitioners and was soon criticized as overly flexible by commentators who believed that it did not mandate sufficiently uniform standards. This criticism and resulting reorganization led to the second private standard-setting organization, the Accounting Principles Board (APB), which was in place from 1959 to 1973.

Like the CAP, the APB included accounting academics and practitioners who served on a part-time basis. However, the APB made a deliberate decision to include representatives from all the eight biggest accounting firms at the time so that each firm would ensure that its clients followed the APB's accounting standards and norms. Unfortunately, the inclusion of these representatives created other conflicts, as the accounting firms' clients lobbied for standards favorable to their interests.[72] In the end, three of the eight accounting firms stated they had lost confidence in the APB, leading to the establishment of a study group that recommended that the APB be replaced with an independent, full-time standard-setting body.

The Financial Accounting Standards Board (FASB) began in 1973 and still exists today. Although still subject to criticism and by no means perfect, FASB has been considerably more successful than its predecessors.[73] Some key differences include a smaller board with full-time members,[74] a large research staff, and a considerable budget. The board members represent a broad swath of users of accounting information, including auditors, government regulators, investors, and accounting academics. To minimize the conflicts that plagued the APB, FASB's members are required to sever all ties with their prior firms or institutions upon joining the organization.[75] Its sizable budget allows it to compensate board members for this loss. For example, in 2019, FASB's parent organization received funding of almost $57 million, coming from publication and subscription revenues and fees from public companies and brokerages.[76] Although FASB has not been immune from either industry or political pressures,[77] its relative financial independence and political insulation as a private entity have allowed it to survive and enact meaningful standards. As with its predecessors, FASB sets the standards, but the SEC mandates that US public companies follow them.

If financial reporting is politically controversial and subject to immense lobbying, imagine the potential controversies related to ESG reporting. At a minimum, any ESG standard setter must be a financially independent institution with significant research capacity and full-time, well-compensated board members who represent a broad swath of stakeholders. For all the current interest in creating common standards, we have not seen any significant movement to create an independent standard-setting body.

Part 4: The Need for Reporting Infrastructure

Thus far, we have discussed ESG reporting standards and the standard-setting body, but the focus on standards alone is incomplete. To produce high-quality metrics also requires concurrent improvements in internal and external ESG reporting infrastructures.[78] Internal reporting infrastructure refers to the reporting systems and internal controls that companies rely on to produce data; external reporting infrastructure refers to the auditing and regulatory enforcement mechanisms that verify reporting accuracy and correct misreporting.

Internal Mechanisms

Much evidence from financial reporting demonstrates the need for strong internal reporting infrastructure. In the context of financial disclosures, companies rely on financial reporting software and internal controls to generate the inputs for financial statements.

Internal controls are the processes and procedures that companies put in place to provide reasonable assurance that the reported numbers are correct. At the simplest level, internal controls separate duties related to recordkeeping (e.g., an individual who uses petty cash should not be the one to record the receipt for their purchases) and safeguarding assets (e.g., putting that petty cash in a locked safe). The vast majority of financial restatements[79] result from internal errors rather than fraud,[80] and there is strong evidence that internal controls improve the quality of reported information.[81] Indeed, in the financial context, they are so important that large public companies must provide a separate audit attestation regarding the quality of their internal controls.[82]

Internal controls are equally essential for ESG reporting. As a simple example, imagine employees at different manufacturing plants within the same company recording emissions. Without formal processes and procedures, the reported data may be inaccurate because employees used inconsistent measurement methods.[83] Yet, despite their importance, companies often lack the internal control mechanisms necessary to produce accurate ESG information. For example, consider the difficulties companies face in reporting under the "conflict minerals" standard required by Section 1502 of the Dodd-Frank Act. Although companies were given three years to prepare for this disclosure, one study found that nearly 80 percent of the 1,300 corporations that reported in 2014 and 2015 were unable to trace the country of origin for conflict minerals in their supply chain.[84] By 2018, these disclosures had improved, but problems still remained; a Government Accountability Office study of one hundred randomly selected companies found that "almost all companies reported that, after conducting due diligence, they could not determine whether their conflict minerals financed or benefited armed groups."[85]

The difficulties related to internal data management are not limited to supply chains. For example, when Section 953(b) of the Dodd-Frank Act required that companies report the ratio of the median employee's pay to that of the CEO, companies objected, saying that it would be extremely expensive to identify the median employee's pay. Indeed, the SEC estimated that this rule could cost $1.3 billion in initial compliance costs and $526 million annually in ongoing costs.[86] This seemingly simple disclosure highlights the inability of companies' internal data systems to analyze ESG data in the way that users demand.[87]

There is reason to believe that technology could improve companies' internal reporting systems. In the realm of financial accounting, there is evidence that reporting software has increased the accuracy of reported information and improved business operations based on this information.[88] We are not aware of any comparable software for ESG reporting, which is instead compiled through separate, ad hoc systems;[89] but it seems likely that such a system will be developed as demand for ESG information increases. In addition, blockchain technology has the potential to improve reporting quality in accounting in general and with respect to social issues such as supply chain management in particular. Although these technologies will likely lead to long-term improvements,[90] they ultimately rely on the quality of data that is fed into them.

External Mechanisms

The most prominent external mechanisms are assurance (i.e., auditing) and regulatory enforcement, which serve to verify reported data.[91] There is ample evidence that properly conducted audits can improve the quality of reported information.[92] Yet it is unclear whether ESG audits will provide these benefits, as many such audits are of much lower quality than their financial counterparts.[93] Unlike financial reporting, which is currently dominated by the Big Four accounting firms, there are many ESG accounting firms, and it is difficult for consumers to know the reputation associated with each firm. Standards vary across the industry, as does the training (and auditing) of auditors. Although the industry is attempting to professionalize and develop more consistency, much work remains.

Furthermore, even the most highly qualified auditors face an uphill battle. Without reliable internal data, companies cannot establish a reliable audit trail, which is a significant challenge for any external auditor. Thus, the weaknesses of internal data systems inevitably compromise external mechanisms. The lack of quality internal information is likely the reason for the high frequency of "limited assurance" audits in publicly available ESG reports. Because the auditors are unable to access reliable internal data, their audits provide a standard of assurance far below that provided in financial audits. In other words, the low-quality internal reporting environment reduces the effectiveness of one of the most effective mechanisms for inducing compliance with standards.

Next to auditing, regulatory enforcement of financial reporting is the most prominent external mechanism. In this context, enforcement refers to regulatory sanctions brought against companies and individuals who do not adhere to reporting standards. As an example of the value of enforcement, in the early years of the twenty-first century, many European countries unified their financial reporting standards by mandating that companies follow International Financial Reporting Standards (IFRS). This unification was thought to be a huge advancement in financial reporting since a greater number of companies were expected to make comparable, high-quality disclosures. Yet adherence to the standards, and the resulting benefits, turned out to be highly dependent on the strength of each country's regulatory enforcement. Countries that lacked sufficient legal and regulatory enforcement to ensure that companies adhered to the new standards saw few if any benefits.[94]

These studies are among the many indicating that the regulatory landscape, particularly the strength of local enforcement practices, significantly affects the implementation of reporting standards. In the context of US financial reporting, public enforcement most commonly occurs through regulatory actions by the SEC, with assistance from other agencies, such as the Department of Justice. However, although the SEC has deep financial accounting expertise, it lacks the environmental and social expertise necessary for strong regulatory enforcement of ESG reporting. Therefore, if the SEC is to take the lead in ESG reporting as it has with financial reporting, the agency must either develop internal expertise in ESG-related areas or coordinate with other agencies such as the Environmental Protection Agency.

In theory, private litigation could be an additional tool to increase the quality of reported information. In the context of financial reporting, shareholders almost always sue company managers and directors following a material accounting error, plausibly incentivizing managers to avoid such errors. However, given that it is exceedingly rare for managers to pay out-of-pocket for such errors,[95] it is not terribly surprising that the empirical evidence is inconsistent about whether litigation risk improves financial reporting outcomes.[96] Assuming that private litigation functions similarly for ESG reporting, there is every reason to think that such litigation would be frequent and costly, but it is uncertain whether it would significantly improve the quality of the disclosed information.

Of course, litigants, regulators, and auditors are only some of the external actors that play a role in enforcement. There are two emerging forces worth noting. First, environmental activism, in which shareholders pressure management to improve a firm's environmental impact, is becoming increasingly common. Recent work suggests that these campaigns are effective in reducing target firms' air pollutants.[97] Second, proxy advisors, whose recommendations carry great weight with institutional investors, have become increasingly ESG focused. For example, Institutional Shareholder Services (ISS) issues annual sustainability proxy voting guidelines.[98]

Conclusion

The preceding discussion suggests one obvious reason why the correlation of a company's ESG metrics with its financial value is uncertain and the correlation among ratings services is extremely weak. One cannot escape the phenomenon of garbage in, garbage out. Indeed, given their multifarious natures, ESG metrics as a whole will never have the accuracy, validity, reliability, and commensurability of financial metrics.

Yet the considerable efforts to improve ESG metrics described here reflect the increasing interest in them as indicators not only of companies' financial performance but also their impact on people and the planet. In the spirit of not letting the perfect be the enemy of the good, it makes sense to rely on the particular metrics that have reached maturation while working to bring the others up to their level, and to treat the integration of the widely disparate E&S metrics as highly aspirational. However, the burden of the last sections of the chapter is that without an independent standard setter to update metrics, and strong reporting infrastructure to induce compliance and accuracy, a company's reports on its metrics cannot be taken at face value. These features are essential components of a robust and useful ESG framework.

FOR FURTHER READING

For readers interested in the current state of ESG reporting and proposed approaches for improving reporting, we suggest several articles. In "The Current State of Sustainability Reporting: A Work in Progress" (*CPA Journal*, July 30, 2018), Jill M. D'Aquila provides a critical survey of existing reporting standards and their implementation. For a short, accessible description of the measurable dimensions of a company's social and environmental impacts, see Ronald Cohen and George Serafeim, "How to Measure a Company's Real Impact" (hbr.org, September 3, 2020, https://hbr.org/2020/09/how-to-measure-a-companys-real-impact). For an excellent academic paper that summarizes the empirical literature on the costs and benefits of imposing a mandatory ESG reporting regime, see Hans B. Christensen, Luzi Hail, and Christian Leuz, "Adoption of CSR and Sustainability Reporting Standards: Economic Analysis and Review" (SSRN working paper, 2019, https://privpapers.ssrn.com/sol3/papers.cfm?abstract_id=3427748). The IRFS Foundation has written a detailed description of a proposed ESG standards board and priorities for such a board ("Consultation Paper on Sustainability Reporting," IFRS Foundation, September 2020, https://cdn.ifrs.org/-/media/project /sustainability-reporting/consultation-paper-on-sustainability-reporting.pdf). For readers interested in learning about a proposed collaboration among global disclosure and reporting organizations, see Impact Management Project, "Statement of Intent to Work Together towards Comprehensive Corporate Reporting" (Impact Management Project, 2020, https://impactmanagementproject.com /structured-network/statement-of-intent-to-work-together-towards-comprehensive -corporate-reporting/). For those attempting to anticipate the SEC's actions in the ESG space, a speech delivered by acting chair Allison Lee, "A Climate for Change: Meeting Investor Demand for Climate and ESG Information at the SEC" (March 15, 2021, Securities and Exchange Commission), provides the best roadmap. A description of efforts to monetize social and environmental impacts is provided in George Serafeim, T. Robert Zochowski, and Jen Downing, "Impact-Weighted Financial Accounts: The Missing Piece for an Impact Economy"

(Harvard Business School, 2019, https://www.hbs.edu/impact-weighted-accounts
/Documents/Impact-Weighted-Accounts-Report-2019.pdf). Finally, fairly detailed
suggestions for ESG disclosures have been assembled by the World Economic
Forum, "Measuring Stakeholder Capitalism: Towards Common Metrics and
Consistent Reporting of Sustainable Value Creation" (World Economic Forum,
2020, http://www3.weforum.org/docs/WEF_IBC_Measuring_Stakeholder
_Capitalism_Report_2020.pdf).

Notes

We greatly appreciate the research assistance of Kevin Li and David Liou, and
comments on drafts from Matthew Bannick, Iris Brest, Michael Callahan, Richard
Danzig, Ronald Gilson, Thomas Heller, William Meehan, Curtis Milhaupt, Paul
Pfleiderer, Kristen Savelle, Alicia Seiger, Russell Siegleman, and Mark Wolfson.

1. Although the term "sustainable" connotes "environmental," it is commonly
used to refer to social performance as well. As of year-end 2019, $17.1 trillion in
assets were managed according to sustainable investing strategies, a 42 percent
increase from the $12.0 trillion two years earlier. See US Sustainable Investing
Foundation (USSIF), *Report on US Sustainable and Impact Investing Trends 2020*,
USSIF, 2020, 1, https://www.ussif.org/files/Trends/2020_Trends_Highlights
_OnePager.pdf.

2. Business Roundtable, "Statement on the Purpose of the Corporation," press
release, August 19, 2019, https://www.businessroundtable.org/business-roundtable
-redefines-the-purpose-of-a-corporation-to-promote-an-economy-that-serves-all
-americans; BlackRock, "A Sense of Purpose: Larry Fink's 2018 Letter to CEOs,"
https://www.blackrock.com/corporate/investor-relations/2018-larry-fink-ceo-letter.

3. Prior research has shown that ESG-related disclosures can lead to real
benefits regarding these measures. See Hans B. Christensen, Eric Floyd, Lisa Yao
Liu, and Mark Maffett, "The Real Effects of Mandated Information on Social
Responsibility in Financial Reports: Evidence from Mine-Safety Records," *Journal
of Accounting and Economics* 64 (2017): 284–304. See also Benedikt Downar, Juergen
Ernstberger, Stefan Reichelstein, Sebastian Schwenen, and Alexander Zaklan, "The
Impact of Carbon Disclosure Mandates on Emissions and Financial Operating
Performance," working paper, November 2020.

4. Studies have shown weak correlations among ratings services and IWAI's
explanation that they rate activities rather than outcomes or impact. See Aaron K.
Chatterji, Rodolphe Durand, David I. Levine, and Samuel Touboul, "Do Ratings
of Firms Converge? Implications for Managers, Investors and Strategy Researchers," *Strategic Management Journal* 37 (2016): 1597–1614, https://doi.org/10.1002
/smj.2407.

5. At least some ratings agencies retroactively readjust their own ratings. See
Florian Berg, Kornelia Fabisik, and Zacharias Sautner, "Rewriting History II: The
(Un)Predictable Past of ESG Ratings," European Corporate Governance Initiative
Working Paper Series in Finance, January 2021, https://dx.doi.org/10.2139/ssrn

.3722087; Goldman Sachs, "2021 US Equity Outlook: Roaring '20s Redux," November 11, 2020, 29 (discussing pros and cons, noting that "investors currently assign a modest but statistically insignificant valuation premium to E&S scores" but stating that their impact on stock valuations has increased sharply).

6. World Economic Forum, *Measuring Stakeholder Capitalism: Towards Common Metrics and Consistent Reporting of Sustainable Value Creation* (Cologny, Switzerland: World Economic Forum, 2020), http://www3.weforum.org/docs/WEF_IBC _Measuring_Stakeholder_Capitalism_Report_2020.pdf. Although we focus on E&S, some aspects of G play important roles as well. Traditionally, the criteria for governance have centered on factors that directly or materially affect its financial performance. As E&S outcomes emerge as having independent value, however, good governance encompasses the accuracy and transparency of those factors as well.

7. Though the G, or governance, factors encompass a broad range of issues, we will focus on their role in supporting E&S outcomes.

8. See part 3.

9. Jill M. D'Aquila, "The Current State of Sustainability Reporting: A Work in Progress," *CPA Journal*, July 2018, https://www.cpajournal.com/2018/07/30/the -current-state-of-sustainability-reporting.

10. Sustainability Accounting Standards Board, *The State of Disclosure 2017: An Analysis of the Effectiveness of Sustainability Disclosure in SEC Filings* (San Francisco, CA: Sustainability Accounting Standards Board, 2017), https://www.sasb.org/wp -content/uploads/2017/12/2017State-of-Disclosure-Report-web.pdf.

11. Martha C. Wilson, "A Critical Review of Environmental Sustainability Reporting in the Consumer Goods Industry: Greenwashing or Good Business?," *Journal of Management and Sustainability* 3, no. 4 (2013): 1–13, http://dx.doi.org/10 .5539/jms.v3n4p1.

12. For criticisms of SA8000, see Richard M. Locke, Fei Qin, and Alberto Brause, "Does Labor Monitoring Improve Labor Standards? Lessons from Nike," *Industrial and Labor Relations Review* 61, no. 1 (2007): 3–31, https://doi.org/10.1177 /001979390706100101.

13. Casey O'Connor, "A New Approach to Evaluating Company Social Perfor- mance," *Center for Business and Human Rights* (blog), Stern School of Business, New York University, June 14, 2018, https://bhr.stern.nyu.edu/blogs/2018/6/14/a-new -approach-to-evaluating-company-social-performance.

14. Impact Management Project, *Statement of Intent to Work Together towards Comprehensive Corporate Reporting* (Stamford, CT: Impact Management Project, 2020).

15. IFRS Foundation, "Consultation Paper on Sustainability Reporting," September 2020, https://cdn.ifrs.org/-/media/project/sustainability-reporting /consultation-paper-on-sustainability-reporting.pdf.

16. World Economic Forum, *Measuring Stakeholder Capitalism*, 14 (noting that "[m]ateriality is a dynamic concept, in which issues once considered relevant only to social value can rapidly become financially material. In this sense, sustainable value creation lies at the intersection of social and corporate value").

17. International Federation of Accountants, *Enhancing Corporate Reporting: The Way Forward* (Geneva, Switzerland: IFAC, September 2020), https://www.ifac.org /system/files/publications/files/IFAC-Enhancing-Corporate-Reporting-The-Way -Forward.pdf.

18. Harvard Business School, "Impact-Weighted Accounts," accessed January 12, 2021, https://www.hbs.edu/impact-weighted-accounts/Pages/default.aspx.

19. Sir Ronald Cohen and George Serafeim, two leaders of IWAI, note that "many companies are creating environmental costs that exceed their total profit (EBITDA). . . . Of the 1,694 companies [in IWAI's database] which had positive EBITDA in 2018, 252 firms (15%) would see their profit more than wiped out by the environmental damage they caused, while 543 firms (32%) would see their EBITDA reduced by 25% or more. For certain industries, including airlines, paper and forest products, electric utilities, construction materials, containers and packaging, almost all firms would see more than a quarter of their EBITDA eliminated." See Ronald Cohen and George Serafeim, "How to Measure a Company's Real Impact," hbr.org, September 3, 2020, https://hbr.org/2020/09/how-to -measure-a-companys-real-impact.

20. Ben Smith and Graham Cooper, *Green Bond Funds: Impact Reporting Practices* (London: Environmental Finance, 2020), https://www.environmental-finance.com /content/focus/creating-green-bond-markets/publications/green-bond-funds -impact-reporting-practices-2020.html.

21. While many of the elements parallel those described by IWAI, our terminology is not always identical. IWAI describes the ultimate goals of such a framework as (1) a company's impact can be measured and compared, (2) impact should be measured within an accounting framework with the aim of harnessing our economy to improve our society and planet, (3) impact measurement must be scalable, and (4) to be scalable, the measurement of impact must be actionable and cost-effective. See George Serafeim, T. Robert Zochowski, and Jen Downing, *Impact-Weighted Financial Accounts: The Missing Piece for an Impact Economy* (Boston: Harvard Business School, 2019), 30, https://www.hbs.edu/impact-weighted -accounts/Documents/Impact-Weighted-Accounts-Report-2019.pdf.

22. George Serafeim and Katie Trinh, "A Framework for Product Impact-Weighted Accounts," Harvard Business School Accounting & Management Unit Working Paper Series, January 2020, http://dx.doi.org/10.2139/ssrn.3532472.

23. For example, a thermometer that measures tenths of a degree is more accurate than one that measures only degrees.

24. For example, the amount of a company's carbon dioxide emissions is a valid indicator of its contribution to global warming, but the number of employee complaints about a company's unsafe working conditions is less so, because the number of complaints may be affected by matters other than safety.

25. David Freiberg, D. G. Park, George Serafeim, and T. Robert Zochowski, "Corporate Environmental Impact: Measurement, Data and Information," Harvard Business School Accounting & Management Unit Working Paper Series, April 2020, http://dx.doi.org/10.2139/ssrn.3565533. This seems a plausible common metric for comparing companies in the same industry, and one that can be extended

beyond environmental costs. Unless the products of different industries are reasonably substitutable, however, the comparisons are limited to a particular industry; for example, there seems little point in comparing the environmental intensity of an airline to that of an apparel manufacturer.

26. Serafeim, Zochowski, and Downing, *Impact-Weighted Financial Accounts*, 27.

27. Goldman Sachs has attempted to reduce a host of E&S factors to a single score. See Goldman Sachs, "2021 US Equity Outlook," 25.

28. Serafeim, Zochowski, and Downing, *Impact-Weighted Financial Accounts*, 5.

29. Global Reporting Initiative, "Our Mission and History," accessed January 2, 2021, https://www.globalreporting.org/about-gri/mission-history/.

30. Social Accountability Accreditation Services, "SA8000 Certification," accessed January 2, 2021, http://www.saasaccreditation.org/certification; World-wide Responsible Accredited Production, "Certification Process," accessed January 2, 2021, https://wrapcompliance.org/certification/.

31. Fair Labor Association, "Safeguards," Transparency, accessed January 2, 2021, https://www.fairlabor.org/transparency/safeguards.

32. B Lab, "Certification," accessed January 2, 2021, https://bcorporation.net /certification. To receive certification, companies must also make their impact reports public and their legal governing documents must "require their board of directors to balance profit and purpose." See generally Christopher Marquis, *Better Business: How the B Corp Movement Is Remaking Capitalism* (New Haven, CT: Yale University Press, 2020).

33. See, for example, B Lab, "B Impact Assessment of Seventh Generation," B Impact Report, accessed January 11, 2021, https://bcorporation.net/directory /seventh-generation.

34. "Greenhouse gases" generally refers to the seven gases covered by the Kyoto Protocol: carbon dioxide (CO_2), methane (CH_4), nitrous oxide (N_2O), hydrofluoro-carbons (HFCs), perfluorocarbons (PFCs), sulfur hexafluoride (SF_6), and nitrogen trifluoride (NF_3). See United Nations Framework Convention on Climate Change (UNFCCC), *Kyoto Protocol Reference Manual* (Bonn, Germany: UNFCCC, 2008), 106, https://unfccc.int/sites/default/files/08_unfccc_kp_ref_manual.pdf.

35. The protocol was jointly convened in 1998 by the World Resources Institute and the World Business Council for Sustainable Development. The steering group was comprised of members from environmental groups and industry. See Green-house Gas Protocol, "About Us," accessed December 21, 2020, https://ghgprotocol .org/about-us.

36. World Resources Institute and World Business Council, *GHG Protocol: A Corporate Accounting and Reporting Standard*, revised edition (Washington, DC, and Geneva, Switzerland: WRI and WBC, 2004), https://ghgprotocol.org/sites /default/files/standards/ghg-protocol-revised.pdf.

37. World Economic Forum, *Measuring Stakeholder Capitalism*, 14.

38. The specific distinction between direct and indirect emissions is beyond the scope of this chapter.

39. World Resources Institute and World Business Council, *GHG Protocol*, 25.

40. Ibid., 29.

41. Ibid., 30.

42. Greenhouse Gas Protocol, "Calculation Tools," accessed January 2, 2021, https://ghgprotocol.org/calculation-tools. Calculations of Scope 1 emissions (direct consumption of fuels) are based on standard CO_2, CH_4, and NO_2 emission factors applied to consumption of various fuels. These direct emissions will likely not apply to most office-based organizations but may be substantial for many manufacturing-oriented organizations. Scope 2 emissions (indirect emissions from electricity consumption) are based on regularly updated emission factors specific to individual utility subregions, reflecting the fuel composition used to generate electricity in any given subregion.

43. While the specific price of emissions is a product of regulatory decisions and market regimes, investors and other stakeholders can value a company's relevant emission levels. Recent research has found a statistically significant relationship between higher levels of emissions (for all three scopes) and higher required equity returns, implying that investors are pricing a "carbon premium" into the market as they evaluate the risk exposure associated with carbon emissions. See Patrick Bolton and Marcin Kacperczyk, "Do Investors Care about Carbon Risk?," European Corporate Governance Initiative Working Paper Series in Finance, June 2019, http://dx.doi.org/10.2139/ssrn.3398441.

44. The TCFD was created by the Financial Stability Board (FSB) at the request of the G20 finance ministers and central bank governors and charged with developing climate-related disclosures that "could promote more informed investment, credit [or lending], and insurance underwriting decisions" by enabling financial stakeholders "to understand better the concentrations of carbon-related assets in the financial sector and the financial system's exposures to climate-related risks." See TCFD, *Recommendations of the Task Force on Climate-Related Financial Disclosures* (New York and London: TCFD, 2017), 2, https://assets.bbhub.io /company/sites/60/2020/10/FINAL-2017-TCFD-Report-11052018.pdf. In the several years since the TCFD was established, many major corporations have begun to meet its disclosure standards.

45. See, for example, World Economic Forum, *Measuring Stakeholder Capitalism*, 55 (recommending that a company disclose whether it has set GHG emission targets in line with the goals of the Paris agreement, including a plan to achieve net-zero emissions before 2050 and meet interim emission reduction targets).

46. Perhaps some third-party provider will eventually develop the capacity to assess TCFD disclosures and develop a rating system that makes it possible to compare companies, but the notoriously poor correlation of ratings by conventional ESG ratings firms does not provide cause for optimism. See Chatterji et al., "Do Ratings of Firms Converge?"; F. Berg, J. F. Koelbel, and R. Rigobon, "Aggregate Confusion: The Divergence of ESG Ratings," Cambridge, MA, MIT Sloan School of Management Working Paper 5822-19, 2019.

47. Global Sustainability Standards Board, *GRI 303: Water and Effluents* (Amsterdam, Netherlands: GRI, 2018), 7, https://www.globalreporting.org /standards/media/1909/gri-303-water-and-effluents-2018.pdf.

48. Ibid., 22.

49. Social Accountability International, *Social Accountability 8000: International Standard* (New York: Social Accountability International, June 2014), 9, https://sa -intl.org/wp-content/uploads/2020/02/SA8000Standard2014.pdf.

50. Global Sustainability Standards Board, *GRI 403: Occupational Health and Safety* (Amsterdam, Netherlands: GRI, 2018), 9, https://www.globalreporting.org /standards/media/1910/gri-403-occupational-health-and-safety-2018.pdf.

51. Ibid., 19.

52. Occupational Safety and Health Administration, US Department of Labor, "OSHA Injury and Illness Recordkeeping and Reporting Requirements," accessed January 11, 2021, https://www.osha.gov/recordkeeping.

53. The fraction is multiplied by 200,000 or 1,000,000 (based on the approximate size of the workforce) to avoid difficult-to-read small numbers.

54. For social accounting purposes, it may be useful to separate costs borne by the company itself and external costs imposed by the company on employees and others. With respect to the former, even if a company fully compensates employees for workplace injuries, whether directly or through insurance, a high injury rate may adversely affect its reputation to the detriment of its ability to recruit employees or may reduce its financial value in the eyes of investors who are concerned with the company's ability to manage risks.

55. "Workers' Compensation," US Department of Labor, accessed January 11, 2021, https://www.dol.gov/general/topic/workcomp.

56. Standards for child labor and forced labor, covered by GRI 408 and 409, respectively, have many of the same features. At least with respect to child labor, it is feasible to estimate the costs per child per year for social accounting purposes. See Global Sustainability Standards Board, *GRI 408: Child Labor* (Amsterdam, Netherlands: GRI, 2016), 9, https://www.globalreporting.org/standards/media/1023 /gri-408-child-labor-2016.pdf. For example, a 2004 study by the International Labor Organization estimates "the added productive capacity a future generation of workers would enjoy due to their increased education, and the economic gains anticipated from improved health due to the elimination of the worst forms of child labor." See International Program on the Elimination of Child Labor, *Investing in Every Child: An Economic Study of the Costs and Benefits of Eliminating Child Labor* (Geneva, Switzerland: International Labor Organization, 2004), 3, https://www .ilo.org/wcmsp5/groups/public/—dgreports/—dcomm/—webdev/documents /publication/wcms_071311.pdf. The report (p. 67) notes that "there are many other benefits of eliminating child labor, such as enhanced opportunities for personal development and social inclusion, that are resistant to economic quantification."

57. EUFIC, "Measuring Burden of Disease: The Concept of QALYs and DALYs," last modified December 1, 2011, https://www.eufic.org/en/understanding -science/article/measuring-burden-of-disease-the-concept-of-qalys-and-dalys.

58. With respect to monetization, it should be noted that VSL varies significantly among countries based on their levels of wealth. The current VSL in the United States is estimated to be $8–10 million, but the VSL in poor countries is as low as $100,000. Compare Jonathan M. Lee and Laura O. Taylor, "Randomized Safety Inspections and Risk Exposure on the Job: Quasi-experimental Estimates of

the Value of a Statistical Life," *American Economic Journal: Economic Policy* 11, no. 4 (2019): 350–374 at 352, https://doi.org/10.1257/pol.20150024; W. Kip Viscusi and Clayton J. Masterman, "Income Elasticities and Global Values of a Statistical Life," *Journal of Benefit-Cost Analysis* 8, no. 2 (2017): 226–250 at 244, https://doi.org/10.1017/bca.2017.12.

59. Paul Brest and Linda Hamilton Krieger, *Problem Solving, Decision Making and Professional Judgment* (New York: Oxford University Press, 2010), 377. Willingness to pay (WTP) can be determined through surveys of people's stated preferences or through revealed preferences based on actual trade-offs between compensation and workplace injuries. Although WTP is commonly used for contingent valuation, it is highly vulnerable to psychological biases (p. 421).

60. Global Sustainability Standards Board, *GRI 403*, 16. For this reason, the GRI states that the company "has a responsibility to make efforts, including exercising any leverage it might have, to prevent and mitigate negative occupational health and safety impacts that are directly linked to its operations, products or services by its business relationships. In these cases, the organization is required, at a minimum, to describe its approach to preventing and mitigating significant negative occupational health and safety impacts and the related hazards and risks."

61. Global Sustainability Standards Board, *GRI 408*, 8.

62. Social Accountability International, *Guidance Document for Social Accountability 8000* (New York: Social Accountability International, 2016), 7, https://sa-intl.org/wp-content/uploads/2020/02/SA8000-2014-Guidance-Document.pdf. SA8000 adds that child labor "can jeopardize a country's reputation and productivity, as well as global acceptance of its exports." GRI 408 similarly states that "child labor is work that 'deprives children of their childhood, their potential and their dignity, and that is harmful to their physical or mental development including by interfering with their education." See Global Sustainability Standards Board, *GRI 408*, 4.

63. Social Accountability International, *Social Accountability 8000*, 8.

64. Ibid., 8.

65. International Program on the Elimination of Child Labor, *Investing in Every Child*, 3. The report notes that "there are many other benefits of eliminating child labor, such as enhanced opportunities for personal development and social inclusion, that are resistant to economic quantification."

66. Global Sustainability Standards Board, *GRI 406: Non-discrimination* (Amsterdam, Netherlands: GRI, 2016), 4, https://www.globalreporting.org/standards/media/1021/gri-406-non-discrimination-2016.pdf. See also SA8000 standard 5.1, which specifies prohibited forms of discrimination. An employer "shall not engage in or support discrimination in hiring, remuneration, access to training, promotion, termination or retirement based on race, national or territorial or social origin, caste, birth, religion, disability, gender, sexual orientation, family responsibilities, marital status, union membership, political opinions, age or any other condition that could give rise to discrimination." See Social Accountability International, *Social Accountability 8000*, 10.

67. Many other countries have similar laws and analogous procedures. For a discussion of equal treatment legislation and enforcement in the European Union,

see Tamas Kadar, "Equality Bodies: A European Phenomenon," *International Journal of Discrimination and the Law* 18, nos. 2–3 (2018): 144–162, https://doi.org/10.1177/1358229118799231. However, it would be difficult for a US company to apply the standard to foreign suppliers because of the vast differences in what different countries treat as discrimination as well as in their enforcement procedures. Although a US company certainly can demand some minimal standards of its suppliers, it would be difficult to enforce all US standards in developing countries with very different cultures and traditions.

68. Global Sustainability Standards Board, *GRI 405: Diversity and Equal Opportunity* (Amsterdam, Netherlands: GRI, 2016), 6, https://www.globalreporting.org/standards/media/1020/gri-405-diversity-and-equal-opportunity-2016.pdf.

69. For example, although the GRI has comprehensive standards regarding energy (GRI 302), water use (GRI 303), biodiversity (GRI 304), emissions (GRI 305), and waste (GRI 306), their applications depend on contextual factors that are not readily comparable among businesses. See Global Sustainability Standards Board, *GRI Standards Glossary* (Amsterdam, Netherlands: GRI, 2020), 2, https://www.globalreporting.org/standards/media/2594/gri-standard-glossary-2020.pdf.

70. At present, firms currently face myriad standards and reporting frameworks. The introduction of a centralized and, ideally, global standard-setting body could reduce confusion over which framework to select, particularly for multinational firms that currently face different reporting norms in different regions.

71. Although the SEC has relied on the private sector to set the standards, it has retained a pivotal role. Among other things, it advises on changes in FASB's advising and disclosure standards, provides guidance on interpreting those standards, and enforces compliance with such standards. It has threatened to establish its own standards when the private standard setters were moving too slowly, has on occasion declined to fully endorse standards with which it disagrees, and has attempted to preserve FASB's independence when industry and political leaders sought to exert more control. See Stephen A. Zeff, "Evolution of US Generally Accepted Accounting Principles (GAAP)," working paper, Rice University, 2004, https://www.iasplus.com/en/binary/resource/0407zeffusgaap.pdf.

72. Zeff, "Evolution of US Generally Accepted Accounting Principles (GAAP)." In one year alone, 1971, the APB was successfully pressured not to proceed with three accounting opinions after members of industries that expected to be affected by the new standards lobbied their accounting firms and Congress.

73. For example, some commentators argue that fair value accounting exacerbated the 2008–2009 financial crisis. See, for example, Jennifer Hughes and Gillian Tett, "An Unforgiving Eye: Bankers Cry Foul over Fair Value Accounting," *Financial Times*, March 13, 2008, https://www.ft.com/content/19915bfc-f137-11dc-a91a-0000779fd2ac; Nicholas Rummell, "Fair Value Rules Get More Blame for Crunch," Financialweek.com, March 24, 2008, https://web.archive.org/web/20080327092504/http://www.financialweek.com/apps/pbcs.dll/article?AID=/20080324/REG/854569832. Although academic work largely disputes this account, FASB is by no means perfect. See Robert M. Bowen and Urooj Khan, "Market Reactions to Policy Deliberations on Fair Value Accounting and Impairment Rules

during the Financial Crisis of 2008–2009," *Journal of Accounting and Public Policy* 33, no. 3 (2014): 233–259, https://doi.org/10.1016/j.jaccpubpol.2014.02.003. Some GAAP standards are incomplete, confusing, or present information in a form that does not reflect economic reality. Even aside from political interference, which seems likely to increase the risk of error, it is inevitable that any ESG standard setter will likewise be imperfect.

74. FASB has seven full-time board members, whereas the APB had eighteen to twenty-one part-time members. Each FASB board member is paid close to $1 million annually. See Non Profit Light, "Financial Accounting Foundation," accessed January 11, 2021, https://nonprofitlight.com/ct/norwalk/financial -accounting-foundation.

75. Financial Accounting Standards Board, "About the FASB," last modified July 2020, https://www.fasb.org/jsp/FASB/Page/SectionPage&cid=1176154526495.

76. Financial Accounting Foundation, *2019 Annual Report* (Norwalk, CT: Financial Accounting Foundation, May 2020), 29.

77. Perhaps the most well-known example of political interference in accounting standards concerns accounting for stock options. In 1972, the APB issued ABP Opinion 25, which allowed companies to issue stock options without a correspond-ing expense, provided that the strike price of the option was equal to the current stock price (i.e., the standard did not value the option characteristic that makes the option valuable to its owner). It soon became abundantly clear that allowing companies to issue at-the-money options without an accounting charge did not reflect financial reality. Recognizing fault with its earlier standard, in 1984 FASB initiated a review of stock option accounting and in 1993 was ready to require companies to take an annual expense for the value of stock options. However, that proposed revision met Senator Joe Lieberman, who argued that expensing stock options would harm high-growth technology firms. Senator Lieberman sponsored a nonbinding resolution opposing the revision, and the resolution passed by a vote of eighty-eight to nine. Following that success, Senator Lieberman proposed legislation forcing the SEC to vote on every statement issued by FASB, a proposal that would have effectively killed FASB's independence and reason for existence. Rather than make itself obsolete, FASB caved. In 1995, it issued SFAS 123, a revised standard requiring only that companies disclose the expense associated with stock options in the footnotes to the financials, not in the actual financial statements. In was not until roughly one decade later that, in the wake of a scandal related to stock option backdating, FASB was finally able to require that companies take a charge for options in their financial statements. See Nicholas G. Apostolou and D. Larry Crumbley, "Accounting for Stock Options: Update on the Continuing Conflict," *CPA Journal*, August 2005, http://archives.cpajournal.com/2005/805/essentials /p30.htm.

78. For example, with respect to financial standards, Ray Ball, Ashok Robin, and Joanna Shuang Wu state that they view "the focus on standards as substantially and misleadingly incomplete." See Ray Ball, Ashok Robin, and Joanna Shuang Wu, "Incentives versus Standards: Properties of Accounting Income in Four East Asian Countries," *Journal of Accounting and Economics* 36, nos. 1–3 (2003): 235–270 at 236,

https://doi.org/10.1016/j.jacceco.2003.10.003. For a summary of this literature, see
Hans B. Christensen, Luzi Hail, and Christian Leuz, "Economic Analysis of
Widespread Adoption of CSR and Sustainability Reporting Standards: Structured
Overview of CSR Literature," SSRN working paper, November 2018, http://dx.doi
.org/10.2139/ssrn.3313793. These authors and others have noted that financial
reporting is profoundly affected by economic and political forces (e.g., compensation, firm capital requirements, and external pressure from stakeholders) and that
companies need internal and external mechanisms to constrain these forces.

79. A financial restatement is a revision of a company's previous financial
statements to correct a misstatement.

80. Marlene A. Plumlee and Teri Lombardi Yohn, "An Analysis of the Underlying Causes Attributed to Restatements," SSRN working paper, June 2009, 11,
http://dx.doi.org/10.2139/ssrn.1104189.

81. See, for example, Jeffrey T. Doyle, Weili Ge, and Sarah E. McVay, "Accruals
Quality and Internal Control Over Financial Reporting," *Accounting Review* 82
(2007): 1141–1170 at 1166, http://dx.doi.org/10.2139/ssrn.789985; Peter Iliev, "The
Effect of SOX Section 404: Costs, Earnings Quality, and Stock Prices," *Journal of
Finance* 65 (2010): 1163–1196 at 1166, https://doi.org/10.1111/j.1540-6261.2010
.01564.x.

82. Section 404(b) of the Sarbanes-Oxley Act of 2002. Despite research on the
benefits of internal controls, this requirement has been heavily criticized because
of its implementation costs. See, for example, Joseph A. Grundfest and Steven E.
Bochner, "Fixing 404," *Michigan Law Review* 105, no. 8 (2007): 1643–1676, https://
repository.law.umich.edu/mlr/vol105/iss8/2.

83. In theory, a software system could address some of these concerns by, for
example, requiring users to input the unit of measurement.

84. Yong Kim and Gerald F. Davis, "Challenges for Global Supply Chain
Sustainability: Evidence from Conflict Minerals Reports," *Academy of Management
Journal* 59, no. 6 (2016): 1896–1916 at 1897, http://dx.doi.org/10.5465/amj.2015
.0770.

85. Cydney Posner, "GAO Issues Annual Report on Conflict Minerals Filings,"
Cooley PubCo, Cooley LLP, October 16, 2019, https://cooleypubco.com/2019/10
/16/gao-annual-report-conflict-minerals/ ("as in prior years, almost all companies
reported that, after conducting due diligence, they could not determine whether
their conflict minerals financed or benefited armed groups").

86. LaDawn Naegle and R. Randall Wang, "SEC Adopts Pay Ratio Rule,"
Lexology, August 7, 2015, https://www.lexology.com/library/detail.aspx?g=c2d34e09
-4ccb-4194-8582-19a614b7df1c-19a614b7df1c. In response to these concerns, the
SEC adopted a watered-down rule that allowed companies to identify the median
employee's pay using an array of approaches. This approach is cheaper for companies to implement but limits comparability. See US Securities and Exchange
Commission, "SEC Adopts Interpretive Guidance on Pay Ratio Rule," press
release, September 21, 2017, https://www.sec.gov/news/press-release/2017-172.

87. To understand why it is so difficult to identify the median employee's
compensation, consider that compensation includes many different buckets

(e.g., wages paid, equity, benefits). The systems tracking each component of compensation are often independent and not easily linked. This process becomes more difficult when using a broader definition of employees. For example, if part-time and international employees are included, linking the systems to calculate median pay is even more arduous.

88. To study the effect of reporting systems, most research examines the introduction of such a system. Because established US companies have had systems in place for decades, most research is international and examines firms in countries that have more recently introduced such systems. See, for example, A. T. Moghaddam, S. H. Baygi, R. Rahmani, and M. Vahediyan, "The Impact of Information Technology on Accounting Scope in Iran," *Middle-East Journal of Scientific Research* 12, no. 10 (2012): 1344–1348, http://dx.doi.org/10.5829/idosi.mejsr.2012.12.10.1643; Ahmad Adel Jamil Abdallah, "The Impact of Using Accounting Information Systems on the Quality of Financial Statements Submitted to the Income and Sales Tax Department in Jordan," *European Scientific Journal* 1 (2013): 41–48, https://doi.org/10.19044/esj.2013.v9n10p%25p; Olive Chepkorir Sugut, "The Effect of Computerized Accounting Systems on the Quality of Financial Reports of Non Governmental Organizations in Nairobi County, Kenya" (thesis, Masters of Business Administration University of Nairobi, October 2014).

89. Brendan O'Dwyer, "The Case of Sustainability Assurance: Constructing a New Assurance Service," *Contemporary Accounting Research* 28 (2011): 1259–1260, https://doi.org/10.1111/j.1911-3846.2011.01108.x.

90. For a discussion of the potential of blockchain technology in financial accounting, see David Yermack, "Corporate Governance and Blockchains," *Review of Finance*, 21, no. 1 (2017): 24–28, https://doi.org/10.1093/rof/rfw074 (describing the potential implications of blockchain for financial recordkeeping and corporate governance generally); Enrique Bonson and Michaela Bednárová, "Blockchain and Its Implications for Accounting and Auditing," *Meditari Accountancy Research* 27, no. 5 (2019): 725–736, https://doi.org/10.1108/MEDAR-11-2018-0406 (describing the history and potential difficulties with blockchain in financial reporting). For a discussion of the benefits and limitations of blockchain and social audits, see Axfood, Axfoundation, and SIM Supply Chain Information Management, "Blockchain for Social Compliance in the Moroccan Strawberry Supply Chain," Spring 2019, https://www.simsupplychain.com/wp-content/uploads/2020/03/Blockchain-Moroccan-strawberry-supply-chain.pdf.

91. In financial reporting, auditors are tasked with assuring that the reported results are in compliance with prevailing accounting standards and free from material misstatement. Auditors are not tasked with correcting errors, as this is the company's responsibility, and it is a violation for them to prepare financial statements themselves. However, they may help to correct misreporting indirectly (e.g., by helping the company interpret the applicable standard).

92. See, for example, Ross L. Watts and Jerold L. Zimmerman, "Agency Problems, Auditing, and the Theory of the Firm: Some Evidence," *Journal of Law and Economics* 26, no. 3 (1983): 613–633, https://doi.org/10.1086/467051; Randolph P. Beatty, "Auditor Reputation and the Pricing of Initial Public Offerings,"

Accounting Review 64, no. 4 (1989): 693–709, https://www.jstor.org/stable/247856; David W. Blackwell, Thomas R. Noland, and Drew B. Winters, "The Value of Auditor Assurance: Evidence from Loan Pricing," *Journal of Accounting Research* 36, no. 1 (1998): 57–70, https://doi.org/10.2307/2491320; Michael Willenborg, "Empirical Analysis of the Economic Demand for Auditing in the Initial Public Offerings Market," *Journal of Accounting Research* 37, no. 1 (1999): 225–238, https://doi.org/10.2307/2491405; Joseph Weber and Michael Willenborg, "Do Expert Informational Intermediaries Add Value? Evidence from Auditors in Microcap Initial Public Offerings," *Journal of Accounting Research* 41, no. 4 (2003): 681–720, https://doi.org/10.1111/1475-679X.00120; Michael Minnis, "The Value of Financial Statement Verification in Debt Financing: Evidence from Private U.S. Firms," *Journal of Accounting Research* 49, no. 2 (2011): 457–506, https://doi.org/10.1111/j.1475-679X.2011.00411.x; Mark DeFond and Jieying Zhang, "A Review of Archival Auditing Research," *Journal of Accounting and Economics* 58, nos. 2–3 (2014): 275–326, https://doi.org/10.1016/j.jacceco.2014.09.002; Colleen Honigsberg, "The Case for Individual Audit Partner Accountability," *Vanderbilt Law Review* 72, no. 26 (2019): 1871–1922, http://dx.doi.org/10.2139/ssrn.3470414.

93. Samantha Ross and Gordon Seymour, "The Developing World of Assurance on Sustainability Reporting" (unpublished manuscript, July 15, 2019), Microsoft Word file.

94. For a summary of the many papers on IFRS adoptions, see Christian Leuz and Peter D. Wysocki, "The Economics of Disclosure and Financial Reporting Regulation: Evidence and Suggestions for Future Research," *Journal of Accounting Research* 54, no. 2 (2016): 525–622, https://doi.org/10.1111/1475-679X.12115. For two specific, well-done studies showing that regulatory enforcement was a necessary condition to experience the benefits of IFRS adoption, see Hans B. Christensen, Luzi Hail, and Christian Leuz, "Mandatory IFRS Reporting and Changes in Enforcement," *Journal of Accounting and Economics* 56, nos. 2–3 (2013): 147–177, http://dx.doi.org/10.1016/j.jacceco.2013.10.007; Wayne R. Landsman, Edward L. Maydew, and Jacob R. Thornock, "The Information Content of Annual Earnings Announcements and Mandatory Adoption of IFRS," *Journal of Accounting and Economics* 53, nos. 1–2 (2012): 34–54, https://doi.org/10.1016/j.jacceco.2011.04.002.

95. Bernard Black, Brian Cheffins, and Michael Klausner, "Outside Director Liability," *Stanford Law Review* 58 (2006): 1055–1159.

96. For a survey of this literature, see Ahsan Habib, Haiyan Jiang, Md. Borhan Uddin Bhuiyan, and Ainul Islam, "Litigation Risk, Financial Reporting and Auditing: A Survey of the Literature," *Research in Accounting Regulation* 26, no. 2 (2014): 145–163, https://doi.org/10.1016/j.racreg.2014.09.005. However, litigation over misreporting in ESG reports is an important topic worthy of consideration. ESG disclosures are likely relevant to a broader base of stakeholders than financial disclosures, and it is not clear which of those stakeholders will have standing to sue.

97. See S. Lakshmi Naaraayanan, Kunal Sachdeva, and Varun Sharma, "The Real Effects of Environmental Activist Investing," working paper, London Business School, September 2020, 32, http://dx.doi.org/10.2139/ssrn.3483692; Carrie Driebusch, "The Next Wave in Shareholder Activism: Socially Responsible

Investing," *Wall Street Journal*, March 8, 2020, https://www.wsj.com/articles/the
-next-wave-in-shareholder-activism-socially-responsible-investing-11582892251.

98. Institutional Shareholder Services, *United States Sustainability Proxy Voting
Guidelines: 2020 Policy Recommendations* (Rockville, MD: Institutional Shareholder
Services, December 2019), https://www.issgovernance.com/file/policy/active
/specialty/Sustainability-US-Voting-Guidelines.pdf.

5

Powering the Social Project

The Structural Changes Needed to Fund Social Progress

Bernadette Clavier

Social entrepreneurs are increasingly approaching their impact work from a for-profit angle. Between 2014 and 2019, the proportion of social entrepreneurs applying to the prestigious Echoing Green fellowship with a for-profit business model increased from 20 percent to 30 percent.[1] Whether they are hoping to do well by doing good or have ambitions to demonstrate that our capitalist system can deliver opportunity for all with the appropriate leadership, they assume that a for-profit organizational structure is the best way to plan for long-term, scaled, and sustained impact. The reasoning is that they can access significant capital to fuel their growth by raising funds from the very large pool of traditional private investment funds, including impact investing capital, some of which may tolerate concessionary returns.

Indeed, the legal structure of the organization is a strong determinant for its ability to access growth capital.[2] We compared the fundraising outcomes of Stanford Graduate School of Business (GSB) social entrepreneurs to that of mainstream GSB entrepreneurs over their entire entrepreneurial journey. A study of 1,003 alumni-led companies, including ninety social ventures, shows that social ventures overall are less successful at raising funds than mainstream startups. At the same time, for-profit social ventures are much more successful at fundraising than nonprofits. Over the span of the company's life, for-profit social ventures access nine times more funding than their nonprofit counterparts, with an average deal size nine times greater as well.[3]

However, this story obscures the inadequate role of the impact investing world for seeding for-profit social entrepreneurs and developing a tide of impactful companies that can serve communities around the world in ways that traditional financial markets have not. While the legal environment has evolved[4] to enable for-profit companies to embrace a social mission, the funding world is not making significant movement in that direction. New forms of incorporation are available in a majority of US states and in several countries around the world that allow an organization to enshrine its purpose in statutes and give directors agency to pursue its mission. However, commercial funding in essence continues to be profit driven, and prioritizes financial outcomes that are difficult to reconcile with the realities and purpose of a social venture.

In this chapter, I explore the realities of the fundraising experience of for-profit social entrepreneurs and ask what it would take to generate the resources needed to truly power the social enterprise, how to allocate them effectively, and who should be allowed to lead and take part in our collective social project.

The Social Entrepreneur's Fundraising Experience

Often, the operations of social ventures have to contend with challenging environments such as conflict zones, inadequate public infrastructure, and a lack of skilled labor. Traditional for-profit funders come

BIOGRAPHY

BERNADETTE CLAVIER is executive director of the Center for Social Innovation at the Stanford Graduate School of Business, which educates insightful leaders for social and environmental change. Before transitioning to academia, she had a ten-year business career in procurement with French hypermarket chain E. Leclerc, during which she witnessed firsthand the challenges of our global economy, including social and environmental issues, and took part in the early days of the responsible supply chain movement.

EXECUTIVE SUMMARY

For-profit social entrepreneurs are not accessing capital in sufficient amounts to adequately address social needs. Voluntary private funding sources such as philanthropy and impact investing are not rising to the necessary scale. This chapter takes a macro perspective to explore how the incentives of our economic system could be harnessed to fuel social projects. It also offers principles for the effective and inclusive allocation of resources to set our collective social project on a path for success. Market-based solutions to social problems have both potential and limits. Government plays a crucial role in designing effective systems for society.

with expectations of quick market-rate financial returns. Venture capitalists favor high-risk and high-valuation business models that can return their entire fund in one exit and compensate for the expected high failure rate of the majority of the fund's portfolio. Social ventures don't fit the coveted venture profile, and they fail to meet expectations in two ways:

- As detailed by Steve Davis in chapter 7 of this volume, they need time to refine a solution that may involve a complex web of stakeholders, changing people's behaviors, or reforming a failed system. For founders of social ventures, the short-term pressures of traditional investment capital are detrimental when designing one's impact model. Time pressure compromises their ability to develop trust with beneficiaries and other critical actors and to go through the necessary steps to develop and refine an effective theory of change. Social entrepreneurs don't just optimize a business model to achieve product-market fit; they also optimize an impact model. A product or service with a viable unit economics that people want is not the whole story. As detailed by Gloria Lee in chapter 8 of this volume, social entrepreneurs also design for a social outcome.

- The business may not produce financial returns at market-rate levels while optimizing for something other than profit. How much the market can support the solution varies widely from providing marginal revenue to funding overhead and launching new programs. The return profile is not typical and necessitates setting different expectations for investors.

Those evaluating social ventures by traditional measures will categorize them as bad businesses, or subcommercial investments, as defined by Matt Bannick in chapter 6 of this volume. Success often requires holding both the impact and the business models in tension. With rare exceptions, for-profit social entrepreneurs need to resolve the contradictions between expectations of financial performance and the mission of the organization.

Impact investors have emerged over the past ten years, with the purpose of fueling the social enterprise movement. The volume of impact investing capital has been growing very quickly, which has led to enthusiastic forecasts about the future of the field of impact investing and hope that an impact revolution is around the corner. However, rapid rates of growth for a small pool of capital aren't enough to reach the scale of change that we need. Assets managed with this philosophy remain very limited, in 2020 amounting to $715 billion globally.[5] By comparison, in the United States alone, pure philanthropic donations totaled $471 billion in 2020.[6]

In addition, while all impact funders seek impact, only 7 percent of impact investing assets under management are invested with a tolerance for subcommercial returns.[7] The vast majority of impact investors uphold risk-adjusted levels of return and limit risks by investing after a venture has proven its concept. As a result, the promise of the for-profit form doesn't materialize for all early-stage for-profit social entrepreneurs, especially not for those that fail to meet traditional expectations of return and rapid scaling. As shown in table 5-1, based on self-declared funding data by Echoing Green fellowship applicants from 2012 to 2020, early-stage social entrepreneurs' access to capital is not significantly better for seed-stage for-profit organizations compared to their nonprofit counterparts. Furthermore, social entrepreneurs looking to protect their mission with hybrid forms of incorporation or with a combination of nonprofit and for-profit organizations in tandem or subsidiary structures struggle to find funding[8] at all, as these forms and other mission-anchoring mechanisms remain misunderstood by both philanthropists and for-profit funders.

Instead, most social entrepreneurs rely on bootstrapping, gifts, grants, fellowships, and competition prizes to get through the first couple of years. To support the first few phases of social venture development,

TABLE 5-1

Characteristics of Echoing Green fellowship applicants

Organizational form	Proportion of the applicant pool (2012–2020)	Average funds raised at the time of application[a]
Nonprofit	50.0%	$75,015
For profit	27.8%	$89,557
Hybrid	22.2%	$46,690

[a]Funds raised generally one to three years from time of founding. Excludes organizations whose legal structure is "other" or "undecided."

which include an exploration of the problem, the development of an impact model, and the creation of a proof of concept, philanthropy is critical to foster innovation and enable risk taking for subcommercial for-profit social ventures.

Some social entrepreneurs turn to advocacy and partnerships as a way to reduce the need to deploy costly operations by attacking the problem at the source. Addressing societal issues sometimes means repairing harms and collateral damage from commercial activities, such as cleaning the oceans of the plastic produced and released through industrial production, providing mental health services to a generation of children who developed behavioral issues as a result of lead exposure in apartment buildings, and connecting low-income students to the internet to provide the opportunity their parents cannot afford with their minimum wages. Social entrepreneurs work to compel business leaders to address social issues by embracing stakeholder capitalism as part of the solution. Far from a fundraising strategy, this approach has the potential to significantly reduce the scale of the needs to be addressed through social entrepreneurship. With resources allocated to cover the costs related to stakeholders' needs and to operations' externalities, inequality gaps are likely to shrink and communities are likely to face fewer challenges.

Philosophies for Funding Impact

Various types of private sources of funding approach resourcing social projects with distinctive philosophies and respective limitations.

Philanthropy: "Not My Problem"

The role of philanthropy to fuel the nonprofit world is well understood and established. Less obvious but nonetheless crucial is the role that philanthropic capital has to play in enabling innovation while protecting the mission of seed-stage subcommercial for-profit social ventures.

Social issues such as refugee rights, child abuse, or homelessness involve market failures or impact people with no ability to pay. Entrepreneurial models that address these issues can rarely rely on generating revenue to support the solution and generally incorporate as nonprofit organizations. The fragmentation of philanthropy provides an effective early-stage funding ecosystem that encourages and rewards experimentation and innovation and has fueled the creation and launch of many nonprofit programs or ventures.

Philanthropists have traditionally seen their role as being limited to the nonprofit sector. However, gifts, grants, fellowships, and even program-related investments (PRIs) expecting below-market financial returns, from nothing to slightly less than risk-adjusted returns, can support outsized risk and subsidize trade-offs between financial return and impact. Philanthropy can serve a role analogous to what we see in the commercial sector when public investments made in fundamental research by government entities such as the Defense Advanced Research Projects Agency (DARPA) or the National Institutes of Health (NIH) create the conditions for private enterprise to derisk business, identify uses, and create a market for new products and services that deliver commercial value. In the context of the social enterprise and in the absence of governmental funds focused on domestic social intervention experiments, philanthropic capital can enable the creation of long-term sustainable public good while catalyzing new markets and possibly enabling private wealth.

Although new actors are breaking ranks with traditional models,[9] philanthropy is primarily focused on charity and is culturally misaligned with the idea of investing. In chapter 3, Bill Meehan provides a critique of philanthropy and offers insights into why it has not been scaling with social needs despite the rapidly expanding resources of individuals with high net worth.

Impact Investing: "Working against the Grain"

I argue that impact investing, which is generally assumed to be the future of finance and our most promising foot forward to address the needs of society,[10] relies on voluntary mechanisms and is therefore unlikely to unleash the resources we need.

Recognizing that the nature of the social enterprise requires making a trade-off between impact and financial return is a prerequisite to finding effective ways to make resources flow to where society needs them most. Professional impact investors often point to the supply issue to justify the current size of the available impact investing capital. There aren't enough social entrepreneurs with good ideas likely to generate market-rate returns to justify the creation of more or larger impact investment funds, they say. Judging by how frequently funds that position themselves as "society positive" refuse the label of "impact investor" for fear of signaling a tolerance for concessionary returns, it is clear that a strong motivation of many actors gravitating toward social investing remains the promise of market rates of financial return. As demonstrated by the success of the ESG investing space, capital owners are attracted by more-ethical ways of continuing to make money at similar rates. In other words, the popular approach is to "do no wrong" as opposed to proactively making a positive impact. While until recently investors thought that corporate social responsibility was a waste of resources and ran counter to shareholders' interest, in 2016 Harvard professor George Serafeim's research highlighted the first evidence for the financial materiality of ESG issues.[11] Taking care of the most relevant stakeholders in any given industry is shown to boost financial performance, so large volumes of capital ($40.5 trillion in assets in 2020 worldwide[12]) naturally flow to ESG funds even though, as described in chapter 4 of this volume by Paul Brest and Colleen Honigsberg, ESG reporting is still in its infancy and needs to mature.

In chapter 6 of this volume, Bannick shows that it is possible, although not easy, for investors to support some social entrepreneurs through commercial investments that are not market validated. However, market-rate returns are precisely not the point of the social enterprise. The point is to create social value; it is hoped without losing money and possibly while producing a little bit of financial return. We don't have a social ventures supply issue. Rather, we have a demand issue for the social enterprise value proposition, the vast majority of which is subcommercial. The "doing well while doing no harm" opportunity is quite large, but the "doing well by doing good" proposition is overhyped.

The remarkable growth of impact investing capital we have seen is the result of individuals making a statement for what areas of society they believe are worthy of investment and in some cases exercising their values to justify lower rates of return. Impact finance pioneers are developing innovative funding mechanisms such as revenue-based financing, most of which require capital willing to trade off financial return for impact. The growth of impact investing has dovetailed with the social enterprise movement. Because impact investing relies on capital owners' personal motivations to choose impact over profit, it could disappear in the same way it appeared. All it would take is for actors exploring this space to decide to change course. The impact investing model leaves investing in society to the moral imagination of capital owners and trusts that investors are naturally inclined to do the right thing. It would be naive to believe that true concessionary impact investing can continue to grow much longer despite a fundamental misalignment with the market incentives that organize the sector. At the heart of the impact investing movement are mission-driven impact professionals who are working to realign the purpose of business with meaningful human needs and to provide an ethical framework for how business is done. However, when understanding social entrepreneurship as a way to soften the edges of our capitalistic system by addressing the societal needs that it does not take into account, it becomes obvious that impact investing as a field with its current capitalistic incentive structure is inadequate to address the need.

Stakeholder Capitalism: Heroism

Stakeholder capitalism relies similarly on voluntary action on the part of corporate CEOs to take account of all stakeholders in business operations. Some but not all stakeholder needs are aligned with a corporation's best interests. In a seminal 2011 article, Michael Porter and Mark Kramer argued that companies can gain competitive advantage by including social and environmental considerations in their strategies.[13] Since then, Serafeim's research clarified that not all kinds of alignments with societal needs have the same positive effect on company value.[14] Concretely, it makes good business sense for Pepsi to collaborate with local communities to proactively manage groundwater reserves when scarce water supplies would increase the cost of operations and threaten profits.[15] It makes less sense, however, for oil and gas companies to be concerned about soiled rivers unless constrained by regulations with significant costs for noncompliance. Workers are too grateful for employment opportunities to complain about the impact on their environment, and communities with the least resources tend to tolerate the trade-off.[16] Market incentives influence the corporation to direct resources to pro-social endeavors in win-win circumstances. In the case of issues that don't intersect with business operations, it is unrealistic to expect that CEOs would willingly disregard their fiduciary duty to maximize profits for the benefit of their shareholders. Therefore, stakeholder capitalism, although more cognizant of societal needs, still relies on goodwill and, as put by Unilever's former CEO Paul Polman, a good dose of "CEO heroism"[17] as a solution to address them.

In sum, philanthropists don't see a role for themselves in funding private social enterprise, and investors who decide to allocate resources to subcommercial social investments, or CEOs who direct business resources to commercially unproductive social causes, are resisting the incentives of the free market system. It takes a combination of rebel spirit, extra effort, creativity, and courage to accomplish something that our existing capitalist system is not designed to achieve. Under these conditions, it's not reasonable to expect that these behaviors could become mainstream without structural changes and proper incentives in place to foster them, reinforce them, and celebrate them. The combination of philanthropy, impact investing, and stakeholder capitalism that is generally assumed to be the way forward to address the needs of society relies primarily on voluntary mechanisms and is therefore unlikely to unleash the resources we need. To get us there, we should instead build on the powerful forces of market incentives proven to routinely move trillions of dollars.

Designing for Abundance

Pioneers such as Sir Ronald Cohen act as role models, show the path, and tilt the twentieth-century investing culture focused on risk and return to a twenty-first-century paradigm of risk-return-impact.[18] However, to adjust their investment behaviors, investors need both the willingness and a supportive environment. Behavior change requires more than just will power. A focus on motivating others to do the right thing will not be enough to create a tide of subcommercial impact investing if not accompanied by efforts to remove obstacles in the way of everyday investors and to create strategic nudges that render the desired investing behavior effortless.

What if, instead of working against the grain, we could harness the profit motive and use it as an engine to meet societal needs? To generate a much larger flow of capital for the social enterprise, we need to build on existing financial behaviors and systematically direct them toward investments in our future and in our communities. What if the government could subsidize subcommercial investments to make them attractive to commercial investors and effectively eliminate any trade-off between social endeavors and commercial activities? What if every time a dollar was invested in a commercial endeavor anywhere in the world, ten cents was automatically invested in a subcommercial social enterprise as the price for doing business? What if by law every investment opportunity was systematically paired with a subcommercial investment? We need to make subcommercial investing an embedded fixture of traditional investing or more broadly of doing commercial business—a logical consequence of normal economic activities, not a choice for a small group of individuals between more financial returns or more social good.

It is government's role to create the structures within which society can flourish, and the role of democracy is to organize a healthy discussion about what those structures might look like. Over time, the role of the US government has evolved with ideologies. After World War II, the US government took a strong hand in creating the conditions for a thriving society in which every successive generation could expect to be better off than the previous one, and it was effective at reducing, at least for its white population, the inequalities that had fractured American society during the Gilded Age. Since the 1980s, however, faith in the "invisible hand" of the market has taken hold among most American governing institutions, justifying years of deregulation and weakening the government to the point of irrelevance.

The principles by which resources are allocated are critically important and have forever been the topic of passionate debates. Specific rules such as those described in the tax code create incentives and opportunities that drive individual and institutional spending, saving, investing, or giving behaviors in powerful ways. The UK government's "Nudge Unit" is the world's first government institution that uses behavioral economics to examine and influence human behavior and "nudge" economic actors into making better decisions. This approach has demonstrated results in various domains, including taxes, health care, pensions, employment, crime reduction, energy conservation, and economic growth.[19]

The relative sizes of the US commercial (measured in trillions) and impact (measured in billions) capital pools give direct evidence of the inadequacy of existing incentives to direct private investments to societal needs. Government intervention in the form of subtle nudges, including subsidies, tax breaks, advance commitments, or investment mandates, could be transformative as the country tries to rebuild after multiple Covid-19 shutdowns.

Tax Breaks and Subsidies

Every year, Americans are ready to give away over $400 billion[20] with no expectation of returns but are unable to gather nearly as much for projects that could do as much good, do so sustainably in the long run, and provide a little return along the way. Largely because of misaligned incentives created by the US tax code, what would otherwise be sensible behavior doesn't happen. Allowable tax deductions for giving create a de facto unbeatable rate of return for philanthropy over investing, let alone impact investing. In the same way that tariffs distort markets by artificially making the origins of some products or services more cost-effective than others or subsidies give one source of energy a competitive advantage over another, for the majority of people with disposable income, the 501c3 tax exemption generates savings higher than the return opportunity afforded by financial markets.

Considering the willingness of society to subsidize philanthropic donations, there is a clear rationale for subsidizing subcommercial impact investments as well. The sacrifice of risk-adjusted returns made by a subcommercial investment is the equivalent of a philanthropic grant. Tax breaks for subcommercial impact investments could boost the financial return on investment made by everyday people in community projects, deliver public value, and help small investors create a financial safety net for themselves in the process.

This approach has been tested in the world of foundations in the form of program-related investments (PRIs).[21] The US Internal Revenue Code allows foundations to make loans, equity investments, or guarantees in pursuit of their charitable mission to both nonprofit organizations and for-profit business enterprises. Unlike investments made from their endowments, foundations do not expect PRIs to produce market-rate returns. Like traditional grants, PRIs count toward a foundation's qualifying distribution—the required annual payout of 5 percent of its endowment.[22] In essence, foundations already receive a tax incentive for subcommercial investments. Foundations like those of Ford, Bill & Melinda Gates, John D. and Catherine T. MacArthur, and Packard have used PRIs to support non-market-validated startups in developing environments, to scale up enterprises that serve the poor, or to encourage biotech companies to focus on neglected diseases. Because of strict restrictions and cumbersome reporting requirements designed to eliminate the temptation to reclassify poor endowment investments as PRIs, the instrument has not been broadly adopted. Revised regulatory guidance could make it easier for foundations to make PRIs and unleash massive amounts of capital for subcommercial impact investing. Transposing this experiment in the realm of private investing would similarly require designing social investment qualification mechanisms that clearly set subcommercial social ventures apart from others. Although attitudes would need to be tested, such tax breaks could be a winning proposition for small individual investors along the entire political spectrum, satisfying those who favor individual agency over government intervention as well as those supporting social expenditures.

Guarantees

Similarly, government guarantees could derisk subcommercial investments and channel higher volumes of money to areas of need. We have seen this work before. During the Great Depression, the administration of Franklin Delano Roosevelt made a major effort to stimulate the housing sector. Created in 1934 by the National Housing Act, the Federal Housing Administration (FHA) backed mortgage insurance that derisked lending for banks and other lending institutions so they would extend private credit to more borrowers. This effort is credited with creating the white middle class in the United States. If the Covid-19 recession is anything like the Great Depression, it's time for a *new* New Deal with similar guarantees but this time with an inclusive impact agenda.

Permitting or Mandating New Hybrid Saving Instruments

Less costly for the state than tax breaks or subsidies, the creation of new savings instruments can also drive significant investments to community projects. For example, France adopted a unique regulatory framework providing a state mandate that corporate-sponsored pension funds allocate a portion of their investable capital in social ventures. The framework's cornerstone is a 90-10 solidarity fund retirement savings mechanism. Ninety-ten savings funds must invest 5 to 10 percent of their equity or debt in nonprofits, social ventures, and other socially focused projects. According to the 2014 law, all companies with more than fifty employees are required to offer their workers 90-10 pension plan options. As of 2018, close to one million French individuals had invested more than €12 billion in 90-10 funds, leading to more than €1 billion in financing for social impact organizations. The main area supported by solidarity-based financing is addressing unemployment, poverty, and affordable housing, a cross-sector issue regarded as France's main social problem. Financing also goes toward organic farming and clean energy generation and provision, and supporting development projects in emerging economies.

In the United States, just 2.9 percent of 401(k) plans include investing options tied to environmental, social, and governance (ESG) issues.[23] This is a result of strict fiduciary provisions of the Employee Retirement Income Security Act of 1974 (ERISA), the federal statute that oversees employee pension and benefit plans. ERISA prevents pension trustees from engaging in any investment behavior that might sacrifice fund returns, even if such behavior is supported by an overwhelming majority of beneficiaries. In a 2016 survey by Natixis, 62 percent of retirement plan participants said they would increase their contributions if they knew their investments were doing social good, and the percentage bumped up to 72 percent among millennials, who now represent more than 50 percent of the American workforce.[24] We can only imagine how many more people would be willing to increase their retirement savings if they knew not only that their investments were working to increase the quality of their lives but also that the majority of their money would get a market-rate return. Indeed, people are on the receiving end of both kinds of benefits of such hybrid investment instruments: the financial benefits in the form of distributions and the nonfinancial benefits, such as clean air and rivers, universal health care, and other services that enhance quality of life and relieve the pressure of financial needs. It's only fitting that people's money would be used to further the social project in addition to economic growth that negatively impacts communities by putting downward pressure on wages and contributes to a toxic environment and warming climate. Yet today, despite the domination of ownership of oil and natural gas companies by middle-class households through their pension and retirement accounts (47 percent of the value of all US-based oil and gas company shares in 2014 was held in retirement accounts, 29 percent in pension plans, and 18 percent in 401(k)s and IRAs),[25] people have no control or say over the scientifically established negative externalities of the oil industry on the health of people and the planet. Even if nothing changed in individuals' saving behavior, a reform of ERISA could direct a sizable amount of money to support our collective social project. In the final quarter of 2019, Americans held a collective $32.3 trillion in their retirement accounts.[26] That is larger than the gross domestic product of the United States and more than one-third of the world's.[27]

Options to generate new capital for the social enterprise abound in the form of tax collection relief, advanced commitments, or new investment vehicles. Finding the resources is possible and is a matter of political will. The market system we depend on was set in place through a political process and can be modified through the democratic process as well.

We should not leave it to the goodwill of private capital owners to choose lower rates of return over the best that markets have to offer. The market-oriented system they work within is motivated and structured for profit, not social impact. It will take government intervention to revisit the incentive structures of our economy and to rebalance resources between the creation of public and private goods. Markets remain the best economic engines we have; it's up to us to decide to harness their power for society.

Efficient Capital Allocation: Qualifying Social Investments

Regardless of the amount of resources available to address societal needs, identifying social solutions worthy of investment is its own challenge. The risk when relaxing expectations of returns is to allow sloppy investing without a clear articulation of the financial return versus impact trade-off. Social impact bonds offer an accountability mechanism that puts the risk on investors and rewards impact results only when proven. This social investment qualification approach is limited in its applications, especially when it comes to early-stage solutions. Assuming that distributing new resources for social projects is best done by leveraging our existing financial sector and infrastructure, evaluating the potential for impact of social investments will require new talent and new approaches in the finance industry. Pioneering impact investing firms such as the Omidyar Network and Bridges Fund Management are developing the tools, experience, and mindsets required to maximize impact for society and collaborate on initiatives such as the Impact Management Project to create industry standards.

In contrast, a lot of new entrants who are trying their hand at impact investing continue to leverage old and inadequate frameworks and can hardly demonstrate any impact at all.[28] Unless created by people or organizations rooted in a philanthropic culture, when a fund management company or a corporation starts exploring impact investing, the tendency is to start small, explore, and learn. Investing managers may be asked to take on a firm's impact fund as a reward for service or because they have a genuine interest and are willing to get started. They often don't have the same resources they usually have for traditional funds. They rarely have had the chance to develop an instinct for impact through pattern matching over years of interaction with impact organizations, and they approach this work with a financial return mentality. Besides limited innovation in a variety of asset classes, impact investors are stuck in venture capital mental models that hope large returns with one or more of the investments will make up for the losses incurred on the rest of the portfolio. They quickly confront the reality that, except in specific impact areas such as energy and health care, social ventures tend to produce rather low returns. There are rarely opportunities to invest in "unicorns," those startup companies capable of reaching $1 billion in valuation.

When it comes time to make their first hire to power their impact fund, finance professionals new to impact investing often continue to prioritize people with a finance skill set who understand the investing part of impact investing but don't have experience with the impact part. In 2017, we at the Center for Social Innovation examined the hiring preferences of impact funds and found that hiring managers underappreciated the social impact experience of prospective employees.[29] Many fund managers assume that people can learn about social impact quickly but that accumulating investing experience takes years. The result is that 80 percent of the impact investors we studied had a background in finance before landing an impact investing job, while only 45 percent had experience in social impact. The more-recent hiring decisions put more of an emphasis on impact skills and knowledge as the impact investing job market became very competitive, with a groundswell of interest from millennial professionals and as pioneering impact investors developed the profession and established standards.

Qualifying social investments requires that finance professionals completely reframe their traditional selection criteria and processes. The lack of a single objective function to optimize makes it difficult to engage with impact in a way that is rigorous and unbiased. We need ways for fund managers to understand which of their investment options will generate the most impact and whether a well-intentioned social program can also have a negative impact on society. Academics rely on randomized controlled trials to assess social and environmental effects, both short term and long term, of so-called interventions or programs. But carefully designed studies are costly and aren't always practical, especially when trying to assess a seed-stage venture deal. Evaluating the future impact potential of a product, service, organization, or policy absent study results and serious modeling capabilities is an art and the privilege of longtime experts who can draw from a robust set of experiences to inform their judgment.

Absent an impact compass[30] such as the one developed by the Center for Social Innovation, which I detailed in chapter 9, it's hard to imagine how reliance on traditional financial measures of success could be effective at delivering social value to communities if there were a massive transfer of capital into social investing instruments. To accelerate the transition from a workforce trained in the mindsets of stock price and profit maximization to one fluent in evaluating both financial and impact returns, the finance profession will need to hire large numbers of impact professionals with nonprofit and foundation backgrounds. Talent combining both impact and finance skills and mindsets is a rarity, as being proficient in both requires being able to hold opposing goals in tension. Business schools have a key role to play to accelerate a convergence of the social and the financial talent pools.

Community Empowerment: Helping Communities Help Themselves

The many different communities that make up our society are facing a vast array of challenges, all of which are competing for limited time and resources. The fair allocation of funds across communities is equally as important as generating sufficient resources and identifying effective solutions to address the issues. Assuming that all communities will have the same entrepreneurial drive to address their own challenges, a fair allocation system should provide similar access to all entrepreneurs based on the merit of their project and regardless of their community of origin. This is not how capital is allocated in the United States today. Rather, we see that the communities with the most critical rates of poverty and proximate knowledge of the issues are the least able to access capital. Who gets to prioritize founders worthy of investment and who gets to design entrepreneurial solutions is critically important for the quality and relevance of the outcome. Empowering entrepreneurs with no proximate knowledge of the issues is akin to making a bad investment if the expected impact return doesn't materialize for lack of empathy with the issue. The pursuit of the social enterprise requires empowering communities to address their own needs, and the best way to do that is to fund their social entrepreneurs.

Philanthropists and impact fund managers deciding where to direct their resources generally consider their personal fit and passion for the issue or that of the capital owners on behalf of whom they are managing the funds. As a society, we are relying on the individual preferences of people who may not be representative of society as a whole to decide how to allocate resources.[31] While this arrangement supports innovation, individual agency ultimately limits our collective ability as a society to prioritize resources where they are most needed. Philanthropy and impact investing ultimately empower those with resources to set the social agenda for all and fail to empower economically disadvantaged populations to help themselves.

In the United States, the predominantly white and higher socioeconomic status of philanthropists and finance professionals has had a non-negligible impact on the kind of social ventures that get funded as well as on the kind of founders backed. People of color, who are disproportionately affected by many social and environmental issues and are best positioned to design solutions that work for their communities, have a harder time raising funds for their social entrepreneurship work. Particularly badly represented in the lucky circle of social entrepreneurs who receive funding support for their social ventures are founders at the intersection of identities, whose groups experience compounded social issues and discrimination. Self-declared funding data by Echoing Green fellowship applicants from 2012 to 2020 shows that regardless of their choice of structure model, founders of color have a harder time raising money. The experience of Echoing Green's large pool of applicants provides strong evidence of barriers[32] to capital based on race, with Blacks raising 29 percent of funds while accounting for 47 percent of applicants and whites raising 44 percent of all funds while accounting for 34 percent of applicants.

Racial inequities have reached such degrees in the United States that supporting a Black-led enterprise and its promise to create opportunities for Black communities, whether by a social entrepreneur or not, has a social impact in and of itself. Yet, those founders are not gaining the same access to capital as their white counterparts in traditional capital markets either. Only 1 percent of venture-backed founders are Black and 1.8 percent are Latinx,[33] even though in 2015 Black and Latinx entrepreneurs made up 14 percent and 8 percent of all entrepreneurs in the United States, respectively.

There is a complicated and deeply rooted set of factors that explain this reality and prevent the empowerment of social entrepreneurs of color to address the social issues faced by their communities. Studies show that the pattern-matching approach that many investors rely on to evaluate the success potential of entrepreneurs broadly makes it difficult to break away from past models. When the academic degrees, skin color, gender, and/or nationality of those that successfully walked the entrepreneurial path in the past define the profile of the ideal future investee, access to capital becomes very difficult for already underrepresented founders. A preference for serial entrepreneurs in innovation ecosystems such as Silicon Valley makes it harder for capital to flow toward new entrants. Even for fund management teams that embrace affirmative action in the name of diversity and inclusion, race exceptionalism that favors immigrants of color, including Blacks from Africa and founders of Indian descent, over African Americans confuses the issue of diversity and obfuscates the underrepresentation of African Americans.[34] Finally, race also influences the financial judgment of professional investors and leads them to require more from and to put more obstacles in front of funds led by people of color even after they have proved themselves to be strong performers.[35] The resulting lack of representation in the predominantly white world of fund management reinforces stereotypes for what success looks like, introduces implicit biases in selection processes, and exacerbates communication challenges between funders and prospective investees.

Kapor Capital, Reach, New School Ventures, and Camelback Ventures are among the pioneers of impact investing that are finding solutions to connect with communities of color and their entrepreneurial leaders. They are shifting how they evaluate opportunities and are transforming the makeup of their boardrooms, staffs, and leadership teams to make sure they can facilitate the flow of capital to the communities most in need. These measures are self-imposed by fund managers and have been embraced as a movement as awareness of racial inequity has increased. It is unclear how far relying on cultures and norms will take us as a society toward channeling resources to the communities of greatest need. The world of international development has a number of community empowerment models to offer that could provide inspiration to develop democratic structures that put the social agenda back into the hands of communities and generate much-needed civic engagement.

Conclusion

The health of societies depends on their ability to balance the creation of private wealth on the one hand and the public good on the other. The vision that doing well by doing good will become the way we do business and that traditional and impact investing will converge has blinded us to the real nature of the social enterprise—addressing market failures and repairing inequities created by an imperfect economic system tilted primarily in the direction of the creation of private wealth.

In their current forms, philanthropy, impact investing, and stakeholder capitalism won't solve the world's biggest social problems. In particular, expecting a market-oriented economy and a finance industry optimized for financial returns to embrace subcommercial world-saving opportunities is pure fantasy, as a market system does not incentivize prosocial outcomes. A better system would channel new resources to the public good by default, without effort by economic actors, foster new impact-savvy talent, and provide a democratic process to preside over the allocation of these resources.

The pipeline of social entrepreneurs is actually quite robust when the proper expectations of speed and returns are set, when the social value of what they deliver can be clearly articulated, and when color filters are removed. Growing the share of private investment capital allocated to fueling the social enterprise will require intentional design. Government intervention will be needed to create new financial instruments and incentives that harness market forces to channel resources in the service of societal needs alongside private interests.

The impact revolution will not happen on its own. We need to invest in society again. Our failure to do so is threatening democracy. This is no longer a choice; let's not make it one.

FOR FURTHER READING

In *Inside the Nudge Unit: How Small Changes Can Make a Big Difference* (W. H. Allen, 2016), behavioral scientist David Halpern provides insights into what's possible when removing frictions and designing systems with incentives in mind. For readers wanting to keep abreast of the state of impact investing around the world, the Global Impact Investing Network's *Annual Impact Investor Survey* provides regular updates. Finally, for readers interested in the intersection of social innovation and social justice, I recommend *The Color of Money: Black Banks and the Racial Wealth Gap* by Mehrsa Baradaran (The Belknap Press of Harvard University Press, 2019), which explores the history of the exclusion of people of color from the distribution of financial resources in the United States.

Notes

I thank Paul Brest, Russ Siegelman, Neil Malhotra, Stuart Coulson, and Noopur Vyas for comments on earlier drafts of this chapter.

1. Echoing Green, "The State of Social Entrepreneurship," 2020, https://echoinggreen.org/news/state-of-social-entrepreneurship-2020.

2. Sarah Soule and Todd Johnson, *Social Enterprise Legal Structure*, Stanford, 2017, https://stanford.edu/dept/gsb-ds/Inkling/CSI_Legal_Structures/index.html.

3. "PitchBook Data Inc.," LinkedIn.

4. Soule and Johnson, *Social Enterprise Legal Structure*.

5. Global Impact Investing Network, *2020 Annual Impact Investor Survey* (New York: Global Impact Investing Network, June 2020).

6. Giving USA Foundation, *Giving USA 2021: The Annual Report on Philanthropy for the Year 2020* (Chicago: Giving USA Foundation, June 2020).

7. Global Impact Investing Network, *2020 Annual Impact Investor Survey* (New York: Global Impact Investing Network, June 2020).

8. Julie Battilana, Matthew Lee, John Walker, and Cheryl Dorsey, "In Search of the Hybrid Ideal," *Stanford Social Innovation Review* 10, no. 3 (Summer 2012), https://ssir.org/articles/entry/in_search_of_the_hybrid_ideal#.

9. Dana Brakman Reiser, "Is the Chan Zuckerberg Initiative the Future of Philanthropy?," *Stanford Social Innovation Review* 16, no. 3 (Summer 2018), https://ssir.org/articles/entry/the_rise_of_philanthropy_llcs.

10. Global Impact Investing Network, *Roadmap for the Future of Impact Investing* (New York: Global Impact Investing Network, March 2018).

11. David Freiberg, Jean Rogers, and George Serafeim, "How ESG Issues Become Financially Material to Corporations and Their Investors," working paper 20-056, Harvard Business School, Boston, November 2019 (revised November 2020).

12. Sophie Baker, "Global ESG Data-Driven Assets Hit $40.5 Trillion," *Pensions and Investments*, July 2, 2020, https://www.pionline.com/esg/global-esg -data-driven-assets-hit-405-trillion#:~:text=The%20value%20of%20global%20 assets,to%20%2440.5%20trillion%20in%202020.

13. Michael Porter and Mark Kramer, "Creating Shared Value," *Harvard Business Review*, January–February 2011, https://hbr.org/2011/01/the-big-idea-creating -shared-value.

14. Freiberg, Rogers, and Serafeim, "How ESG Issues Become Financially Material to Corporations and Their Investors."

15. Pepsico, *2019 Sustainability Report* (Purchase, NY: Pepsico, 2019).

16. Arlie Russel Hochschild, *Strangers in Their Own Land: Anger and Mourning on the American Right* (New York: New Press, 2016).

17. Sarah Butler, "Ex-Unilever Boss Seeks 'Heroic CEOs' to Tackle Climate Change and Inequality," *The Guardian*, July 21, 2019, https://www.theguardian.com /business/2019/jul/21/ex-unilever-boss-seeks-heroic-ceos-to-tackle-climate-change -and-inequality-paul-polman.

18. Sir Ronald Cohen, *On Impact: A Guide to the Impact Revolution* (London: Sir Ronald Cohen Publications, 2018).

19. David Halpern, *Inside the Nudge Unit: How Small Changes Can Make a Huge Difference*, reprint edition (London: W. H. Allen, 2016).

20. Giving USA Foundation, *Giving USA 2020*.

21. Paul Brest, "Investing for Impact with Program Related Investments," *Stanford Social Innovation Review* 14, no. 3 (Summer 2016), https://ssir.org/articles /entry/investing_for_impact_with_program_related_investments#.

22. Internal Revenue Service, *Program Related Investments*, http://www.irs.gov /Charities-&-Non-Profits/Private-Foundations/Program-Related-Investments.

23. Plan Sponsor Council of America (PSCA), *63rd Annual Survey Report* (Chicago: PSCA, 2020).

24. Natixis Global Asset Management, *Running on Empty: Attitudes and Actions of Defined Contribution Plan Participants* (Boston: Natixis Global Asset Management, 2016).

25. Robert Shapiro and Nam Pham, *Who Owns America's Oil and Natural Gas Companies: A 2014 Update*, www.senecon.com.

26. Investment Company Institute, "Retirement Assets Total $32.3 Trillion in Fourth Quarter 2019," March 19, 2020, https://www.ici.org/research/stats/retirement /ret_19_q4.

27. World Bank, "World Development Indicators: Structure of Output," accessed May 1, 2020, http://wdi.worldbank.org/table/4.2.

28. Paul Brest and Kelly Born, "When Can Impact Investing Create Real Impact?," *Stanford Social Innovation Review* 11, no. 4 (Fall 2013), https://ssir.org/up_for_debate/article/impact_investing.

29. Bernadette Clavier and Neil Malhotra, "Valuing Social Impact Expertise in Impact Investing," *Stanford Social Innovation Review*, Fall 2017, https://ssir.org/articles/entry/valuing_social_impact_expertise_in_impact_investing.

30. Stanford Graduate School of Business, Center for Social Innovation, *The Impact Compass* (Stanford, CA: Stanford Graduate School of Business, 2018).

31. Rob Reich, *Just Giving: Why Philanthropy Is Failing Democracy and How It Can Do Better* (Princeton, NJ: Princeton University Press, 2018).

32. Echoing Green, "The State of Social Entrepreneurship."

33. The Knight Foundation, "Diversifying Investments: A Study of Ownership Diversity and Performance in Asset Management Industry," 2019, Miami, Florida.

34. Arun Venugopal, "The Making of a Model Minority," *The Atlantic*, January–February 2021, https://www.theatlantic.com/magazine/archive/2021/01/the-making-of-a-model-minority/617258/.

35. Sarah Lyons-Padilla, Hazel Rose Markus, Ashby Monk, Sid Radhakrishna, Radhika Shah, Norris A. "Daryn" Dodson IV, and Jennifer L. Eberhardt, "Race Influences Professional Investors' Financial Judgments," *Proceedings of the National Academy of Sciences* 116, no. 35 (August 27, 2019): 17225–17230.

6

Market Creation

Catalyzing New Markets with Early-Stage Impact Investments

Matt Bannick

We cannot solve our problems with the same
thinking we used when we created them.

—Albert Einstein

The prevailing market economy, fueled by an efficient, return-maximizing financial system, has brought stunning advances in science, human longevity, and global prosperity. Financial markets, and the capitalist system they support, however, have done less well in other critical areas, such as serving the needs of disadvantaged populations and protecting the environment. Impact investing has generated optimism that "investing for good" can help address some of these market failures. In this chapter, I describe how two segments of the impact investing market, "commercial, non-market-validated" investments and "subcommercial" investments, can catalyze new, high-impact markets by supporting transformative, market-creating innovations eschewed by mainstream return-maximizing investors. By jump-starting entire new markets for social change, investments in market innovators can generate impact substantially greater than that generated by any single firm.

This chapter first describes three distinct segments of impact investments—(1) commercial, market-validated investments; (2) commercial, non-market-validated investments; and (3) subcommercial investments—outlining how each segment varies in the key dimensions of risk, expected financial return, and impact. Commercial, market-validated impact investments are those commercial investments where expectations of high returns are "validated" by the existence of other commercial investors. Commercial, non-market-validated investments are those commercial investments where expectations of high returns have *not* been validated by the existence of other commercial co-investors. This is usually because the investor who expects commercial returns has specific expertise or knowledge that other commercial investors lack. Subcommercial investments, in contrast, accept concessionary rather than commercial returns. Critically, both commercial, non-market-validated investments and subcommercial investments generate substantial impact that would not have happened without the investment.

After segmenting the impact investing market, the chapter highlights the transformational impact of a type of entrepreneurial venture referred to as a "market-creating innovator." The impact of market-creating innovators extends well beyond their direct impact on customers. Indeed, by creating entirely new high-impact markets, market innovators can generate a massive "impact multiplier," as their early success attracts competitors, accelerating innovation while delivering improved quality at a lower cost and inspiring similar innovations in other markets. In addition to creating new markets, "market innovators" can lay the foundation for the next generation of innovators and help create a more robust entrepreneurial ecosystem, fueling continued innovation, impact, and economic growth. One of the best-known examples of a high-impact

BIOGRAPHY

MATT BANNICK is the former managing partner of the Omidyar Network, a philanthropic venture capital firm and pioneering impact investor. Under his leadership, the Omidyar Network invested more than $1.3 billion in early-stage for-profit and social ventures, impacting tens of millions of lives and helping to create new high-impact markets. Prior to joining the Omidyar Network, he served in various senior executive roles, including president of PayPal and president of eBay International. He is a lecturer at the Stanford Graduate School of Business.

EXECUTIVE SUMMARY

Impact investors tend to focus on the impact of an individual company and on financial returns. Frequently absent from consideration is how an investment—or a series of investments from a range of investors—can create entirely new high-impact markets. This chapter highlights how specific types of early-stage investments—those that leverage unique investor insights and those that provide a form of subsidy—can generate market-creating impact beyond what would be created by return-maximizing capital markets. The chapter uses examples from across frontier, emerging, and developed markets to illustrate key points and emphasize the critical role that individuals with ultrahigh net worth can play in market creation.[1]

market-creating innovator is the Kenyan mobile payments company MPesa. MPesa's digital payment platform, created with the support of a $1 million grant, has accelerated innovation and economic development across Kenya. MPesa has also inspired the launch of more than three hundred mobile money deployments around the world, which collectively serve more than three hundred million active users and have reduced the cost of financial services by 80 percent or more in most markets.[2]

After describing the impact multiplier created by market innovators, the chapter turns to the critical role that commercial, non-market-validated investments and subcommercial investments can play in fostering those high-impact market innovators that are often overlooked by traditional commercial capital markets. Though relevant across all stages of investments and all geographies, these investments play a particularly catalytic role in early-stage investing and in emerging and frontier markets, where venture capital markets are more nascent, disposable incomes are lower, infrastructure is less developed, and perceived risks are higher. The catalytic role of early-stage commercial, non-market-validated, and subcommercial investments is illustrated with case studies from across developed, emerging, and frontier markets.

The chapter concludes with an analysis of potential sources of relatively scarce market-catalyzing impact capital, highlighting the tremendous potential of market-catalyzing investments from individuals having ultrahigh net worth, many of whom generated their wealth through market-creating innovations.

This chapter draws on the insights and lessons learned during my twelve years as managing partner at the Omidyar Network, a leading early-stage impact investor. It builds on three published reports I coauthored, "Priming the Pump: The Case for a Sector Based Approach to Impact Investing,"[3] "Frontier Capital: Early Stage Investing for Financial Returns and Social Impact in Emerging Markets," and "Across the Returns Continuum."[4]

Segmenting Private Market Impact Investments

Impact investments, generally defined as "investments made with the intention to generate positive, measurable social and environmental impact alongside a financial return,"[5] continue to grow rapidly, reaching an estimated $715 billion in assets under management (AUM) globally in 2020.[6] Impact investments occur in both private and public markets, as debt or equity, and at all stages of investment. For the balance of this chapter, however, *the focus will be on equity investments in private markets and on early-stage investments*, as they are most likely to support the creation of new markets.

This chapter focuses on three distinct segments of impact investments. The key points of differentiation in these segments are whether the investor expects commercial returns (defined here as risk-adjusted market-rate financial returns) and whether co-investors (regardless of whether they consider themselves impact investors) expect commercial returns. Each of these impact investing segments varies not only in terms of returns but also in terms of positive social and/or environmental impact and "additionality." "Additionality" refers to impact that was created by a given investment that would not have been created but for that investment.[7]

Figure 6-1 is adapted from an article authored by Matt Bannick, Paula Goldman, Michael Kubzansky, and Yasemin Saltuk, entitled "Across the Returns Continuum,"[8] which described the conditions under which an investor might choose to invest at different points along a continuum of financial returns. The element of additionality has been added to the original "Returns Continuum" illustration, which has also been simplified. Figure 6-1 illustrates how each of the segments described here varies in terms of expected returns and additionality.

FIGURE 6-1

Across the returns continuum with additionality

Expected financial return

| Commercial, market-validated impact investments | Commercial, non-market-validated impact investments | Subcommercial impact investments |

Additionality

Commercial, Market-Validated Impact Investments

In this segment, an impact investor's expectation of commercial returns in a particular investment is "validated" by the existence of multiple co-investors in the investor syndicate who are also expecting commercial returns. These investors are typically investing in well-developed capital markets characterized by an abundance of return-maximizing capital. Most venture capital (VC) and private equity investments in the United States, for example, would be considered "commercial, market-validated investments" because they typically involve multiple co-investors, all of whom are expecting risk-adjusted returns on their investments. Commercial, market-validated investments have helped generate enthusiasm and momentum for impact investing by demonstrating that an impact investor does not need to accept below-market financial returns. Eighty-eight percent of self-declared impact investors[9] report meeting or exceeding their financial goals.[10] The growth of impact investing has been driven largely by commercial, market-validated investments, which account for the majority of the sector's AUM.[11]

It's important to note that "risk-adjusted" returns must consider the risk of investing in a specific country, sector, and stage of investment. "Risk premiums" can vary dramatically. Aswath Damodaran of NYU's Stern School of Business, for example, estimates that the equity risk premium varies from 4.72 percent in the United States to 7.63 percent in Brazil and 10.05 percent in Kenya.[12] In other words, an investor's return on an investment in Kenya should be 5.33 percentage points higher than on a similar investment in the United States to fully compensate for country risk alone. In reality, the risk premium in Kenya is likely to be substantially more than 5.33 percentage points given that industry risks and market-segment-specific risks of an investment in Kenya are likely to be greater than in the United States.

Expected financial returns. Risk-adjusted market rates of return.

Additionality. It is not clear that market-validated commercial investments generate substantial incremental impact beyond what would have occurred without them. If the expected returns on an impact investment are market rate, the argument goes, then the investment would have attracted commercial capital from nonimpact investors. In this case, there would be no "financial additionality."

The question of additionality then turns to whether market-validated commercial impact investments can generate *nonfinancial* value. Here the answer is less clear-cut. Most concur that the nonfinancial impact provided by an investment in public markets is modest, though there may be opportunities for activist impact investors to influence critical governance matters. Most private equity and venture capital investors, meanwhile, argue that their firms deliver substantial nonfinancial value to investees in the form of industry and/or geographic expertise, networks or relationships, and strategic and financial acumen. The threshold for additionality, however, would seem to be not whether an investor generates nonfinancial value but rather whether they generate *more* value than an alternative investor—regardless of whether that investor is an impact investor.

One potential "value add" of an impact investor would be to ensure, typically through governance, that a mission-driven impact company does not veer away from its impact mission in pursuit of greater profit, a phenomenon frequently referred to as "mission drift." For example, a return-centric board member may encourage a firm to generate greater profits by developing higher-margin products for wealthier customers, while an impact-oriented board member may resist such a move up market, as it might hinder a company's ability to serve lower-income segments. In this case, an impact investor's insistence on maintaining "mission alignment" may face resistance from nonimpact investors if it potentially reduces financial returns. This is not merely a hypothetical example; many impact-oriented investors can describe boardroom debates involving tension between impact mission and financial returns.

It's important to note that some companies do not position themselves as "impact" companies, as they fear that such a positioning would narrow their sources of funding, even though they may be working with lower-income, underserved, or excluded populations.

Commercial, Non-Market-Validated Impact Investments

In this segment, an investor's expectation of commercial returns in a particular investment is not "validated" by the presence of other commercial co-investors. These deeply committed impact investors tap their specific knowledge, networks, and/or geographic proximity either to develop a proprietary deal flow or to be able to price risk more effectively. Such investors bet on promising companies that are either overlooked or eschewed as too risky by other commercial investors. Many of these investments are in emerging and frontier markets, where capital markets are less developed, particularly for early-stage investments. Non-market-validated commercial investments are far less common than market-validated commercial investments, as relatively few investors are willing to incur the cost and challenges associated with gaining proprietary insights in difficult markets.

Expected financial returns. Risk-adjusted market rates of return.

Additionality. Non-market-validated investments generate substantial additionality. The absence of other commercial investors suggests the company either would have had to pay a much higher price to raise capital or may not have been able to raise capital at all but for the investor. In addition to financial capital, the investor's contributions in areas such as governance, industry expertise, networks, and general human capital are also likely to be highly additional, as the investee is unlikely to be receiving such support from other investors.

Numerous impact investors seek market returns while investing, frequently at an early stage, in often challenging geographies and/or sectors. Among these are Aavishkar (India), Bamboo Finance (Africa, India, Latin America), Bridges Fund Management (United Kingdom, United States), Ceniarth (Global), Elevar Equity (India, Latin America), Flourish Ventures (United States, Africa, South/Southeast Asia, Latin America), Ignia (Mexico), Imaginable Futures (United States, Global), Leapfrog

(India, Africa), LGT Impact Ventures (Africa), Lok Capital (India), and the Soros Economic Development Fund (United States). Most of these investors make commercial, market-validated and commercial, non-market-validated investments. In other words, they are willing to invest alongside purely commercial investors as well as to invest in companies that are not receiving capital from other commercial investors. A smaller subset of investors will consider subcommercial investments in addition to commercial ones.

It's important to note that many investors making commercial, non-market-validated investments do not consider themselves impact investors. Many are simply using market knowledge and expertise to invest in underappreciated companies that can generate risk-adjusted returns regardless of impact. Indeed, many return-maximizing investors—and some impact investors—avoid the term "impact investor," as it may make it more challenging to raise capital from potential investors who associate the term "impact investor" with below-market returns.

Subcommercial Impact Investments

In this segment, an investor is willing to accept outsized risk and/or lower financial returns in order to generate substantial impact.

Expected financial returns. Returns ranging from slightly less than risk-adjusted returns to preservation of capital.

Subcommercial investments subsidize businesses that deliver social good. Subsidies can be particularly valuable when prevailing "amoral" market-based systems underinvest relative to societal value, including markets serving disadvantaged or low-income populations, products and services with positive externalities (e.g., health care and education), and public goods (e.g., clean air). For example, in the United States, community development financial institutions subsidize housing for lower-income families.

Some subsidies support businesses that need upfront capital in order to become sustainable. Subsidized investments can also help develop markets by, among other things, creating industry infrastructure (e.g., a credit rating agency in financial services) or demonstrating the commercial viability of innovations that may straddle the public and private sectors (e.g., "career impact bonds" issued by the not for profit Social Finance, which enable low-income customers to pay for education costs through an innovative income-sharing model). Each of these types of subsidies can generate strong positive social impact. For the remainder of this chapter, however, the focus will be on the subset of subcommercial investments that strive to create or accelerate *entire markets* by investing, typically at an early stage, in individual for-profit companies. These investments will be referred to as "market catalyzing," as they seek to catalyze new markets for social impact.

Additionality. Well-executed subcommercial investments have high additionality. In addition to providing access to otherwise unobtainable capital, many subcommercial investors are also willing to invest in a first-time fund or to hold an investment for a longer period of time, a particularly important factor in emerging and frontier markets and in sectors such as clean energy and health care, where a business may take more time to scale and/or exit options take longer to develop. In addition to financial capital, subcommercial investors typically provide additional assistance by, inter alia, assuming board seats, providing industry expertise and strategic guidance, and leveraging their networks. The networks of subcommercial impact investors can be especially valuable to entrepreneurs in emerging and frontier markets, enabling them to connect with other subcommercial impact investors and also commercial investors once their business begins to get traction.

Some impact-oriented private investors, such as the Acumen Fund, Ceniarth, Global Partnerships, the Soros Economic Development Fund, and the Omidyar Network and its successor organizations, make market-catalyzing impact investments. Some foundations, such as the Ford Foundation, the Gates Foundation, and the MacArthur Foundation, also make subcommercial investments, typically through an investment vehicle called a program-related investment (PRI). In addition, many development finance institutions (DFIs), such as the United Kingdom's CDC Group, and international financial institutions (IFIs), such as the World Bank, have invested successfully in emerging and frontier markets while taking outsized risk.

Subcommercial development investments can often generate strong, if not entirely risk-adjusted, returns. Returns on investments made by the World Bank's International Finance Corporation (IFC) since 1961, for example, have exceeded the returns of the S&P 500 by 15 percent.[13] Though impressive, it is unlikely that these returns fully compensate for the disproportionate risk that the IFC has taken, which is why these investments would technically be referred to as subcommercial for the purposes of this chapter. It's worth noting that investment fund managers who target strong but not risk-adjusted returns typically do not refer to themselves as subcommercial investors, lest they scare off potential capital providers.

Subsidized investments have their critics. Some argue that they open the door to "sloppy investing," where relaxing the financial hurdle enables an investment decision to be based on an often-flimsy promise of future impact. A focus on impact can thus lead to an investment in a subpar, nonviable company unable to raise or generate the capital to scale and have substantial long-term impact. Subsidies also have the potential to distort markets, hindering—rather than accelerating—their growth. Well-intentioned subcommercial investors risk tilting the playing field in an already commercially viable market by providing below-market financing. The distortion could be particularly damaging if it enabled a weaker firm to survive against stronger, more agile competition.

On the other hand, there are many instances where a market simply does not yet exist and the investment-seeking entrepreneur is innovating in order to *create* a market. In many ways, the more disadvantaged the population being served, the less likely that a commercially viable market exists and the more essential a subsidy might be to kick-start a market. This was evident in many of the early investments by impact investing pioneers such as the Acumen Fund (founded in 2001 by Jacqueline Novogratz), which intentionally invested in businesses serving lower- and middle-income communities, even when returns were likely to be low and/or uncertain. Acumen's early investment in d.light, for example, helped jump-start the market for affordable home solar lanterns and eventually home solar systems, which are increasingly replacing the noxious and expensive kerosene used by many low-income customers in Africa and India and enhancing electricity access, livelihoods, and educational opportunities for millions. Notably, d.light has been able to scale by tapping into all three impact investing segments over time, including investors seeking risk-adjusted returns.

The financial cost of Acumen's early subsidy is a small percentage of the value of the impact generated by d.light. Most impact measurement tends to focus on the impact of an individual investment. Frequently absent from the conversation is the extent to which an investment—or a series of impact investments from a range of investors—can create impact at the level of a market rather than just a firm. If an entire new market can be kick-started, then an early financial subsidy in a company such as d.light may end up being a tiny fraction of the total impact generated by a "market-creating innovator."

The Extraordinary Impact of Market-Creating Innovators

Market-creating innovators are entrepreneurial ventures that spark entire new markets by developing and commercializing a product or service well before its profit (and impact) potential is obvious to others. While market innovators have an important direct impact on their customers, their most significant impact is through market creation. The early success of a market innovator incentivizes competitors to enter the market, jump-starting a flywheel of innovation that continuously drives costs down and quality up, accelerating market growth and increasing customer value and social impact. From an impact perspective, it is not important whether the market innovator prevails against its competition. Indeed, competitors may come and go, but a thriving market, once ignited, will continue to scale, creating a multiple of impact well beyond the impact of any one firm. Some market innovators create a foundation or "platform" on which additional entrepreneurs can innovate, creating an additional multiplier effect.

One excellent example of a market innovator is Kenyan mobile money platform MPesa. MPesa not only created an entire new market for digital payments but also developed a platform on which other innovations were built and inspired similar market creation around the world. The innovation behind MPesa was funded by a $1 million grant from the United Kingdom's Department for International Development (DFID), which hoped that digital payments could reduce costs and improve the security of repaying microfinance loans. MPesa's early success was based on its ability to enable domestic remittances, a $400 billion global market, as highlighted in its tagline, "Send Money Home." The benefits of a mobile wallet quickly extended beyond person-to-person payments, providing ordinary Kenyans access to a range of financial services and enabling merchants to safely and affordably accept digital payments. Moreover, by providing customers with an easy, affordable, and secure way to pay, MPesa's payment platform facilitated the creation of new markets in Kenya, including high-quality affordable private education (Bridge Academies) and home solar systems (d.light).

MPesa's impact extends well beyond Kenya; it has inspired the creation of mobile money deployments in ninety-five countries, which collectively have signed up more than one billion accounts and have dramatically improved financial inclusion.[14] The reach of mobile money agents is now seven times that of ATMs and twenty times that of bank branches, and the cost of providing basic financial services has fallen by 80 percent or more in most markets.[15]

The MPesa example highlights the role of mobile technology in facilitating and accelerating market innovations, particularly in emerging and frontier markets. As increasingly affordable mobile technology has spread to all but the most poor or remote areas of the globe, it has become perhaps the single biggest development platform in emerging and frontier markets, enabling new business models to be born and to scale much more rapidly than possible just five to ten years ago.

MPesa also illustrates how market innovators can even create a more vibrant entrepreneurial ecosystem, fueling successive rounds of innovation. The existence of an efficient, effective digital payment platform has encouraged entrepreneurs to invest in Kenya, creating a hotbed of innovation and earning Kenya the nickname of "Silicon Savannah." Frequently, innovative entrepreneurs help nurture the next generation of entrepreneurs and foster a robust entrepreneurial ecosystem by, among other things, becoming venture investors. Yibo Shao, for example, an early internet pioneer in China, went on to invest in multiple Chinese unicorns—privately held startups valued at more than $1 billion—as a partner in Matrix China. Similarly, Avnish Bajaj cofounded Matrix India after selling his e-commerce platform to eBay. Marcos Galperin, the founder of Mercado Libre, the leading e-commerce and payments platform in Latin America, has been instrumental in fostering a vibrant entrepreneurial ecosystem in Latin America. Nicholas Szekasy and Hernan Kazeh, two members of the founding team of Mercado Libre, later founded Kascek Ventures, one of the most successful VC firms in Latin America. The alumni of the Egyptian ride-hailing service Careem, meanwhile, have gone on to found or play leadership roles in numerous startups across the Middle East.

The MPesa example and others like it demonstrate that the impact of market innovators extends well beyond the "direct impact" they have through such things as the provision of goods and services and the creation of jobs. Indeed, the "indirect impact" represented by the innovator's creation of or contribution to the development of powerful new markets, platforms, and networks must also be considered when thinking about the total impact of a market innovator. To put it simply:

Total Social Impact of a Market Innovator
= Direct Impact of the Market Innovator
+ Indirect Impact of the Market Innovator[16]

When thinking about the potential impact of a market innovator, it is useful to think of a "market multiple" of impact. Consider, for example, the extent to which Boeing's impact on commercial aviation has been a multiple of the impact it has had in serving its direct customers. How much credit should go to Netscape for the subsequent waves of innovation triggered by its browser or to eBay and Amazon for pioneering e-commerce? How much market value creation can be attributed to the now-defunct Lotus 1-2-3 spreadsheet application, which helped drive the popularity of desktop PCs in the 1980s?

While there are a plethora of tools and metrics for measuring the direct impact of a firm, it has proven far more difficult to measure a firm's indirect impact, largely because of the challenges of measuring a firm's contribution to what economists refer to as positive externalities. The inability to measure or perhaps even recognize the market-level impact of innovations has profound implications for impact investors. If impact investors are drawn to the highest impact returns on their dollar and *if* they only count those impacts that are both measurable and attributable to their investments, then they are likely to systematically underinvest in companies—particularly early-stage, high-risk innovative firms—that have the potential to create entire new markets for social change.

If market innovators can indeed have extraordinary but underestimated impact, the question for the impact investing community is: How can impact investments—across a spectrum of expected returns—help spark, nurture, and scale such market innovators? In particular, what role can each investment segment play in driving market innovation beyond what already happens through traditional return-driven commercial capital markets? And how does the role played by each of these segments vary according to factors such as geography and the income level of the population being served?

Catalyzing New Markets through Impact Investments in Market Innovators

Each of the three segments of impact investments supports market innovators in different, often complementary, ways that play out over the life cycle of an investment. The easiest path is for market innovators who have strong financial prospects and can thus attract early-stage capital from commercial, market-validated investors such as venture capitalists. Market innovators with strong financial prospects working in underappreciated sectors or geographies meanwhile may not be on the radar of traditional VC firms but are frequently able to secure financing through commercial, non-market-validated investors.

Often, an early grant or subsidy is essential in kick-starting an idea or company or in demonstrating the financial viability of a geography, sector, or income segment deemed by commercial investors as too risky. After the viability of the business model has been demonstrated, investors with strong sector-specific or geographic-specific knowledge or expertise (e.g., commercial, non-market-validated investors) can provide larger tranches of capital to help the idea gain early scale and a path to profitability. Once a path to profitability is discernible, commercial, market-validated investors, who represent the largest pool of capital, may provide the financial resources necessary for the innovation to scale massively. Microfinance is perhaps the best-known example of a sector that required substantial subsidized capital before being able to attract the commercial capital required to reach massive scale.

Figure 6-2 is adapted from Bannick and Goldman's "Priming the Pump,"[17] which, among other things, describes the role that various investor segments play in nurturing, developing, and scaling new high-impact markets. The three impact investment segments highlighted earlier have been added to the original "Priming the Pump" illustration, which has also been simplified to focus on the early stage of market development and on the financing of individual firms rather than markets. Figure 6-2 underscores the potential complementarity of impact investing segments and also illustrates the extent to which the segments frequently overlap: at each stage of development, a market innovator may be supported by different types of impact investments.

Of course, the real world is complicated, and most market innovators do not tap into a clear, sequential set of subsidized, commercial, non-market-validated and then commercial, market-validated investments.

FIGURE 6-2

The potentially complementary role of impact investment segments in market development

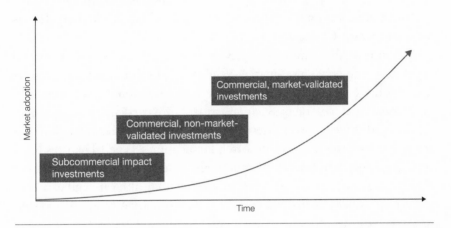

However, there are numerous examples of market innovators benefiting from more than one of these often-complementary investment types.

While the three segments of impact investments are highly complementary in most markets, their relative importance in supporting market innovators varies by market and is largely driven by the relative wealth of a market and the maturity of the local venture capital sector.

Catalyzing New Markets in Developed Economies

In developed economies, such as the United States, most market innovators are supported through traditional for-profit, "impact agnostic" early-stage investors, particularly venture capital firms. US venture-backed companies attracted more than $150 billion in the first half of 2021 alone.[18] Some commercial, market-validated VC firms in developed markets, such as Spero Ventures, apply a "mission filter" before making an investment but otherwise act like a typical return-driven VC. Other VCs go further, pledging to maintain an impact focus even after making an investment. Impact-focused investors may appeal to an impact entrepreneur who wishes to avoid mission drift and may prefer to have like-minded investors on its board. Some mission-driven companies have created an "impact advisory board" composed of impact-oriented investors. Handshake, for example, which assists college students in getting jobs, received early investments from traditional VC firms such as Kleiner Perkins and subsequently established an impact advisory board composed of impact-oriented investors such as Imaginable Futures, Emerson Collective, Chan Zuckerberg Initiative, and Reach Capital.

Notwithstanding the preponderance of commercial VCs in developed markets, commercial, non-market-validated and subcommercial investors can still drive significant innovation beyond what would be generated by traditional capital markets. Such investments are particularly impactful in sectors with high positive externalities, such as health care and clean energy. The Juvenile Diabetes Research Foundation's Type 1 Diabetes Fund and Breakthrough Energy Ventures are among the numerous impact funds designed to catalyze market innovation in health care and clean energy, respectively, by making commercial, non-market-validated and subsidized investments—and occasionally by providing grants as well.

I present in boxes 6.1 through 6.8 miniature case studies that provide examples of the various impact investing concepts discussed in the chapter.

BOX 6.1

Case Study: The Juvenile Diabetes Research Foundation's (JDRF) Type 1 Diabetes (T1D) Fund, Health Care, Disease Treatments, and Cure

Location: United States and Global

Systemic challenge: Type 1 diabetes, the more prevalent and life-threatening form of diabetes, affects millions of people around the world. Historically, the only treatment for type 1 diabetes has been insulin injections; little money has gone to innovative treatments or cures.

Market-creating investor: Sean Doherty, a former Bain Capital executive who has a son with type 1 diabetes, created the $100 million T1D fund in 2016 to catalyze private investment in innovative cure-oriented therapies such as immunotherapies and beta cell therapies. Investments include both commercial, non-market-validated and subcommercial investments.

Market-creation potential: Doherty notes that the JDRF has "demonstrated that a mission-driven, non-profit market participant can de-risk a disease area for the venture community and draw capital to the field, enabling real progress towards a cure."[19] The fund attracts six dollars for every dollar it invests, and one of its investees, Semma Therapeutics, was acquired by Vertex Pharmaceuticals for almost $1 billion. Returns from T1D's investments are reinvested in the fund rather than being returned to investors.

BOX 6.2

Case Study: Breakthrough Energy Ventures, Clean Energy

Location: United States and Global

Systemic challenge: Though the need for innovations in clean energy is urgent, many high-potential energy innovations require significant upfront costs, have long development periods, and are high risk, making them unattractive for most traditional commercial, market-validated investors.

Market-creating investor: Breakthrough Energy Ventures (BEV) was launched in 2016 as a $1 billion fund spearheaded by Bill Gates and supported by more than two dozen other wealthy philanthropists. It invests in scientific breakthroughs that have the potential to deliver cheap and reliable clean energy. It focuses on aspects of clean technology that have attracted less commercial investment, hoping to demonstrate the viability of certain market segments and to catalyze additional investment and innovation. BEV has a high risk tolerance and an investment time frame of twenty years, more than twice as long as most traditional VC firms. It also uses grant funds for research and policy, recognizing that these tools can be complementary in driving systems and sector-level change.

Market-creation potential: BEV has made more than thirty investments, ranging from battery storage to fusion energy, and raised an additional $1 billion in 2021. It has been credited with helping to lead a resurgence in clean tech investing.

Catalyzing New Markets in Emerging Economies

Venture capital has grown rapidly in emerging economies such as China, India, Brazil, and South Africa. Though "emerging markets" are frequently lumped together, they represent great diversity in terms of things such as income, infrastructure, and growth rates. Per capita income ranges from about $10,000 in China and Brazil to about $5,300 in South Africa and $2,200 in India. The Chinese VC market is second only to that of the United States in size, with the overwhelming majority of investments being market-validated commercial ones. Venture capital funding in India and Latin America has grown rapidly in recent years and includes more commercial, non-market-validated impact investors than in China.

Historically, most emerging-market VC firms have funded startups focused on upper- and middle-income customer segments, frequently with mobile-based offerings, and have shied away from firms serving lower-income segments or working in challenging sectors such as agriculture. It is in these areas that commercial, non-market-validated investors and subcommercial investors can play a particularly catalytic role.

The potential market-creating innovations highlighted in boxes 6.3 through 6.8 come from the portfolio of just one impact investor, the Omidyar Network and its successor organizations, demonstrating the breadth of impact that a single committed investor can have. Each case study not only highlights the market innovation itself but also identifies the funders and funding types and describes how each innovation might spark new high-impact markets. Many of these innovations, particularly those in sectors such as education and health care, have positive externalities that create substantial value for society as well as for the individual being served. Such investments can also help fill an institutional void when government has failed to provide a basic good at a minimum quality threshold.

BOX 6.3

Case Study: Mapan, Last-Mile Distribution, Financial Inclusion, and Livelihoods

Location: Indonesia

Systemic challenge: The mostly poor rural citizens in the far-flung islands of Indonesia lack access to high-quality goods and services.

Market innovator: Mapan (formerly PT Ruma) has pioneered a replicable, cost-effective, technology-enabled, agent-based model, delivering financial services and high-quality goods and services to lower-income rural Indonesians while also providing employment and income for local communities. Mapan now has more than 1.5 million members and employs more than 1,000 full-time employees and 120,000 commission-based agents in sixty cities across Indonesia.

Funding: Mapan began as a grant-based project of the Grameen Foundation's technology innovation lab, focused on creating livelihoods by enabling lower-income women to sell airtime. As it evolved, Mapan received funding from the impact-first venture fund Patamar and the Omidyar Network. After strong growth and margins demonstrated the commercial viability of its model, Mapan received a strategic investment from a firm backed by Chinese tech giant Tencent. In 2017, Mapan was acquired by Go-Jek, a ride-hailing, logistics, and digital payments company valued at about $9 billion.

Market-creation potential: Many countries have poor infrastructure, creating barriers to access for the rural poor. In expanding its footprint across difficult terrain, Mapan has created a model that can be replicated and adopted in other similar markets, providing hundreds of millions more people with access to financial services and high-quality products while also creating significant employment opportunities.

BOX 6.4

Case Study: Dr. Consulta, Health Care

Location: Brazil

Systemic challenge: Health care in Brazil is ostensibly "free," but patients face long wait times, poor quality, and hidden fees. In Sao Paulo, where Dr. Consulta started, there are sixteen public clinics for the city's fifteen million residents. Only one in four Brazilians can afford private health care.

Market innovator: By standardizing care, leveraging technology, and ensuring high doctor and facility utilization, Dr. Consulta provides high-quality, low-cost specialty health care and diagnostic services to Brazil's low- to middle-income population. Dr. Consulta now has more than fifty clinics, serving more than one million patients, and continues to expand rapidly.

Financing: Dr. Consulta received early funding from Kascek Ventures, a commercial VC firm, which later brought in impact-centered investors such as LGT Venture Philanthropy and the Omidyar Network.

Market-creation potential: Poor-quality, inaccessible health care is a major problem in many, if not most, emerging and frontier markets. Dr. Consulta offers a promising blueprint for delivering high-quality, affordable health care, which can also relieve the stress on public systems. As founder Thomaz Srougi notes, "I don't think that the solution for global health care will come out of wealthy economies. It is probably going to come out of places like Brazil and Asia."[20]

BOX 6.5

Case Study: Doubtnut, Education

Location: India

Systemic challenge: India's non-English-language speakers, who represent more than 80 percent of its population, are not well served by the country's education technology offerings, which are English-language focused. This risks increasing the education and income gap between better-educated, higher-income urbanites and less-affluent, less-educated rural communities.

Market innovator: Doubtnut's mission is to "democratize education across India." The Doubtnut app enables students from sixth grade to high school to solve and understand math and science problems in local languages. A student can take a picture of the problem, share it with Doubtnut through its app, website, or WhatsApp, and receive a short video providing the answer and illustrating how to solve the problem. Eighty-five percent of Doubtnut users come from outside the top ten cities in India, where local languages predominate. Doubtnut already serves more than thirteen million active users monthly and is growing rapidly.

Funding: Doubtnut received an initial commercial, non-market-validated investment from the Omidyar Network, with subsequent funding provided by commercial investors such as Sequoia Capital India and Tencent.

Market-creation potential: Doubtnut has demonstrated the vast potential of underserved language communities in India, which is likely to encourage others in India to move beyond serving primarily higher-income English-language speakers. Doubtnut's innovative approach and platform can also be adapted for use in other multilingual countries.

Catalyzing New Markets in Frontier Economies

Despite significant growth, VC activity in frontier economies is much less than in emerging or developed markets. Annual VC investments in all Africa, for example, are about $1 billion to $1.3 billion, much of it in relatively developed South Africa. Private equity investments are more prevalent but tend to provide growth capital to well-established ventures rather than funding early-stage innovations.

Many frontier markets have poor infrastructure, costly and ineffective supply chains, challenging regulatory and governance environments, and limited disposable income, making returns more speculative and unpredictable, particularly for early-stage investments. Investment sizes tend to be smaller and due diligence costs higher, raising the prospect that even solid financial returns can be offset by transaction and human capital costs. Even if an enterprise is successful, frontier capital markets remain relatively immature, and exit opportunities are often limited.

On the other hand, there is no shortage of entrepreneurial talent in regions such as Africa, and VC activity is picking up considerably, particularly in hotbeds such as Nairobi. The increasing ubiquity of mobile technology is fueling continued growth and innovation.

Given the relatively low income levels in frontier markets, most market innovations are likely to have significant social impact; in order for a market innovation to reach scale, it must be able to reach down into the typically underserved emerging middle- or even lower-income segments and to deliver a product or service that makes a meaningful difference in a person's life. Indeed, many of Africa's most active VC firms are impact-focused investors, such as Goodwell, Novastar, Blue Orchard, and LGT Ventures. Grant dollars and subsidized investments also tend to be more prevalent in frontier markets.

BOX 6.6

Case Study: d.light, Energy Access

Location: Primarily Africa, also India

Systemic challenge: Globally, 1.3 billion people lack access to electricity, including 600 million in India and 300 million in Africa. Hundreds of millions rely on toxic and expensive kerosene for lighting.

Market innovator: d.light sells solar lanterns and home solar systems in Africa and India, providing clean electricity and lighting while reducing carbon emissions associated with kerosene and diminishing the need for future lighting based on fossil fuels. d.light's pay-as-you-go model enables customers to acquire a home solar system at a daily cost below what they typically pay for kerosene. d.light has directly impacted the lives of more than 100 million people across seventy countries.

Funding: Early on, d.light received more than $10 million of grant funding, as well as investments from impact-centered subcommercial investors, including Acumen and Grey Matters Capital. Later rounds included the Omidyar Network as well as sector-focused investors such as Inspired Evolution. d.light has now raised more than $100 million, in debt and equity.

Market-creation potential: d.light has pioneered new markets in solar lanterns and low-cost "pay-go" home solar systems. Robust competition is driving continued innovation, reducing costs, and helping to grow the market by educating consumers about the benefits of solar power. d.light and its competitors are now shipping hundreds of thousands of home solar systems per year in Africa alone.

BOX 6.7

Case Study: Bridge Academies, Education

Location: Primarily Africa

Systemic challenge: Public education in Africa is generally of poor quality even as the percentage of the world's children who live in Africa is set to increase from about 21 percent today to about 40 percent by 2050.

Market innovator: Bridge Academies provides affordable private and public education to primary and preprimary students in Africa and India, demonstrating that well-run schools can deliver higher-quality education at a lower cost than they do today. Sophisticated use of data and technology enables Bridge and its teachers to develop and deliver consistent, high-quality instruction while also streamlining school administration and classroom management. Test results consistently show Bridge students outperforming their non-Bridge peers. Bridge currently educates more than 100,000 students through its company-owned schools in countries such as Kenya as well as in government-funded schools in Liberia; Lagos, Nigeria; and Andhra Pradesh in India.

Funding: Bridge has received more than $100 million of grant and investment capital from across the continuum of expected returns. Bridge received early grants from organizations such as the Mulago Foundation and the Omidyar Network. The Omidyar Network subsequently invested in Bridge alongside other impact investors (e.g., LGT Impact Ventures, Gates Foundation, Chan Zuckerberg Initiative, King Philanthropies), VC firms (e.g., Learn Capital, NEA, Khosla Ventures), and DFIs (e.g., OPIC, DFID).

Market-creation potential: Bridge has demonstrated that it is possible to deliver high-quality education at reasonable cost even in the most difficult environments. Many of the insights from Bridge can be learned, replicated, and improved on by other entrepreneurs committed to high-quality affordable education. In addition to pioneering an innovative education model, Bridge has also sparked important debates about the role of private education in frontier and emerging markets.

BOX 6.8

Case Study: Pula Advisors, Agricultural Productivity and Insurance

Location: Africa and South Asia

Systemic challenge: Two-thirds of the world's working poor make their living in agriculture, and smallholder farmers typically struggle with low productivity, limited access to high-quality inputs such as seed and fertilizer, and exposure to potentially calamitous weather events, which are becoming more frequent because of global warming.

Market innovator: Pula provides farmers with free insurance bundled with inputs (such as seeds and fertilizer) and farmer advisory services to help increase their yields and boost (and protect) their income. Agricultural input companies pay the premium to differentiate their product from the competition, and the insurance is underwritten by third-party insurers. Pula uses satellite data and farm yield measurements to understand how weather affects yield and then uses this information to automate compensation in the case of loss. The company also provides farmers with targeted agronomic advice via SMS messaging, helping them increase yields. Pula facilitates insurance coverage to more than four million farmers.

Funding: Pula's seed round was led by Accion Venture Lab, which often makes high-impact subcommercial investments. The next round included several impact-first investors, including Omidyar Network/Flourish Ventures, Mulago Foundation, Choiseul Africa Capital, Mercy Corps Social Venture Fund, and several angel investors. In 2020, Pula raised $6 million from Pan-African venture capital firm TLcom Capital and the nonprofit Women's World Banking.

Market-creation potential: Pula's model has the potential to dramatically reduce global poverty by increasing the efficiency and income of the world's 500 million smallholder farmers. Increased crop yields can also accelerate economic growth.

Activating Impact Capital to Drive Market Innovation

The appeal of generating risk-adjusted commercial returns while doing good helps explain why impact capital is concentrated in commercial, market-validated investments rather than being evenly distributed across the continuum of financial returns. The preceding examples illustrate the massive potential that "high-additionality" early-stage commercial, non-market-validated and subcommercial investors can play in nurturing the innovations that can catalyze entire new markets for social impact.

Notwithstanding the potential impact, the amount of "market catalyzing" capital being deployed across commercial, non-market-validated and subcommercial investments is quite modest. According to a survey by the Global Impact Investing Network (GIIN),[21] investors reported committing $3.5 billion of "catalytic capital"[22] in 2019, representing less than 10 percent of the $47 billion of new impact investments.

Industry observers often cite three key investor segments as important sources for investments in market innovators: development finance institutions (DFIs)/international financial institutions (IFIs), US foundations, and individuals with ultrahigh net worth.

As part of their mission, DFIs and IFIs invest in challenging markets, and some are venturing into earlier-stage investing, where there is a higher potential for creating new markets. The United Kingdom's CDC, for example, is making a series of "catalyzing investments" that bear more risk than CDC's main commercial portfolio. DFI/IFIs are also supporting market innovation by providing capital to independent VC and impact funds operating in emerging and frontier markets. However, most DFI/IFI capital continues to be focused on later-stage investments, and overall DFI funding is not expected to increase substantially in the coming years.

As noted previously, several large US foundations, including the Ford Foundation, the Gates Foundation, and the MacArthur Foundation, make both commercial, non-market-validated and subcommercial investments. The Gates Foundation has committed $1.5 billion for program-related investments (PRIs), while the Ford Foundation has earmarked up to $1 billion of its endowment for mission-related investments (MRIs). Meanwhile, members of the Catalytic Capital Consortium, led by the MacArthur Foundation, have demonstrated that foundations can come together to advance an important set of ideas, raise capital, and invest behind impact in a dynamic, flexible way. Notwithstanding leadership from several key foundations, total commitments to impact investing remain modest. Only about 2 percent of foundation endowments have historically been committed to investment vehicles focused on impact (MRIs and PRIs). Moreover, only a small percentage of MRI/PRI capital is invested in equity, which is the type of capital typically invested in early-stage firms with high impact potential.

Individuals with ultrahigh net worth represent perhaps the greatest potential for increased impact-first investments, not only because of the enormous wealth they control but also because most lack the institutional constraints represented by a government mandate or a somewhat narrowly defined (grant-centric) philanthropic charter. Many of the ultra-wealthy made their money through entrepreneurship and thus may more readily understand the transformative power of market innovation. Innovative philanthropists such as Pierre Omidyar, Laurene Powell Jobs, Mark Zuckerberg, Laura and John Arnold, George Soros, and others have invested in promising high-impact ventures. One group of high-net-worth individuals that seems particularly well suited to venturing into the realm of impact-first investing are the signatories to the Giving Pledge, who have already committed to deploying at least 50 percent of their wealth for the betterment of humanity in their lifetimes. Since signing the original Giving Pledge in 2010, the collective wealth of the original forty signatories has more than doubled, and the combined wealth of the current 200 plus signatories is greater than $1.2 trillion. Deploying just 1 percent of this amount each year for catalytic capital would free up $12 billion for market-creating impact investments, more than three times what is currently being devoted to catalytic capital according to the GIIN. Effectively invested, this money would earn a financial return, enabling a recycling of funds. And with fewer bureaucratic constraints, this capital can be deployed more nimbly, with a focus on higher-risk innovation and underserved populations.

The fundamental challenges facing our global community were clear before the Covid-19 pandemic. The pandemic not only made these issues more evident but also made tackling them more urgent. Impact pioneers have demonstrated the potential of catalytic, market-creating impact investments. Now is the time to build on this progress to overcome obstacles and accelerate the path for catalyzing market innovation and driving profound positive social impact.

FOR FURTHER READING

This chapter is based on my experience in early-stage impact investing and builds on insights from three papers I coauthored while leading the Omidyar Network. "Priming the Pump: The Case for a Sector Based Approach to Impact Investing" (coauthored with Paula Goldman, *Stanford Social Innovation Review*, 2012) describes how impact investors can help spark, nurture, and scale entire new high-impact markets by investing in innovative for-profit companies (market innovators), industry infrastructure, and policy. "Frontier Capital: Early Stage Investing for Financial Returns and Social Impact in Emerging Markets" (coauthored with Paula Goldman and Michael Kubzansky, Omidyar Network, 2015) focuses on the challenges and opportunities of impact investing in emerging markets, outlining which market segments might receive venture capital funding and which are likely to require some form of financial subsidy. "Across the Returns Continuum" (coauthored with Paula Goldman, Michael Kubzansky, and Yasemin Saltuk, *Stanford Social Innovation Review*, 2017) describes how impact investors can invest across a continuum of financial returns in order to maximize social impact. In particular, the article outlines the conditions under which a sophisticated impact investor might consider accepting lower returns or higher risk in exchange for higher potential impact—typically in the creation of a new market.

Notes

1. I am grateful for substantive feedback on this chapter, particularly from Sarah Frandsen.

2. Simon K. Andersson-Manjang and Nika Naghavi, *State of the Industry Report on Mobile Money 2021* (London: GSM Association, 2021).

3. Matt Bannick and Paula Goldman, "Priming the Pump: The Case for a Sector Based Approach to Impact Investing," *Stanford Social Innovation Review,* September 25–October 6, 2012.

4. Matt Bannick, Paula Goldman, Michael Kubzansky, and Yasemin Saltuk, "Across the Returns Continuum," *Stanford Social Innovation Review* 15, no. 1 (Winter 2017).

5. Global Impact Investing Network, https://thegiin.org/impact-investing /need-to-know/#what-is-impact-investing.

6. Dean Hand, Hannah Dietrich, Sophia Sunderji, and Noshin Nova, *2020 Annual Impact Investor Survey* (New York: Global Impact Investing Network, 2020). The 294 respondents represent $404 billion of assets under management (AUM), or about 57% of estimated total impact investing AUM. Of this amount, two-thirds is in commercial investments.

7. For a comprehensive treatment of the question of additionality in impact investing, see Paul Brest and Kelly Born, "When Can Impact Investing Create Real Impact?," *Stanford Social Innovation Review* 11, no. 4 (Fall 2013).

8. Bannick et al., "Across the Returns Continuum."

9. There is no independent third party that determines that an investment qualifies as impact investing.

10. Hand et al., *2020 Annual Impact Survey.*

11. Ibid. This is an estimate. Two-thirds of impact investors reported seeking risk-adjusted returns. This two-thirds, however, would encompass both the commercial, market-validated and the commercial, non-market-validated segments. Given that the commercial, market-validated segment is much larger than the commercial, non-market-validated segment, I estimated that the commercial, market-validated segment represents more than half the total impact investing market.

12. Aswath Damodaran, *Country Risk: Determinants, Measures and Implications— the 2020 Edition* (New York: NYU Stern School of Business, July 14, 2020).

13. Shawn Cole, Martin Melecky, Florian Mölders, and Tristan Reed, *Long-Run Returns to Impact Investing in Emerging Market and Developing Economies* (Washington, DC: World Bank Group, August 2020).

14. GSM Association, *State of the Industry Report on Mobile Money.*

15. Ibid.

16. This builds on the assertion that the total impact of a firm equals the direct impact of the firm plus the sector-level impact of the firm, outlined in Bannick and Goldman, "Priming the Pump."

17. Ibid.

18. PitchBook Data, Inc., *PitchBook-NVCA Venture Monitor* (Seattle: Pitchbook Data Inc., July 13, 2021).

19. Impact Alpha interview with Sean Doherty, "How Disease-Focused Venture Philanthropy Can Accelerate Cures," October 21, 2020.

20. Daniel Galls, "Creating Startups against the Odds in Brazil," BBC News, September 2, 2018, https://www.bbc.com/news/business-45020473.

21. Hand et al., *2020 Annual Impact Survey*.

22. Ibid. For the survey, the GIIN defines catalytic capital as "debt, equity, guarantees, and other investments that accept disproportionate risk and/or concessionary returns relative to a conventional investment in order to generate positive impact and enable third-party investments that otherwise would not be possible."

7

The Decade of Delivery

New Opportunities for Scaling*
Social Innovation

Steve Davis

Nearly every problem has been solved by someone, somewhere. The challenge of the twenty-first century is to find out what works, and scale it up.

—President Bill Clinton

Living in the Asterisk

The PowerPoint presentation is polished. The pitch is perfect. Another great social enterprise is about to launch in order to bring the world a game-changing innovation. Maybe it's a new health product that could save millions of people from avoidable death, a new service that might improve education around the globe, or a novel idea for business financing that will allow marginalized populations to participate in the global economy as never before. It has been proven to work. It clearly matters. The team is fantastic. What could go wrong?

Then, at the lower right-hand corner of the final slide of the business plan sits a small asterisked statement that reads: *then scale up.*[1] As if it were as simple as flipping a light switch: the no-brainer part of the social innovation journey, or someone else's problem to solve.

Ignore that asterisk at your peril. During the past few decades, as technological invention has surged and social enterprises of both the for-profit and nonprofit variety have flourished, most innovators have focused on devising and launching ever-newer ideas, typically leaving to others the messy nuances of bringing their inventions to the world. As a result, we have foundations, think tanks, entrepreneurs, and academics treating the work of scaling as an afterthought. This mindset has left thousands of potentially life-saving innovations to languish in the social innovation pipeline, and it represents an enormous risk for any enterprise aiming to create significant social impact. Successful innovation involves more than brilliant ideas. To truly transform society, an innovation must move from an idea to a solution that can be deployed—at scale.

That deceptively small word, *scale*, is defined differently by different audiences. The most common metric is big numbers—billions of units sold or distributed. Other innovators will define scale as reaching profitability or ensuring a sustainable method for financing. Still others do not consider an innovation to have successfully scaled until it achieves broad public distribution or market share. But achieving scale is not merely about growing the size of an organization; it is also about ensuring that the impact of an advance matches the level of need. For the purposes of this chapter, I adopt the most inclusive definitions of both social innovation[2] and scale.

The art of scaling refers to a vast and complex undertaking that involves developing, adapting, and financing an innovative product or service; securing approvals, whether regulatory, procurement, or other critical gateway decisions; generating demand and building channels

BIOGRAPHY

STEVE DAVIS currently serves as a senior strategic adviser and the interim director of the China Country Office at the Bill & Melinda Gates Foundation. He is also a lecturer at the Stanford Graduate School of Business, a Distinguished Fellow at the World Economic Forum, and a member of the Council on Foreign Relations. He serves as cochair of the World Health Organization's Digital Health Technical Advisory Group and is a member of numerous boards and advisory committees. He is the former president and CEO of PATH, a leading global health innovation organization; former Director of Social Innovation at McKinsey & Company, a global consultancy; former CEO of Corbis, a digital media pioneer; and former attorney at the law firm now known as K&LGates.

EXECUTIVE SUMMARY

After several decades of increased investment in, focus on, and celebration of early-stage social innovation and social entrepreneurship, new forces are pushing for more research, resources, and commitment to scaling that innovation—taking proven ideas through the challenging middle stages of the innovation value chain so they can reach many people who need them the most. This chapter discusses the requirements for social innovators to cross the challenging valleys of death on this path, outlines some of the key factors for successfully scaling social innovation, and frames the opportunity for the social innovation field to pave the way for the "decade of delivery."

for distribution on the ground; and ensuring the product or service reaches the intended users and incorporates the feedback of those in need. Innovators often bemoan this "unsexy middle" of the innovation journey, referring to this gauntlet as the "valleys of death," and crossing them can take years, sometimes decades. It involves a complex set of cross-disciplinary undertakings not easily contained within an asterisk.

Of course, the challenges of scaling innovation are not limited to the social sector; almost every commercial and public enterprise can describe the difficulties of moving great ideas to large markets or populations that need them.[3] And we find many instructive common elements between those innovation journeys and the work of social innovators. While this chapter is not a comparative study between scaling commercial and social innovations, some of the key differences will be highlighted, such as the frequent presence of market failure (and corollary lack of market incentives and strategic capital) in pulling social innovation forward; the limited structural mechanisms (e.g., mergers and exits, financing products, established metrics) that constrain investors and discourage social innovators from relinquishing solutions to more able distribution partners; the varied and dynamic cross-sectoral requirements in complex multistakeholder environments; and the complicated work of demand creation for public goods and services in many hard-to-reach communities, to name a few. These create unique challenges for scaling social innovation; they should not, however, disguise the fact that many of the opportunities or challenges along the innovation journey are similar whether the goal is business profits, social impact, or both.

Nevertheless, today thousands of proven and effective social innovations that could solve many of the world's problems are sitting unused on laboratory shelves or languishing on the drawing board of a social enterprise. Some may be too expensive to mass-produce for the target market, others would need to be adapted for specific populations, and some require behavior change among key stakeholders. But it's jaw-dropping to consider the vast sums of money and years of work that have gone into discovering new products, or devising new services, without devoting equal energy toward ensuring that these innovations see the light of day. As Judith Rodin, former president of the Rockefeller Foundation, puts it, "Solutions to many of the world's most difficult social problems don't need to be invented, they need only to be found, funded, and scaled."[4]

This realization has begun to shape new contours in the field of social innovation, redirecting the attention of a growing number of social innovators, institutions, and investors, who are now committed to focusing more on the asterisk and increasingly building scaling into their business plans. This includes folding implementation science into their programs—a welcome innovation in itself. This added expertise includes a deeper understanding of partnership models and preparation for regulatory and procurement hurdles. It has begotten a keener appreciation for operational research and the critical role of policy makers in spreading innovation, particularly when driving demand for products in places where markets have failed. While the hard work of scaling may lack the crackling energy or seductive elegance of a brilliant idea, a new generation of social activists sees "the asterisk" as their battleground. For them, this is where the real work of positive change gets done.

This chapter explores the challenges and opportunities in taking a social innovation to scale. It offers insight on what "living in the asterisk" means, and it aims to inspire more social activists to focus on this part of the innovation journey. It will discuss why the work of scaling is often overlooked and underresourced, and why that must change. Finally, it posits that scaling large solutions is a growing current in social activism as we move into the "decade of delivery" in pursuit of the United Nations' Sustainable Development Goals.[5] Using case studies and other examples, this chapter provides a framework for thinking about the elements of scaling social innovation and describes lessons learned from the practice to date.

FIGURE 7-1

The process of social innovation

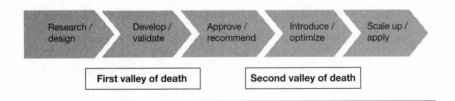

Research / design | Develop / validate | Approve / recommend | Introduce / optimize | Scale up / apply

First valley of death   Second valley of death

The Twin Valleys of Death

As illustrated in figure 7-1, innovation—both social and commercial—is not a moment but a process, one frequently analyzed using the value chain model.[6] Borrowed from the field of for-profit business strategy, this model illustrates the movement of an idea from its inception to its full-scale application. While there are flaws in applying this schematic to social innovation—which is rarely linear, often confronts complexities outside traditional market forces, and is usually context specific—it provides a useful point of reference for grasping the many stages, and potential sinkholes, along the social innovation journey to scale.

The junctures on this route are described with varying nomenclature, depending on the sector from which an innovation was generated, the context for which it is envisioned, or even the consulting firms hired to help shape the process. But, in general, at one end of the chain is the initial research (or "ideation"): developing a new gadget, process, enterprise, or cure to solve a problem. Everyone loves this part. It is creative and exciting. It inspires words such as "breakthrough," "genius," and "founder." Though this first-mile portion of the trek is typically fraught with difficulty, it is also the part that creates Nobel Prize winners and generates MacArthur Genius awards. The last-mile delivery at the other end of the chain—bringing products and services to people who need them—is also immensely gratifying for anyone who wants to see change happen "on the ground." These two points, the moment of discovery inside an inventor's garage and the sound many years later of clean water arriving in a rural household for the first time, are full of undeniable heroics. They are the stuff of splashy news stories and bestselling books.

The distance between the first and last stages is the part we rarely see, the slog through the middle. It is usually erratic, often consumes decades, and looks more like a zigzagging pinball than a smoothly bowled strike. Successful completion of the journey almost always involves complex partnerships, frustrating setbacks, and financial pain. Along the route from blueprint to impact, innumerable crevasses can swallow brilliant ideas whole.

Two points across the middle of the value chain are particularly difficult to cross, hence the twin "valleys of death." The first comes after a product or service has passed the proof-of-concept point and been demonstrated to work, at least at subscale. Then comes the partnership-building phase, when innovators must secure funding, subject their idea to numerous rounds of testing, refinement, and adaptation, and then convince others of its value. This is when more investment is required, pilot projects or prototypes are created, and regulatory requirements are addressed. Not surprisingly, this complex and treacherous first valley of death has been the final resting place for the dreams of many social innovators.

The struggle to scale global use of thermal-sensitive stickers on vaccine vials illustrates the hurdles that even simple ideas must clear. This one was conceived to address the problem of vaccine wastage—tens of thousands of vials discarded every year because health workers had no way of reliably determining whether they had become overheated and nonviable during the journey from a manufacturer's laboratory to the doctor's office. Affixing small heat-sensitive stickers to vaccine vials, a simple technology adapted from the food-safety industry, would allow health workers to immediately determine whether a vial was usable. Yet it took decades for vaccine vial monitors (VVMs) to become an industry standard. Part of the problem was the lack of a clear value proposition. These monitors would add costs to the manufacture and distribution of vaccines without providing any additional financial rewards to companies. Overcoming that challenge required years of negotiation between the World Health Organization (WHO) and vaccine manufacturers. Then there were normative standards and regulatory approvals to be secured. In all, it took more than thirty years to scale the VVM innovation, but today these monitors are standard in most of the world, and more than seven billion units have been distributed.[7] The next-generation VVMs have been essential in the unprecedented distribution of some Covid-19 vaccines that need to be kept very cold to be effective.

Another historic and remarkably familiar social innovation, car seatbelts, traveled a comparable journey. It took nearly a hundred years before the idea conceived and proven effective by English engineer George Cayley in the 1850s was offered as a safety option by the Ford and Saab car companies. In 1956, only 2 percent of Ford buyers chose it, but within thirty years, US laws made seatbelt wearing compulsory. Even in more contemporary automobile examples, the time line to adoption is surprisingly long; life-saving electronic stability control technology (ESC) was first developed in 1989 and took until 2011 and beyond for it to be mandated for all new cars in the United States and elsewhere.[8]

In the case of VVMs, seatbelts, and ESCs, all of which are vital public health advances, broad deployment hinged on buy-in from manufacturers (without significant financial benefits) and strong advocacy from policy makers and consumer groups, and each took extensive work in educating end users and encouraging considerable behavior change to enable their use at scale.

The second "valley of death" is less often discussed but equally challenging: after an innovative product or service has been approved or adopted—sometimes in the form of a first major customer, a regulatory license, or through a major business deal—the innovator must navigate numerous pitfalls in its long-term distribution and uptake. This includes creating demand among users through education, training, and sometimes culture change. This stage can be particularly challenging within the social innovation space, since many innovations with high social impact do not have strong market forces pulling them forward, or the intended users are in communities and markets that have traditionally been difficult to reach. For this reason, demand must be created in new ways, such as ensuring that country health systems are willing to adopt the innovation, school districts incorporate it into their curricula or procurement budgets, or community leaders become champions for the innovation. This second valley of death requires a whole new skill set, one that is outside the bounds of what most original innovators imagine when envisioning the journey to scale.

These hurdles afflict established multinational enterprises as much as they do small social entrepreneurs. In advancing the world's first malaria vaccine, for which there was no significant commercial marketplace but enormous social and scientific impact,[9] pharmaceutical giant Glaxo-SmithKline (GSK) worked with several social sector and government partners to develop a vaccine that was partially effective, fully approved, and endorsed by the stringent European regulatory authority. However, even with demand from governments across Africa and Asia, lack of traditional market forces and uncertainty about how this malaria prevention tool would fit alongside other tools (e.g., bed nets and insecticides) presented both operational and economic headwinds formidable enough that even after the $700 million invested through 2019, this innovation could still stumble and languish in the valley of death.

The problem can best be described as a financial catch-22: to complete critical phase 3 trials for a malaria vaccine and begin producing it at mass scale, the manufacturers needed to pump out tens of thousands of vials. They then invested still more money to train health workers for data collection and built an infrastructure to store and analyze it. Forecasts suggest it will have cost some $1 billion over thirty-five years of research and development before the malaria vaccine is available for widespread use—and that will be in countries where the value proposition for such investments is not immediately clear.

David Kaslow, vice president for essential medicines at one of GSK's critical partners, PATH, has called for more formalized alignment between research funders, producers, regulators, and distributors in developing vaccines that are "socially justified but that have no business case."[10] According to Kaslow, those donors and research groups supporting the "first-mile phase" of vaccine research—laboratory discoveries—must come together to make concrete plans for a handoff to usher it through both valleys of death. Otherwise, despite our formidable scientific and technological abilities, millions of people will continue to needlessly suffer and die.

At the other end of the social innovation spectrum are small social enterprises such as Dimagi, a company founded out of the Harvard-MIT Health Sciences and Technology programs, which developed Comm-Care, one of the first scalable software platforms to allow community health workers to manage patient records and health data in remote corners of rural Africa and India. Despite demand for this innovation, the second valley of death is threatening Dimagi, just as it has pharmaceutical giant GSK. While CommCare had proven its utility and had initial buyers, global procurement standards and increasing competition have slowed the scaling of what was conceived initially as a public good. Though Dimagi had successfully deployed CommCare for use across several states in India, the challenge of securing a second or third major customer posed a major business problem for this social enterprise. Only after Covid-19 created new levels of urgent need for CommCare's track-

and-tracing capabilities across US states did Dimagi see a wave of renewed interest in its product.[11]

To be sure, both valleys of death serve an important function in both
commercial and social innovation. In many commercial environments,
these stages of product or service innovation truly separate the winners
and losers, testing viability, fitting product to market, demand, competitive positioning, and profitability, not to mention the teams' capabilities
to execute and adapt to changing markets and environments. Social innovators should embrace these difficult chasms not as unique to their
social impact missions but rather as important steps to weed out bad ideas
and as positive moments in their product or institutional life cycle to
adapt and improve. However, the chasms are undoubtedly wider for social sector actors. For one, many social innovations are directed at low-
resource communities or humanitarian situations where market forces
don't provide enough capital or incentives to pull the idea forward without significant government or philanthropic subsidies. In addition, many
of the mechanisms that have been created to streamline pathways to
scale—regulatory, commercialization, financial services—are optimized
for commercial players, so they often fail to meet the needs of social impact solutions. New models are being created to adapt to these challenges; for instance, Gavi, the vaccine alliance, was created as a mechanism to aggregate demand, provide advanced market commitments and
other financing, and serve as a conduit for moving commercially developed vaccines to the poorest communities in the world, but these unique
and well-funded mechanisms are few and far between.[12] And, of course,
there are social innovations that inherently do not require scaling: tools
or services focused on small target-user populations or narrowly focused
problems, or where pilot projects suffice as useful learning opportunities for the field without further expansion.

Therefore, to many social innovators, navigating such gauntlets is not
an attractive prospect. So, it is hardly surprising that the billions of dollars and media buzz circling around social innovation recently focused
almost exclusively on the big new idea and less on its implementation.
In fact, the popularity of international competitions, accelerators, and
incubators aimed at spurring social innovation has sharply increased in
the twenty-first century. Many of these gatherings offered significant
prize money to winners, funded by groups such as the Grand Challenges, Nesta Challenges, European Social Innovation Competition,
the Chivas Venture, the Earthshot Prize, The Trinity Challenge, and

Tata Social Enterprise Challenge. The surge in interest and projects is now such that some social entrepreneurs are questioning the ever-increasing fanfare against a backdrop of hazier results.

"Is our landscape of capital and other support for social ventures really enabling the potential of the best social entrepreneurs to ideate, proto-type, launch, and grow new businesses that provide answers to the world's systemic challenges at the scale we need?" wrote Julian Cottee, an as-sociate director at the Skoll Center for Social Entrepreneurship during summer 2020. "Even since the inception of the Skoll Venture Awards in 2012, the number and breadth of organisations (corporates, governments, nonprofits, and academic institutions) building awards that catalyze so-cial ventures has grown exponentially."[13]

No doubt, some of these ideas will change the world—humanity des-perately needs more breakthroughs in medicine, education, clean energy, and other areas—but it is not nearly enough. With few exceptions, unless a program or tool can be replicated and sustained for use at scale by broad populations, it will never be transformational. It is therefore imperative that future social innovators spend more time in "the unsexy middle."

Keys to Successful Scaling

What allows some ideas to scale, whereas others fail? Certainly, part of the answer is money. A 2018 paper from the leaders of the Tides Foun-dation notes that while most philanthropic grants range between US$50,000 and $500,000,[14] it takes a lot more than that to build the in-frastructure, hire teams, develop models, undertake research, navigate a regulatory process, and sustain the multisector partnerships required to bring an idea from inception to fruition on the ground. The struggle to find investors after the proof-of-concept stage in innovation is well studied.[15] In social innovation, traditional philanthropists and social impact investors have followed suit: operational research and imple-mentation science in the social sector has not been a priority, and the grant-making model and mindset of large philanthropic organizations often prioritize shorter-term and less risky opportunities.[16] In many cases, the lack of clear and measurable impact metrics and a quantifiable value proposition can doom a prospective innovation, and frequently the innovative solutions simply remain too expensive for the targeted com-munity or buyers or require costly adaptation or messy behavior change for that access to be meaningful.

But capital is not the whole story. Many well-intentioned ideas stall because of inventors' failure to listen to their intended users and the communities' needs, a lack of government approval, a poor fit between a product and its target market, a dearth of infrastructure to build out the innovation, spotty or nonexistent data demonstrating its value, or partnership management problems. Of course, some ideas are just plain bad, and the valleys of death serve as sorting grounds for products or services that don't solve critical problems appropriately and affordably.

Consider the One Laptop Per Child initiative from the MIT Media Lab, which promised to transform education by distributing low-cost, low-power laptops to children across the developing world. This is the kind of idea that social entrepreneurs love. It was catchy, high profile, and frugal. It involved many companies sharing the load and would evangelize for computer literacy worldwide, which spoke to the economic interests of every firm involved. Yet many of the communities targeted for this program had problems far more pressing than learning to work a trackpad—such as a lack of reliable electricity. The anticipated results never materialized.

More often, social sector innovators fail to devote sufficient focus to creating a market that will drive demand for their product or service. They are even less inclined to hand off a beloved pilot project to some other organization—either another nongovernmental organization (NGO), a private sector group, or government—that might be able to spread the impact more effectively. This problem plagues the social sector, which has a distinctly different orientation than that of private enterprise, where entrepreneurs routinely advance ideas with the expectation that they will eventually sell their invention to an organization with a bigger reach. (It is extremely rare that a new commercial product or service is created and scaled by the same company.) And because founders in the private sector are well compensated for these handoffs, the idea of an "exit" is built into their business models. Not so among most philanthropies and research institutions in the social sector, where many ideas are targeted to the world's poorest and therefore have little or no market value. In other words, there are few incentives, valuation models, or sources of financing available for mergers, acquisitions, or other necessary handoffs.

As the seatbelt example illustrates, the private sector is not merely desirable in scaling innovation, it is often essential. There is simply no efficient means for public and social sectors to develop and distribute all the interventions in health care, education, and climate at the scale required without incorporating expertise, practices, resources, and market incentives from the business world. The notion of involving commercial interests in social innovation often provokes ambivalence, which is understandable. For many in the social sector, it raises important questions regarding conflicts of interest, drivers of economic inequality, and market-driven priorities, but the private sector is already making a difference in the lives of people across the developing world—as GSK's commitment to a malaria vaccine shows—and it can do much more. Businesses that engage with social innovation may need to measure the value of these enterprises with metrics beyond sheer profit, loss, or access to new markets. They likely will be firms that embrace corporate social responsibility goals, improved reputation, and stronger customer communities.

Consider the struggle to bring the antiseptic chlorhexidine for umbilical cord care into widespread use. This workhorse formulation, used in more than sixty products from mouthwash to skin care, has been around since the 1950s and is widely available in drugstores and hospitals across the United States and Europe. Chlorhexidine is easy to apply. It requires minimal training and no equipment. In fact, few interventions have shown such promise for saving lives at such low cost. In low-resource settings, chlorhexidine could prevent hundreds of thousands of infant deaths from sepsis and infection from newly cut umbilical cords. Clinical trials have demonstrated that application of a chlorhexidine gel in the first day of life reduced newborn deaths by 23 percent.[17] Yet, in the developing world, chlorhexidine umbilical care is not widely used.

Initially, scientific evidence proving its utility was slow; the World Health Organization did not add chlorhexidine to its list of Essential Medicines for Children until 2013, decades after its discovery. Then, in-country commercial providers in places such as Nigeria and Nepal agreed to adopt the product for their communities. Even then, chlorhexidine faced resistance—in part because of a lack of training among health-care workers, who preferred to use traditional methods of umbilical care such as cow dung or blessing coins. With a lack of good information, some instead administered chlorhexidine to children's eyes and ears—with adverse outcomes that further discouraged its use. Better product labeling was critically necessary.

In 2012, social innovators representing nineteen governments, social sector organizations, and private firms—including GSK and Johnson &

Johnson—formed the Chlorhexidine Working Group to address these issues and advance the treatment,[18] which in three years led to a more than tenfold increase in use of the product for umbilical cord care. Five years after the working group was formed, twenty-five countries were moving forward with national scale-up programs.

Scaling this important innovation required deployment of every tool in the social innovator's kit: product testing and modification for new markets; education, policy, and advocacy work to get national and local systems to endorse the treatment; market shaping and demand creation; logistics and supply chain adaptation to ensure availability; and, finally, behavior change.

While chlorhexidine gel is finally beginning to scale, it was long side-lined in the second valley of death. The innovation pipeline is loaded with similar wallflowers, yet social innovators have many exemplars in use around the world that point the way forward.

The nutritional product Ultra Rice is one of them, and its journey to scale demonstrates the critical importance of multisector partnerships.[19] Like all successful social innovations, Ultra Rice was developed to address a specific problem, in this case stunting caused by malnutrition. This condition affects two billion people worldwide, and the consequences—including impaired cognitive function—have been well known to health authorities for nearly a century. They are particularly profound for children, with the ramifications affecting educational outcomes, job prospects, and ultimately a community's quality of life. In India, nearly half of all children suffer stunted growth. Researchers estimate that the condition curtails GDP by 12 percent globally.[20]

Thirty-five years ago, a father-and-son team of American inventors hypothesized that it might be possible to address the global problem of malnutrition by grinding broken rice into flour, mixing it with nutrients such as calcium, zinc, folic acid, and iron, and then extruding the fortified powder through a machine to create enriched rice kernels for worldwide distribution. As with VVMs, this seemingly straightforward idea took decades to develop and is only now beginning to see uptake at scale.

First, the developers had to create a product that looked, smelled, and tasted like regular rice when cooked. It took a decade. And that was the easy part.

Marketing the product would require navigating a maze of international regulatory and economic obstacles, so its original inventors handed off their formula to a global health NGO, which took another eleven years to adapt the prototype kernels and ancillary milling processes into something that could be evenly spread throughout a rice sack rather than sinking to the bottom. That advance alone required inventing a special milling machine to blend the enriched and regular rice together. Then the milling process had to be customized for each country where Ultra Rice might be sold, because people in different countries eat different types of rice.

But was the new product a medicine—subject to health regulations—or a type of food? The answer varied, depending on the country in question, with unique rules for each. Thus, to get Ultra Rice approved for delivery at farm stands and schools around the world, its original NGO champions had to forge partnerships with a half dozen health ministries and clear the hurdles for each. Even then, the journey was not complete. Ultra Rice's special milling requirements made it more expensive to produce, a fact that could have dashed its chances in the poorest regions of the world—the very places that needed it most—had not several national governments agreed to subsidize its production.

India, Myanmar, and Brazil each agreed to purchase Ultra Rice for school feeding programs. In India, that commitment manifests in the form of seventy-nine trucks dispatched daily to make deliveries at twenty-eight schools in time for lunch hour. The United Nations World Food Program is bringing Ultra Rice to ninety-eight thousand children in the east Indian state of Odisha. Another 450,000 students across the southwestern state of Karnataka also get Ultra Rice in school.[21] Nearly three thousand miles away in Myanmar, a similar government-powered distribution network is distributing Ultra Rice in orphanages. Public education campaigns urge factory workers in the capital city of Yangon to buy it for their families. In Brazil, government support brought Ultra Rice to 2.5 million customers in two years, most of them middle and low income.[22]

Other than economic, cultural, or regulatory challenges, a sticking point less often noted is the reluctance of public, private, and social sector groups to collaborate, though each brings unique talents and tools to the puzzles of scaling innovation. This hesitation shows up most obviously in attitudes toward the public sector—particularly from business. While the road to scale almost always requires some sort of public policy endorsement—as the Ultra Rice example demonstrates—innovators frequently look askance at government involvement, seeing regulators as little more than traffic cops on the superhighway toward innovation.

This viewpoint, widespread among Silicon Valley social innovators, is simplistic and overlooks the public sector's role as often being the biggest champion, funder, and procurer of many education and health tools. In other words, public sector actions—whether in the form of policy-making, purchasing plans, or a bully pulpit—often determine whether a social innovation flies at scale. As Patrick McCarthy, the former CEO of the Annie E. Casey Foundation, writes, "[I]nevitably, the road to scale goes through the public sector."[23]

Why Is Scaling Social Innovation at the New Frontier?

The challenges of "scaling" are not new. They have bedeviled the social sector for more than a century. Even the straightforward advance of simple handwashing during surgery—proven by 1867 to dramatically lower rates of fatal infection among patients—was ignored until the turn of the twentieth century because it required a change in doctors' routines.[24] But we are at a moment in history—one of simultaneous urgency and technological ability—that portends a new era of commitment to adapting our know-how and bringing more solutions to scale.

Some of this momentum was driven by Covid-19, which made clear how vulnerable we are to all manner of disasters and how quickly our systems can respond when necessary. Within weeks of the WHO's declaration of a global pandemic, the social sector had developed hundreds, perhaps thousands, of new tools to help scientists and policy makers track and analyze medical data as never before. Even progress toward a Covid-19 vaccine—typically a four- or five-year process—has been fast-tracked to reach this goal in less than half that time.[25]

But a focus on scaling had begun to grow well before the pandemic. One reason is investment cycles. During the past twenty years, governments and philanthropic institutions have funneled hundreds of billions of dollars toward advancing global health and development. New players such as the Bill & Melinda Gates Foundation, Bloomberg Philanthropies, Wellcome Trust, and Dangote Foundation, not to mention new mechanisms for government aid, supported the generation of hundreds of new products and services to improve human well-being. To see these extraordinary investments pay off, we now need to move beyond the curse of pilot projects—that plethora of one-off projects that may benefit a discrete population but never get sustainably financed—to target innovations worth pushing across the valleys of death.

The phenomenon of "pilotitis" has in fact become so frustrating to some countries that they are declaring moratoria on anything other than end-to-end solutions that can be seamlessly integrated into existing systems. We see evidence of this trend toward solutions at scale through the relatively recent phenomenon of "Big Bet Philanthropy,"[26] collaborative efforts by consortia of major donors to target problems in education, energy, agriculture, and health and fund solutions from conception to implementation. Examples include such programs as the TED Conference's Audacious Project,[27] the Rockefeller, Gates, and Skoll Foundations' Co-Impact collaborative giving model,[28] Blue Meridian's transformative model for finding and funding scalable solutions,[29] and the MacArthur Foundation's 100&Change competition, which offers a $100 million grant to the group proposing ways of making "real and measurable progress" in solving the critical problems of our time. The digital revolution further accelerates the focus on scaling; most of the big bet ideas are enabled by significant digital and data platforms that make possible the kinds of partnerships and opportunities for nonlinear growth critical to successfully scaling new social innovations and enterprises.

Urgency around bringing solutions to scale also is increasingly palpable. That is partially because of worldwide recognition about the need to do something—quickly—about climate change and growing economic inequity. As the 2030 deadline approaches to meet at least some of the aspirations outlined in the UN Sustainable Development Goals (SDGs)—such as eradicating extreme poverty, protecting the oceans, and ensuring universal access to reproductive health care—multisector stakeholders across the globe have begun to refer to the 2020s as the "Decade of Delivery."[30] It offers amazing opportunities for social innovators of all stripes to live in the asterisk and realize social impact at great scale.

Key Lessons for Scaling Social Innovation

There is no simple algorithm that can ensure a social innovation will scale. Each journey is marked by its own list of opportunities and challenges. The variables are immense and the pathways often unclear, but there are some predictable stages that all social innovations go through and issues each must address.

Focus on the Innovation, Not Only the Enterprise

Social innovations often birth social enterprises and vice versa. Indeed, an innovation can give an enterprise its raison d'etre, but innovators too often conflate the two, which frequently leads to problems in scaling. Whereas commercially motivated startups usually create innovations with plans to hand off their invention to someone else for production and distribution, social sector innovators have traditionally been reluctant to do this, and that resistance almost always undercuts their success. Scaling an innovation often requires that an owner or founder partner or let go of it by licensing their formula to others or finding another organization to handle distribution. Many of our greatest advances have no clear lineage or single owner at all—remember the seatbelt?—but have instead been shaped by many different organizations on the journey to scale, each adding value. This obsession to see the innovative service or product get into the hands of many is critical.

Think Cross-Sector Partnerships

To scale successfully, virtually every social innovation has needed engagement from practitioners in all three sectors: public, private, and social. The future of social innovation as a field lies in developing expertise around forging these multisector alliances across global governments, industries, philanthropies, academic institutions, and nonprofits. Each of these stakeholders offers important capabilities to usher innovation along the road to scale, and underappreciation of that fact is a persistent barrier. Solving the increasingly enormous problems we face as a planet, however—from climate change to health crises and threats to democracy—will increasingly require mutual reliance. To innovate at scale, the art of conceiving, building, and managing cross-sector partnerships will be critical.

Focus on Demand Creation and Behavior Change

Many social impact projects struggle with fitting product to market, making the journey across the second valley of death exceedingly difficult. New models and capabilities for addressing the psychological, cultural, or economic assumptions that might inhibit adoption or procurement are increasingly vital to scaling social innovation. For example, successful innovators work hard to understand what behavior change might be required to incorporate an innovation into a community or individual's regular routine, and they bring in expertise on the science and art of implementing effective behavior change programs when introducing a product or service. More-recent examples have involved deploying new dissemination channels, such as social media,[31] and new techniques, such as "nudging" clients or patients to motivate them differently or retrain them.[32] Given that market incentives alone are often not available to scale social impact, using alternative demand-creating models becomes even more important.

Align Impact Measurements Early and Often

To ensure that such partnerships thrive, it is essential to make sure that the various stakeholders' metrics for impact are aligned. Measuring social impact can be messy and complicated; there is no single model or formula. Too often, the lack of a clear template becomes an excuse to avoid important discussions about outcomes. The good news is that the need for these metrics—including in corporate environmental, sustainability, and governance (ESG) goals—is beginning to generate new measurement tools, and those are likely to facilitate more scaling of social innovation. A priority for social innovators focused on "living in the asterisk" should be to develop more-sophisticated means to analyze social impact.

Look to the Horizon

In thinking about the many elements of scaling innovation, one mantra bears repeating: anticipate what is coming and plan for it early. The value chain model provides a useful road map, enabling innovators to see where they are on the journey and anticipate their next steps, identify potential obstacles, and plan for contingencies. Far too often, regulatory and distribution concerns go ignored until late in the process, or customer research and demand creation do not begin until the product is ready for launch. But successful scaling is like playing chess: it requires that innovators think three or four moves ahead and adapt accordingly. And, like other forms of innovation, it often finds more opportunity and power in nonlinear opportunities: scaling technology platforms, building vertically integrated service models, or optimizing available network effects in shaping distribution. Forecasting these opportunities and hurdles while still in the early stages of the value chain portends greater results. For young innovators and entrepreneurs, there is no advice more important to ensuring a payoff than to look to the horizon and plan.

Find Relentless Champions

Finally, the role of individuals and leaders in scaling social innovations cannot be overlooked. The technology behind VVMs never would have made it into seven billion doses without relentless advocacy from the NGO officials who initially conceived these labels. Ultra Rice would not exist at all were it not for the obsession of two inventors who wanted to ensure that their idea got into the correct global channels. Having supporters who are in it for the long haul and willing to steer a product through each phase of its journey to scale, celebrating its partnerships and helping it across the valleys of death to last-mile success, is the distinguishing feature of social innovations now used by hundreds of millions of people.

Conclusion

Living in the asterisk and committing to bringing the best ideas for humanity to scale will rarely generate glittering publicity for social activists. Nor is it likely to net shiny awards. But contributing behind the scenes to the advent of innovation is among the most important work of social innovators in the twenty-first century. It draws on a broad range of expertise and skill, far beyond the purview of one innovator. At its very core, this work depends on collaboration, a handoff process through which the communities of our world unite to fit the puzzle pieces together and push humanity forward—at scale.

FOR FURTHER READING

Literature on scaling innovation abounds, from the more descriptive and anecdotal (Atul Gawande, "Slow Ideas," *New Yorker*, July 19, 2013; Steve Davis, *Undercurrents: Channeling Outrage to Spark Practical Activism*, Wiley, 2020), to the more analytical (Kriss Deiglmeier and Amanda Greco, "Why Proven Solutions Fail to Scale Up," *Stanford Social Innovation Review*, 2018), to the more prescriptive (Patrick McCarthy,

"The Road to Scale Runs through Public Systems," *Stanford Social Innovation Review*, 2014; USAID, *A Guide To Impact: A Guide to Introduction and Scale of Global Health Innovations*, USAID, 2015). Two of many important books are Paul Bloom and Edward Skloot's *Scaling Social Impact: New Thinking* (Palgrave MacMillan, 2012) and Christian Seelos and Johanna Mair's *Innovation and Scaling for Impact: How Effective Social Enterprises Do It* (Stanford University Press, 2017).

Notes

1. Working on the asterisk is further described in Steve Davis, "The Surprisingly Sexy Middle: Crossing the Valleys of Death to Scale Innovations," chapter 6 in his *Undercurrents: Channeling Outrage to Spark Practical Activism* (Hoboken, NJ: Wiley, 2020). See also Steve Davis, "Social Innovation: A Matter of Scale," *Huffington Post* (January 2012), https://www.huffpost.com/entry/social-innovation_b_1109920.

2. For the purposes of this chapter, social innovations are products or services that are a significant or disruptive change in model or approach; designed for positive social impact, usually touching the most vulnerable or low-resource communities; will have enduring and sustained positive impact; and almost always involve some multisector collaboration (across public, private, and social sector organizations).

3. Countless books and articles describe the opportunities, challenges, lessons, and methods for scaling innovation. Some foundational ideas can be found in Morten T. Hansen and Julian Birkinshaw, "The Innovation Value Chain," *Harvard Business Review*, June 2007; Geoffrey Moore, *Crossing the Chasm* (New York: Harper Collins, 1991); Christian Seelos and Johanna Meir, *Innovation and Scaling for Impact: How Effective Social Enterprises Do It* (Stanford, CA: Stanford University Press, 2017); Jeffrey Bradach, *Scaling What Works* (Boston: Bridgespan Group, June 2010).

4. Muhammad Musa and Judith Rodin, "Scaling Up Social Innovation," *Stanford Social Innovation Review* 14, no. 2 (Spring 2016), https://ssir.org/articles/entry/scaling_up_social_innovation.

5. See "The Decade of Delivery: Can We Still Meet the SDGs for 2030?," *Eco-Age*, March 2020, https://eco-age.com/resources/the-decade-of-delivery-can-we-still-meet-un-sustainable-development-goals-2030.

6. Various models have been used to illustrate innovation value chains, with different stages and taxonomies. See Hansen and Birkinshaw, "The Innovation Value Chain," *Harvard Business Review*, June 2007; Marc de Jong, Nathan Marstan, and Erik Roth, "The Eight Essentials of Innovation," *McKinsey Quarterly*, April 2015, https://www.mckinsey.com/business-functions/strategy-and-corporate-finance/our-insights/the-eight-essentials-of-innovation.

7. See Steve Davis and Debra Shifrin, "Vaccine Vial Monitors: The Little Big Thing," Case SI145, *Stanford GSB Case Studies*, 2016, https://www.gsb.stanford.edu/faculty-research/case-studies/vaccine-vial-monitors-little-big-thing-taking-social-innovation-scale.

8. See Ludgar Myer, *25 Years of Electronic Stability Program* (Gerlingen, Germany: Bosch Publications, 2020), https://www.bosch.com/stories/25-years-electronic-stability-program-esp/.

9. Over 600,000 people die annually from malaria. See Roll Back Malaria Partnership, https://endmalaria.org/.

10. David Kaslow, "Vaccine Candidates for Poor Countries Are Going to Waste," *Nature* 564, no. 7736 (2018): 337–339, https://www.nature.com/articles/d41586-018-07758-3.

11. See Dimagi CommCare Application, https://www.dimagi.com/commcare/; Zach Winn, "A Mobile Tool for Global Change," *MIT News* (March 2020), https://news.mit.edu/2020/dimagi-commcare-health-0309.

12. See Gavi, the vaccine alliance, https://www.gavi.org/.

13. Julian Cottee and Chris Blues, "Rethinking Social Impact Competitions," Skoll Foundation (blog), July 2020, https://skollcentreblog.org/article/rethinking-social-impact-competitions#/. Systematic examination of the winners' impact at scale is less robust. Not since 2009, when McKinsey & Company studied two hundred international innovation contests, has there been a detailed and broadly publicized study. See Kevin Starr, "Dump the Prizes," *Stanford Social Innovation Review*, August 22, 2013, https://ssir.org/articles/entry/dump_the_prizes#.

14. Kriss Deigmeier and Amanda Greco, "Why Proven Solutions Struggle to Scale Up," *Stanford Social Innovation Review*, August 10, 2018, https://ssir.org/articles/entry/why_proven_solutions_struggle_to_scale_up#.

15. Martin Zwilling, "10 Ways for Startups to Survive the Valley of Death," *Forbes*, February 23, 2013, https://www.forbes.com/sites/martinzwilling/2013/02/18/10-ways-for-startups-to-survive-the-valley-of-death/?sh=6b9320b369ef.

16. See elsewhere in this volume, Brest and Honigsberg (chapter 4) and Bannick (chapter 6).

17. See Healthy Newborn Network, "Chlorhexidine for Umbilical Care Cord," https://www.healthynewbornnetwork.org/issue/chlorhexidine-for-umbilical-cord-care/.

18. Patricia Coffey, Steve Hodgins, and Amie Bishop, "Effective Collaboration for Scaling Up Health Technologies: A Case Study of the Chlorhexidine for Umbilical Cord Care Experience," *Global Health: Science and Practice* 6, no. 1 (2018): 178–191, https://www.ncbi.nlm.nih.gov/pmc/articles/PMC5878071/pdf/178.pdf.

19. Kristi Heim, "Ultra Rice: Whatcom County Invention Holds Hope for Health," *Seattle Times*, July 24, 2010, https://www.seattletimes.com/seattle-news/ultra-rice-whatcom-county-invention-holds-hope-for-health/. See also Abbott, "Wonder Grain," https://www.abbott.com/responsibility/social-impact/access-to-healthcare/ultra-rice.html.

20. M. E. McGovern, A. Krishna, V. M. Aguayo, and S. V. Subramanian, "A Review of the Evidence Linking Child Stunting to Economic Outcomes, *International Journal of Epidemiology* 46, no. 4 (2017): 1171–1191, https://www.ncbi.nlm.nih.gov/pmc/articles/PMC5837457/.

21. See Abbott, "Our Science, Kid's Health," https://www.abbott.com/corpnewsroom/sustainability/ultra-rice.html.

22. See PATH, "Assessing Ultra Rice," 2007, https://path.azureedge.net/media/documents/MCHN_ultrarice_fs.pdf.

23. Patrick T. McCarthy, "The Road to Scale Runs through Public Systems," *Stanford Social Innovation Review* 12, no. 2 (Spring 2014), https://ssir.org/articles/entry/the_road_to_scale_runs_through_public_systems.

24. Atul Gawande, "Slow Ideas," *New Yorker*, July 29, 2013, https://www.newyorker.com/magazine/2013/07/29/slow-ideas.

25. For further discussions of social innovation and Covid-19, see in this volume, Davis (chapter 13) and Singer et al. (chapter 14).

26. Bridgespan Group, *Unleashing Philanthropy's Big Bets for Social Change* (Boston: Bridgespan Group, Spring 2019), https://ssir.org/articles/entry/introduction_to_unleashing_philanthropys_big_bets_for_social_change.

27. The Audacious Project, https://audaciousproject.org/.

28. Olivia Leland, "A New Model of Collaborative Philanthropy," *Stanford Social Innovation Review*, November 15, 2017, https://ssir.org/articles/entry/a_new_model_of_collaborative_philanthropy.

29. Nancy Roob and Mark Edwards, "From Promising Model to Major Investment," *Stanford Social Innovation Review* 17, no. 2 (Spring 2019), https://ssir.org/articles/entry/from_promising_model_to_major_investment.

30. Political statement from the UN SDG Summit, May 2019, https://www.un.org/pga/73/wp-content/uploads/sites/53/2019/05/Zero-draft-Political-Declaration-HLPF-17.5.19_.pdf.

31. Lauren Pfeifer, "Digital Green: Training Partners with Videos and Social Media," *ONE* (blog), November 21, 2012, https://www.one.org/international/blog/digital-green-training-farmers-with-videos-and-social-networks/.

32. Yannick Biker, "The 7 Most Creative Examples of Habit-Changing Nudges," *Medium*, August 15, 2019, https://medium.com/swlh/the-7-most-creative-examples-of-habit-changing-nudges-7873ca1fff4a. See also Richard H. Thaler and Cass R. Sunstein, *Nudge: Improving Decisions about Health, Wealth & Happiness* (New Haven, CT: Yale University Press, 2008).

8

The Impact Triangle

Maximizing Efficacy, Financial Sustainability, and Scale

Gloria Lee

It has been a roller coaster of a year for LaShawn. She leads the National Equity Project (NEP), a nonprofit leadership-development organization based in Oakland, California, that helps US K–12 schools eliminate racialized student outcomes. After Covid-19 caused schools nationwide to close in March 2020, she forecasted a 50 percent reduction in training revenue and immediately began planning scenarios that included staff reductions. A few months later, after George Floyd's death and the resulting national call for racial justice, the NEP team saw a deluge of interest in their services and received several unsolicited general operating grants. By June, they were expecting a 50 percent increase in revenue. LaShawn was excited at the potential to expand their impact but, knowing how much time it took for new team members to become skilled at facilitating emotionally charged discussions about race, also worried about how they would continue to maintain the quality of their work.

Across the bay in San Francisco, as she looked across the sea of mortarboards, Beth was so proud of her students. She'd been CEO of KIPP Bay Area long enough that she had known many of the graduates when they started at KIPP schools as fifth graders and was excited to see that so many of them had been accepted into four-year colleges. Compared to a decade ago, when she became CEO, she was more confident that this group of students would also make it through college. It was the first graduating class to benefit from the new "KIPP Through College" program for their entire high school career. She thought that the extra benefit to the KIPPsters was worth the pressure on her of raising an additional $1.5 million in funding annually.

In Sacramento, Heather was outwardly confident but inwardly nervous as she stood at the podium in the state capitol, ready to address the California Commission on Teacher Credentialing (CCTC). The Alder Graduate School of Education, a teacher residency program that she founded and led, needed permission from the CCTC to grant teacher licenses. While Alder had great initial results and lots of interest both from would-be teachers and school districts, a similar organization had been denied a few months earlier. Most of Alder's teacher "residents" were people of color who earned under $30,000 per year, and many had previously worked as teaching assistants or after-school staff. They couldn't afford tuition unless they were able to secure Free Application for Federal Student Aid (FAFSA) loans. Alder had successfully raised grants from foundations to get started, but without the tuition revenue, it wouldn't have the resources to grow and serve more communities across California.

Like LaShawn, Beth, and Heather, every social entrepreneur strives to maximize the impact of their organization, and to do that they need to address three dimensions simultaneously: efficacy, sustainability, and scalability.

BIOGRAPHY

GLORIA LEE is a serial entrepreneur who has founded and led multiple mission-focused K–12 education organizations, including Educate78 (a grant-making and leadership development organization based in Oakland, California), Teaching Channel (professional development video platform), Yu Ming Charter School (California's first Mandarin immersion charter school and now a National Blue Ribbon school), and Aspire Public Schools (national charter management organization). She was also president of NewSchools Venture Fund, overseeing $20 million in annual grant-making and mission-related investing in innovative education ventures. She is a lecturer on education entrepreneurship at the Stanford University Graduate School of Business and Stanford University Graduate School of Education.

EXECUTIVE SUMMARY

The "impact triangle" encompasses the three intertwined elements essential for every social enterprise: efficacy, financial sustainability, and scalability. This chapter describes the components of the impact triangle, provides tools and frameworks to maximize each element, and weighs trade-offs between the three elements. The ideas in this chapter will be useful to prospective and current social entrepreneurs, students with an interest in social enterprise, board members of mission-focused organizations, and donors.

Alone, each of these is challenging to achieve. They can also often be in tension, requiring difficult trade-offs and persistent management of risks—as illustrated by these three examples. Sometimes organizations are wildly successful at one but fail at another. As organizations mature, the challenges in each area change. As each area is addressed, the organization's current and potential positive benefits to society grow.

Definitions

Each social sector organization is designed to address a particular social ill: house the unsheltered, reduce carbon emissions, close the educational opportunity gap, increase legal rights for an oppressed minority, bring beauty to a community, protect an endangered species, or one of many other admirable goals. An organization's *efficacy* is how well it serves its intended beneficiary or changes conditions in its chosen arena. (Most of the "impact dimensions" in the impact compass described by Bernadette Clavier in chapter 5 of this volume are aspects of efficacy.)

To operate, social change organizations need resources—dollars, talent, supplies. *Sustainability* describes an organization's ability to garner the resources it needs to do its work. Financial sustainability is relevant regardless of whether the organization is structured as a for-profit, B corporation, or not-for-profit public benefit corporation. It's important even when an organization relies heavily on volunteer labor. Being sustainable also means the organization has the resources it needs to cover its administrative work and the resource acquisition function itself. (Elsewhere in this volume, chapter 5 by Bernadette Clavier and chapter 3 by

Bill Meehan provide in-depth pictures of two different and important revenue sources fueling social innovation.)

Nearly all social change organizations aspire to grow—to benefit more individuals, more communities, more aspects of the cause. This requires *scalability*: the ability to augment the societal benefit of the organization through expansion, replication, or extension. Steve Davis writes extensively about the opportunities and challenges of scaling in chapter 7 of this volume.

Increasing Efficacy

Organizations that are highly effective tend to have a clear theory of change, an aligned operating model, and the discipline to measure progress and continually improve. We'll discuss each in turn.

A Clear Theory of Change

Entire books have been written about theory of change, and many consultants make a good living helping organizations create or iterate theirs. Some philanthropic foundations consider it a prerequisite for their funding, so much so that funders like the Edna McConnell Clark Foundation help grantees refine their theory of change before they scale up. At its simplest, a theory of change articulates what societal benefit the organization aims to create and how it will occur. Along with a mission or vision statement and stated organizational values, the theory of change helps all stakeholders—staff, volunteers, donors, and directors—understand what they must believe and work toward.

However, the first major challenge is often to establish a shared understanding of what a good theory of change looks like, how comprehensive it needs to be, and what level of detail would be most useful. Given the complexities and challenges of any social change effort, authors of an organization's theory of change must decide whether to favor a more compact document and risk oversimplification or err on the side of comprehensiveness and risk opaqueness.

The simplest formats for a theory of change are linear, sequential if-then infographics that depict the organization's major inputs, processes, and outputs along with the ultimate desired goal: "given these conditions, if we do these things, then this will happen, and then these benefits will be achieved." In a *Stanford Social Innovation Review* article, Moaz Brown makes a strong case that a good theory of change should also articulate the underlying rationale for the goal and process (i.e., why the impact is possible and why the activities are important).[1] Others want a theory of change to include assumptions, context, supporting factors, externalities, and unintended consequences. Alas, the visual elegance desired by graphic designers and the uncomplicated pithiness that works well in a fundraising pitch can lead to oversimplification, leaving open questions and mysterious "black boxes" encompassing unarticulated steps in the change process. But then, in an attempt to capture some of the complexity and nuance of social change, many a theory of change author adds more words and components to the originally simple boxes-and-arrows chart, reducing the font size and margins until they have an impenetrable wall of spaghetti.

Those who wish to create a documented theory of change that is both clear and thorough may consider embracing hyperlinks. Definitions, frameworks, explanations and caveats, and other details can be covered in one or more connected supplemental documents so any audience member can understand the theory of change at the level of detail appropriate to their use.

An Aligned Operating Model

In the literature on social impact organizations, much less has been written about operating models, which describe how the many parts of an organization work in alignment with each other and in the service of the organization's goals. This is often just as important as a well-crafted theory of change. As Jim Collins and Jerry Porras put it succinctly in their bestseller *Built to Last*, "Building a visionary company requires one percent vision and 99 percent alignment."[2]

Many frameworks applied to private sector companies are helpful for describing the inner workings of social sector organizations. For example, McKinsey's 7S Framework, created by Robert H. Waterman and Tom Peters, includes structure, strategy, systems, skills, style, staff, and shared values. Bain's five-part operating model framework includes structure, accountability, governance, ways of working, and capabilities.[3]

Fleshing out an operating model that is aligned internally and with the organization's goals not only helps maximize efficacy; it's also a prerequisite to scaling. A health-care organization may have developed a treatment with a 100 percent cure rate, but it won't achieve its mission without distribution channels, suppliers, partnerships, marketing, trained clinicians, political savvy, and cultural sensitivity to support widespread adoption of the treatment.

The operating model also needs to be aligned with the external context—an approach that is well designed for a particular time or place may not be well suited for other geographies or when conditions change. For example, Fresh Lifelines for Youth, which prevents juvenile incarceration through legal education and mentoring and typically works with high school students, created a new program for youths age eighteen to twenty-one in response to the passage of a new law.

A Robust, Well-Integrated Approach to Measuring Progress

Social impact organizations also need to regularly ascertain that what they are doing is working—not only to garner support from external parties such as donors or governments but also to inform adjustments to the approach and motivate staff. At first, anecdotal and self-administered measures are often sufficient. Some organizations can get by with participant satisfaction surveys, quotations from beneficiaries, and captivating photos. Some can also gather, analyze, and publish efficacy data themselves using widely agreed indicators. For example, a program to employ formerly incarcerated men might track and share recidivism rates, while a prenatal care innovator may celebrate a reduction in infant mortality. Many organizations eventually seek validation from an external third party such as a university researcher or independent evaluator—usually requested by others who may provide new funding or enable growth. In fact, some governmental funding programs require or embed third-party evaluation into their requests for proposals and grants. Eventually, some organizations initiate a randomized controlled trial (RCT), which is widely considered the gold standard of experimental methods. But, to some, even that is not the pinnacle of demonstrating efficacy. In their "standards of evidence" framework, Geoff Mulgan, Ruth Puttick, and Simon Breakspear encourage mission-focused organizations to make sure they understand why the intervention is effective and to evaluate efficacy in different contexts and over time.[4]

Ultimately, efficacy in achieving public benefit is what distinguishes a social sector organization from a private sector corporation, but proof of efficacy doesn't guarantee the opportunity for growth. Studies of charter management organizations by the Center for Research on Education Outcomes (CREDO) at Stanford used matched student samples to determine the size of the effect of attending charter schools. They found significant effect sizes in many cities, with students accelerating by many additional months, yet politically motivated opposition to charter schools has nevertheless stymied the expansion of even schools with the most demonstrated efficacy and parent demand. The world is also littered with ineffective "solutions" that, despite not working, nonetheless become widespread (and lucrative). Units of Study, a set of resources for teaching English language arts to elementary school students, used methodologies that contradicted well-established scientific findings regarding how children learn to read. Yet this program was widely adopted by school districts across the country. The program, created by Lucy Calkins at the Teachers College Reading and Writing Project at Columbia University and published by Heinemann Publishing, captured a 16 percent market share in 2019. The founder of the program, Lucy Calkins, finally recanted assertions of the efficacy of its methodology, but during the thirty years in which it was a dominant approach to teaching young children in many schools, it undoubtedly contributed to the dismal literacy rates and persistent racial reading proficiency gaps across the United States.[5]

Increasing Sustainability

Every organization needs resources to do its work, and social sector organizations are no exception. People—whether volunteers, employees, or contractors—need to be recruited, supported, and retained. The stuff that is essential to the organization's work—whether books, technology, land, medical equipment, or other things—must be procured. Whatever the mission, an organization needs to ensure that the resources that come in are at least as much as the resources expended in doing the work. Just like any business, a social impact organization needs to identify a viable revenue model, manage costs, and ensure sufficient cash flow.

A Viable Revenue Model

Identifying and developing a model that is financially sustainable—one that provides a steady stream of resources that grows commensurately with the organization's expansion—is a major challenge for almost all social sector organizations. Social entrepreneurs have a variety of options for achieving financial sustainability, but each potential source of funds requires different capabilities, organizational characteristics, and risks. Dollars may be earned from customers, secured as charitable donations, or received from the government.

Donations. Many social entrepreneurs automatically look to philanthropic donations for their first—and often only—source of funds. Many individuals see charitable giving as an important part of citizenship, and some impact organizations rely on many smaller donations from individuals. Churches promote tithing (giving 10 percent of one's income), colleges use peer pressure via alumni class gift committees, and others send mail solicitations. The 2014 ALS Ice Bucket Challenge was a social media campaign that went viral, which prompted millions of individual donations and raised an astonishing $115 million to find a cure for amyotrophic lateral sclerosis (ALS), a progressive nervous system disease. Individuals with a personal connection to a charitable cause also give donations in the context of fundraising events such as bake sales, marathons, galas, and auctions. Foundations are organizations specifically designed for charitable giving at a larger scale and are often operated by grant-making professionals. Private foundations are typically established by high-net-worth individuals and families as the vehicle for their charitable giving, many corporations have foundations to advance their corporate citizenship goals and brand, and community foundations help aggregate and distribute capital in specific geographies. Much has been written about the unfortunate reluctance of foundations to adequately resource administrative expenses, and in some circles giving by billionaires is subject to suspicion rather than gratitude (see Meehan, chapter 3, this volume). Unfortunately for many social entrepreneurs, securing sufficient donations to operate is a source of great stress. For instance, BUILD was created to teach entrepreneurship to young people and was so successful that the organization continued to grow by adding locations in new cities. Eventually, it had a national footprint. It relied heavily on donations, causing founder Suzanne McKechnie Klahr to observe, "My job is to raise a quarter of a million dollars every single week."

Earned revenue. Over the past twenty years, more social impact organizations have sought to establish an earned revenue model—a way of securing revenue in the form of product sales, service fees, or contracts. Sometimes those revenue streams are a direct result of activities essential to the organization's core social benefit—they essentially monetize their impact. Customers with a sweet tooth pay Rubicon Bakery for the baked goods produced as part of training workers, the government pays a health clinic for treatments, opera aficionados pay for show tickets, and members pay public radio stations for a steady stream of news. Bangladesh Rural Advancement Committee (BRAC) has reduced poverty and helped people become self-sufficient in Bangladesh by using earned revenue from its microfinance lending and social enterprises. Other organizations sell products or services that are less directly related to their impact-focused activities, although a disconnect between the revenue-generating activities and the impact-producing activities can lead to misalignment and friction within the organization.

An Understanding of Cost Structure

For many scrappy organizations, a dollar saved is as good as a dollar earned. Many social impact organizations operate on a shoestring—particularly those that are small, local, and provide social services. They rely on volunteer labor, underpaid employees, used furniture, and decommissioned equipment to deliver services to a vulnerable population. This approach is usually not sustainable over time and is not scalable, as this practice essentially underestimates the real cost of doing the work.

Any impact-focused organization wishing to manage its budget needs to understand the costs of delivering its social benefit, often at multiple unit levels, especially as the organization grows. For example, a health clinic would need to understand cost per patient as well as costs per healthcare provider. Before adding additional locations in the same city, it would also need to understand cost per site; before expanding to another city, it would need to calculate cost per geography. Calculating unit costs usually requires making assumptions about how staff time is allocated. To ensure a complete understanding, leaders need to make sure that unit cost calculations are "fully loaded." It's not enough to know the cost of the raw materials and labor that go into producing the new low-cost infant warmer; an entrepreneur also needs to calculate the costs of sales, distribution, training, maintenance, fundraising, and administration. Geographically distributed service providers and multiprogram organizations often struggle with how to allocate costs of shared services (such as a finance department), which are often administrative but nevertheless essential to understanding the full price tag for delivering the social benefit.

Strong Cash Flow

Many startup and high-growth organizations, including mission-oriented ones, find that cash flow is more important to corporate survival than profitability on a GAAP (generally accepted accounting principles) basis. Assurances from a foundation program officer that a grant will be approved at the next quarterly board meeting may not be sufficiently soothing for frontline workers who need to pay rent. Securing a huge government contract is a win—until that bureaucratic government agency is ninety days in arrears on its invoices for services already rendered. It's not unusual for founding social entrepreneurs to forgo their own pay when their nascent organizations face cash shortfalls. To manage cash flow, entrepreneurs need to plan ahead. They may borrow to ensure sufficient cash by securing a line of credit before they need it or by tapping governmental loan programs. A mission-focused organization that is structured as a for-profit corporation and has a plan for accelerated high growth within a large market may also be able to secure funding from individual private investors, venture funds, private equity firms, or strategic corporate investors.

Legal Structure

The organization's legal structure—whether for-profit, B corporation, or nonprofit public benefit corporation—somewhat affects the sources of funds that are available to it. However, the lines have become increasingly blurred. Some not-for-profits now earn revenue for their services—sometimes the same services offered by for-profit companies. TalkingPoints and Remind are similar text-messaging tools that facilitate communication between schools and families, and both earn revenue when schools and districts pay for the service, but TalkingPoints is a not-for-profit and Remind is a venture-backed for-profit. Both for-profit and not-for-profit organizations are usually eligible for government funding, in the form of competitive grants or payments for specific services. Health clinics, services for immigrants or veterans, and post-secondary education are all fields within which organizations with different governance structures can receive government funding for similar services. Even in the world of philanthropy, mission-focused for-profit corporations have sometimes received "nondilutive capital" to support their activities. NewSchools Venture Fund, a venture philanthropy focused on education entrepreneurs, created its Ignite program to provide early-stage grants to organizations—both for-profit and not-for-profit—that are developing education technology products that address identified gaps. Large foundations can also use their endowment funds to make mission-aligned investments ("program-related investments"), although arguably they do so far too infrequently. However, some types of capital (e.g., venture funding, strategic partnership investments, and private equity) are only available to companies with equity stakes that could eventually provide a return to investors. As a result, social entrepreneurs organized as for-profit corporations are more able to access larger amounts of capital for hypergrowth than not-for-profit public benefit corporations (as described by Clavier in chapter 5 of this volume). Some entrepreneurs even create multiple connected organizations to maximize their access to different types of capital.

Ultimately, traditional labels may not be sufficiently informative. Some not-for-profit organizations are quite profitable, and plenty of venture-backed for-profit companies operate for years with sizable operating losses. In any case, any organization regardless of incorporation type needs to manage resources wisely over the long term to achieve its mission.

Increasing Scalability

Social sector leaders imagine a better future as a result of their work. That vision usually requires an ever-bigger reach for their organizations. Scaling is often considered a penultimate goal of social impact organizations. Many initiatives have struggled to attain the scale needed to do more than put just a small dent in widespread and complex societal problems. Increasing scalability requires understanding whether an organization is ready for scale, figuring out a suitable approach to scaling, and configuring operations for scale.

Readiness for Scale

An important first step is simply determining whether a social impact organization is ready to scale. Many organizations scale too soon—because of overambition, the urgency of the cause, time-sensitive opportunities, and/or pressure from funders. Bruce Holley and Wendy Woods provide six good questions to ask about an organization's readiness to scale: (1) Have you earned the right to grow? (2) Do you manage your costs effectively and understand what will change with expansion? (3) Are the conditions for success in place? (4) Can you fund the growth? (5) Do you have the right people and leadership in place? (6) Is your organization model scalable?[6] In general, both efficacy and financial sustainability need to be strong before scaling, since scaling will put pressure on both. If the program model isn't refined, adding more staff and more locations is likely to make quality problems worse, not better. If the financial model doesn't work, trying to serve more beneficiaries will usually result in an even deeper fiscal hole.

A Model for Scaling

Many social entrepreneurs assume that adding a new geography is the only way to scale their impact, but that is just one of many approaches for scaling. Jeffrey Bradach and Abe Grindle provide an excellent framework for considering a wider variety of approaches to scale that go far beyond geographic replication, including recruiting others to deliver the solution, unbundling, field building, and policy advocacy.[7]

Kingmakers of Oakland was originally a program within the Oakland Unified School District in which Black men mentored Black male students. When other school districts asked them to replicate the program, it "spun out" to do so. As demand grew, Kingmakers of Oakland eventually created a curriculum so that other districts could deliver the program themselves.

Configuring Operations for Scale

Increasing scale requires purposely configuring the way a social impact organization works to reach more beneficiaries. As illustrated in figure 8-1, an organization's leaders should consider two important questions in conjunction:

1. What drives its social impact? (In other words, is it principally a service, product, or idea?)

2. How much control is needed to produce the desired benefit? (In other words, how much flexibility could there be in how the impact is achieved?)

FIGURE 8-1

Configuring for scale

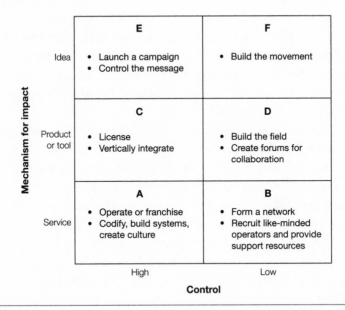

		High	**Low**
		E	**F**
Idea		• Launch a campaign • Control the message	• Build the movement
		C	**D**
Product or tool		• License • Vertically integrate	• Build the field • Create forums for collaboration
		A	**B**
Service		• Operate or franchise • Codify, build systems, create culture	• Form a network • Recruit like-minded operators and provide support resources

Mechanism for impact

Control

Based on these two decisions, entrepreneurs may take different approaches to configuring their activities for scale.

A service organization with a control-oriented approach might scale through a franchise approach or by directly operating all its sites (see cell A in figure 8-1). In order to scale, this type of organization needs to codify what is nonnegotiable in its approach, build strong systems for managing mission-critical activities (especially those related to the people delivering the services), and cultivate a strong culture to facilitate aligned decisions and behaviors. Over a fifteen-year period, the charter management organization Success Academy grew from a single school serving 157 students to forty-seven schools serving 20,000 students and yet maintained its extraordinary academic results. (In 2019, 99 percent of students were proficient in Math and 90 percent were proficient in English Language Arts compared to about 50 percent for all other New York City public school students; although almost all Success Academy students are children living in poverty, academic proficiency rates of its schools are much higher than New York City public schools serving affluent students.) Success Academy accomplished this by tightly managing every aspect of the educational program.

A social entrepreneur operating a service organization who believes that a variety of means could get a similar result may instead choose a network design for scaling, and then focus its resources on building the tools to support other groups delivering similar services (see cell B in figure 8-1). The NACA Inspired Schools Network takes this approach to creating high-performing charter schools serving Native American students. Rather than directly operating dozens of schools, they operate a fellowship program for aspiring school founders, a teacher training program, and a resource hub.

Social impact organizations that create an impact through a product or technology tool are in many ways more inherently scalable than service-oriented ones. Scaling models for this type of organization center on how the product or tool is distributed. More control-oriented organizations seeking scale may revise the product to ease adoption, reduce customizations, streamline the manufacturing process, expand the supply chain, closely manage distribution, and provide user support to ensure correct use of the tool (see cell C in figure 8-1). The Miraclefeet brace to correct the debilitating clubfoot condition in children (described in more detail by Stuart Coulson in chapter 11 of this volume) configured its operations to increase scalability by establishing industry partnerships for manufacturing and distribution.

Products and tools that produce benefit even with modifications and variations can increase scalability by building the field to help others to produce similar tools, facilitating collaboration among providers to increase use, enabling use in multiple languages, increasing user-friendliness, lowering culture-specific barriers, adding uses for application, and accelerating adoption (see cell D in figure 8-1). Social impact investors like Reach Capital facilitate convenings among the education technology entrepreneurs in their portfolio to build momentum for the field, encourage sharing successful practices, and facilitate partnerships.

Organizations that are focused on an idea—changing attitudes or behavior rather than delivering a product or service—may build scale through a variety of communication and advocacy strategies. Some will desire tighter control over messaging, messenger, and form (see cell E in figure 8-1). PATH, an NGO, worked for thirty years to secure global adoption of heat-sensitive stickers on vaccine vials to monitor viability of vaccine doses and reduce waste. (For more details, see Davis's discussion of scaling in chapter 7 of this volume.) In contrast, those comfortable with loosely affiliated groups that reach shared goals by a variety of means scale by building a movement (see cell F in figure 8-1). Black Lives Matter has influenced public perceptions of race relations but is a collection of independent actors with a shared purpose rather than a single organization with a hierarchical structure.

Regardless of scaling model or scalability, organizations seeking to scale need to ensure there is sufficient demand and that their approach is applicable in the new context.

Tensions and Trade-offs

Needless to say, efficacy, sustainability, and scalability are not standalone concepts. In the context of a social impact organization, they are often intertwined. Increasing one may require giving up gains in another. An intervention that is very complex may be highly efficacious, but an organization that wants to serve many others with that intervention may need to simplify the procedure—giving up some efficacy for more scalability. Many scrappy social impact organizations can think of 101 ways to increase their efficacy with more resources, but expensive interventions tend to be both less sustainable and less scalable. Organizations reliant on philanthropic contributions sometimes add new programs or innovations to attract funding from donors who gravitate toward new ideas—temporarily increasing financial sustainability but perhaps at the expense of the efficacy of its core work. Organizations seeking to establish an earned revenue stream to increase sustainability and reduce reliance on philanthropy can also fall victim to "scope creep" or distraction. Growth can sometimes cause a decline in efficacy as management shifts its focus to new markets rather than maintaining quality in the original ones. The sudden shift to remote everything during Covid-induced shutdowns illuminated both sacrifices and unexpected wins in efficacy by using digital technology to scale up place-based in-person programs.

An important part of the art of leading a social sector organization is understanding *how to mitigate risks* inherent in the tensions between efficacy and sustainability, efficacy and scalability, and/or sustainability and scalability, *when to make trade-offs* in service of the larger mission, and *which strategies are mutually reinforcing* across the three parts of the impact triangle.

Mitigating Risks

The difference between successful and less successful organizations is often the ability to mitigate the downside risk of actions that improve one dimension of the impact triangle but strain the other. As a service-focused organization, the National Equity Project's value is provided by highly trained professionals—typically one of the hardest types of organizations to scale. Historically, the NEP team had been extremely deliberate about maintaining the quality of the learning experience, investing heavily to ensure its own staff had sufficient time apprenticing under more experienced facilitators. That initial investment paid off after Covid eliminated the possibility of immersive in-person retreats, as it enabled the team at the National Equity Project to rapidly pivot all its programming to be completely virtual without losing the essential qualities of the participant experience. The experienced team was creative and purposeful in every aspect of the remote-only program design and facilitation, enabling participants to build a sense of community, be vulnerable, and have authentic dialogue even over a video call. This has created a pathway for the organization to expand its virtual programs, which both provides a financially self-sustaining earned revenue stream and reaches many more educators with a compelling learning experience.

Evaluating Trade-offs

Sometimes there is no way to lessen the tension, and leaders must choose to prioritize one dimension of the impact triangle over another. The KIPP Through College program was created after the renowned charter network found, in 2011, that 31 percent of KIPP alumni graduated from college within six years—a much higher rate than the national average for low-income students but a rate that was still very disappointing to KIPP leaders (for information on US college graduation rates, see Rob Urstein's discussion in chapter 12 of this volume). They reworked their college counseling program, created partnerships with colleges that had a track record of providing effective support to first-generation college students, and increased outreach to KIPP alumni. All this came at a cost of $850 per alumnus, which required the organization to raise more donations to supplement government per-pupil funding. However, the investment in this program enhancement paid off: "summer melt" (when students have been admitted to college but subsequently do not attend) decreased from 35 percent to 2 percent, and the graduation rate for KIPP alumni has been steadily climbing ever since.

Creating Mutually Reinforcing Strategies

What every social entrepreneur strives for is an approach in which the activities of the three dimensions of the impact triangle are mutually reinforcing, so an investment that increases one dimension also benefits the others. Creating this "virtuous cycle" was the reason the Alder Graduate School of Education prioritized securing approval to grant teacher credentials from the California Commission on Teacher Credentialing (CCTC). With this important milestone, teacher "residents" were able to secure FAFSA loans to pay tuition to Alder, whereas many teacher residency programs rely heavily on philanthropic subsidies to operate the core teacher training program. Alder GSE graduates could then almost double their income by becoming a fully credentialed teacher. School partners could provide a career pathway for their instructional aides and after-school staff and pay a living stipend to residents during their training period. Alder GSE was then able to focus philanthropic resources toward resident support and statewide expansion. For Alder GSE, securing this approval was the key to increasing efficacy, sustainability, and scalability.

Coda

The world is much better. The world is awful. The world can be much better. All three statements are true.

—Max Roser

In many ways, for many individuals, communities, and ecosystems, our world is better today than it was a few decades ago—in part because of leaders like Heather, Beth, and LaShawn. At the same time, we still have too many suffering through indignities, injustices, and disasters both natural and man-made. With their boundless creativity, social entrepreneurs—through the effective, sustainable, and scalable social impact organizations they create—can make our world so much better.

FOR FURTHER READING

For readers interested in understanding some of the challenges in American public education, TNTP (formerly known as The New Teacher Project) has published a number of excellent white papers, including "Opportunity Myth,"[8] "The Irreplaceables,"[9] and "Greenhouse Schools."[10] Additionally, Bellwether Education Partners, a consulting firm focused on US public education, has written numerous case studies, policy recommendations, and tool kits. McKinsey & Company has a Public & Social Sector practice that has published reports on drivers of student performance and school improvement globally. For any aspiring social entrepreneur, I recommend *The Cathedral Within*,[11] an inspiring book by Bill Shore, the founder of antihunger organization Share Our Strength, about his leadership journey. For leaders interested in applying for-profit business ideas to impact-oriented organizations, see Jim Collins's monograph *Good to Great and the Social Sectors*,[12] a follow-up to his bestseller *Good to Great*. For students weighing career options in the social sector, Harvard Business School professor Rosabeth Moss Kanter wrote a lovely short article called "The Happiest People Pursue the Most Difficult Problems."[13]

Notes

1. Moaz Brown, "Unpacking the Theory of Change," *Stanford Social Innovation Review*, Fall 2020, https://ssir.org/articles/entry/unpacking_the_theory_of_change#.

2. Jim Collins and Jerry Porras, *Built to Last* (New York: Harper Business, 1994).

3. Marcia Blenko, Eric Garton, and Ludovica Mottura, *Winning Operating Models That Convert Strategy to Results* (Boston: Bain & Company, 2014), https://www.bain.com/insights/winning-operating-models-that-convert-strategy-to-results/.

4. Geoff Mulgan, Ruth Puttick, and Simon Breakspear, *From Good Intentions to Real Impact: Rethinking the Role of Evidence in Education Businesses* (London: NESTA, 2014).

5. Sarah Schwartz, "Lucy Calkins Says Balanced Literacy Needs 'Rebalancing,'" *Education Week*, October 19, 2020, https://www.edweek.org/teaching-learning/lucy-calkins-says-balanced-literacy-needs-rebalancing/2020/10.

6. Bruce Holley and Wendy Woods, *Is Your Nonprofit Ready to Grow?* (Boston: BCG, July 2016), https://www.bcg.com/publications/2016/is-your-nonprofit-ready-to-grow.

7. Jeffrey Bradach and Abe Grindle, "Transformative Scale: The Future of Growing What Works," *Stanford Social Innovation Review*, February 19, 2014, https://ssir.org/articles/entry/transformative_scale_the_future_of_growing_what_works.

8. "The Opportunity Myth: What Students Can Show Us about How School Is Letting Them Down—and How to Fix It," white paper, TNTP, 2018, https://tntp.org/assets/documents/TNTP_The-Opportunity-Myth_Web.pdf.

9. "The Irreplaceables: Understanding the Real Retention Crisis in America's Urban Schools," white paper, TNTP, July 30, 2012, https://tntp.org/publications /view/retention-and-school-culture/the-irreplaceables-understanding-the-real -retention-crisis.

10. "Greenhouse Schools: How Schools Can Build Cultures Where Teachers and Students Thrive," white paper, TNTP, March 27, 2012, https://tntp.org /publications/view/retention-and-school-culture/greenhouse-schools-how-schools -can-build-cultures-where-teachers-thrive.

11. Bill Shore, *The Cathedral Within: Transforming Your Life by Giving Something Back* (New York: Random House, 2001).

12. Jim Collins, *Good to Great and the Social Sector* (Boulder, CO: HarperCollins, 2005).

13. Rosabeth Moss Kanter, "The Happiest People Pursue the Most Difficult Problems," hbr.org, April 10, 2013, https://hbr.org/2013/04/to-find-happiness-at -work-tap.html.

PART THREE

LEARNING AND INCUBATING

9

Social Impact Leadership Development

Lessons from Fifteen Years of Developing Educational Programs and Mentoring Aspiring Leaders for Social Impact

Bernadette Clavier

Approximately 36 percent of students join the Stanford Graduate School of Business (GSB) with the express goal of exploring how social innovation fits into their careers. The vast majority of the class has different priorities for their time at school. Despite a critical mass, aspiring social impact leaders find themselves working against the tide of mainstream worldviews just as they would in society. As they contemplate their career options, they are up against herd mentality, a well-known campus phenomenon that compels students to turn their attention to what seems to be the most appealing career aspiration for the majority of their peers. This is a powerful and hard-to-resist call that has sent generations of students into careers in consulting, finance, and technology. The Center for Social Innovation (CSI) gives impact-minded students a home and a sense of cohort, helping them share their voice and make it count in the business school community.

The Center for Social Innovation was created in 2000 to develop insightful leaders for social and environmental change. It was the first center of its type in a business school context and since then has inspired the creation of similar centers and institutes at many business schools around the world. It fosters the development of a cutting-edge social innovation curriculum, offers experiential activities, and facilitates real-world impact through a robust portfolio of fellowships. It has launched many programs that have been replicated by others, such as Board Fellows, an opportunity for business students to familiarize themselves with nonprofit board governance; the Summer Immersion Management Fund, which supports students in acquiring social sector experiences over the summer; and the GSB Impact Fund, an experiential learning program that introduces its participants to impact investing. The center launched the *Stanford Social Innovation Review*, the go-to magazine for impact professionals, which is now part of the Center for Philanthropy and Civic Society (PACS) at Stanford. Over the years, the CSI has worked with thousands of aspiring social innovators. Its participants leave prepared to become corporate executives who transform large industries from within, government leaders who can bridge the public and private worlds, social entrepreneurs who leverage markets and business for the greater good, effective nonprofit executives and board members, and skillful advocates who move social and environmental agendas forward.

Soon after setting foot on campus, students start organizing to create a healthy conversation with their classmates that challenges the way business is done, calls into question the very structures of our economic system, highlights compelling causes to get invested in, and benefits the entire student body. This ongoing community conversation takes the form of coffee chats and small group dinners with peers, speaker events highlighting issues of societal importance, challenging status quo

BIOGRAPHY

BERNADETTE CLAVIER is director of the Center for Social Innovation at Stanford University, which educates insightful leaders for social and environmental change. She has led the design, launch, and growth of a social enterprise incubation program, an impact investing fund, a mentorship program, and a traditional classroom curriculum, as well as certification, internship, and fellowship programs.

EXECUTIVE SUMMARY

Students hoping to leverage business skills for social good—or even to revolutionize capitalism itself—are a strong constituency in business schools today. Responding to their interests and needs is a matter of relevance for all MBA programs. It's also a matter of excellence. Today's CEOs may have considered engaging with social issues as optional while at school, but they are now called to step in and lead. This chapter provides key impact and leadership frameworks for the professional development of aspiring social innovators, shares examples of programs from the Stanford Graduate School of Business's Center for Social Innovation, and describes the transformative role these students play in a business school community.

thinking in the classroom, deep scholarly work, and active learning experiences. Students' engagement in the campus social innovation conversation is foundational in many ways. It provides aspiring social change leaders with the chance to develop their field-building chops in a learning environment; deepens their understanding of social issues; equips them with the skills and frameworks needed to design impact solutions and run purpose-driven organizations; gives them an opportunity to develop a network of lifelong supporters eager to connect them with experts and resources that can propel their work to the next level; and, most importantly, advances the discussion about the purpose of business where it matters most, among the leaders of tomorrow.

A center legitimizes and supports these ongoing conversations, provides continuity to the collective endeavor, and every year helps new student groups build on the shoulders of previous cohorts. Designing a forum in which those conversations can take place productively requires the creation of a shared language. It also requires wrestling with issues of both engagement format and curriculum substance.

In this chapter, we will focus on the importance of defining impact. We will also share the critical set of skills, mindsets, and values we believe enable the success of social impact endeavors and serve as our North Star to develop a relevant learning experience for aspiring social innovators in a business school setting. Although your organization will have its unique set of challenges and opportunities, this chapter will provide a blueprint for designing productive environments for incubating social innovation and impact.

Getting on the Same Page about Language

Students in a business school class express a rainbow of impact philosophies, from the carefully measured and proven impact approach to the less-stringent "do no harm" mantra. With such a wide-ranging understanding of what impact is or should be, communicating without a shared language is challenging, if not impossible, when conversations quickly move into moral judgment territory and arguments are easily dismissed for lack of rigor.

At the Center for Social Innovation, we have defined social innovation as *the process of developing and deploying effective solutions to challenging and often systemic social and environmental issues in support of social progress.* Social innovation is not the prerogative or privilege of any organizational form or legal structure. Solutions often require the active collaboration of constituents across government, business, and the nonprofit world. In this context, impact is the measurable change (either positive or negative) experienced by people and communities that happens as a result of a deliberate activity or service and wouldn't have happened otherwise.

The need to evaluate the impact of an organization or intervention without access to insider information or published impact measurement data comes up often in the context of the social innovation education endeavor, from discussing social innovation cases in the classroom, to selecting program partners for students to learn from, to advising on career options and guiding job searches. In all these situations, only a predictive framework can help assess the impact potential of interventions or organizations that have yet to prove their impact. The CSI's impact compass[1] (detailed in box 9.1) identifies three big "no's" and six dimensions as particularly helpful for gauging the relative impact potential of organizations when data is limited. The impact compass captures the collective wisdom about predictors of impact and turns it into a helpful framework to assess the relative social impacts of various organizations. The framework was leveraged for student advising and put to use in the design of the CSI's programs. In particular, it supported the design of the GSB Impact Fund's impact thesis. Since its creation, the impact compass has been adopted and customized by a variety of philanthropists and impact investors to help center impact as the main criterion for decision-making.

Box 9.1 Impact Compass Framework

Zeroing factors. Some interventions have no impact at all. Others have a negative impact on society. Still others may violate the set of ethical standards pertaining to issues of environmental preservation, natural resource management, working conditions, health safety and security, property rights, labor conditions, governance transparency, and others. In other words, in a Kantian approach, there are some actions and behaviors that are unacceptable to socially conscious individuals. For the purpose of the impact compass, those solutions receive a potential impact score of zero. Organizations that clear this initial screening are analyzed along six impact dimensions.

Impact dimensions. How much impact a program, social venture, investment, or philanthropic opportunity generates for society is a function of its critical importance for society, its intentionality and focus on delivering societal value, whether the solution actually works, its depth and scale, and the social, environmental, and governance performance of the operations involved.

Impact potential score. Using the six dimensions of the impact compass allows us to compare the significance and nuances of the potential for impact of various organizations. We use a three-point scale to calibrate the evaluation on each of the impact dimensions. An impact potential score is obtained by multiplying an organization's scores on the six different three-point scales.

The impact compass model focuses on solutions with no proven failures, adverse effects, or ethical weaknesses and evaluates six impact dimensions. The end product is an impact potential score that helps compare the promise of various solutions to identical problems.

Organizations that clear the three zeroing factors typically maximize their impact when they address a dire societal need, design effective interventions, address the issue in-depth, can deliver at scale, anchor their mission through organizational features that will carry them for the long haul, and operate in a way that adds value to all constituents involved. As described by Gloria Lee in chapter 8 of this volume, some of these impact dimensions are often in tension with each other, particularly efficacy, scale, and the long-term continuity or sustainability of the solution.

The model emphasizes the need for all impact dimensions to be in place to make progress toward impact. It represents the amplifying and interactive power of each of the six dimensions of impact on all others (in contrast to a simple additive sum). It makes no assumption as to whether a dimension might be more powerful than the others at amplifying impact. Further refinement of this model could look into the relative importance of the six impact dimensions for a variety of different issue areas.

Beyond the notion of impact, the social innovation space is rich in contradictory jargon and poor in standards. While shared language is important, it's equally important to resist the temptation to pick winners and simplify. Every word carries a philosophy that requires contextualizing, not standardizing. By keeping the dogma out and bringing the debate in, we expose students to the richness of perspectives and approaches of the world. By creating a microcosm of society in the classroom, we equip these students to deal with the world's ambiguities.

A Critical Set of Skills, Mindsets, and Values for Success in Impact Work

Effectiveness in the social innovation world requires holding and leading with deeply held values, developing skills, and cultivating mindsets that support working in a complex world—characterized by human behavior, structures of power, interconnected systems, and entrenched issues. Social sector leadership demands fueling one's own strength and ability to show up with conviction and courage to sustain a long-term effort that often has no finish line to cross.

I have had the privilege of working with students, mentoring them, and helping them develop into effective agents of change since 2004. Staying in touch with them over the years has afforded unique and well-informed perspectives about their needs, successes, and challenges, and about how to develop future leaders for society.

Our approach at the CSI is not only inspired by excellence in social impact work but also informed by the leadership expertise and philosophy of the Stanford GSB; the study of activism, movement building, social entrepreneurship, impact investing, philanthropy, and public service; and constant attention to the best practices developed by organizations that incubate early-stage social ventures.

Social change leaders are inherently in the service of people. This is not about you, about being a good person, or about clearing one's soul by giving back after benefiting from an unfair or corrupt system. It's about empowering others to access equal opportunities. This work requires a human-centered philosophy based on values of equity, inclusion, and accountability. Social issues require more than temporary fixes. They call for whole new systems that can support lasting solutions, where people have gained the agency to provide for themselves and can generate the resources needed to sustain the solution for the long haul. Finally, in a world of finite resources, human and planetary destinies are deeply interdependent and command a sustainability mindset.

We recognize that professional and personal development are intimately intertwined and that learning is a lifelong journey. Students are better served by understanding the skills and mindsets taught in business school as the work of a lifetime that requires practice and relentless introspection rather than as a tool kit they acquire during their one- or two-year educational program. What follows is what we offer aspiring social innovators as a framework for their lifelong development as leaders dedicated to the betterment of society. We also provide an illustration of how the "secret sauce" of social impact leadership success can be instilled in a business school program, and we hope it can help inform the work of professionals in incubational settings broadly.

Leadership for Social Change

Leadership is the art of inspiring and enabling others in the pursuit of a shared vision. Leading social change requires the ability to make informed and effective decisions where others have not yet forged a path; the understanding of one's unique character; the social intelligence to perceive the perspectives of others and enter into productive relationships across deeply entrenched and sometimes dangerous divides; the sensitivity to the ways social and environmental contexts and dynamics influence thinking and human behavior in sometimes new and unprecedented circumstances; and the effective use of verbal and nonverbal expression with a broad set of stakeholders. High stakes, urgency, and truth to power dynamics stretch social impact leaders' competencies along multiple dimensions to meet the complexity and plurality of the environment in which they operate. It requires the courage to go where others wouldn't dare go and the strength to make and sustain long-term commitments. Stanford GSB social entrepreneurs develop their leadership competencies in the context of the school's acclaimed suite of leadership courses and use their projects as a laboratory to apply their learning and practice rallying support, talent, and resources to their work.

Critical Analysis

Impact leaders gain the rigorous theoretical grounding and analytical tools necessary to make informed and effective decisions. When faced with complex, variable, interdependent, or conflicting sources of information—as is often the case when working on social and environmental issues—a commitment to evidence and to identifying root causes, and the skill to synthesize, organize, and formulate strategic perspectives and action are critical. Effective social change leaders embrace the complexity and messiness of reality and understand the world in terms of systems and trade-offs. They resist the temptation to optimize for one variable over all others, can hold opposing values and goals in tension, and work on reaching an acceptable system equilibrium.

Social entrepreneurs developing in an academic environment gain a critical appreciation for science and the importance of evidence-based knowledge. They learn to read studies and to seek insights that can support their decisions. Over the years, the CSI developed a number of electives that help students get up to speed with the research on critical social and environmental issues such as poverty and inequality, access to education, health-care equity, and climate and environmental protection topics. Students have demonstrated interest in many more issue areas and have been able to partner with faculty members to take a deep dive into related research through independent study projects.

Self-Awareness

Impact leaders understand and begin to embrace their unique character. It is helpful to gain clarity about one's personal motivations, strengths, opportunities for growth, and effect on others. Leaders who understand why they do the work they do and what they need to do to show up as their best selves have an easier time staying authentic, grounded, focused, and nourished to weather setbacks and sustain efforts. They are clear about the limits of their understanding of the issue they are trying to address and proactive about correcting gaps in knowledge. Based on an honest evaluation of their abilities, they seek the help and advice they need and form teams that complement their expertise and style. Social impact leaders observe how they come across to others, including those they seek to serve, those they need to fund their work, and those they lead. They seek, hear, and grow from ongoing feedback so they can lead with confidence, humility, and self-discipline.

Stanford GSB students develop their self-awareness in the required Leadership Labs class during their first year in the MBA program. The GSB culture submits students to constant peer, instructor, and administration feedback and reframes feedback as a gift, an opportunity to grow. Social innovation coaches support students in determining what kind of social innovation career might be a fit for their skill set, social and emotional needs, and career aspirations. An early decision to reject the creation of social enterprises as a metric of success for the CSI is responsible for our ability to truly enable students' self-awareness. Even our coaches specializing in developing social entrepreneurs have no incentives to push the participants in the Social Entrepreneurship Program to become social entrepreneurs. On the contrary, they often challenge students enamored with "heropreneurship" ideas to think deeply about whether social entrepreneurship is for them by exposing them to the harsh realities of the day-to-day life of social entrepreneurs. Seeing ourselves as a school of leadership rather than as solely an incubator of social ventures gives us a unique chance to put aspiring social innovators on a path of introspection and self-awareness.

Interpersonal Acumen

Leaders develop the social intelligence to perceive the perspectives of others around them in order to better interpret viewpoints, thoughts, motivations, intentions, and/or emotions as they relate to them or the situation at hand. This helps them manage, motivate, and mentor others more effectively—whether direct report or volunteer workers—and is critical for developing influence in contexts where they don't have authority within and outside their organization. The ability to navigate relationships proves particularly important for social change leaders reaching across cultures, geographies, or political viewpoints and building bridges across differences. They often need to engage with a broad set of stakeholders, including funders with a variety of profiles and preferences. They marshal resources across sectors, build movements, and design public-private partnerships. They benefit from learning about the languages, motivations, strengths, constraints, and measures of success of various actors across sectors. This awareness helps them understand what they can contribute and when and how to collaborate with other players. For leaders compelled to help solve the problems of others, accurately hearing and valuing the voices of those impacted by the issue they are trying to solve is critical for ensuring the relevance of the solution they design. Empathy requires listening beyond what is being said to uncover all that remains unsaid. It takes humility and willingness to let others be key actors in solving their own problems. It prioritizes an accompaniment over a hero mindset while building stronger, more-resilient relationships.

GSB students develop their interpersonal skills in the highly acclaimed Interpersonal Dynamics elective class. Every experiential activity in the CSI's portfolio provides students with another chance to lead teams and interact with a diverse group of students from all over the world and with professionals of the impact world. For example, the GSB Impact Fund exposes students to impact investing by putting them in charge of running a real fund's operations, empowers them to make investment recommendations for real investable companies, and challenges them to deliver value to the fund's portfolio of companies. Every year, over sixty fund participants embrace various roles, from investment analyst, to deal team leader, to fund CEO, and practice interacting with peers with different skills and backgrounds and with a variety of actors of the social impact field, from entrepreneurs, to impact investors, to fund donors.

Situational Awareness

Leaders are attuned to the ways in which variable contexts and evolving social and environmental dynamics can influence their behavior and that of others. Social change leaders can navigate with fluidity and sensitivity the differentiated cultural contexts of a multitude of stakeholders, including their direct beneficiaries and a rainbow of different sources of capital, each with their own incentives, preferences, and untold engagement rules. They understand how identities, societal hierarchies, cultural norms, and privileges affect a situation. They are aware of the power they impart to them and others. They know how to use their power with care and purpose to create safe spaces for productive conversations, collaborations, and negotiations. Finally, they can decipher the zeitgeist and seize opportunities to meet the moment.

A small-grant program can underscore the importance of being attuned to and meeting the moment and can encourage students to develop service projects addressing immediate societal needs in reaction to current events in the world. In general, experiential service-oriented programs provide powerful teachable moments for students to become aware of the power they hold in a variety of situations and to understand how it might interfere with clear communications. Send students into a rural community of any developing economy with the promise of generating ideas and providing manpower to help, and suddenly these students find themselves on a pedestal in the eyes of the community that welcomes them. They are instantly challenged to develop a true relationship that would allow them to receive actionable feedback on their suggestions from the people who best understand the need. In truth, the poor have wasted their time way too often on the promising ideas of leaders who failed to recognize the effects their position of power has over them. As a result, many useless and sometimes costly charitable solutions sit unused or go straight to the landfill. The risk of transforming communities into guinea pigs for the development of the world's elite is high. You don't want to send students into any community anywhere in the world without an existing relationship with the community, proper infrastructure, thoughtful project scoping, and copious student guidance. It's easy to underestimate the level of preparation and time required to develop the trust required to keep well-intentioned student learning programs from turning into poverty tourism.

Holistic Communications

Leaders learn the most effective verbal and nonverbal methods for managing perceptions, communicating information, and orchestrating events so they can effectively inspire and influence others while achieving their goals. Social change leaders are called to share their personal connection to their cause with authenticity. They create and promote a narrative that can amplify the voices of those they advocate for. They dream of a better story for society and, in sharing that story, transform their vision into hope, movements, and reality. The most influential social change leaders develop into thought leaders with a perspective and a strong public presence. They serve as beacons for others, and their voice becomes an instrument to attract attention and resources to the cause they care about. They practice a vast array of communication forms to engage beneficiaries, clients, donors, potential partners, and the media.

The GSB's annual demo day and signature social innovation fellowship competition provide unique opportunities for aspiring social entrepreneurs to practice conveying their vision with passion and authenticity and sharing their proposed solution under pressure. Both events bring their work to the attention of philanthropists and investors in a position to make commitments to their projects. To prepare for these high-stakes opportunities, students practice sharing their work with countless instructors and advisers throughout the year, participate in the GSB's acclaimed Low Keynote program, which trains them in the art of presentation, and work on their pitch with communication coaches.

Persistence and Resilience

Impact leaders develop habits and mindsets that will keep them engaged for the long haul with the work of solving vexing social and environmental issues despite setbacks and difficult-to-measure progress. Social sector leaders allow themselves to think differently. They are aware of, but not burdened or constrained by, the current reality. They have the courage to break away from the traditional measures of success, institutional or personal, such as prestige and financial success. By redefining success and prioritizing alignment with their values over competing pressures and the judgment of others, they unleash creativity and hope and open themselves to taking risks on unproven paths. To be able to persist through challenges and sustain long-term struggles, confront opposition, be challenged, and possibly face retaliation or legal consequences, they build their strength by investing in self-care, celebrating milestones, and creating an intellectual, emotional, and/or spiritual space for themselves that promotes resilience, sustains their passion, honors their purpose, and helps them thrive. Finally, they surround themselves with a network of champions and supporters to sustain the work.

We found that facilitated peer groups provide the best environment for aspiring social innovators to think about their personal mission, envision their life's work, and explore the first steps in what will likely become a cross-sector career. Away from the distractions of other career options they already decided to ignore, and free of the judgment of those who may look at them as soft, naive, or idealistic, participants validate each other's aspirations and worldviews and emerge with a support system that is hard to reproduce independently. The business of changing the world can be lonely, and a year or two in business school is a privileged time to find one's people.

Entrepreneurial Skills and Mindsets

Social innovators, whether activists, policy makers, funders, intrapreneurs working to transform organizations from within, or entrepreneurs, are in the business of inventing the future. It's not enough to reject the status quo. Social impact leaders have a bias for action, let the work teach them, embrace failure as an opportunity to learn, focus on assets, build on what works, iterate, and navigate with agility from the strategic to the tactical. Designing effective solutions and gathering momentum requires an ability to take a step back and start understanding the world in terms of systems; to master the tools of human-centered design; to develop both an impact and a business model in parallel and manage the tensions between the two; and to develop the management skill set to lead mission-driven organizations. As described in box 9.2, the CSI developed a series of teaching materials for social entrepreneurs that explore these skills areas and can be incorporated into courses, workshops, and experiential learning programs by instructors around the world or taken by independent learners at their own pace. These assets, developed under the leadership of Sarah Soule, are available for free to anyone using them for noncommercial purposes.[2]

Systems Thinking

Impact entrepreneurs move beyond linear thinking and become system thinkers who can identify external factors and influences likely to impact desired outcomes, anticipate patterns, recognize system archetypes, and harness forces outside their immediate control. System thinkers consider the broader landscape and integrate new findings into their impact and business models. They map stakeholders and their influences on the problem. They map the comprehensive ecosystem of existing solutions relevant to the people they want to help, including identifying top organizations trying to create similar interventions, and articulate areas of differentiation and gaps. They can interpret regulations, trends, and

---

Box 9.2　Free Teaching Modules for Social Entrepreneurship Instructors and Social Entrepreneurs

The following are examples of educational and planning tools that can be found at http://sehub.stanford.edu:

Strategy for social change. A guided step-by-step process to understand the problem, build and iterate on a theory of change, and monitor and refine your work to create the impact you seek. This module includes written and video content, as well as a downloadable workbook.

Impact business model canvas (IBMC). The IBMC is a framework for visualizing, evaluating, and refining your business model to achieve both social and financial value. Stanford professor Sarah Soule presents the canvas in short video modules. The canvas and prompting questions push deep thinking about each facet of your model and the flow of value that will create your intended impact.

Social enterprise legal structure. Legal expert Todd Johnson explains structuring options within the US legal system and highlights key trade-offs between the legal forms available to you. Miniature case studies and interviews illustrate these choices and bring to life the dilemmas you may face. The legal structure of your venture and the legal design tools you use will govern key stakeholder relationships and can shape your financing options, market interaction, growth options, liabilities, and governance.

---

social and market forces and can anticipate how they will impact user needs or create new opportunities. This helps them identify key leverage points within complex systems where they should focus their efforts. They collaborate effectively within the nonprofit, for-profit, and government sectors to further amplify impact. They distill and disseminate key insights to inform and motivate the public agenda and exert influence beyond their organization.

Creating the space for students to understand the big picture of how our society works is easier said than done at a business school. The fear of missing out on activities and opportunities results in busy schedules, sleepless nights, and little time for the thoughtful reflection required to develop one's vision as a leader. The drive to start up something, excitement of a new idea, and false sense that speed is essential have blinded more than one entrepreneur and allowed too many bad social solutions to see the light of day.

While a business school doesn't offer a Master of Public Policy (MPP) degree, business students benefit from exposure to the landscape of public institutions and their strengths and weaknesses as they relate to serving society. They gain from developing an understanding of the policy-making process and public finance. Students need to develop a keen awareness of the necessity and challenges of trisector collaborations and proactively identify and develop the skills needed to facilitate public-private and multilateral partnerships.

User-Centered Design

Impact entrepreneurs train themselves in the design thinking methodology and put the people they hope to help at the center of their work. Effective solution creators develop clear problem statements, interact with key stakeholders, innovate, and iterate quickly based on their needs. They generate hypotheses around user needs and run experiments to test their assumptions. They let go of perfection, develop low-cost prototypes resourcefully, and gather authentic and actionable feedback to refine their plans and better meet needs. Finally, they embed ongoing stakeholder input into all their operations, not just at the ideation stage, to enable course correction at any time during the life of a project. They value the time and honor the trust that their survey participants or potential users have invested in them by ensuring the sustainability of their solutions. They set targets and measure progress along the way.

Stanford GSB students have multiple opportunities to practice Stanford d.school's tried-and-true design thinking methodology, including courses such as StartUp Garage or Design for Extreme Affordability (described by Stuart Coulson in chapter 11 of this volume), and a summer immersion program between the first and second years of the MBA program, the Impact Design Immersion Fellowship (IDIF), which provides both educational workshops and financial support to students who developed a thoughtful user experience exploration plan to inform their understanding of a social issue. In all these experiences, students apply user-centric design principles and develop an informed perspective and clear problem definition.

Impact-Focused Business Model

Impact entrepreneurs understand how to develop both an impact and a business model and anticipate how they will support each other and/or be in tension with one another. On the impact side, effective social innovators identify the ultimate outcome that meaningfully solves the problem for the population they are serving and can articulate a clear theory of change to reach it (as detailed by Gloria Lee in chapter 8). They anticipate the consequences of their activities on stakeholders and account for their impact on existing systems. On the business side, they can develop a value proposition for their solution based on the stakeholders' points of view. They can explore how a product fits its market. They know how to calculate the unit economics of a product or service. They can identify payers beyond the users themselves, develop revenue streams, size a market, and create a funding model. They can determine key risks and assumptions associated with their impact model and with a product or service (e.g., liability, technical infeasibility) and develop approaches to address them. Overall, they constantly consider trade-offs between finding a market and delivering social impact. They hold their impact goals as a North Star and measure their progress on both impact and financial dimensions for evaluation, reporting, and strategy development purposes.

When designing an entrepreneurship curriculum, we often come back to the question of whether courses for social entrepreneurs should be separate and supplemental to those designed for mainstream entrepreneurs. Our approach has evolved over time as a result of gradual changes in people's appreciation for issues of societal importance and with the fluctuation of available resources. Bringing all entrepreneurs under one roof helps inspire the entire group of learners to reach for meaningful entrepreneurial goals and for responsible and sustainable products, services, and supply chains. On the flip side, the pressure to fit a product to a market from instructors whose primary expertise lies in the private sector has derailed more than one aspiring social entrepreneur. A traditional entrepreneurship curriculum prompts ventures to pivot to users who can afford the product or to ideas for new products and services that may address a different need for the user rather than to solutions that the target beneficiary or related stakeholders can afford and that solve the problem initially identified. Social ventures trying to address market failures are not well served by guidance on fitting product to market. Devising a fully integrated entrepreneurship course takes more than bringing every type of entrepreneur under one roof. It requires careful curriculum adaptation and the addition of new expertise to the teaching team. To support that process, our teaching modules guide social entrepreneurs through the development of their impact and business models. "Developing a Strategy for Social Change" leads to the creation of their impact model and theory of change. "Impact Business Model Canvas,"[3] adapted from the original business model canvas by Alexander Osterwalder and Yves Pigneur,[4] supports students through the development of an impact business model.

Management Skills

Impact entrepreneurs develop an understanding of core business functions (e.g., finance, accounting, operations) to operate effectively in an organizational context and hone their operational skills to run projects, partnerships, or ventures. Social innovators can harness an extensive management tool kit with extra emphasis on talent management, resource magnetism, and lean management.

- **Talent management.** They define, find, and retain the talent they need to bring to bear on the issues. They set the stage for healthy cofounder or partner relationships, they develop high-performing teams, and they approach new relationships with curiosity and are creative about turning new connections into allies to create a rich ecosystem of expert advisers and supporters around them to guide their work.

- **Resource magnetism.** They get prospective funders excited about playing a part in bringing their vision to life and develop and maintain relationships with them. They design productive governance structures and know how to identify the organizational environment and legal form best suited to protect their mission. They understand the pros and cons of various types of capital to fuel their work at all stages of development and can conduct due diligence on investors with an impact lens.

- **Lean management.** Impact entrepreneurs budget their resources strategically and structure and manage nimble and effective administrative systems (accounting, payroll, databases, etc.). They learn to operate within the current reality while pushing the boundaries and keeping an eye on the long-term vision. Managing change requires the humility to start with what's possible while working to build what is ideal and the ability to navigate back and forth from the mundane to the strategic. Social change leaders can develop long-term strategies to scale reach while retaining impact. They understand how to maximize value to stakeholders and mitigate unintended consequences along the entire value chain.

Developing management skills has forever been the bread and butter of business schools. In large part, a center can rely on traditional business courses for the broad management education of social impact leaders. Overlooked differentiated skills in the area of talent and finance and fiscal management can be addressed through the creation of dedicated workshops and individual advising sessions. For example, a self-paced online module available to all for free supports students in the selection of the right legal structure for their social entrepreneurial projects.[5]

A concluding case study will synthesize several of the concepts in this chapter. Gayatri Datar's mission to help the world started long before her journey as an MBA student. She chose Stanford's Graduate School of Business hoping that the Design for Extreme Affordability course (described by Coulson in chapter 11) could catalyze her ability to effect change on a large scale, but she had no idea how her life would transform over the next two years. At the inception of the course, she and her teammates—two medical students and a mechanical engineering postgrad—were tasked with improving health within the home for low-income Rwandans. They traveled to Africa to learn about the issue, and while leaky roofs appeared to be the chief complaint, Datar noticed mats covering muddy patches on the dirt floors and saw residents wash anything that accidentally touched the ground. Through observing these actions, the team deduced that mud flooring was the real issue. Muddy floors brought in bugs that would bite children and cause diseases, while paved floors reduced childhood diseases by nearly 50 percent and some infections by more than 75 percent. Datar and her team began to understand that mud flooring was not only a health hazard but also a symbol of poverty and distress. To have no affordable way to improve the place where they spent most of their time, their homes, was a constant reminder of their lack of upward mobility. With this in mind, Datar and her team set their sights on improving floor quality to enhance health and reverse the feeling of helplessness. Datar emerged as team leader through the tiresome prototyping phase. Earth Enable was born with the mission to "make living conditions healthier and more dignified for the world's poor."[6] Datar purchased a one-way ticket to Rwanda, where she opened an office and hired a team of locals.

If you visit Rwanda today, you may find Datar visiting clients' houses, her favorite element of the job. She enters each house with a keen awareness of who she is and how the people she is visiting might see her. Her goal is to ensure that the solution works for them. She carefully designed her interactions to create dynamics that foster a transparent exchange of information. She charges a fee for EarthEnable's services, which is significantly cheaper than concrete but still a significant expense for most of her customers. Treating people as clients and not as beneficiaries ensures that she gets honest feedback. Her clients don't feel obligated to demonstrate unconditional gratitude as they do for charities. Whether their feedback revolves around the payment plan, the referral bonus, or the floor itself, Datar understands that any small improvement on her end can improve the lives of the 300 million people still living with dirt floors.

Datar, who didn't see herself as a social entrepreneur when she joined the Stanford GSB, discovered her strengths during her MBA experience and internalized many of the competencies of successful impact leaders. EarthEnable is on track to install floors for a million people by 2025, and with Gayatri Datar as leader, they certainly will. Datar's social entrepreneurship journey, which started at the GSB, is grounded in human-centered principles and exemplifies traits of leadership that will continue to serve her and the millions of people she has served over the years.

FOR FURTHER READING

For readers interested in more details about "the impact compass," a framework for understanding impact, see https://www.gsb.stanford.edu/faculty-research/centers-initiatives/csi/impact-compass and https://www.gsb.stanford.edu/sites/gsb/files/whitepaper-csi-impact-compass.pdf. Jacqueline Novogratz's *Manifesto for a Moral Revolution* beautifully describes the qualities of social impact leaders in the context of their groundbreaking work.

Notes

1. Stanford Graduate School of Business, Center for Social Innovation, *The Impact Compass* (Stanford, CA: Stanford GSB, CSI, 2018), https://www.gsb.stanford.edu/faculty-research/centers-initiatives/csi/impact-compass.

2. Stanford Graduate School of Business, Center for Social Innovation, *Stanford Social Entrepreneurship Hub* (Stanford, CA: Stanford GSB, CSI, 2021), http://sehub .stanford.edu/.

3. Bernadette Clavier, Amanda Greco, Cari Keller, and Sarah Soule, *Impact Business Model Canvas*, 2018, https://stanford.edu/dept/gsb-ds/Inkling/ibmc.html.

4. Alexander Osterwalder and Yves Pigneur, *Business Model Generation: A Handbook for Visionaries, Game Changers, and Challengers* (Hoboken, NJ: Wiley, 2010).

5. Sarah Soule and Todd Johnson, *Social Enterprise Legal Structure*, 2017, https://stanford.edu/dept/gsb-ds/Inkling/socialimpact.htm.

6. EarthEnable mission statement, https://earthenable.org.

10

Social Innovation Practicum

Designing New Interventions and Social Ventures for Outsized Impact

Kim Starkey

If you don't know where you are going, you might wind up someplace else.

—**Yogi Berra**

The journey to create and launch a new social innovation can be long and circuitous, full of unexpected detours and even dead ends. Designing a new intervention that works is hard; ensuring that it will be widely adopted is even harder. The social sector is littered with interventions that haven't turned out to be effective and organizations that haven't been able to disseminate at scale. For those aspiring entrepreneurs who attempt to turn their social innovation into a new nonprofit organization, for example, the odds aren't great. Approximately 30 percent of nonprofits cease to exist within ten years,[1] and those that do survive tend to remain small. Two-thirds of public charities have budgets of less than $500,000,[2] and only 5 percent have budgets of $10 million or more.[3] Those that attempt to turn their social innovation into a new for-profit social venture also face daunting odds. Most venture capitalists assume that only one or two of every ten new for-profit ventures will be successful; adding a social mission often makes things more complex and challenging, not less. As is the case when setting out on any arduous journey, it is essential to have good directions and the right roadmap at the outset to increase the likelihood that you will successfully arrive at your destination.

This chapter provides a clear map as well as expert guidance drawn from the experience of entrepreneurs who have traveled the social innovation road. It is intended for those who are embarking on this exciting journey or considering it, for teachers and mentors who seek to guide them along the way, and for funders who support social entrepreneurs. My aim is to provide essential tools, healthy doses of inspiration, and encouraging examples of leaders who have successfully navigated the path of social innovation. My hope is that readers will vicariously experience the exciting process of designing and launching a new intervention—and gain the information and insights they need to set out on their own journey.

In setting forth this map, I will draw heavily on the curriculum for a class I have taught at the Stanford University Graduate School of Business (GSB), an institution known for fostering entrepreneurship in the private and, increasingly, social sectors. The course, Social Innovation Practicum: Designing Interventions and Social Ventures for Outsized Impact, offers a rigorous, step-by-step process for pursuing social innovation. First expertly developed nearly a decade ago by Bill Meehan (who has a four-decade track record teaching, mentoring, and advising successful social entrepreneurs) and Gina Jorasch (who is now Director of Career Advising at GSB), the practicum is an interactive, learn-by-doing workshop relevant to anyone who aspires to develop a new social innovation. After I began teaching the course, I took the lead in enhancing its already-strong syllabus, including providing examples from the experiences of many of our grantees at King Philanthropies. Over the decade that the practicum has been taught, it has spawned more than fifty social ventures and generated impact across the globe. (You can see examples of many of these social ventures at www.kingphilanthropies.org/course-alumni-ventures.)

BIOGRAPHY

KIM STARKEY is president and CEO of King Philanthropies and lecturer in management at the Stanford Graduate School of Business. She is coauthor, with Bill Meehan, of *Engine of Impact: Essentials of Strategic Leadership in the Nonprofit Sector.*

EXECUTIVE SUMMARY

This chapter provides a front-row seat to the journeys that leading social innovators undertook as they designed trailblazing new interventions and social ventures. It includes essential tools, healthy doses of inspiration, and encouraging examples of intrepid leaders who have successfully navigated the challenging path of social innovation. Readers will vicariously experience the exciting process of designing and launching a new intervention—and gain the information and insights they need to embark on their own social innovation journey or advise others who aspire to begin theirs.

The viewpoint taken here will be that of someone who designs a new intervention—someone who, if the intervention proves compelling and merits advancement, will become the founder of a new social venture (be it nonprofit, for profit, or hybrid) or will find a way to get the intervention adopted by an existing organization. You will gain insight on how to rigorously research and analyze a problem, how to use key tools to conduct your analysis, and how to design, test, and refine a new intervention to address the problem. Along the way, we will explore the elements of a successful intervention in the social sector—elements that can enable you to achieve outsized impact—while also considering pitfalls that you may encounter on your journey.

This is a truly opportune time to be contemplating social innovation. The world has entered a crucial moment, and unmet needs are apparent everywhere one looks. Indeed, in late 2020, the World Bank predicted that global poverty would rise for the first time in two decades, as the consequences of the Covid-19 pandemic pushed an additional 88 million to 115 million people into extreme poverty that year alone—a number expected to rise to 150 million in 2021.[4] The world, unfortunately, has more than enough problems that need solving. At the same time, it provides ample opportunity for those with the right set of interests and skills to design new ventures that will deliver substantial impact.

Step 1: Take Stock

As you start on your journey of social innovation, you must pick a particular problem that *you* want to solve and then identify a feasible, high-impact intervention to address it. To select that problem, you should first take stock of what you bring to both the problem and the proposed solution. Simply focusing on the need, or your own passion for addressing it, is not enough.

Taking stock of what you bring means considering your unique skills, knowledge, experience, and interests, and then brainstorming—including seeking input from others—how you might have real impact on the issue you aim to address. While passion is important in this process, it can also be problematic. As bestselling writer on leadership and well-being at work Tom Rath once tweeted, "the problem with pursuing passion: it presumes the world's need should revolve around your interests."[5] Stanford University researchers, too, have found that the advice to "find your passion"—popular with social sector consultants and commencement speakers alike—can be detrimental because it implies that once a passion is found, pursuing it will be easy.[6] This, of course, is rarely the case, so when challenges invariably arise, many people simply give up.

Instead, I recommend that you start your journey—as all my students start the practicum—by taking an honest inventory of your interests and skills. First, list the one to three unmet needs in the world that most interest and concern you; if possible, also briefly explain what led you to care about each area of need. Then list your top one to five skills or areas of expertise, as well as any areas in which you believe you might excel with further training or experience. This should help you match your interests with your skills so you can assess the impact you might make. Your goal here is to answer these questions: Who am I best positioned to serve? What do I bring to the social sector?

Next, you should ask: Where can I do the most good? The answer to this question requires looking not inward, at your interests and talents, but outward, at the social landscape, to identify the highest-impact opportunities. This process typically entails rigorous analysis of things such as the extent of unmet need, the efficacy of various interventions, the degree to which others are already addressing the need, and the likelihood of success. Throughout this process, you should pause to reflect on whether a new venture is what is needed or whether there is an existing organization where you could contribute your talents and skills. All too often, there is momentum to start a new organization when a more effective approach would involve embedding innovations into, or improving programs in, an existing organization.

Finally, I suggest going to YouTube and watching an extraordinarily inspirational speech that the Reverend Dr. Martin Luther King Jr. gave to a group of Philadelphia middle school students in 1967.[7] The students he addressed were Black, and many of his comments were meant to encourage these young men and women to value themselves in a world that often degraded them, disparaged them, and denied them opportunity. But the broader message of the speech—which is widely known as "What's Your Life's Blueprint?"—applies to all of us.

According to Dr. King, when someone sets out to construct a building, they generally have a blueprint—and as you set out to construct a life, or some portion of it, you need a blueprint, too. This starts with what he called "a deep belief in your own dignity, your own worth and your own somebodiness" and is followed by a determination to achieve excellence. In his words:

> Set out to do a good job and do that job so well that the living, the dead, and the unborn couldn't do it any better.
>
> If it falls to your lot to be a street sweeper, sweep streets like Michelangelo painted pictures. Sweep streets like Beethoven composed music. Sweep streets like Leontyne Price sings before the Metropolitan Opera, and sweep streets like Shakespeare wrote poetry. Sweep streets so well that all the hosts of heaven and earth will have to pause and say, "Here lived a great street sweeper who swept his job well."

According to Dr. King, the blueprint of life must include a commitment to the eternal principles of beauty, love, and justice. "You have a responsibility to seek to make life better for everybody," he said. "And so you must be involved in the struggle for freedom and justice."

I can't think of any better advice for those beginning the journey to create and launch a social innovation.

Step 2: Go Deep

Once you define your interests and determine how your skill set and experience will help you address a particular problem, you must undertake a period of intense research aimed at understanding the problem in all its dimensions. I advise that you guard against the all-too-common mistake of anchoring on a solution before you have put in the time needed to truly understand the problem—a potential pitfall that could lead to dead ends and time-consuming detours that require you to turn back and retrace your steps.

PlayPump International is a cautionary example of a venture that made this mistake. With the goal of bringing drinking water to thousands of African communities, this organization sought to scale a simple innovation that harnessed the energy created by children at play. Each PlayPump consisted of a wheel as on a merry-go-round, attached to an underground water pump and an accessible, elevated water storage tank. As children spun on the merry-go-round, water pumped into the tank, ready for use.

The core technology won the World Bank Development Marketplace Award in 2000, and it subsequently attracted significant funding, publicity that included a PBS *Frontline* feature in 2005,[8] and support from First Lady Laura Bush, the US Agency for International Development (USAID), and rap artist Jay-Z, among others. PlayPump International was established as a nongovernmental organization (NGO) in order to facilitate partnerships with governments, businesses, and nonprofits, and by 2008 it had installed a thousand PlayPumps in five southern African countries. It aimed to expand to additional countries and to install another four thousand PlayPumps by 2010, and its lofty goal was to bring water to more than ten million people in the region.[9]

Unfortunately, the expansion did not go as planned, as revealed in numerous postmortem reviews by stakeholders. Reports commissioned by the Mozambique government[10] and UNICEF[11] highlighted numerous problems: operational difficulties, maintenance challenges, user preferences for existing hand pumps over the new technology, and a failure of the technology to access water in locations where groundwater was scarce. The core challenge, though, was the use of a technology dependent on children spinning a large merry-go-round wheel to access water from the storage tank—an activity that was fun for a few minutes but became onerous when demand for water required pumping for multiple hours a day. It was a situation ripe for child exploitation, and children were sometimes paid or forced to keep "playing" in order to pump enough water to meet demand. By 2010, when the organization finally shut down, hundreds of abandoned or uninstalled PlayPumps littered the African landscape. Though the PlayPump team and the community of funders who supported them were well meaning, smart, and passionate, the initiative failed because the solution was rolled out without a comprehensive understanding of either the problem or the landscape.

In-Depth Research

After identifying a problem, you should invest time in conducting deep, on-the-ground research both on the problem and on options for solving it. At this stage of the process, there is no substitute for going out into the field to see how potential beneficiaries experience the problem in their daily lives.

That was the approach taken by Kola Masha, the founder of social enterprise Babban Gona, which is based in Nigeria, Africa's most populous country. Babban Gona, which means "Great Farm" in Hausa, has a mission to end financial insecurity among smallholder farmers—who are part owners of the enterprise—by enabling them to make more money. It aims to offer youth a path to a viable agricultural livelihood by supporting them through development and training, credit, agricultural inputs, marketing support, and other key services. Masha received a master's degree in mechanical engineering at MIT and an MBA from Harvard University before moving back to Nigeria in 2007. Around this time, Nigeria had twenty million youth entering a labor force that was already oversaturated. This led to skyrocketing youth unemployment, which, in the eyes of many observers, triggered three major insurgencies (including the infamous Boko Haram) that tore through the country.

Masha believed that the best way to address the problem of conflict was to create more jobs in agriculture, a field that requires large numbers of low-skilled workers. He went to work with Onajite Okoloko, an entrepreneur who had established Notore Chemical Industries, and spent six months traveling through the countryside and demonstrating the efficacy of the company's fertilizer to smallholder farmers. (Nigerian smallholder farmers used one-tenth as much fertilizer as their peers in other nations, in part because fertilizer products were often adulterated with sand.) Through this work, he gained a much deeper understanding of the problems that farmers faced, and he learned how to earn their trust. Afterward, he became chief of staff to Nigeria's agricultural minister, helping to develop an agricultural transformation agenda for the country. In 2011, he traveled around the United States and visited agricultural cooperatives on an Eisenhower Fellowship. That experience led him to see that such enterprises can operate at scale only if they have grassroots leadership, professional management, and access to capital.[12]

After accumulating all this knowledge, Masha moved to Saulawa, a farming community in northern Nigeria, and launched Babban Gona. In doing so, he avoided the common pitfall of developing an enterprise in the United States and then trying to transfer it to another country without a deep understanding of the local context, culture, and norms. To better understand the challenges faced by smallholder farmers, he even bought his own small plot of land to cultivate. As Masha demonstrates, success as a social entrepreneur involves a never-ending process of researching the problem one seeks to solve.

Problem Analysis

To design a social venture that will prove effective and sustainable over time, you should analyze your target problem from numerous angles to develop a multidimensional understanding. A number of tools exist to enable a structured approach to analyzing and articulating key aspects of a problem. The impact gaps canvas,[13] created at Oxford University, is a framework that helps map out a problem as well as current solutions in the field. As shown in figure 10-1, answering specific questions about a problem or "challenge" (what is holding the current status quo

FIGURE 10-1

Summary of Daniela Papi-Thornton's impact gaps canvas

Challenge mapping	Impact gaps	Solutions mapping
How do you describe the challenge?	Where are the gaps between the challenge and solutions?	What is happening locally?
What is the impact of the challenge?	Where are the gaps within the solutions?	What is happening globally?
What is the cause of the challenge?	Where are the unaddressed obstacles?	What is working, and what is not?
What are the history and future of the challenge?	What are the key lessons learned?	Where is the focus and the future?

Source: http://tacklingheropreneurship.com/the-impact-gaps-canvas.

FIGURE 10-2

Development impact and you: causes diagram

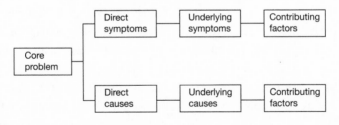

Source: https://diytoolkit.org/tools/causes-diagram/.

in place, what other issues this problem is related to, what the history of the problem is, etc.) and about current solutions (what has already been tried, what has worked and what hasn't, what future efforts are planned, etc.) produces a comprehensive diagnosis. Insight on "impact gaps" emerges in the space between the challenge map and the solutions map.

The causes diagram offers another approach to breaking down a complex issue. As shown in figure 10-2, this tool encourages the deconstruction of all possible causes of a problem—not just the obvious ones—and it differentiates causes from effects or symptoms. This parsing of information helps highlight solutions that can address not only root causes but also address those causes over the long term.

CAMFED is an international nonprofit that has excelled at analyzing a problem as a means of informing specific solutions. The acumen of CAMFED leaders in this area is illustrated in an impact gaps canvas and a causes diagram that are available on the King Philanthropies website.[14] (CAMFED is part of King Philanthropies' highly selective portfolio of grantees.) CAMFED's mission is to multiply educational opportunities for girls and empower young women to become leaders of change. More than four million children in Ghana, Malawi, Tanzania, Zambia, and Zimbabwe have benefited from its innovative approach to educating and empowering girls, and these results stem in part from CAMFED's comprehensive understanding of the problem it aims to solve.

CAMFED leaders recognized early on that girls in the poorest rural communities in sub-Saharan Africa were not receiving a quality education. Poverty, the out-of-pocket costs of attending school (such as uniforms and school supplies), and gender inequality led families to prioritize sending boys to school over girls. The long distance to schools—particularly secondary schools—in remote areas posed further logistical difficulties and safety risks for girls. When girls dropped out of school early, they became more likely to enter early marriage, to have earlier-than-expected pregnancies, and to raise less-healthy children. These outcomes in turn compounded the pressures that keep girls at home. In addition, because mothers in these communities were largely undereducated, there were few parents who actively encouraged school attendance, few female role models in these communities, and few women in positions of influence.

Landscape Analysis

In addition to analyzing your problem using tools such as the impact gaps canvas and the causes diagram, you should undertake landscape analysis. It is important to identify both the landscape of needs that your intervention will address and the interventions that already exist in that space.

Before starting their organization, CAMFED leaders studied the range of educational programs that governments and civil society organizations were already providing in the field. Government schemes were inconsistent, and while they might cover direct school fees, they failed to overcome other barriers to education. Nonprofits filled some gaps—for example, by providing sanitary products, offering scholarships, and even constructing boarding schools—but these interventions had limited reach and were insufficient to address all the constraints facing young girls. CAMFED leaders found that even when educational solutions were available, they were of poor quality, they generally failed to serve girls in the poorest, hardest-to-reach communities, and they provided little or no transition support for girls who had completed their schooling.

CAMFED leaders' deep understanding of the landscape for girls' education in Africa helped them hone a model that targeted gaps they saw within that landscape. Of particular note, they saw that schooling alone would not be enough to improve the lives of girls and young women. They concluded that long-term mentoring and support was also important. This insight spawned the emergence of the CAMFED Association, a powerful network of former CAMFED clients who have gone on to become leaders in their communities. CAMFED Association members include teachers, entrepreneurs, lawyers, doctors, social workers, and local political leaders, and they share an understanding that allows them to speak on behalf of girls and young women who face the same disadvantages that they did. Importantly, many of them live in the same communities where they grew up, and they form a powerful cadre of female mentors and role models for the younger generation. Because CAMFED graduates understand both the challenges facing young women and the benefit of the education and mentoring support that they received, they give back to the program on a truly impressive scale. On average, each CAMFED graduate financially supports more than three girls to attend secondary school, creating a multigenerational multiplier effect that I call "pay-it-forward scaling."[15] This virtuous cycle reflects a principle that CAMFED places at the center of its work: "When you educate one, you educate many."

CAMFED has continued to refine its model and expand its reach over multiple decades, achieving substantial economic and social returns at both the individual and societal levels. Its investment in analyzing the problem has reaped dividends that include improvements in school enrollment, retention, and attainment among girls; increased financial assets among young women graduates; and a delay in the age at which women enter marriage and begin motherhood.

Competitive Analysis

An important variation of landscape analysis is competitive analysis. It is essentially an effort to examine "competing" actors in your field to understand what they do, how they do it, and how your intervention will differ from theirs. One excellent means of assessing the competitive position of your planned intervention is to use Sharon Oster's six-forces model (see figure 10-3),[16] an adaptation of Michael Porter's five-forces model.[17] Porter's model was intended to help businesses assess their competitive position, and Oster adapted it to the dynamics of the nonprofit sector. To Porter's five forces—threat of new entrants, bargaining power of suppliers, threat of substitute products or services, bargaining power of buyers, and rivalry among existing competitors—Oster added a sixth force: funders. She also changed Porter's "rivalry among" to "relations among" to account for the fact that, while businesses compete with each other, nonprofits often collaborate with other organizations to achieve their missions, and she replaced the term "buyers" with "users."

FIGURE 10-3

Oster's six forces

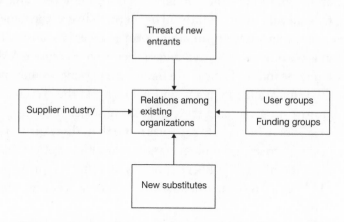

Source: Sharon M. Oster, *Strategic Management for Nonprofit Organizations: Theory and Cases* (Oxford: Oxford University Press, 1995).

In our book *Engine of Impact*,[18] Bill Meehan and I demonstrated how Oster's model works by applying the model to Eastside College Preparatory School, a nonprofit high school in East Palo Alto, California, founded by Chris Bischof and Helen Kim in 1996. Eastside's mission is to open doors for young people who have been historically underrepresented in higher education. When Bischof and Kim founded Eastside Prep, East Palo Alto had no high school of its own, and its students were bused to several schools in other communities. Eastside Prep therefore had essentially no direct competitors in its market. But it did have to compete for funders, who were critical to the school's existence and could give their money to any number of other causes. It also had to compete for suppliers—teachers in its case—who could get jobs at other schools, conceivably with better pay. It had to build its reputation among users—students and their families—so it could grow and sustain its enrollment. It would also need to build assets, such as buildings, dorms, and sports facilities, so it could retain its position in the likely event that other competitors entered the market.

As Eastside Prep demonstrates, even an intervention intended to provide essential services to underserved populations must consider the multiple forces that might impact its ability to build a strong position from which to fulfill its mission. Identifying these forces is a critical part of the research process, and this analysis should inform your evaluation of the market context in which you intend to operate.

Target Population Analysis

It is essential to conduct a needs analysis of your target population. In lay terms, this means working to understand the specific needs of the people who stand to benefit from your proposed intervention. First, you must have a very clear idea of who comprises this population, and then you must dig deeply into the unmet needs that you hope to address. Since these needs are likely to change continually—especially if your intervention proves to have an impact—this process must be ongoing.

Proximity Designs, a social enterprise that focuses on Myanmar's thirty-five million farmers, offers an inspiring example of how to approach this process. Proximity, which was launched by Debbie Aung Din and Jim Taylor in 2004 and has been a grantee of King Philanthropies for many years, designs and delivers affordable tools and services that will help small family farms become profitable. Proximity has served more than one million customers and adds 100,000 new ones annually; farm families that work with the enterprise see an increase in average annual net income of $300, a significant amount in rural Myanmar.[19] To better understand its customers as well as the broader ecosystem of rice cultivation and distribution in Myanmar, the organization interviews thousands of farmers each year, with Aung Din and Taylor personally speaking to hundreds of customers annually.

In 2015, for example, Proximity decided to explore the attitudes, perceptions, and practices regarding paddy farming in Myanmar. There are three million paddy growers in Myanmar, and by building a base of deep knowledge of the country's paddy-to-rice ecosystem, Proximity aimed to improve its ability to develop products and services that would benefit those farmers. A team of twelve researchers worked over a six-week period to conduct on-the-ground interviews with 120 people using qualitative, empathic research techniques. Interviewees included rice farmers, day laborers, service providers, brokers, traders, millers, and consumers. In-depth contextual interviews lasted from one to two hours; ad hoc interviews with people the researchers met along the way lasted from five to fifty minutes. In addition to talking with participants in the paddy ecosystem, researchers visited shops and warehouses, applied fertilizer, learned how to test the moisture and yield of a paddy, sampled a variety of rice products, and even brewed moonshine! "Research is not just for researchers," Proximity wrote in *From Paddy to Plate*, its report on findings from the project. "Talking with and listening to the people for whom you are designing provides the foundational understanding on which great products can be built."[20]

As Proximity demonstrates, an aspiring social enterprise must conduct very many interviews before launching an intervention. Before starting the interview process, you should undertake ample preparation; Proximity, for example, took six months to prepare for its interviews with members of the paddy farming ecosystem. It also undertook considerable exploratory research with experts in the field in order to refine the protocol it would use for interviews.

Needs analysis must be an ongoing process. Proximity originally focused its research on rice paddy farmers—in part because rice is by far the most popular crop in Myanmar. But as farmers saw their businesses become more mature, they started asking about sesame (a very high-margin cash crop) and about repurposing Proximity technology to address that opportunity. Yet, before deciding to go into the market (by customizing its tools and services or by creating new ones), Proximity undertook deep-dive research on sesame farming, demonstrating the importance of continually listening, learning, and evolving.[21]

In conducting research on your target population, be sure to follow interviewing best practices. Go into every interview with your questions identified and ranked in importance. Then, before ending each interview, make certain that you have covered your top three questions. (Of course, you should also be open to conversation that diverges from your question list, and it's fine to engage in genuine topical conversation that may open up new paths of inquiry.) Frame your questions smartly by leaving them open ended, and always avoid leading questions (meaning those that include or imply a desired response). Take good notes and, when the interview is over, codify and synthesize what you learned.

Proximity divided its postinterview process into in-field synthesis, which consisted of informal debriefings with field teams after each research session; daily debriefings to discuss findings, possible process improvements, and goals for the next day; and on-site meetings to create a high-level, synthesized summary of findings for each location. It also employed a data manager to catalog and back up interview content and other data. Of course, not all social ventures will have a research team of this size, but the basic approach is still worthy of emulation.

Systems Change Analysis

Another form of analysis that has steadily gained currency in recent years involves assessing how a problem or proposed solution fits into an over- all system. Should you seek to start a social venture, funders are likely to ask how your idea applies a "systems change" lens. Answering that question may not be easy, especially because there are so many different definitions of the term "systems change." Some use it to underscore the idea of attacking the root causes of a problem and not just its symptoms. Others mean an approach that identifies aspects of the problem that interact with each other. By mapping the parts that form a whole— including all the stakeholders, interdependencies, and mechanisms that make a system operate in a particular way, these social sector leaders aim to create an intervention that will produce lasting change. To be sure, it is important to map and understand a system at the outset. But many social entrepreneurs start by focusing on direct service delivery and then move toward systems change later—after they have achieved success with service delivery and have developed on-the-ground experience to inform their worldview.

Evan Marwell is one social entrepreneur who chose to target the system he aimed to change rather than focus only on a narrow oppor- tunity or technical challenge.[22] His goal was a big one—to bring broad- band internet access to every public school classroom in the United States—and he realized that to succeed he would have to change the entire system that constrained internet access. He understood that he needed to engage governors and state governments, early and often, and he did it. Indeed, at the outset, he developed an "influencer map" that helped him identify all parties that he would need to engage both in the private sector and in government, and at both federal and local levels. By 2020, Marwell's organization, Education Super Highway, had helped more than forty million students gain access to high-speed internet.

"Every societal problem is embedded in a system," Sally Osberg, the first president and CEO of the Skoll Foundation, told students when she appeared as a guest in my practicum class, adding, "Any system is infi- nitely complex and connected to other systems. Part of the challenge is to scope your problem and define the equilibrium [or] status quo that has led to the injustice that you are studying." In *Getting beyond Better*, the seminal book that Osberg wrote with Roger Martin, she and Martin emphasize the importance of understanding the equilibrium in a system in a really deep way before attempting to change it. "The most successful change agents must truly understand how and why an equilibrium works, while remaining steadfast in their mission to shift it," Martin and Osberg write.[23] This means charting the actors, their roles, and the interactions between actors that reinforce the equilibrium.

Step 3: Design Your Intervention

You might think that it took a long time to reach the fun and exciting phase of designing a new intervention. The process of going deep in understanding a problem can feel like a very long road trip indeed. Yet, in the case of social innovation, it is the best way to travel; the time you invest upfront in understanding the problem will get you closer to your goal of developing an intervention that actually works.

Ideation

One way to generate ideas for potential solutions is by employing tools from design thinking (see also Stuart Coulson's chapter 11 in this volume). Consider, for example, creating an "affinity diagram"—a tool that gathers large amounts of language data (ideas, opinions, issues) and organizes it analytically into groups based on their natural relationships.[24] You could also create a "beneficiary journey map"—a simple framework that helps you think through key moments for your customer or beneficiary as they experience your solution.[25] A well-fleshed-out journey map will reveal needs, gaps, and pain points, helping you identify and improve key features of the product, experience, or service you're designing.

As you develop ideas for your intervention, ask yourself how you would evaluate the success of each one. At this stage, you will still have a number of ideas, and you will begin to narrow them down to those that seem most promising—a process called convergence. But even as you go through that process, do not let yourself get fixated on just one idea; indeed, to do so is another potential pitfall. Instead, continue to explore a wide range of ideas and look beyond the obvious. Many ideas will not pan out, and that's absolutely fine. It's also important to note that ideation—like research—continues even after a social innovation is up and running, because there are always ways to make an intervention better.

One organization that excels at generating and honing new approaches to social innovation is Pratham, a nonprofit founded in Mumbai in 1995.

It provides educational solutions for children throughout India. Propelled by its mission, "Every Child in School and Learning Well," it has grown into one of the country's largest NGOs. It develops programs on the basis of innovation and rigorous evaluation, often working in tandem with the Abdul Latif Jameel Poverty Action Lab (J-PAL) to design and execute randomized controlled trials (RCTs) and to build a body of evidence for the impact of Pratham's work.

Through Read India, its flagship program, Pratham offers short, intensive periods of remedial education in reading and math to children in grades three through five who are behind in basic skills. Underlying the program is a Pratham-developed pedagogical approach called Teaching at the Right Level (TaRL), in which children are grouped by ability rather than age or grade. Its proven results, as measured by J-PAL, show that it "consistently improves learning outcomes when implemented well and has led to some of the largest learning gains among rigorously evaluated education programs."[26]

Even as Pratham took pride in these results, it also continued to experiment. A key area of innovation focused on expanding its work to include mothers and young children in settings within and outside formal school environments. In the hope that intervening with children at a younger age would reduce the need for remedial intervention in primary school, Pratham created Early Years, a program that aims to improve learning among children in preschools and in grades one and two. Significantly, this program—if it proved to be effective—would disrupt Pratham's own Read India model.

I had worked with the talented leaders of Pratham and J-PAL over many years, and in 2018, my colleague Cindy Chen and I approached Pratham to discuss its early childhood education program and opportunities to scale that work. Considerably more evidence was needed to determine the efficacy of Early Years, but with testing and time, it was possible that this new model could scale across India and beyond and thereby impact millions of children worldwide. To implement the Early Years approach, Pratham proposed a program called Hamara Gaon ("Our Village"), a model that would target learning interventions for young children while strengthening community ownership. By working in each village over a period of three years, the main objective of Hamara Gaon was to ensure that preschool and early primary school children would secure foundational learning skills that would be sustained over time, leveraging the power of community involvement, especially with mothers. A robust set of measurement tools, including "village report cards" and periodic assessments of both preschool and elementary school children, would be in place to monitor results and assess a comprehensive set of research questions.

Pratham also worked closely with J-PAL to plan for an RCT that would evaluate the impact of Early Years on basic reading and math skills. If results prove to be positive, Pratham aims to partner with state governments to scale the program through deployment in public schools. King Philanthropies initiated and made a grant to implement Hamara Gaon in eight hundred villages across the states of Gujarat, Odisha, and Rajasthan, and work on the ground began in December 2018. Early results are promising.

Theory-of-Change Development

Once you have explored a range of ideas for addressing your problem and narrowed them down to the best ones, it is time to design one or more compelling interventions based on evidence of what works and what kind of impact will be achieved. This will require that you have a theory of change that explains how the desired impact will come about. (At this stage, you might want to design multiple intervention hypotheses—each with its own theory of change—to prevent you from locking down a solution too early.)

A theory of change is a logical description of *how* the particular strategies you intend to use will solve the problem you aim to address. The Center for Social Innovation at the Stanford GSB has a helpful online guide to developing a theory of change (authored by Paul Brest, Laura Hattendorf, and Bernadette Clavier[27]), and in this volume Gloria Lee's chapter 8 addresses this topic as well. The process of articulating a theory of change is not just for startups; on the contrary, every established social sector organization needs a theory of change to explain how its strategies will help achieve its mission. A theory of change should ideally be based on a detailed, comprehensive, and rigorous explanation of the empirical evidence that makes you believe your intervention will work. It should be tested rather than intuited. As Paul Brest and Hal Harvey note in their book *Money Well Spent: A Strategic Plan for Smart Philanthropy*, "A theory of change is only as good as its empirical validity. An intuitively plausible theory of change is better than none at all—but the not-for-profit sector is littered with programs based on theories of change that seemed intuitively plausible but were not valid. Therefore, the more tested the theory of change, the sounder its use as the basis for strategy."[28]

As you design your potential interventions and craft the theories of change that underlie them, it is important to consider the value proposition that your intervention offers to its target customers. Eastside Prep, for example, offers its students multifaceted support to ensure that they will have a very high probability of being admitted to a four-year college. Today, twenty-five years after the school's founding, more than 99 percent of its graduates have been accepted to four-year colleges or universities and, importantly, 80 percent have earned a bachelor's degree or are on track to do so. Even more remarkably, 99 percent of Eastside Prep students are in the first generation of their family to attend college. By comparison, nationwide in the United States, 11 percent of first-generation low-income students have earned a bachelor's degree.

According to the Social Security Administration, American men with bachelor's degrees earn approximately $900,000 more in median lifetime earnings than their counterparts who have only a high school diploma; among American women, the difference in median lifetime earnings comes to $630,000. So, the value proposition of Eastside Prep is strong.[29] Eastside Prep also supports its alumni (including those in college and those who have graduated from college) by connecting them to each other. One criticism of other programs that promote college attendance is that their participants get into college but then drop out and are left with significant debt. Eastside Prep works to ensure that its students obtain a college degree.

Evaluation. As you contemplate interventions and the theories of change that undergird them, you should also consider how you might evaluate or measure the effectiveness of each intervention in the short, medium, and long term. Building a culture of evaluation and measurement from the outset is essential to creating a successful and enduring intervention. After all, if you don't measure the impact of your intervention, how can you know whether it works? Skipping this step, while not uncommon, is a major pitfall. *Engine of Impact* contains a chapter ("Count What Counts") that provides guidance for evaluating the impact of your intervention.[30]

Randomized evaluations, pioneered in the social sector by J-PAL and Innovations for Poverty Action, are considered the gold standard of impact evaluation, but such efforts are extremely costly and often are not feasible in the early stages of an intervention. One alternative used by many in the early stages is the "lean data" method developed by Acumen.[31]

Choice of Organizational Structure

Once you have designed a compelling intervention, you can follow any of several possible pathways to impact, as shown in figure 10-4.

You will need to decide whether your innovation can be adopted by an existing organization or whether a new social venture must be established. There are significant advantages to leveraging the distribution footprint and economies of scale of an existing organization. However, as Kevin Starr, managing director of the Mulago Foundation, underscored in a *Stanford Social Innovation Review* article coauthored with Sarah Miers, most large NGOs are reluctant to adopt the new innovations of social entrepreneurs.[32]

For those who decide to disseminate their innovation by launching a new social venture, a new journey is just beginning. *Engine of Impact* provides actionable guidance for the many decisions that you will have to make in building your organization, particularly with respect to elements such as mission, strategy, impact evaluation, funding, managing talent,

FIGURE 10-4

Social innovation: pathways to impact

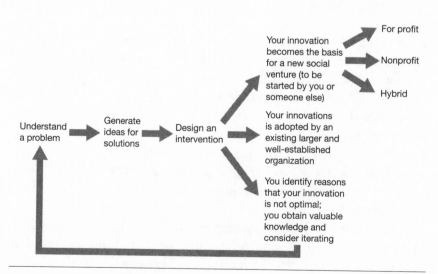

and board governance. In chapter 2 of this volume, I provide advice for leaders wielding these elements to build their organizations. In chapter 7 of this volume, Steve Davis provides astute and relevant insights as well.

If you decide to create a new social venture, one of the most important—and often one of the most difficult—early decisions that you make will involve structure: Should your organization be a for-profit company, a nonprofit organization, or a hybrid? I encourage students to spend considerable time and energy making this decision because taking a wrong turn at the outset can be very difficult to reverse and brings real challenges. The Center for Social Innovation at GSB has assembled useful resources—including insights from professor Sarah Soule and legal expert Todd Johnson—for those wrestling with decisions about legal structure.[33] Kevin Starr and Laura Hattendorf's article "The Doer and the Payer: A Simple Approach to Scale" provides especially helpful guidance.[34]

In recent years, we have seen a trend in which an increasing number of our practicum students opt to structure their social ventures as for-profit enterprises. Take heed, we warn them, and make sure that the unit economics justify this decision.[35] Look closely at your revenue model: As you produce each additional unit of whatever your product or service may be (in this context, it will likely take the form of delivering your intervention to additional beneficiaries), will you make more money or will you lose more money? If the latter, you need to consider structuring your organization as a nonprofit. You must also ask yourself if the anticipated profits of a for-profit enterprise will be sufficiently compelling that external investors will be motivated to invest? If external investors do come on board, will you be comfortable with the time line and financial targets that they expect? If the expectations of external investors will lead you to change the target segment or problem that you are addressing in a way that generates less overall social impact, then you must carefully weigh the trade-offs.

Be prepared for the possibility that your idea will prove not to be compelling for one reason or another. In that case, it is easy to fall into the pitfall of stubborn reluctance to pull the plug, not least because you have invested considerable time and energy in your venture. Please view that time and energy as "sunk costs" and view your learning as a significant "return" that you will get to keep and that no one can take away from you! There are always opportunities to join another organization and contribute your talents, knowledge, and skills as you continue to hone your model and potentially restart the innovation process.

The Next Step: Be Ready for the Long Haul

By now, if you have followed the steps outlined in the chapter, you have minimized and (I hope) prevented the unexpected detours and dead ends that threaten to impede the launch of your social innovation. Even so, the road will always be difficult at times, and you have my hearty congratulations for having traveled this far.

I leave you with a reminder that designing a new social innovation is just the beginning. The road ahead is long, and you will be traveling it for years to come. This is really a lifelong journey. Henceforth, you will need to embark on continuous improvement and maintain an ample supply of perseverance to sustain you on the long haul to your ultimate destination: impact at scale.

FOR FURTHER READING

For a deeper dive into the material in this chapter, please see *Engine of Impact: Essentials of Strategic Leadership in the Nonprofit Sector* by William F. Meehan III and Kim Starkey Jonker (Stanford Business Books, 2017). For examples of students who have launched more than fifty social ventures through the Stanford GSB course Social Innovation Practicum, please see www.kingphilanthropies.org/course -alumni-ventures. For those who wish to read more on the "how to" of social entrepreneurship, I recommend *Getting beyond Better: How Social Entrepreneurship Works*, by Roger Martin and Sally Osberg (Harvard Business Review Press, 2015), and "The Doer and the Payer: A Simple Approach to Scale," by Kevin Starr and Laura Hattendorf (*Stanford Social Innovation Review*, August 21, 2015).

Notes

1. Tracy S. Ebarb, "Nonprofits Fail—Here's Seven Reasons Why," National Association of Nonprofit Organizations & Executives (NANOE), September 7, 2019, https://nanoe.org/nonprofits-fail/#:~:text=The%20real%20data%20from%20 National,of%20a%20strategic%20plan%2C%20among.

2. National Center for Charitable Statistics, "The Nonprofit Sector in Brief 2019," June 4, 2020, https://nccs.urban.org/publication/nonprofit-sector-brief -2019#the-nonprofit-sector-in-brief-2019.

3. Ibid.

4. World Bank, "COVID-19 to Add as Many as 150 Million Extreme Poor by 2021," press release, October 7, 2020, https://www.worldbank.org/en/news/press

-release/2020/10/07/covid-19-to-add-as-many-as-150-million-extreme-poor-by -2021#:~:text=The%20COVID%2D19%20pandemic%20is,severity%20of%20 the%20economic%20contraction.

5. Tom Rath (@TomCRath), "the problem with pursuing passion: it presumes the world's need should revolve around your interests," Twitter, February 5, 2020, https://twitter.com/TomCRath/status/1225052506482450432.

6. Melissa De White, "Instead of 'Finding Your Passion,' Try Developing It, Stanford Scholars Say," *Stanford News*, June 18, 2018, https://news.stanford.edu /2018/06/18/find-passion-may-bad-advice/#:~:text=While%20.

7. Video excerpt of Martin Luther King Jr.'s speech "What Is Your Life's Blueprint?," (3.00–20.15), posted by Beacon Press, May 2015, https://www.youtube .com/watch?v=zmtogxretou.

8. PBS *Frontline*, 2005.

9. Stefanos Zenios, Lyn Denend, and Edward Sheen, "PlayPumps International: Gaining User Buy-in," *Global Health Innovation Insights*, April 2012, https://www.gsb .stanford.edu/sites/default/files/publication-pdf/playpumps-gaininguserbuy-in.pdf.

10. Ana Lucia Obiols and Karl Erpf, "Mission Report on the Evaluation of the PlayPumps Installed in Mozambique," Rural Water Supply Network, April 2008, https://www-tc.pbs.org/frontlineworld/stories/southernafrica904/flash/pdf /mozambique_report.pdf.

11. UNICEF, *An Evaluation of the PlayPump® Water System as an Appropriate Technology for Water, Sanitation and Hygiene Programmes* (New York: UNICEF, 2007), https://www-tc.pbs.org/frontlineworld/stories/southernafrica904/flash/pdf /unicef_pp_report.pdf.

12. "Babban Gona Helps Subsistence Farmers in Nigeria," B The Change, March 27, 2017, https://bthechange.com/sponsored-babban-gona-helps-subsistence -farmers-in-nigeria-c6bdd1450fa3.

13. Daniela Papi-Thornton, "The Impact Gaps Canvas," Tackling Heropre-neurship, accessed January 29, 2021, http://tacklingheropreneurship.com/the -impact-gaps-canvas/.

14. King Philanthropies, *Example "Impact Gaps Canvas" and "Causes Diagram" on CAMFED* (Menlo Park, CA: King Philanthropies), https://kingphilanthropies.org /wp-content/uploads/camfed-impact-gaps-canvas-and-causes-diagram.pdf.

15. Kim Starkey, "Pay-It-Forward Scaling: A Powerful New Approach Exempli-fied by CAMFED," *Forbes*, February 6, 2020, https://www.forbes.com/sites /kimjonker/2020/02/06/pay-it-forward-scaling-a-powerful-new-approach -exemplified-by-camfed/?sh=31ca5b6e3b5c.

16. Sharon M. Oster, *Strategic Management for Nonprofit Organizations: Theory and Cases* (Oxford: Oxford University Press, 1995).

17. Michael Porter, *Competitive Strategy: Techniques for Analyzing Industries and Competitors* (1980; New York: Free Press, 1998), and Michael Porter, "The Five Competitive Forces that Shape Strategy" *Harvard Business Review*, January 2008.

18. William F. Meehan III and Kim Starkey Jonker, *Engine of Impact: Essentials of Strategic Leadership in the Nonprofit Sector* (Stanford, CA: Stanford Business Books, 2017).

19. Jim Taylor, email message to the author, January 29, 2021.

20. Proximity Designs, *Paddy to Plate—the Rice Ecosystem in Myanmar: Challenges and Opportunities* (Yangon, Myanmar: Proximity Designs, 2016), https://proximitydesigns.org/wp-content/uploads/PaddyToPlate-BookonlineAA .pdf.

21. Jan Chipchase, "When It Rains, It Pours," Medium, November 16, 2019, https://medium.com/studio-d/when-it-rains-655bbf8869bc.

22. Vanessa Kirsch, Jim Bildner, and Jeff Walker, "Why Social Ventures Need Systems Thinking," *Harvard Business Review*, July 25, 2016, https://hbr.org/2016/07 /why-social-ventures-need-systems-thinking.

23. Roger L. Martin and Sally R. Osberg, *Getting beyond Better: How Social Entrepreneurship Works* (Boston: Harvard Business Review Press, 2015), 84.

24. Balanced Scorecard Institute, *Basic Tools for Process Improvement* (Cary, NC: Balanced Scorecard Institute, n.d.), https://balancedscorecard.org/wp-content /uploads/pdfs/affinity.pdf.

25. Sarah Gibbons, "Journey Mapping 101," Nielsen Norman Group, December 9, 2018, https://www.nngroup.com/articles/journey-mapping-101/. See also IDEO, "Journey Map," Design Kit, accessed February 28, 2020, https://www .designkit.org/methods/63.

26. Abdul Latif Jameel Poverty Action Lab (J-PAL), "Teaching at the Right Level to Improve Learning," accessed January 29, 2021, https://www.poverty actionlab.org/case-study/teaching-right-level-improve-learning.

27. Paul Brest, Bernadette Clavier, and Laura Hattendorf, "Developing a Strategy for Social Change," Stanford Graduate School of Business and Stanford Center on Philanthropy and Civil Society, https://stanford.edu/dept/gsb-ds /Inkling/socialimpact.html.

28. Paul Brest and Hal Harvey, *Money Well Spent: A Strategic Plan for Smart Philanthropy* (New York: Bloomberg Press, 2008), 48.

29. Social Security Administration, "Education and Lifetime Earnings," November 2015, https://www.ssa.gov/policy/docs/research-summaries/education -earnings.html.

30. Meehan and Starkey Jonker, *Engine of Impact*, 77–100.

31. Acumen, *The Lean Data Field Guide* (Acumen, 2015), https://acumen.org/wp -content/uploads/2015/11/Lean-Data-Field-Guide.pdf.

32. Kevin Starr and Sarah Miers, "Nowhere to Grow," *Stanford Social Innovation Review*, October 22, 2020, https://ssir.org/articles/entry/nowhere_to_grow#.

33. Online resources located at http://sestructures.stanford.edu/.

34. Kevin Starr and Laura Hattendorf, "The Doer and the Payer: A Simple Approach to Scale," *Stanford Social Innovation Review*, August 21, 2015, https://ssir .org/articles/entry/the_doer_and_the_payer_a_simple_approach_to_scale.

35. For a helpful resource, see "Top-Down and Bottom-Up Unit Economics: The Basics," Stanford University Graduate School of Business Case study, 2015.

11

Design for Extreme Affordability

Considerations When Providing a Social Innovation Educational Experience with Real-World Challenges

Stuart Coulson

The moving spirit of the Founders in the foundation and endowment of the Leland Stanford Junior University was love of humanity and a desire to render the greatest possible service to mankind . . . While the instruction offered must be such as will qualify the students for personal success and direct usefulness in life, they should understand that it is offered in the hope and trust that they will become thereby of greater service to the public.

—Jane Stanford, address to the Board of Trustees, October 3, 1902, subsequently adopted by resolution as an amendment to the founding grant of Leland Stanford Junior University[1]

It is not very often that you can find the inspiration for an individual program, albeit with hindsight, within the original founding documents of a university. Without specific knowledge of Jane Stanford's wishes, Design for Extreme Affordability, affectionately known simply as Extreme, exists to try to fulfill some of those aspirations. As with all lofty goals, the road to achievement is a bumpy one, but reaching the destination can be incredibly fulfilling. This chapter provides an inside look into Stanford's famed Extreme course, which has been crucial in spreading the idea of design thinking to social entrepreneurship. The lessons and takeaways from Extreme are broadly applicable to all social innovators.

First offered as an elective class at Stanford in 2003, Extreme has developed into a program incorporating a two-quarter course sequence; a summer incubator to support continuing projects, Social E Lab; and a follow-on accelerator program for projects requiring additional runway through the following academic year. Products and services designed and developed by students within the program have touched the lives of well over a hundred million people globally.

Each year, the forty places available in the class are oversubscribed multiple times, often with students who want to make Extreme a core aspect of their Stanford experience, and even some who have made a choice to attend Stanford in order to take the class. Months before class starts, the teaching team begins the process of working with and selecting prospective partners, who provide "challenge spaces" within which they hope a student team will identify a problem to work on and a solution to that problem. The focus is on poverty and inequality in low-income economies around the world and more recently in Stanford's own neighborhood around the San Francisco Bay Area.

If there is an easy way to create and present a university program, the inherent design of Extreme almost always dictates the hard way. As a Graduate School of Business and School of Engineering cross-listed elective course, hosted at the famed Institute of Design (the d.school), and open to students from all Stanford schools, the very fabric of a univer-

BIOGRAPHY

STUART COULSON is an adjunct professor at Stanford University's d.school and a lecturer at the Stanford Graduate School of Business, where he has taught and now leads the Design for Extreme Affordability program. He was previously an internet entrepreneur, pioneering technology that powers many of the world's largest airline reservation websites. He is a mentor, adviser, and investor in early-stage for-profit and social impact ventures and is a member of Trinity College Dublin's Provost's Council.

EXECUTIVE SUMMARY

Design for Extreme Affordability ("Extreme") is an iconic program at Stanford's equally iconic d.school. Multidisciplinary student teams use a design thinking approach to address issues of poverty around the world, often producing solutions that have real impact. This chapter outlines some of the deeply embedded philosophies and tenets of the program and how they are used to design an innovation learning experience focused on real-world social impact challenges.

sity school-siloed system pushes back on scheduling, grading, funding, and access to resources. With the dual and equal missions of educating future social entrepreneurs and creating direct social impact, there is constant rebalancing and compromise between the students' needs, projects' trajectories, and partners' expectations. And by choosing to work on real-world challenges provided by external partners and not tidy, well-defined academic problem sets, there is a level of ambiguity and variation that is the enemy of regular and repeatable academic development and success.

As is often the case, the struggle is where the gratification lies, and each of these challenges provides vital opportunities to add value to the student and partner experience. Multidisciplinary teamwork is at the core of best practice in innovation and is a basic tenet for both class and teaching team makeup at the d.school. What could be more inspiring and motivating as a student than seeing a direct pathway from your academic work to potential social impact? And how much more useful is a solution prototype, supporting business model, and applicable implementation plan to a partner?

In this chapter, we will look at some of the big themes that the Extreme teaching team focuses on to make this experiential, team-based, multidisciplinary, real-world, multiplayer production work each year.

Inspiration and Motivation

The entry point into the Extreme program is a two-quarter elective class often considered some of the hardest credits a Stanford student will earn. For the teaching team, student recruitment is one-half of a

FIGURE 11-1

Profile of Extreme students

Our students are:

Committed to the course
You will make Extreme your #1 priority for Winter and Spring quarters

Passionate
You have a passionate soul, even if it's not yet dedicated to a specific topic

Humble
You know that you don't have the answers yet, but you will empathize with and learn from those who experience the problems

Self-aware
You recognize your own strengths and weaknesses, as well as how you project them

Adaptable
You are willing to move through challenges with a commitment toward impact

Resourceful
You are inspired—not discouraged—by constraints and scarcity of resources

A rookie/veteran mix
We admit students who have experience with content and process as well as students who don't

Team players
You realize that personal success is tied to team success

Collaborative
You look forward to sharing creative experiences with others

Seeking an experience
You are seeking a deep personal experience and growth, not just units, a grade, or a line for a résumé

Willing to try our approach
You are open to learning and practicing our design process, regardless of preexisting knowledge and experience

Comfortable in an introvert/extrovert mix
We are seeking a healthy balance of personalities

Driven to implement
You are determined to make your project a reality

nervous annual matchmaking process, with the other half being partner and challenge selection. These six-month processes are taken very seriously.

Each year, the Extreme teaching team embarks on a student recruitment roadshow, with videos, interactive information sessions, social media outreach, campus posters, mailing list posts, and alumni word-of-mouth campaigns. During the information sessions, the potentially system-gaming question "what are you looking for in a successful applicant?" gives us the first chance to introduce the ambiguity that will be such an important part of the Extreme experience. We show the slide depicted in figure 11-1 to help address this question.

The student's initial application is by online form, which includes a number of short essay questions and a student's résumé. At this stage, we are primarily trying to detect passion for the mission and commitment to the program. Whenever asked what he would need in order to select an Extreme student, Mechanical Engineering professor Dave Beach, one of the founding members of the teaching team, always gave the engineer's solution, "a detector that you could place on the head of each student and read off their passion score."

A short list of students is invited to attend an in-person application event, where there is a chance to experience a little of the class content in a multidisciplinary, team-based design challenge for a couple of hours. We apologize for the degrading touch of pinning students' names to their backs like ballroom dance competitors, but we are expecting as much movement from the students as you would from the dancers, and we need a way to know who's who in the resulting melee.

At this event, we are looking for all the other characteristics in figure 11-1. Is everyone willing to jump in and try our approach? Do those who "talk to think" pause long enough for those who "think before talking"? Do teammates recognize the ability of others and then contribute when theirs is the skill set needed? For many students, this event may be the first time they have worked in a team with students from different schools or even a different department within their own school. Whether an applicant is successful in gaining a place in the class or not, we hope they experience a little of the methods, tools, and multidisciplinary nature of our innovation approach.

At the same time as we are meeting our new prospective students for the first time, we are also reaching out across our networks for partners who will provide interesting—and we hope worthwhile—challenges for our student teams to work on.

Our basic question to prospective partners is, "If you had a motivated multi-disciplinary team of Stanford students available to tackle the next challenge space you are considering, what would that be?"

Why "challenge space"? As a partner, we bring many constraints, but perhaps the biggest stems from support for our dual missions—educating future social innovators and providing our partners with impactful outcomes. It is human nature to express problems in terms of the solutions we imagine; we all do it. Given a little encouragement, a partner can express the problem they wish Extreme would address, but a "full-cycle" innovation experience requires exposure to the phases of problem discovery and definition, so we step back further with our partners and ask for a "challenge space," an area to investigate that our partner believes has important problems to be found that when addressed can have an impact in support of our partner's mission.

Another of the many constraints we bring to any partnership is the limit on our time and resources. We will start discovery and fluency in January and complete a cycle of innovation through early prototyping of solutions in June, regardless of the partner's timetable. And despite what students might hope for sometimes, there are still only twenty-four hours in their day, and partners must remember that all our students are taking a full class load alongside Extreme. Sizing our challenges appropriately is therefore an important consideration. Our summer and following academic year lab programs give students willing to work for no academic credit the chance to bring their solutions to market.

We regularly receive the question, "Why don't you go after the grand challenges?" First, our student teams are unlikely to get through the innovation cycle within the time and resources available. Second, to the extent we can foresee, challenges need to have a potential "white-space" solution area. If a student team discovers that many large multinational nongovernmental organizations (NGOs) have been working on their challenge for years, they are not likely to be inspired to dig in. For similar reasons, we try to ensure that, for example, a quick Google search does not result in a $2.99 solution readily available from Alibaba—which would not be a very good first day for an Extreme student team.

The initial meeting that perhaps best illustrates our ideal partner and project occurred at the d.school a few years ago. Chesca Colloredo-Mansfeld was introducing MiracleFeet, the organization she cofounded with a mission to eliminate untreated clubfoot, a painful and stigmatizing birth defect. Chesca explained how a low-cost, minimally invasive treatment called the Ponseti Method is perfect for infants in low-income settings, except that it requires the use of a brace to complete the treatment. Existing braces were either too expensive or medically ineffectual. As with all our projects, it's a difficult story to hear. But Chesca's next sentence made our eyes light up: "My problem is that clubfoot *only* affects one in eight hundred babies born, and is not concentrated in any one geography, so nobody is focused on the problem" (emphasis added). Perfect! A neglected social issue, a clear white space between the cost and effectiveness of existing solutions, and, most importantly, a community-connected, experienced, and expert partner.

Student teams have completed a number of projects with MiracleFeet since that first meeting, including the development and launch of the MiracleFeet brace,[2] an affordable, easy-to-use, durable brace with novel design features such as a flat base to allow older kids to stand while wearing it and detachable shoes with interchangeable parts to make it easier for parents to fit and more affordable to resize as the child grows. In the student team's design for the manufacturing phase, plastic injection molding provided low cost and easy replicability, as well as not looking like a "medical device." And a business model including support from industry partners for manufacturing and distribution ensures real-world impact. It's *only* one in eight hundred babies.

Just to get to the point of having a class of students and a cohort of partners and projects takes many hundreds of hours each year, and that's before we prepare and develop any curriculum.

Ambiguity and Constraints

A Google image search for "design thinking" is guaranteed to display many different versions of the five hexagons: empathize-define-ideate-prototype-test. In the embryonic d.school, originally housed in a recycled doublewide trailer with IKEA furniture[3] on the edge of the Stanford campus, the challenge was to quickly convey the design thinking approach to boot camp students. There were seven-step models, circle-based diagrams, some with arrows, some without. One boot camp fellow wondered why so much emphasis was placed on empathy when it did not appear in any of these early graphic representations. A seven-circle model became a five-circle version, empathize-define-ideate-prototype-test. But circles only touch at one tangential point, and the nonlinearity of design thinking was not reflected in an orderly row of activities. On a whim, the circles were converted to tiled hexagons so they would fit together, did not obviously line up in a single row (so as to wrongly suggest a linear process), and could be reconfigured in any order—a design thinking Lego. In the following year's design thinking boot camp, a random wavy layout of "the hexs" was used to introduce the concept, which escaped into the wild, and the rest is the result of that Google image search.[4]

The static hexagons might not be a bad place to start when becoming familiar with the concept, but they do not capture the way in which design thinking is, and should be, practiced. Design thinking is a deeply messy experience, requiring judicious, and often repeated, use of abilities, methods, and tools. Recognizing this, the d.school approach to understanding and mastering design thinking now rests on the eight core design abilities, as illustrated in figure 11-2. (Of course, we have also upped our graphical representation game from the days of the "hexs.")

FIGURE 11-2

The eight design abilities of the Stanford d.school

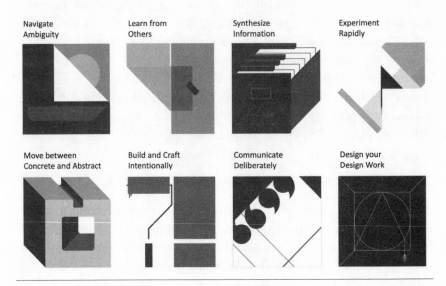

| Navigate Ambiguity | Learn from Others | Synthesize Information | Experiment Rapidly |
| Move between Concrete and Abstract | Build and Craft Intentionally | Communicate Deliberately | Design your Design Work |

Of these abilities, one of the first that Extreme focuses on, and often the hardest for students to internalize, is *navigating ambiguity*.[5] Almost every aspect of the Extreme experience will require a level of comfort with, or at least acceptance of, that unsettling feeling that you are not quite sure what the challenge is and where it will lead you. Open-ended project challenges, unfamiliar environments, ill-specified goals, external partnerships, and team dynamics all contribute to the ambiguity of the students' own experience, the ambiguity of their project, and the potential for a valuable, impactful, real-world outcome.

Why is it so hard for these students to come to terms with ambiguity? They perhaps have spent two decades in an education system that rewards successfully getting the right answer, the first time, to thousands of well-designed, fully constructed questions and problems. Helping our students get comfortable in a messier world is a two-pronged approach: exposure and confidence building.

On the first day of class, students are allocated to multidisciplinary teams and assigned a task to design a large-scale physical prototype that will be needed to perform a measurable task in five days. The current challenge is not described here, since it is intended to be a surprise and more importantly requires the students to produce a first prototype from scratch. We have already had to redesign the assignment because students looked for "inspiration" from course alumni. The previous incarnation was the Monsoon Challenge—design a solution that will catch and store as much water as possible from a "monsoon" (in reality, an irrigation sprinkler attached to the top of a stepladder).

The ambiguity starts with the specification of the criteria for success. In addition to defining the measurable performance of the prototypes in action, the assignment also states that "points will be awarded for designs that exhibit outrageous visual appeal, monstrous complexity, elegant simplicity, infectious team spirit, and multi-sensory engagement. Consideration will be given to the most catastrophic failure, and to the most amazing interpretation of the rules/purpose (that still meets the challenge)."

In addition to ambiguity, the assignment introduces maker skills, rapid prototyping, multidisciplinary teamwork, project planning, affordable design, the importance of testing, and how failure *is* an option (it turns out that water is quite heavy). It also does not hurt that the assignment taps into the students' competitive spirit.

Exposure to ambiguity continues with a design thinking cliché, the whiteboard covered in Post-it notes, and the old d.school joke, "If I'd have known it was going to turn out this way, I would have bought shares in 3M." Space saturation is an important tool in taming ambiguity, team communication, and collecting, processing, and quickly reorganizing large amounts of input, but in the age of word processing, electronic slideshows, and cut-and-pasted images and videos, creating informative, constructive, and engaging physical representations of your information opens up new (or rediscovered) ways of thinking creatively. Students are regularly tasked with saturating their dedicated team studio space with "vast amounts of empathy data—interviews, sketches, photos, maps, physical artifacts, etc." and then synthesizing using "character sketches, maps, diagrams, graphs, flowcharts, timelines, storyboards and more."

The teaching team needs to exercise caution here—introducing ambiguity can be fun. It is easy to enjoy overdoing the reveals and surprises, and even the student's confusion when building familiarity with the topic. We try to resist the temptation. Navigating ambiguity is one of the most powerful abilities future designers will need, and often one of the least comfortable to master.

As part of the process, members of the teaching team need to exhibit their own comfort and willingness to embrace ambiguity. Traditionally, on the evening when students find out which team and project they will work on, and after a rapid-fire in-class project research assignment designed to kick-start their challenge fluency and discovery journey, we make a scary statement: "As of right now, the teaching team no longer knows more about your project than you do." While we do have some domain knowledge, and the experience of working on similar projects for many years, our task is to provide the tools of empathy, innovation, design, and business modeling, not to spoon-feed the information that should come from the student's own discovery processes. Application of these abilities will allow the students to build expertise and arrive at solutions to the challenge itself. Although it can be underwhelming at first for a student to hear, we regularly answer questions with "I don't know, but here's a way to . . . "

It is easy to imagine us all sinking gracefully into a sea of ambiguity, never to reemerge. However, to push the analogy too far, there are some swimming floats out there. First among them are constraints, which usually have a negative connotation, but in design work, constraints are your friend.

Constraints remove some responsibilities, make automatic decisions, and reduce the number of pathways. They are particularly important when narrowing and making choices. In the normal trajectory of the class, this happens at least twice, once when declaring the problem that will be addressed and again when a specific solution strategy must be selected. Both are hard, but deciding which problem to work on has become known as "the lost week" because of the struggle and angst the student teams suffer.

The lost week occurs after teams have spent significant time with their partners and more importantly their end users and stakeholders, gaining empathy and insight into the challenge space and the needs contained within it. They have also become fluent in the challenges, ecosystems, geography, and economics of their clients, and the perceived wisdom, competitive landscape, costs, and applicability of the solutions already available. They have encountered many issues they would like to solve and have built a strong rapport with the people they would like to help. Constraints can help here, but many teams struggle with the idea that introducing and being cognizant of their own constraints—bringing themselves into the design criteria—is somehow wrong.

In addition to many other constraints, selecting on the basis of achievability is important for two reasons. The pedantic one is that we want each student to experience the whole innovation process; attempting too big a project can result in a slow or incomplete journey. The more inspiring reason is that the real-world nature of the projects, and the engagement of the partners, is best served if the student team can produce, at a minimum, a field-testable solution prototype. We often visit and talk to partners who point to the shelf where they keep all the reports and plans that have been generated through university engagements in the past. Our aim is not to be another file on those shelves. We want to provide actual working solutions, which is why sometimes student teams win pitch competitions to support their ongoing work. While most entrants are showing their slide decks, Extreme teams are holding baby incubators and treadle pumps or showing video footage of a donor skin bank in action. The teaching team is also not averse to plopping a solar lantern or a cardboard respiratory inhaler spacer on a dean's conference room table when the need arises.

Empathy and Humility

Some aspects of the design thinking process sound obvious when you say them out loud. For example, discovering what your customer or client wants offers a much higher chance of ultimate success than making assumptions and guesses based on your own experiences, biases, and understanding—in other words, the ability to *learn from others*.

The underlying challenge for students in this context is humility—the willingness and self-awareness to discard their own preconceptions in favor of the experience of their clients. While struggling with the ambiguity of their challenge, they now have to set aside whatever preexisting knowledge they thought they had in favor of the picture they can build and empathetic understanding they can gain for the needs, desires, and world of those they are designing for. Building competence in *navigating ambiguity* and *learning from others* both require a little unlearning.

Perhaps counterintuitively, the projects Extreme students tackle can provide a small advantage in their ability to learn from others. At the time of writing, student teams have worked on challenges in thirty-two low-income countries across the globe. While a few students might have some existing connection to the communities, most will be approaching their challenges with little or no personal experience. In this context, it is somewhat easier to come to terms with the fact that you know very little about the lives or needs of the people you are engaging with and therefore start the empathy process with an open mind and blank sheet.

It turns out that there is a great resource on every university campus that can give students a chance to practice their ability to learn from others. As soon as the first week's assignment is delivered, students are reassigned into new teams and are given a new challenge we call the Stanford Service Corps (SSC) project. Wonderful colleagues across the Stanford campus, working in residential and dining services, building maintenance, grounds and landscaping, transportation and parking, the police department, the bike shop, the athletics department, and many others, volunteer to have our teams practice their design skills on challenges they provide.

Sadly, but in this case to our advantage, while we all benefit from the hard work and professionalism of these colleagues, we know very little about how they operate or even who they are. It is a perfect practice environment, with the advantages of access, safety, insider understanding, and, since most of our clients are repeat volunteers, a more forgiving engagement.

Humility comes early in the relationship. After nearly two decades, patterns and repeating moments emerge that the teaching team enjoys watching for. One often occurs in the first meeting between the student team and an SSC partner—the only meeting that a teaching team member also attends. Invariably, the conversation goes something like this:

Student: We would love to accompany you on your workday to get a better sense of what you do.

SSC Partner: Great! When would you like to do that?

Student: As soon as possible.

SSC Partner: We could do it tomorrow. We like to get our work done before the campus gets too busy. We start at 6 a.m.

This incites a moment of student panic and humility.

Almost every student completes the SSC assignment with a new understanding and respect for the people who make their campus experience happen.

Ethics and Equity

The design of the Extreme program brings together a number of activities and interactions that require specific ethical behavior by the student and teaching teams. Responsible and ethical conduct in academic research, particularly in interacting with human subjects, has long been recognized as an area where students and faculty need awareness and constant vigilance. Ethics in Design also focuses on issues related to collaboration with those for whom we are designing but also brings in responsibilities in how we conduct our work, and the ethical appropriateness of the solutions we produce. In a team- and project-based university course, working cooperatively with teammates of different backgrounds, skill sets, ages, genders, and ethnicities requires an ethical response to ensure everyone receives support and proper academic recognition for their work. On top of all those responsibilities, Extreme's mission to design products and services for the world's poorest citizens is rife with ongoing ethical concerns regarding whether such a mission is appropriate and, if so, how best to accomplish it. Combining a real-world challenge with a student learning experience asks questions concerning whether it is appropriate to ask partners and their communities of clients to spend precious time and resources helping our teams hone the skills they might need to become social innovators.

That is a long list of important issues for a novice designer to address. We do not claim to be able to fully cover all the ethical issues that arise in our work, but we can strive to provide a solid foundational understanding that students will build on in their future careers.

The initial approach is to provide awareness. For many students, Extreme is their first exposure to many of the ethical considerations listed here, and while it could be argued that some should be part of any student's concern, some will certainly be new scenarios.

Some initial insight comes from our emphasis on humility and respect for the knowledge and experience of those we are designing for. Some ethical misbehavior stems from the imbalance of power between the designer and their clients. There is an ugly practice of "parachute research," or in our case "parachute design"—where the all-knowing, tech-savvy, supposedly better-educated designer arrives in a low-resource community, declares what the "obvious" solution should be, and leaves quickly without looking back, leaving the community no better, or, worse, still saddled with an ineffectual solution that at best will eat up scarce time and resources with no result. The humility of our students, their mastery of empathetic problem discovery, and our encouragement and emphasis on co-design are some of the tools we use to avert this behavior.

Building an informed and sophisticated response to the ethical considerations of what we do is hard for students to achieve in a six-month class. Our project partners provide us with many head starts as the students embrace their challenges. The teaching team spends many hours in the fall each year selecting partners and helping develop their challenge statements, including making in-country visits to observe how each partner operates and connects to the communities it serves. One of the many criteria we are there to confirm is how the ethics of the organization manifest in the relationship, working environment, and engagement with the community. As our students get to know both the partners and their clients through available telecommunications and in-person visits, unaccompanied by the teaching team, we want to be sure that there is a healthy environment for the students to inherit.

Another foundational and practical introduction to this topic comes from our friends and colleagues at Stanford's Haas Center for Public Service, whose mission is to connect Stanford students to community service—locally, nationally, and globally. They have consciously focused on the ethics of their work and that of their students, and since 2002 have produced and regularly updated their *Principles of Ethical and Effective Service*,[6] a publication that has proven to be an excellent first step for Extreme students in considering their own behaviors and motivations.

Facilitated by the flexible and dynamic classroom and studio layout possibilities at the d.school,[7] Extreme classes can take on dramatically different formats and can readily incorporate experiential teaching. In focusing on the ethics of designing for low-income environments and communities, one of our class formats includes a "high school debate." Groups of students gather around large tables and are tasked with taking opposite positions on some of the most important and current ethical issues within the space. At the end of the session, the class votes on their support for the various positions. At a basic level, this is an introduction to the topic and instills a desire to know more and consider more. But an outcome that surprises the students every year is that there is never 100 percent agreement on any topic. In fact, there are often very close 50/50 results. The meta message is, we hope, that these are complex and multifaceted issues that require constant work.

Like ethics, there are many facets to considerations of equity within the Extreme ecosystem. Some are inherited from the environment in which we operate and are difficult for a small program to affect significantly. Stanford's faculty makeup and, as an elective class for already admitted students, student body makeup both fall into this category. Luckily, although there is a long way to go, the university, each of the schools we interact with, and particularly initiatives at the d.school are making strides in correcting inequities in these areas.

Within the field of design, and its application to global poverty, there are many inequities for our students to identify, understand, and overcome. The first step is recognition and acknowledgment that it is often as a result of privilege and inequity that our students find themselves at Stanford and in our program. "Designer," "innovator," and "entrepreneur" are not career or skill choices that are equally available to all. The role the students are playing as designers of solutions for communities with significantly different access to resources requires particular focus on how they present themselves in any relationship.

We are fortunate to be surrounded by many colleagues who explore these issues in great depth and can share personal experiences and provide guidance and tools to help our students proceed on their personal equity journeys. In one class session, our students hear from designers and practitioners who have personally battled against inequity in order to be where they are today. We encourage students to share their own difficult journeys if they are comfortable doing so.

Early in the students' journey, we spend time considering how each of us presents ourselves as designers, interviewers, and collaborators, so much of the students' work will revolve around building relationships of trust, where first impressions, knowledge, and power dynamics will all play such an important role. One by-product of our SSC practice project and other team activities is that when our students are in their ultimate Extreme project team, they have classmates around them who have very recent experience of seeing how they present and operate as design team members. On a couple of occasions during the course, we facilitate an opportunity for students to go back to their earlier teammates to check in on these and other team-related issues on which they might want some feedback and advice. This feedback and advice is peer based, coming from a source sharing the same experiences but, importantly, not from current teammates, where the feedback may be more awkward to give or receive.

The reader will have noticed that there can be strong overlap between ethics and equity and our human-centered design approach incorporating humility and empathy. One practice we encourage that brings these together is the concept of co-designing with the end user or client. As an example of how this is facilitated, we place an emphasis on communicating through low-resolution prototypes—physical artifacts that can be used in discovery, problem definition, and solution development. We introduce the idea of shoulder-to-shoulder meetings, not face-to-face ones, with designer and user side-by-side sharing and manipulating a "conversation prototype"—a low-resolution, clearly low-investment artifact inviting criticism, change, and even rejection without dismissing significant effort or hurting anyone's pride. Our students learn to anticipate the most important and useful feedback as soon as a user reaches out to take hold of the simple conversation prototype.

Making for Feasibility, Modeling for Viability

Design thinking and human-centered design are often used interchangeably. Tim Brown, chairman at IDEO, distinguished the two, with human-centered design being the creative approach to problem solving and design thinking being the human-centered approach to innovation—finding the sweet spot between desirability, feasibility, and viability (as illustrated in figure 11-3).[8] Extreme students are presented with this multipronged approach many times, from recruitment information sessions onward.

The early days of Extreme focused on bringing together business and mechanical engineering students to address challenges that might be solved with . . . well . . . business and mechanical engineering skills. Over the years, we have significantly widened the scope for both projects and students (as well as increased the numbers of both that we bring together each year). Students now join Extreme from across all the schools on campus, and projects range from physical products to services—although it is our experience that every viable product needs a service component, and every successful service delivery includes physical artifacts.

Since the foundation of Stanford University, there has always been what we might now call a maker space on the Stanford campus. Jane Stanford was adamant that a "Student Shop" be part of the initial infrastructure of the university. Speaking about her recently deceased son, to whom the university is dedicated, she is quoted as saying, "If my boy were still alive, this is where he would be."

Extreme and our students are privileged to have access to the modern version of that Student Shop, now called the Product Realization Laboratory (PRL).[9] At the PRL's multiple campus locations, our students

FIGURE 11-3

Design innovation: the intersection of desirability, feasibility, and viability

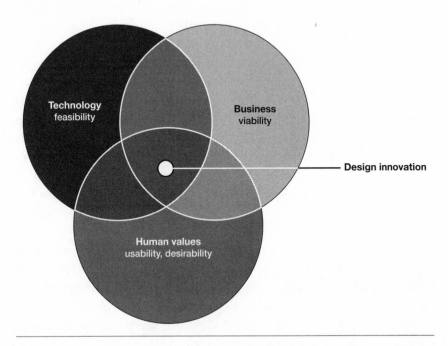

can learn to make things with metal, wood, plastic, foam core, cardboard, soft goods, pink foam, and electronic components. They can glue, nail, weld, form, inject, 3D print, machine, cast, laser cut, sew, solder, and paint. Regardless of their background and major, every Extreme student takes some of our classes at the PRL and is assigned individual and group practice projects that require maker time. Even if one is not already comfortable, crossing the threshold of the PRL and engaging with the very friendly and knowledgeable course assistants more than once is a core part of the course.

Why the focus on maker skills for everyone, particularly since many of the projects may ultimately not need complex fabrication? For some, the answer is straightforward. Our student teams have developed many physical product solutions over the years, and continue to do so, from treadle pumps, drip irrigation systems, and crop processing to foot braces, premature baby warmers, negative pressure wound treatment devices, and low-cost nasoendoscopes. For these solutions, clearly a strong product design and fabrication capability is important, but not just for the engineers or product designers on the team. Knowing the capabilities of raw materials and manufacturing processes, calculating costs and resources, and understanding how to cater for device usability are important for all team members if a truly viable solution is to be developed. In a number of cases, the innovation that has made a product solution viable has not been so much its critical function or usable design but how inexpensively or practically it can be shipped and delivered, with last-mile distribution being a big challenge in the markets we design for. The student teams' insights that dramatically reducing the shipping by volume costs for a stander support for kids with cerebral palsy through designing a collapsible device or modularizing a hazelnut drying solution so it could be transported stacked on the back of a motorcycle through mountainous Bhutan, were the difference between an interesting engineering project and a viable impactful solution.

Many Extreme projects do not need expertise in plastic vacuum forming, TIG welding, or additive manufacturing. Nevertheless, the value of making, or at least thinking and communicating, with your hands is often a novel, instructive, and enlightening skill set.

For their final presentation to their Stanford Service Corps "practice" project clients, the assignment asks students to:

> Craft your story and then think about your audience and what medium might help you convey the message best. Because we cannot guarantee AV setups at in-country partner locations, you will be practicing your "in-the-field" presentation skills (i.e., no digital slideshows allowed), [so] bring artifacts and materials that you can display *without* any digital AV help. Don't just recreate a slide presentation on paper, develop novel and stimulating artifacts that will help you present, as well as engage and inspire your partner audience.

There is newfound power, freedom, and insight when designing and communicating without a computer, reverting to "arts and crafts" skills that a student may not have used since elementary school. If there is any early skepticism about the validity of this approach, we often refer to the initial prototype for one of Extreme's earliest successful projects, the tripod treadle irrigation pump (see figure 11-4).

FIGURE 11-4

Prototyping the tripod treadle irrigation pump

The treadle pump that started as popsicle sticks and dry erase markers has been distributed to over 100,000 farmers in Myanmar by Extreme's partner Proximity Designs, although it is now being replaced with new technologies such as the Lotus solar-powered irrigation pump,[10] also originally designed by Extreme students.

Regardless of the ultimate trajectory of a particular project, we continue to encourage the design ability to *build and craft intentionally*, often for the purpose of *communicating deliberately* as a valuable addition to the designer's tool kit when exploring usability and feasibility.

A possible definition for feasibility as we use the concept is being able to build a single prototype of a product, or deliver one instance of a service, that performs the critical function envisaged. However, for students to be motivated by the possibility of real-world change and for partners to have an opportunity to initiate that change, we need to create viable solutions—for our purposes, solutions that fit within the ecosystem and constraints for which they were designed, which will reach the end users for whom they were designed and can be implemented and replicated at scale to have the impact envisaged. Feasibility is a prototyping journey, but viability is a wider and often more complex systemic challenge, with the added complication of being often impossible to prototype. Consequently, we have to rely on modeling as our design vehicle.

We begin our modeling, perhaps not surprisingly, with an Extreme-modified version of Alexander Osterwalder's business model canvas (BMC).[11] Many students, particularly those from the business school, are familiar with this tool. In the same way that business students might have relied on their engineering or product design classmates in the PRL, it is now time to pay back the favor.

To start, we use the BMC as an analysis tool. One of our liveliest class sessions is when as a class we analyze a nonprofit business that we are all part of—Stanford University. From there, we analyze business models of organizations closer to our domain. An assignment that gives everyone some fluency with the tools while facilitating their discovery journey is the creation of four BMCs. The students select two organizations that operate in their project's economy (usually country) but not necessarily in the same sector as their project and then two organizations that deliver solutions in their project's challenge space but not necessarily in the economy in which the student's solution will be offered. Using publicly available information, contacts, and interviews, the students build pictures of how viable solutions are delivered and how the ecosystems of the country in which they will operate might dictate aspects of their ultimate solution design.

In the same way that our design thinking abilities are nonlinear, feasibility and viability are approached in parallel. As with the cerebral palsy stander and the hazelnut dryer solutions, viability challenges need to be incorporated into a feasible design at an early stage and are often the key innovation that others have missed.

Conclusion

What proceeds is not an attempt to provide a "how-to" for running Extreme but some of the "why" that has guided the teaching team in their ongoing development and enhancement of the program.

Inspiration and *motivation* are powerful sources of energy. *Ambiguity* and *constraints* turn out, perhaps a little counterintuitively, to be strong drivers for innovation and design. *Empathy* and *humility* are the most productive approaches for learning from and creating for others. *Ethics* and *equity* are the twin guiding stars of collaboration. *Feasibility* and *viability* enable hard work to result in real impact.

FOR FURTHER READING

Design for Extreme Affordability utilizes and applies the tools, methods, and abilities developed at the d.school. Details can be found at dschool.stanford.edu and in the d.school's publications. Further information on Design for Extreme Affordability can be found at extreme.stanford.edu and on Instagram @extreme_affordability. Some of the early inspiration for creating the Extreme program came from the late Paul Polak and the ideas expressed in his book *Out of Poverty* (Berrett-Koehler, 2009).

Notes

There is a large community of people who have created, nurtured, and continue to support Extreme, too many to mention here, but some need to be called out. I am joined in the ongoing delivery and design of the program by amazing teaching team colleagues Nell Garcia, Marlo Kohn, Dara Silverstein, Sarah Stein Greenberg, and Manasa Yeturu. Many aspects of the program mentioned in this chapter, such as Stanford Service Corps and Social E Lab, are the creations of former teaching fellow Erica Estrada-Liou. Most importantly, any success we all enjoy is based on the incredible work of the founding teaching team: Dave Beach, Julian Gorodsky, and in particular Jim Patell. Anything important described here is a direct result of these people's imagination and dedication. Finally, each year approximately forty students suspend a little disbelief and start a journey with us that many of them continue with passion and energy long after our support has faded—thank you for your trust and your impactful work.

1. Stanford Digital Repository, Stanford University Library, https://purl .stanford.edu/bz978md4965. Bringing us right up to date, the words of this Jane Stanford address are still included in Stanford's annual *Return of Organization Exempt from Income Tax* (IRS Form 990).

2. MiracleFeet, https://www.miraclefeet.org/the-miraclefeet-brace.

3. Stanford d.school, https://dschool.stanford.edu/redcouch.

4. As told to the author by d.school colleague Scott Doorley, who, along with Perry Klebhan and Thomas Both, have the slightly dubious honor of cocreating "the hexs."

5. Stanford d.school, https://dlibrary.stanford.edu/ambiguity.

6. Haas Center for Public Service, Stanford University, *Principles of Ethical and Effective Service*, https://haas.stanford.edu/about/our-approach/principles-ethical -and-effective-service.

7. Stanford d.school, https://dschool.stanford.edu/resources/make-space-excerpts.

8. IDEO, https://designthinking.ideo.com/faq/whats-the-difference-between -human-centered-design-and-design-thinking.

9. Stanford Product Realization Laboratory, http://productrealization.stanford .edu.

10. Proximity Designs, https://proximitydesigns.org/service/farm-tech.

11. Strategyzer AG, https://www.strategyzer.com.

PART FOUR

APPLICATIONS

12

Disrupting Education

How Social Entrepreneurs Are Bringing Together the Future of Education and the Future of Work

Rob Urstein

For decades, discussions in education have focused on strengthening K–12 public education and closing the achievement gap, arguing that the earlier we can start to level the educational playing field for all children, the more equitable the long-term outcomes will be.[1] While progress has been made, these areas have not been fully ameliorated and demand sustained attention, along with promising pre-K and other early childhood interventions. Such efforts have been complemented by equally compelling college access and affordability initiatives that have sent record numbers of students to postsecondary institutions, from eleven million in 1975 to more than twenty million in 2011.[2] That number has been aided by improved overall high school graduation rates, growing from 57 percent in 1971 to 85 percent in 2018, and an increasing message of "college for all."[3] When President Barack Obama took office in 2009, higher education once again became a national priority, setting 2020 as the year by which the United States would retake the global lead in higher education attainment after having slipped significantly among developed countries. Most significantly, the Obama administration articulated a goal that every American should complete at least one year of postsecondary education, along with expanding the definition of what that education could be, including community college, a four-year degree, or vocational training.[4] While adding two-year institutions and vocational training pleased many advocates, who saw the four-year degree as too narrow a goal, others found it in conflict with the revived commitment to bachelor's degree attainment.

As the US economy recovered in the aftermath of the Great Recession, enrollment slightly decreased, but approximately 19.6 million students were enrolled in higher education programs in 2018, a number expected to remain flat for the next decade because of a number of demographic factors.[5] But in spite of these encouraging enrollment numbers, attainment has remained a challenge. As of 2019, 36 percent of Americans older than twenty-five had completed a bachelor's degree, and more than 40 percent of students in postsecondary education programs leave without completing a degree.[6] While increasing numbers of students have enrolled in college, many are underprepared, poorly supported, financially stretched, and leave school before earning a degree, exiting with no credential, no job, and often significant debt. The equity discussions that dominate higher education today focus on many of these men and women—the more than thirty-six million Americans with some college credit but no degree.[7] Lacking the skills that will provide them with career on ramps in today's economy, and often shut out of jobs by hiring managers who still use the college degree as an inflated and imprecise mechanism to assess applicants' skills and competencies, the challenges and opportunities of serving this population and bridging the gap between education and meaningful work have emerged as a massive social problem in our postindustrial knowledge economy.

While many of these individuals are actively interested in pursuing pathways leading to better futures through education, the structures

BIOGRAPHY

ROB URSTEIN is a lecturer in management at the Stanford Graduate School of Business, where he teaches courses on innovation in higher education and education technology and is cofounder of Gather Learning. He spent many years in senior leadership roles at Stanford University—including associate vice provost for undergraduate education and assistant dean of the Graduate School of Business—before transitioning into building and growing new education technology ventures.

EXECUTIVE SUMMARY

More than thirty-six million American adults have some college credit but no degree. Bridging the gap between education and meaningful work for this population has emerged as a massive social problem in our postindustrial knowledge economy. In recent years, social entrepreneurs have turned their attention to this group of working adults, who have been poorly served by traditional postsecondary education, with strategies to help them attain relevant degrees and credentials at affordable prices. This chapter features three examples of that work, with insights from the social entrepreneurs leading those ventures.

and systems that deliver that education have not been designed with them in mind. When we think about a "typical" college student, we may think of someone moving directly from high school to college, who is eighteen to twenty-two, usually attending a residential college, studying full time, and enjoying all the things that are portrayed as college in popular culture or that we may have participated in ourselves. But that image, if it was ever true, is certainly not true now.[8] With almost twenty million students in postsecondary education, the population of degree seekers is more diverse than ever, but the systems, built for another era, are poorly designed to serve them. This mismatch contributes to longer times to earn a degree and lower levels of completion. Today, 42 percent of students are nonwhite, 40 percent are twenty-five or older, 62 percent work, 28 percent have children, and 33 percent are low income.[9]

A variety of innovative solutions to tackle affordability have been proposed and have received buzz in the popular press (e.g., free tuition and income share agreements). Furthermore, a vast array of "student success" initiatives have proliferated in colleges and universities that have the goal of increasing attainment. Amid these efforts, a number of social entrepreneurs have turned their attention to this large population of working adults who have been poorly served by traditional postsecondary education with strategies to help them earn degrees and credentials at affordable prices so they can get better jobs to support themselves and their families. We know that holders of a college degree will earn 84 percent more over their lifetime than those with only a high school diploma.[10]

The key is therefore making sure not only that people enter college but that they graduate.

The Lumina Foundation, based in Indiana, has been leading the national charge to increase attainment of postsecondary degrees. Recognizing that the long shift from an industrial economy to a knowledge economy has made the necessity of skills and competencies beyond a high school degree essential for both national growth and long-term prosperity for individuals and families, Lumina has invested in numerous initiatives supporting attainment of credentials beyond high school. While the bachelor's degree has been the historic gold standard, Lumina and others, following the Obama administration's expanded definitions, have taken the lead in shining attention on both undergraduate degrees and other credentials beyond high school that will prepare adults for "citizenship and economic success."[11]

For Lumina and others, that focus has turned especially toward the tens of millions of Americans who hold some postsecondary education but no degree or credential. While significant resources have been invested in the college transition process and helping students succeed in college, an equally compelling social problem has been the large number of students who did not complete their education and whose paths to economic mobility are now more limited as a result. There are myriad reasons for noncompletion, but they include affordability; the challenges of juggling life, work, and school; programs designed with a different modal student in mind that no longer reflect the needs of today's student; punitive policies at higher education institutions connected to administrative obstacles such as transfer credit; or disconnects between curricular objectives and an actual job opportunity.

Social entrepreneurs have jumped into this space, building novel ways to solve these challenges by focusing on the levers of *affordability, attainment,* and *relevance.* While the costs of many goods and services have come down over time, college costs have more than doubled at both public and private colleges since the mid-1960s, and the rate of increase has been more than eight times the growth of wages. Additionally, the average student borrower leaves school with more than $30,000 in debt.[12] For adult learners, often managing work and family, the costs of education can be prohibitive. In addition to solving for affordability, developing better strategies to improve completion rates for degrees and credentials remains a challenge, yet we know completers will likely fare better in the labor market. Finally, ensuring that the education adult learners are receiving is relevant—more connected to the jobs and opportunities in the knowledge economy—is essential. These three factors—affordability, relevance, and attainment—are also all heavily dependent on different degrees of support at every level, which adds another dimension to our understanding, as every successful solution requires figuring out how to provide such support at scale.

To get a sense of how social innovation can be applied to higher education, the balance of this chapter considers three examples of social entrepreneurs trying to solve these problems. Each of them has a slightly different focus, approach, and operating model, but collectively they represent attempts to make a dent in this social problem, centered largely on working adults; on education that leads to economic mobility in the modern knowledge economy; and with models that largely depart from the approaches of incumbents. Each has, in a sense, recognized that while good solutions need to be affordable, relevant, and attainable, they can't solve everything, so they need to choose a place to start and recognize that such a choice involves trade-offs. These social entrepreneurs and their ventures also help us understand how they approach a problem space, how they think about social innovation, their organizational models, and some of the methods they use to launch their ventures.

Affordability: Guild Education

Guild Education (hereafter Guild), based in Denver, Colorado, has established itself as one of the most innovative leaders in the education and employment space. With a mission to "unlock opportunity for America's workforce through education," Guild is largely responsible for turning "education as a benefit" into a meaningful phrase and since 2015 has been working with some of the nation's largest and most iconic companies, along with a carefully selected group of nonprofit educational providers, to connect working adults with opportunities to earn degrees and credentials that are affordable and largely funded by their employers.[13] As of 2021, Guild, led by cofounder and CEO Rachel Carlson, has raised more than $378 million in funding from social impact investors with a market valuation exceeding $3.75 billion, a rarity in the education technology space.[14]

Guild works with *Fortune* 1000 companies to help them develop and implement an education benefits program to connect their employees to a selected network of high-quality (mostly online) higher education providers, as well as to Guild's student success coaches, who understand and can help employees find programs that are right for them and their education objectives, move through the application and enrollment process, and advise them regularly as they balance the demands of work and family. Guild's network of academic partners includes institutions experienced in serving working adults, such as Nebraska's Bellevue University, Southern New Hampshire University, and Indiana's Purdue Global University. For these academic partners, Guild reduces the cost of acquiring students by more efficiently matching prospective students to their degree programs; negotiating tuition discounts on their behalf, which in turn help to make the programs more affordable; and supporting those students throughout their educational journey, which exceeds the more minimal support that most online degree programs provide.

Since 2015, Guild has worked with companies with large numbers of frontline employees, including Walmart, Disney, Taco Bell, Lowe's, Discover Financial, and Chipotle. Guild's goal is to take a little-used benefit program and transform it into a powerful strategic tool that companies can use to further their business goals while at the same time providing education to millions of working adults, giving them a chance to learn valuable skills and credentials that will serve them long after their current job. Guild's value proposition to companies is that a strong education benefits program increases recruitment, retention, brand value, and financial return. As of 2021, more than three million students are eligible to participate in education benefits through their employer's Guild-managed program.[15]

Rachel Carlson and Brittany Stich, undergraduate classmates in college and future Stanford Graduate School of Business students, had been working at American Honors in Washington, DC, a company founded by Carlson's father, which developed and ran honors programs for community colleges and helped build strong transfer pipelines to four-year institutions for students. Frustrated by the lack of traction they saw there, both Carlson and Stich began thinking about how to create better solutions for this population of students, especially tackling college affordability, support to help them succeed, and degrees that could lead to good jobs. Affordability was a big insight and motivator. As Stich explained, "[T]he incentives weren't aligned. We knew many students couldn't pay for all of college on their own, and there had to be another payer as an alternative to debt."[16]

During business school, Carlson and Stich began working on potential solutions, first thinking about fixing the gap between education and employment. How could more Americans affordably earn the degrees and credentials that would lead to meaningful job opportunities while also aligning that education with the needs and incentives of employers? Their first effort, Student Blueprint, was launched in 2014 and sought to use technology to match community college students with jobs. While Carlson and Stich learned a lot, they ended up selling the software to another San Francisco educational technology firm. As they continued their research, however, they homed in on an IRS tax provision allowing employers to offer educational assistance to employees of up to $5,250 per year to participate in a "qualified educational program," initially college degrees but expanded since the 1980s to include both degree and nondegree programs, both undergraduate and graduate. The benefit to the employee is that the contribution from the employer is not considered taxable income.[17]

In their research, Carson and Stich discovered a few things that led to what would become Guild. First, while many large companies offered these benefits, mostly in the form of tuition reimbursement, relatively few employees exercised them (3–5 percent). Second, the programs themselves were complex and burdensome to administer for employers and were filled with friction for employees. Employers, lacking the expertise in evaluating and identifying the right academic programs for their employees, provided little guidance and support and were juggling numerous reimbursement requests from employees. Similarly, employees lacked guidance on finding, selecting, and applying to programs, and in many cases had to fund the tuition costs on their own and then go through a lengthy and often complex reimbursement process. For frontline workers, these were significant obstacles. Carlson and Stich also knew that for many schools, especially less selective schools with robust online programs, student acquisition costs were high—averaging more than $3,000 per student. If there were better ways to connect students with accredited high-quality online schools at a lower cost, they thought, an interesting marketplace could be created. So while affordability for students was a driver, one lever they could pull to enable that was to reduce the cost of acquisition for schools.

As Carlson and Stich began this work, they also began thinking about how employers could use educational benefits more strategically, particularly as a way to attract and retain employees, and how individuals could see a job as a pathway to further education instead of the conventional ways we think about education as a pathway to a job. Most importantly, they thought about scale. One of the lessons from American Honors and Student Blueprint was how hard it was to scale education to serve more students, so as they built Guild, they focused on large employers (each with more than ten thousand employees in the United States), especially those with large populations of frontline workers who were seeking further education but who lacked both the resources and the guidance and support to do so.

As Guild developed, its founders also considered operating models and funding sources. When it came time to decide, Stich and Carlson had several options. A large philanthropy offered them $10 million in funding to build Guild as a nonprofit organization. They were also offered seed funding from an existing education and training company that would allow them to operate as a subsidiary under that company's umbrella. Then, one of Carlson's professors, also an investor, encouraged them to consider a venture capital funding structure, which is what they ultimately chose, raising a $2 million seed round of funding in summer 2015. Although they debated whether to build Guild as a for-profit or nonprofit company, Carlson noted that after thinking through their options and evaluating the trade-offs, they decided "that only a venture-backed business could give [them] the needed resources to meaningfully scale."[18] Committed to being a double-bottom-line business, however, Guild would later become a certified B corporation to underscore its commitment to serving the social mission of economic opportunity through education.

Guild's first large customer was Chipotle, a large, fast-casual restaurant. Carlson reached out cold to Chipotle's human resources manager via LinkedIn, which led to Guild's first big contract. What they discovered with Chipotle was a strong social mission and a desire to retain a workforce in an industry with significant churn in a competitive labor market. With its first large customer in place, Guild set up a program where eligible Chipotle employees could exercise their $5,250 in annual education benefits and enroll in online degree programs at one of Guild's academic partners.

Carlson, CEO of Guild, used insights she had gained in the community college space to understand that for working adults to succeed, Guild needed to do more than remove the friction around program selection, application, and payment. Carlson understood that success, especially for nontraditional learners, was often built on support, an insight that has often been hard to scale. Today Guild employs more than three hundred student success coaches, who work with students (who are also employees of Guild's customers) one-on-one at every step of their educational journey, handling some of the tasks that companies were unable to do well and large schools with high ratios of students to advisers were unable to provide.

When asked to reflect on Guild's first five years, both Carlson and Stich take pride in Guild's work in getting people to care about the issue that so many working adults lack the skills and credentials they need to ensure a better future for themselves and their families. Rejecting a winner-takes-all mentality, they are flattered that they have seen new competitors, such as Los Angeles's InStride, enter the space and that in this trillion-dollar market there is plenty of room for multiple companies. They are equally proud that people no longer scratch their head at the phrase "education as a benefit" and that Guild has been a category-defining leader in driving that conversation as it helps unlock opportunity for some of those thirty-six million working adults and make education more affordable.

Relevance: Pathstream

One of the early things that Carlson and Stich recognized in building Guild was that there was a gap between the skills employers were looking for in applicants and the coursework that most colleges were providing and that most students were taking. That's exactly the gap that San Francisco's Pathstream decided to fill. Led by cofounder and CEO Eleanor Cooper, Pathstream partners with leading technology companies to design and build branded digital skills career programs that are delivered through college and university partnerships, bringing relevant technology-specific skills to more learners. Working with companies such as Facebook, Unity, Tableau, and Salesforce, Pathstream develops competency-based online education curricula that teach the most current content and job-specific tools to students and job seekers across the country.[19] Pathstream's team of learning designers works closely with tech partners to build university-level coursework, consulting with industry experts and hiring managers to ensure that there is alignment with industry best practices and real labor market needs. Both adult learners and traditional students can access Pathstream courses through a network of college and university partners, including community colleges and four-year institutions, for both credit and noncredit. Upon completion, students receive a dual-branded certificate from both the university partner and the technology company.

While studying for her MBA, Cooper, a former banker, had been working with formerly incarcerated individuals who were trying to enter the workforce. Lacking degrees and social capital but with a strong desire to move ahead, Cooper realized that the challenges of learning relevant digital skills were compounded even more for this population. At the time, many technology-based skills programs were run mostly through expensive boot camps. Community colleges, traditionally one of the most affordable and accessible routes to education and skills, lacked the resources and expertise to offer the kinds of digital skills education that employers were actually looking for in applicants. Other models existed, but many had prerequisites that this population could not meet. Cooper had been trying to help one formerly incarcerated man access those opportunities and saw firsthand how challenging it was for him, even with her help and support. The man did not want to pursue a traditional vocational path but instead wanted to find work in the modern economy—the knowledge economy. But while the economy was digitizing, few pathways existed for him and for other men and women like him who lacked a college degree or a lot of money. Recognizing that affordable education pathways are often disconnected from employment opportunities, Cooper started Pathstream as a way to tackle that problem.

Cooper says three things motivated her thinking. First was the experience working with one individual and seeing the limited options, especially for someone without a college degree. Boot camps averaged more than $12,000 for a multimonth program and often catered to those with significant prior education, including graduate degrees. Second, in doing a labor market analysis that considered macro trends and a better understanding of the skills gaps, Cooper understood that 70 percent of all open positions require digital skills. Third, a landscape analysis that looked at who was currently working in the space, price points, and where the opportunities might be suggested there was room for something different in the ecosystem.

The early steps to what would soon become Pathstream started with a virtual-reality boot camp that Cooper developed as an interim project for a software company, which allowed her to learn more about digital skills. That project led to a conversation with Facebook, which at the time was interested in doing something oriented toward social impact on a bigger scale related to the skills gap. Working with Facebook, Pathstream developed and launched an online digital marketing certificate program to teach students how to use Facebook Ads and Google Analytics, perform A/B testing, and cultivate other skills that were in demand by thousands of companies, large and small. Originally launched and delivered with twenty community college partners, it was part of Facebook's push to train more than a million people to learn digital marketing skills that could help them secure meaningful employment in the modern economy.[20] As Cooper began seeking college and university partners for Pathstream to work with, she was astonished by the response. Not one school said no. Providing turnkey program content with industry relationships proved a boon for community colleges, which love working with industry but often faced challenges in connecting with technology companies, especially if they were located outside major tech hubs.

Cooper started Pathstream in 2018 as a for-profit company, initially raising $1 million in seed capital, followed a year later by a $13 million second round of funding. When asked about building a venture-backed for-profit company, Cooper explained that, "You can get more significant capital from the venture market. Philanthropic dollars are hard to raise, and if you're serious about scaling, you need capital."[21] She also noted that to attract top talent, especially in building a technology company, she needed to be able to offer meaningful pay and equity. At the same time, she acknowledged that building a social impact business as a for-profit company has its challenges, especially in the world of education, where partners can often be skeptical about your intent. Pathstream understands that employers need job-ready candidates with modern technology skills to remain competitive in their industries. They also know that colleges and universities are not teaching these skills, because they lack the expertise and resources to build and maintain new programs that are current and aligned with industry. Technology companies are motivated to educate new users but do not have the capacity to build accredited college courses or offer a college degree.

Cooper finds the real value in Pathstream's approach as being an intermediary between these communities, who often speak different languages. Pathstream helps students access affordable and meaningful skills and certifications that are hard to access in other ways. Additionally,

Pathstream helps educational institutions provide cobranded and relevant certifications that would be hard to develop on their own. Finally, Pathstream enables technology companies to reach students and institutional partners at scale, since developing and maintaining relationships with individual colleges is difficult and inefficient for most large companies. The dual-branded certificate is proving to be a useful innovation in the space, as certificates are emerging as a leading credential for job seekers.[22] According to Pathstream's data, colleges are embracing certificates because of increased financial pressure to attract and retain students, and federal funding will increasingly be tied to completion outcomes.

When asked where she sees Pathstream today, Cooper replied that "the role we are playing right now is about career discovery and navigation. More people can feel included in the knowledge economy, and can build motivation and confidence, along with skills. We're also teaching digital resilience." In its first eighteen months, more than four thousand students completed Pathstream certifications. When asked where she sees Pathstream tomorrow, she confidently predicted that "in the future, I hope that anyone with a high school diploma and beyond can access a broad enough range of entry level career paths that can open up a huge number of opportunities for self-determination."[23]

Attainment: Rivet School

In the wake of the 2016 US elections, MBA student Eli Bildner had been thinking broadly about the divergent returns of labor and capital, the enormous aggregation of wealth in major cities, and specifically the narrowing of accessible pathways to education and opportunity for more Americans. Prior to business school, Bildner had helped to found an online coding boot camp and also worked for Coursera in the early days of the massive open online course (MOOC) platform company. While the former excited him with its accessibility and the relative affordability of an online curriculum, the latter helped him understand the immense motivational challenges needed to complete an online course or degree that was largely delivered in an asynchronous format for solo learners. A commonly referenced statistic about MOOCs was that 96 percent of students who began a course never finished. In spite of its founders' promise to democratize access to education at scale, it hardly seemed that such a model could be a stand-alone solution for economic inequality and opportunity. The student simply needed more to succeed.[24]

During his last year of business school, Bildner was introduced to someone who had helped start a nonprofit school in Rwanda called Kepler University.[25] Kepler's model combined cohort and place-based in-person academic support and coaching with an accredited competency-based undergraduate curriculum delivered online—specifically an American bachelor's degree program from Southern New Hampshire University. Bildner was being recruited to join and lead Kepler, which wasn't the right fit for him or his family, but the model continued to resonate with him. It wasn't just online, and not just in person, but it blended parts of both to deliver something that was more affordable but also more successful for learner completion. Bildner began to think about how he could replicate that for some of the millions of Americans for whom higher education was both unaffordable and hard to complete.

Bildner started to talk with more people working in the space. He realized early on, as he thought about what a blended or hybrid education program would look like, that there were clear trade-offs between commercial potential and social impact. There were some existing approaches and models, including one that worked with underemployed graduates from lower-selectivity public universities and combined cohort building, social capital building, and skills. But trying to do all this was (and is) hard, and Bildner understood that if he was going to build something successful, he needed to constrain the problem. At about the same time, he connected with a group of current and former board members from KIPP schools in the San Francisco Bay Area, who were frustrated with the lack of success they were seeing in KIPP graduates persisting through college.

Bildner's assessment was that education solutions are easy to talk about at a high level, but education systems are complex, and there are myriad reasons why these problems haven't been solved. As he spoke with more California community college students, he learned more about the barriers they faced as they tried to complete a degree. They were immense. Bildner noted that solutions may seem easy at first. "You see someone who is homeless on the streets," he explained, "and we want to believe that they're one step away from a six-figure salary and a house. And maybe there are people for whom that's true. That there's some easy fix. But for most people twenty things need to happen, and you can't do twenty things at once. What's the one intervention?"[26] Bildner explained that college is often seen as that transformational element in changing lives, but there are many factors that get in the way of someone getting an education. It could be a lack of financial resources. It could be a complicated family situation or home responsibilities. For someone to get through a degree program on top of all those other factors in two to six years, a lot needs to happen.

As Bildner explained:

> It's really hard for most universities to do what we do for a few reasons. When I say, "what we do," what I mean is combining a competency-based online degree program with comprehensive, place-based support. One reason universities offer competency-based programs is that they're less expensive for students than traditional in person synchronous courses. But this is a double-edged sword for the university—it still costs just as much to find students, and if you're charging significantly lower tuition (even if a competency-based model also carries fewer costs), you're going to make less money. I'm not trying to be cynical here—it's just really hard for universities to justify investing in these programs if they're both hard to support on their margins, [and] also might cannibalize students from higher-margin programs. At the same time, most online degree programs just aren't structured in a way where they form place-based partnerships and provide place-based support. It's not the way they're set up, and not in their skill set.[27]

In starting Rivet School (originally called Concourse Education), Bildner went into that work thinking about career, college, and the support students needed to be successful. With seed funding from philanthropic sources, and with an organization of three people, they had some great insights and ideas, some money to get it off the ground, and some choices. They understood that they couldn't solve everything, so they knew they needed to be great at one thing. They chose an accelerated bachelor's degree program, creating shortcuts by partnering with existing low-cost but nonprofit accredited online providers, and bolted onto that the kinds of support they thought could help students be more successful as they managed the rest of their life and school. Bildner and his cofounders realized that the challenges were being able to provide on-demand support, encouragement, and a sense that other students were going through the experience together with them, even if most of their learning was being done online.

Bildner and his small team came to understand that most colleges weren't designed around the needs of real students. The lack of advisers, or the small number of advisers to serve large numbers of students, made understanding credits and course sequences and managing academic life difficult, especially for the demographic that increasing numbers of underserved students looked like: working adults, students who were parents, and first-generation, low-income students. According to Bildner, in California, where Rivet School began, only 23 percent of public university students, 13 percent of community college students, and 3 percent of for-profit online students graduate on time. Founded in 2018 in Richmond, California, in one of the counties lowest in educational attainment in the Bay Area, Rivet School honors the thousands of shipyard workers in Northern California during World War II, including many women and people of color who had previously been discriminated against for employment but found well-paying middle-class jobs there, often represented in popular culture by the "Rosie the Riveter" icon, which Rivet School adopted as part of its brand identity.

Rivet School sees itself as a modern incarnation of that midcentury vision, but instead of jobs in twentieth-century industrial shipyards, Rivet School has developed a program to help more Americans find pathways to economic opportunity and mobility through education in twenty-first century knowledge economy fields such as technology, health care, education, and business.[28] The Rivet School model helps students select and enroll in one of two fully accredited, nonprofit, entirely online bachelor's degree programs through either Southern New Hampshire University or Brandman University. Realizing that solo learning is hard, Rivet School's model puts students into cohorts so they have a group of other students with whom they are progressing and requires a six-week orientation or onboarding process where students get to know others in their cohort, Rivet coaches, and advisers, and are introduced to skills that will be useful in helping them be successful. They also get a personal coach and access to resources to help them stay on track, meet their academic objectives, and progress through a degree program as they manage the rest of their life, which usually includes significant work and family responsibilities.

Today, Rivet School serves about two hundred students across Northern California from its Richmond base. The program has started to see its first bachelor's degree graduates, and the majority of Riveters are on track to earn a bachelor's degree in three years or less, and for less than

$10,000 in out-of-pocket costs, because of its affordable online program and the services that are subsidized by philanthropic support. Their students (and graduates) are almost across the board the first in their families to attend and complete college, are predominately students of color, and, prior to Rivet School, many had unsuccessfully tried to earn a degree.

According to Bildner, "[O]ur goal isn't to get students degrees; it's to enable a broader swathe of Americans to access the opportunity that comes from a knowledge-economy job. And while it's popular to pronounce the death of the degree, Americans without college are increasingly finding themselves shut out of these opportunities."[29]

Bildner noted that

> [W]hat we're doing at Rivet School is making college more accessible, more efficient, and more job-focused for traditionally underserved students. This is particularly important as what we're actually seeing in the market is employers placing more—not less—value on credentials over time. Without a better path to a degree (and other credentials) for "post-traditional" students like working adults and parent learners, for instance, economic mobility will become further and further out of reach.[30]

Conclusion: Affordability, Relevance, and Attainment

When considering these approaches together, each social entrepreneur has indexed more highly on one of these dimensions—affordability, relevance, or attainment. Guild went after *affordability* first, notably by shifting the role of payer from the student to the employer, with these working students exercising company-sponsored tuition benefits; getting a job allows them to get an education. Guild's model, especially focused on frontline workers, has created a more affordable pathway to education. But affordability alone will not solve this problem. Guild has also provided the advice, support, and coaching needed to help drive these working adults toward attainment, which is the hardest part of scaling efficiently. Pathstream started by focusing on *relevance*, building curricula with industry partners but ensuring that those digitally focused certificates are delivered through accredited partners. But Pathstream also recognized that affordability and attainment (an actual academically backed but industry-relevant credential or certificate) is essential to greater economic mobility. Finally, Rivet School focused from the start on *attainment*—getting more students to graduate with degrees—but also understands that for students to persist and complete a degree, programs need to be affordable, flexible, and support the specific needs of working adults, and in fields that have a greater chance of leading to meaningful work.

Most importantly, all these ventures have learned that support—the most resource-intensive part of education—is essential to success for the working adult learner, and while Pathstream and Guild, in particular, have the capital to be able to do that, Rivet School will likely be much harder to scale because of its resource limitations but could be a good model for many other Rivet-like schools on a local or regional level, each of which could be supported by both philanthropy and industry.

Making higher education more affordable, improving time to degree and degree completion rates, and providing better connections between the skills and competencies students learn and labor market opportunities will continue to be areas of concern and focus, especially for more-traditional public and private colleges and universities. But addressing the critical needs of those who have been poorly served by those institutions; who have some credits, some debt, and no degree; and those who have been nonconsumers but seek the kinds of education that will lead to meaningful employment to support themselves and their families remains an equally compelling social problem. Guild, Pathstream, and Rivet School have each approached that problem differently, using different tools and approaches, and to some degree have focused on different segments of that large population that needs to be served. None of these social ventures and their approaches will solve this problem on their own, and choosing one thing often means not working on others. But each of these entrepreneurs has understood that social innovation—whether venture backed or supported by philanthropy—provides an opportunity to contribute to the solution.

FOR FURTHER READING

The single best overview on understanding the changing dynamics of traditional higher education is Goldie Blumenstyk's *American Higher Education in Crisis: What*

Everyone Needs to Know (Oxford University Press, 2015). From the perspective of an education entrepreneur and investor, Ryan Craig's two books *College Disrupted: The Great Unbundling of Higher Education* (Palgrave Macmillan, 2015) and *A New U: Faster + Cheaper Alternatives to College* (BenBella, 2018) document ways that traditional higher education is broken and explore models that provide quality alternatives to traditional degrees. Michael W. Kirst and Mitchell L. Stevens's *Remaking College: The Changing Ecology of Higher Education* (Stanford University Press, 2015) is a useful collection of essays that contextualize the changing demographics of higher education seekers and how those changes need to be understood to better serve the educational needs of contemporary higher education consumers, especially in broad-access universities, community colleges, and alternative programs.

Notes

1. Andy Porter, "Rethinking the Achievement Gap," *University of Pennsylvania GSE News*, https://www.gse.upenn.edu/news/rethinking-achievement-gap.
2. National Center for Educational Statistics, *Digest of Education Statistics* (Washington, DC: National Center for Educational Statistics, 2020), https://nces.ed.gov/programs/digest/d19/tables/dt19_303.10.asp.
3. National Center for Educational Statistics, *The Condition of Education* (Washington, DC: National Center for Educational Statistics, 2020), https://nces.ed.gov/programs/coe/indicator_coi.asp#:~:text=In%20school%20year%202017%E2%80%9318,first%20measured%20in%202010%E2%80%9311.
4. Sara Hebel and Jeffrey Selingo, "Obama's Higher Education Goal Is Ambitious but Achievable, Leaders Say," *Chronicle of Higher Education*, February 26, 2009, https://www-chronicle-com.stanford.idm.oclc.org/article/obamas-higher-education-goal-is-ambitious-but-achievable-leaders-say-1551/.
5. National Center for Educational Statistics, *Digest of Education Statistics*.
6. National Student Clearinghouse Research Center, *Some College, No Degree* (Herndon, VA: National Student Clearinghouse Research Center, 2019), https://nscresearchcenter.org/some-college-no-degree-2019/.
7. Ibid.
8. Goldie Blumenstyk, *American Higher Education in Crisis: What Everyone Needs to Know* (Oxford: Oxford University Press, 2015), 12–15.
9. Gates Foundation, https://postsecondary.gatesfoundation.org/demographics/.
10. Georgetown University Center on Education and the Workforce, *The College Payoff* (Washington, DC: Georgetown University Center on Education and the Workforce, 2013), 2, https://cew.georgetown.edu/cew-reports/the-college-payoff/#resources.
11. The Lumina Foundation, https://www.luminafoundation.org/about/.
12. Ryan Craig, *A New U: Faster + Cheaper Alternatives to College* (Dallas: BenBella, 2018), 11–15, 149–152.
13. Guild Education, www.guildeducation.com.

14. Crunchbase, *Guild Education Funding History*, https://www.crunchbase.com /organization/guild-education.

15. Betsy Corcoran, "Guild's Mission to Create Smarter, Better Workforce Is Just the Beginning," *EdSurge*, August 26, 2020, https://www.edsurge.com/news /2020-08-26-guild-s-mission-to-create-a-smarter-better-workforce-is-just-the -beginning.

16. Brittany Stich and Rachel Carlson, cofounders, Guild Education, interview with the author, September 2020.

17. Internal Revenue Service, *Tax Benefits for Education* (Washington, DC: Internal Revenue Service, 2020), https://www.irs.gov/pub/irs-pdf/p970.pdf.

18. Stich and Carlson, interview with the author, September 2020.

19. Rather than measuring student progress toward completing a course and degree by time, competency-based education approaches focus instead on self-paced mastery of a defined set of competencies that students are able to demonstrate. It has allowed several nonprofit online institutions, such as Western Governors University and Southern New Hampshire University, to offer affordable, timely degree programs at scale.

20. Facebook, "Training 1 Million People and Small Business Owners across the US by 2020," press release, June 8, 2018, https://about.fb.com/news/2018/06 /training-1-million-people-and-small-business-owners-across-the-us-by-2020/.

21. Eleanor Cooper, CEO, Pathstream, interview with the author, October 2020.

22. Paul Fain, "Alternative Credentials on the Rise," *Inside Higher Education*, August 27, 2020, https://www.insidehighered.com/news/2020/08/27/interest-spikes -short-term-online-credentials-will-it-be-sustained.

23. Cooper, interview with the author, October 2020.

24. Daphne Koller, "MOOCs Can Be a Significant Factor in Opening Doors to Opportunity," *EdSurge*, December 13, 2013, https://www.edsurge.com/news/2013 -12-31-daphne-koller-moocs-can-be-a-significant-factor-in-opening-doors-to -opportunity.

25. Kepler University, www.kepler.org.

26. Eli Bildner, Rivet School.

27. Ibid.

28. Rivet School, www.rivetschool.org.

29. Bildner.

30. Ibid.

13

Social Innovation Meets a Global Pandemic

Early Insights on the Challenges and Opportunities in Social Innovation during the Covid-19 Pandemic

Steve Davis

On February 4, 2020, I sat in a stately hearing room in the Russell Senate Office Building in Washington, DC, with a group of senior scientists, politicians, and business and social sector leaders from across the United States to discuss the fragile state of this country's health security. We had gathered to hear the final report from the Center for Strategic and International Studies (CSIS) Commission on Strengthening America's Health Security, which included experts from government, private business, and the social sector, as well as members of Congress from both major political parties. A bipartisan report[1] had been issued for consideration by the White House and Congress on what the United States should be doing to be more prepared for the next disease outbreak. It emphasized the critical role of innovation for advancing the public good and pointed out that new biomedical and digital tools were needed to prepare for and respond to disease outbreaks. Our report urged more investment in this type of social innovation. There was real urgency behind this push, as a novel coronavirus had begun to appear in a few isolated parts of the United States. To the audience of somewhat stunned politicians, the commission suggested that this virus might abruptly change the course of human well-being, business, and politics across the United States and the world in the next few months—as it did.

Covid-19, declared a global pandemic only five weeks after the meeting, sent shockwaves of tragedy around the globe. As of July 2021, it had killed more than four million people across the world.[2] It also has significantly tested health systems, upended economic growth, closed schools and businesses, challenged social norms, isolated individuals and families, and disrupted life across much of the planet. While the full consequences of Covid-19 are yet to be analyzed, the reach and depth of its destructive path and cascading impacts—health, economic, humanitarian, and political—have become painfully clear.

Yet, in the midst of a pandemic for which much of the world was not prepared and that it managed poorly,[3] social innovation has flourished. Social innovators of all kinds have stepped forward, offering meaningful new solutions to address nearly every aspect of the pandemic and its implications for human life. As is often the case with crises that impose enormous upheaval and pain, stories of extraordinary community responses, brilliant new approaches to problem solving, and powerful collaborations have also emerged. Thus, Covid-19 provides a petri dish for the real-time study of social innovation—across products and services and across public, private, and social sectors—needed to reach global scale quickly while offering important lessons for the discipline of social innovation itself as we move beyond the pandemic.

BIOGRAPHY

STEVE DAVIS currently serves as a senior strategic adviser and the interim director of the China Country Office at the Bill & Melinda Gates Foundation. He is also a lecturer at the Stanford Graduate School of Business, a Distinguished Fellow at the World Economic Forum, and a member of the Council on Foreign Relations. He serves as cochair of the World Health Organization's Digital Health Technical Advisory Group and is a member of numerous boards and advisory committees. He is the former president and CEO of PATH, a leading global health innovation organization; former Director of Social Innovation at McKinsey & Company, a global consultancy; former CEO of Corbis, a digital media pioneer; and former attorney at the law firm now known as K&LGates.

EXECUTIVE SUMMARY

While the tragedies of the global Covid-19 pandemic continue to unfold, many insights from the crisis are already being revealed. The pandemic generated enormous opportunities for social innovators, with many critical needs translating into brilliant products and services across every dimension of the crisis. This chapter focuses particularly on the lessons learned in digital health innovation, highlighting both positive trends that should be strengthened and celebrated and challenges that need to be addressed, particularly the incoherency of the global digital health ecosystem and its nascent policy framework, which hindered rather than enhanced the impact of social innovation during the pandemic.

This chapter will explore some of the opportunities, challenges, and lessons learned regarding social innovation during the Covid-19 global pandemic. While these perspectives are constrained by the fact that the pandemic continues to evolve, making it premature to fully evaluate the impact of each innovation, there is already an abundance of data and case studies to allow researchers to begin to unravel their results. To provide concrete examples and insights, this chapter focuses on social innovations in the digital space pertaining to global health, the subset with which I am most familiar, yet many of the same lessons could be extrapolated and applied to pandemic-generated advances in online education, financial services, food security, job development, and other social endeavors. The chapter's themes center on a vibrant moment, created in the wake of inarguable tragedy, for social innovators to rapidly design and scale community-based solutions to answer acute and immediate challenges. Many of the themes go beyond the "black swan" conditions of a once-in-a-century pandemic and have relevance for future social innovators in other contexts and endeavors. I hope that lessons from these experiences will positively impact the broad field of social innovation for many years to come.

Digital Health Social Innovations

Covid-19 was the first global crisis in which such a broad repertoire of digital solutions became essential for responding to the disaster. As such, it can be seen as the world's first "digital pandemic," one that spotlighted the role of digital and data innovations in achieving social impact. The very nature of the pandemic response—requiring ubiquitous social distancing, massive remote capabilities, and the rapid delivery of complex health solutions at scale—bodes well for digital innovators. At first, during mandated "shelter in place" phases of the pandemic, online shopping became the only reliably safe method for purchasing daily goods, including groceries. Zoom and its ilk grew up quickly, moving from tech novelties to daily tools for business meetings, virtual weddings and funerals, cocktail parties, and family dinner and game nights. Schools and universities adapted to provide online education at a scale never seen before, accelerating the long path toward broad-based online learning. Social media engagement reunited families, Amazon flourished (with profits doubling to more than $5 billion over the previous year[4]), and online gaming increased like wildfire. Many leading tech stocks saw growth of 100 to 400 percent.[5]

Nowhere was the power of this digital transformation more apparent than in our engagement with the health crisis itself. Almost everyone with an internet connection was tracking data visualizations of "flattening the curve," while thousands of apps helped us battle the disease itself—teaching and testing people, monitoring temperatures, tracing movement of the sick, and adding depth to our understanding of the illness's spread. Artificial intelligence (AI) predicted new hotspots, which improved our ability to get ahead of Covid-19, even as it helped accelerate drug and vaccine trials.

All this ferment opened extraordinary possibilities for social innovators, and they stepped up. Across the world, visionaries from large companies, public agencies and nonprofits, startups, and research organizations raised their hands to join with social entrepreneurs, individual technologists, and hackers—all offering to help fight the pandemic. Many groups collaborated—breaching traditional boundaries between the public, private, and social sectors—to deploy new products and services. They conceived innovations aimed at attacking every aspect of the disease, from modeling its projected trajectory, to augmenting patient care, to better managing health systems and supplies.[6]

As cochair of the World Health Organization (WHO) Digital Health Technical Advisory Group[7] and a digital health adviser to many global organizations, I have been on the receiving end of this fire hose of proposed solutions and participated in shaping some new initiatives, among them the launch of a clearinghouse for digital and data tools, which became imperative as health and technology communities across the globe assembled a sprawling tech fusillade. The moment proved to be both thrilling and, at times, overwhelming: anyone with the ability to code seemed to have an idea and the desire to pitch in. Yet the nascency and deficits in social innovation models also revealed themselves in dramatic ways: the lack of integrated government response plans, the incoherency across multiple mechanisms, unclear or nonexistent normative policies, and inadequate resources for sustainable impact created considerable obstacles to realizing the impact of these innovations.

In total, this year of blistering digital solutions presented important insights about the huge potential for social innovation during a crisis. Simultaneously, Covid-19 also made clear the challenges of shaping, deploying, and scaling innovation during a fast-moving moment in history. Indeed, the proposition that even the smartest social innovation can flourish and reach the people that truly need it in an uncoordinated, unregulated, and underfinanced ecosystem was severely tested, and arguably it failed.

Broad Dimensions of Social Innovation

Not surprisingly, social innovations[8] generated during the Covid-19 pandemic showed up across every dimension—from early pandemic warning and surveillance tools to new models for testing and treatment; dashboards for tracking data collection and population health management; platforms for handling the challenges of stay-at-home orders; methods for rebooting regional economies; systems for creating immunization yellow cards; and visualizations to predict new outbreaks. Among the most meaningful digital health innovations in 2020 were the spectacular rise in adoption of at-home lab tests, including point-of-care, digitally driven Covid-19 tools; embedded smartwatches and other wearables, including electrocardiograms and other detectors for underlying conditions; the vast use of telemedicine (82 percent of Americans employed such services in 2020); remote mental health services ("telepsychology") supporting growing anxiety and mental health in the pandemic; and artificial intelligence in supporting diagnostics and population modeling.[9] The variety and richness of these innovations will surely be among the most positive outcomes of the crisis; while many of these ideas were driven by Covid-19 specifically, they advanced all these categories significantly.

But none of these advances are useful unless they can be realized at scale, as I discussed in chapter 7 of this volume, on taking social innovation to scale. In talking about methods to ensure that level of broad uptake,[10] a simple framework borrowed from business—the product-development value chain—is helpful for outlining the many different stages, actors, and activities involved in broad-based deployment. It is especially useful when diagnosing why an innovation becomes stuck on its journey toward scale. This value chain model traces the path of an invention from its original ideation and early research through various stages of development, and it provides a guideline for students and practitioners to think through the critical channels, partners, and risks (as well as possible mitigation scenarios) in taking a social innovation to scale. During the first year of the Covid-19 pandemic, each stage of this value chain framework became applicable to social innovations that were surging to the fore. Brand new ideas were generated (e.g., 3-D models and other mask tools; new apps for Covid-19 testing, tracing, and tracking; telemedicine), but others were effectively adapted and reshaped (e.g., converting diagnostic tools to Covid-19 use and redeploying population modeling methods and digital visualization capabilities to Covid-19), others moved quickly through proof-of-concept and regulatory hurdles (e.g., vaccines, diagnostics, and drugs), while still others were more about creating demand, implementing policies, and triggering effective behavior change to ensure scaling (mask wearing, telemedicine, remote diagnostic tools), until we had millions of people adopting multiple tools within a year.

New digital health responses to the pandemic were also notable for their creative collaborations. In recent decades, advances have often failed to scale successfully because of a go-it-alone, our-sector-can-solve-this mentality.[11] That mindset undercuts innovation wherever it originates, whether from the public, private, or social sectors, but during Covid-19, many of those old presumptions crumbled as necessity brought down walls dividing sectors. While private technology companies and for-profit social entrepreneurs led the way by dint of their sheer volume of resources, we saw innovation flowing across social sector organizations and government institutions around the world.[12] Key global organizations that are leading the global vaccine response, specifically Gavi, the vaccine alliance[13] and CEPI (Consortium of Epidemic Preparedness Innovations),[14] will be held out as exemplars of multisector partnerships and collaborations not only in responding to the crisis but also in developing sustainable capabilities and mechanisms for future global health improvements.

Because the Covid-19 crisis remains ongoing, it is difficult to identify obvious winners or prioritize among the many social innovations in digital health that have surfaced, but for the purpose of this chapter several important initiatives merit attention to illustrate what worked and what did not.

The efforts of social entrepreneurs either to create new products and services or retool their existing platforms to address issues generated by Covid-19 were impressive. The World Economic Forum initiated a Covid-19 Action Platform, not only to solicit the best ideas from the innovation community broadly but also to highlight their progress and requirements, with the ultimate goal of attracting more financing, technical assistance, and supportive partnerships for the best of the crop. From some three hundred submissions, the initial WEF Uplink COVID-19 Challenge Cohort issued a report featuring fifteen of the most promising social innovations culled through a competitive review process.[15]

Among those early-stage social innovations spotlighted by the WEF was the German company HelloBetter, a global pioneer in the field of digital mental health research and a leader in digital therapeutics for mental health.[16] HelloBetter offers scientifically validated treatments, all provided digitally, for a broad range of disorders, such as depression, insomnia, burnout, and anxiety. To refine its offerings for Covid-19 in particular, HelloBetter set up an initiative, "Calm through the Crisis," which offered free hotline-based psychological support, a moderated online community, free virtual office hours with a licensed therapist, and an online course targeting those suffering extreme stress because of the pandemic. HelloBetter was recognized as an intriguing model for its ability to pivot a proven platform toward a new challenge: increased mental health needs for a world in which office visits had suddenly become impossible. HelloBetter responded with its versatile and adaptive platform, and it is scaling rapidly. Since its founding in 2015, the company reports that it has subjected its approach to thirty-two randomized controlled trials, tripled the number of staff, and helped tens of thousands of people. It is now seeking additional funding, visibility, and mentorship to identify more applications, markets, and growth opportunities, all while measuring its social impact within a compressed time line.

Many other social enterprises have followed suit, tapping into their core competencies to address needs created by the pandemic. One of the leading social enterprises in digital health, Dimagi, retooled its Comm-Care platform to enable health systems to quickly build and deploy custom mobile applications for every phase of an effective Covid-19 response, from screening and contact tracing to patient monitoring and postcare support.[17] More locally focused solutions showed up across the world: Senegalese students created a "doctor car robot" to lower the risk of infection between patients and caregivers, and a Kenyan entrepreneur developed a wooden money sanitizer that cleans cash notes passed through a slot in the machine.[18] Hundreds more ideas and innovations fill a growing number of compendia and exchange sites serving the innovation community.[19] This list will continue to expand as Tech4-Covid Stream-a-thons[20] and other events, competitions, and initiatives accelerate.

Of course, digital tools and platforms from larger technology companies gained even more visibility. Among the most notable was an unprecedented collaboration between tech giants Google and Apple, which united to create proximity tracking software that state and local health authorities could use for contact tracing and exposure notification. This idea, heralded as a game changer, received widespread attention in large part because it offered proof that tools for public good could come from commercially oriented tech titans, who would work together when societal needs demanded. However, widespread uptake of the tool, announced in April 2020 and rapidly released just one month later, has been slow, primarily because it requires a significant level of Covid-19 testing in a given community (15–60 percent)[21] to be effective.[22] Political divisions coloring the US response to Covid-19 have further impeded the success of this innovation, as it relies on citizen confidence in data privacy and governance in an environment where the rules are unclear. Nonetheless, the Apple-Google partnership offers important lessons for avenues to pursue—and to correct for—in the middle of a crisis. Along parallel lines, Chinese tech giant Tencent created a suite of Covid-19-related tools on its WeChat platform that used AI to analyze billions of pandemic-related queries as a means of forecasting whether patients would become severely ill. It also supported citizens by guiding them through steps to safeguard their health. Tencent made the tool available through an open-source platform, and it has been adopted in India and elsewhere.[23]

The pandemic not only accelerated digital social innovations from entrepreneurs and large companies but also spurred notable innovations at a global level through large multisector collaborations. Two deserve mention for their potential impact and inherent challenges. The first is CommonPass, a promising idea aimed at enabling travel for business and other reasons. Created with the understanding that economies will get back on track only when people can move freely across borders, CommonPass uses a digital model to provide authorities access to confirmed lab records for each traveler (currently these log vaccinations; in the future, they may track antibodies). This is a digital version of the WHO's yellow card already in use by many countries to ensure that each person entering has received the proper immunizations (for yellow fever, cholera, and other widespread diseases). It was generated by the Common Project, a nonprofit public trust dedicated to building global support for trusted data sharing.[24] CommonPass, which is structuring its model with both a nonprofit and for-profit approach, represents a massive collaboration across public, private, and social sector leaders in digital health, epidemiology, data science, law, transportation, and national security. It is already piloting the system at selected international airports.[25]

CommonPass is not alone in undertaking this kind of effort. The government of Estonia, for example, has collaborated with the WHO on another approach to creating a digital vaccine record,[26] and more recently several multinational technology leaders have been investing in similar data tools and platforms.[27]

Here the product-development model for scaling innovation discussed earlier bears repeating. Weeks into the pandemic, the WHO recognized the plethora of digital tools and capabilities being developed from the supply side of the value chain, but there was considerable disconnect with demand, or community needs, at the other end, particularly in low-resource settings. Some places did not have the requisite infrastructure to take advantage of these social innovations. Others were facing stages of the pandemic not addressed by any of the newly available tools. Health authorities across the globe reported that they were being inundated with new ideas and digital instruments, with little capacity to effectively vet, review, source, or finance them. In some cases, health ministries were finding out about devices through Twitter. What all these governments and agencies needed was some sort of mechanism to identify, qualify, and price these digital innovations.

Many initiatives—including the WEF Covid-19 Action Platform discussed earlier and Tech4Covid, a California-based effort to gather and support entrepreneurial ideas—were created to address the problem of overabundance, but none were sufficient. The WHO designed its own effort, the Covid-19 Digital Clearinghouse,[28] to help health ministers and authorities identify tools qualified by its own panel as scalable and proven. That platform was launched in late 2020 and only recently demonstrated the role that normative authorities have in ensuring that the best social innovations reach communities in need. Particularly in a time of urgency and crisis, in order for brilliant innovations to have impact, a proven mechanism for distribution and a reliable set of underlying rules and regulatory standards are needed.

These examples represent the broad range of innovations, players, and activities spawned by the Covid-19 pandemic and, while quite diverse, they share some common themes. Almost every effort was executed through multisector partnerships, with private, public, and social sector players coming together to solve a social problem with a new approach, each demonstrating considerable agility in pivoting to the demands of the day. Given the scale and urgency of the crisis, which has so far sickened more than 100 million people, caused more than four million deaths, and hobbled economies around the globe, this cooperative approach is not surprising, but it is heartening and not to be taken for granted. It showed that there may be more capacity for social innovators to contribute than had been previously acknowledged. The response also underscored our interconnectedness; no longer could rich nations ignore global health problems, as has happened with malaria, where few in the United States or Europe are likely to know anyone who has died of the disease. With Covid-19, everyone experienced the pain of the pandemic in one form or another, and great innovations were generated from every corner of the globe.

What Worked: Impact and Opportunities

In creating a scorecard to evaluate the landscape of digital health social innovation since the start of the pandemic, several themes show up in the success column.

Volume and Intensity

First, and probably most important, was the sheer volume of innovation that emerged during the crisis. This was reflected not only in the number of new products and services but also in their variety, collaborative nature, and financial commitments generated (on social innovation during the pandemic, see also Singer, Memet, Kothari, and Bloom in chapter 14 of this volume). While it will take time to sort through the metrics and actual impact of all this activity, Covid-19 proved to be a heyday for social entrepreneurs and innovators. Germany led the way early, launching its #WeVsVirus online hackathon on March 20, 2020, just nine days after the WHO declared Covid-19 a global pandemic.[29] The response was overwhelming. More than 26,580 social innovators came together to tackle eight hundred Covid-19-related problems in everything from e-learning to neighborhood assistance, to crisis communications, to digitizing public services. The result was the largest government-sponsored hackathon in history. Over a single weekend, these inventors broke into teams and generated 1,494 project ideas. A jury of government officials, academics, and leaders from business and nonprofits chose twenty of the most promising solutions, and the German government launched a program to help develop them. The first tangible result, an online tool to help employers apply for labor grants, went live less than three weeks later.

Of course, many of these efforts will stumble or fail, others will not translate into sustainable projects, and the actual impact of these activities remains unclear, but the cast of players that stepped onto the global health stage during the pandemic has been transformational. They have already contributed new ideas, new engagement models, and refreshing new conversations about the business of health technologies. As one illustration of this extraordinary engagement, forty leading global organizations collectively supporting more than fifteen thousand social entrepreneurs have united to launch the COVID Response Alliance for Social Entrepreneurs to share knowledge, experience, and resources to coordinate and amplify social entrepreneurs' response to Covid-19 and future global health crises.[30]

Beyond ideas, enormous sums of money have been funneled toward digital innovation to confront the pandemic above and beyond the huge global financial commitments to biomedical research, development, and distribution. While realizing enormous financial gains during the pandemic, American digital multinationals all made significant contributions of money, talent, and resources to the response.[31] Google.org committed $100 million and technical expertise to support and scale solutions for immediate relief, long-term recovery, and future preparedness in communities affected by the spread of Covid-19, not to mention building new products and offering the services of hundreds of engineers to global health agencies.[32] Microsoft contributed not only tens of millions of dollars to help with digital skill training to help over twenty-five million people in the Covid-19 economy but also considerable pro bono support to the WHO and others, including its work on mobilizing AI for Covid-19.[33] Intel earmarked $50 million to advance pandemic response technologies, including innovations in online learning.[34] Similar contributions have been made by Facebook, Amazon, Tata, Econet, Tencent, Alibaba, and other players around the world. The Bill & Melinda Gates Foundation promised $250 million to help Africa and South Asia scale their Covid-19 detection and treatment systems while supporting the development of new diagnostics and treatments.[35] After Germany's #WeVsVirus hackathon, three thousand companies said they would be willing to support the winning innovations.[36]

Collaborations

In addition to the volume of innovation and financial support, the pandemic revealed an important trend toward more-effective collaboration among partners within and across sectors. The digital health community came together in unprecedented ways, with United Nations diplomats rolling up their sleeves to work with health experts, corporate leaders, startup incubators, and investors. Through such cooperative efforts as the CommonPass and WHO clearinghouse, social innovators learned a great deal about how to effectively marry supply-side ideas to demand on the ground while building quicker consensus on needs and shaping new cross-sector initiatives. We are already seeing global partnerships forged in the pandemic targeting issues and opportunities that will prevail after the virus is suppressed. The CoWIN digital tool and systems serving as the backbone of India's effort to vaccinate the country promise to address data and health issues for the broader health system.[37] One hopes that, moving forward, this legacy of collaboration between the public, private, and social sectors—and a resulting appreciation for the variety of resources and capabilities each brings to the table—will change the course of social innovation forever.

Scaling

The global spread and vast impact of Covid-19 also demonstrated how essential scaling is to every successful innovation, as discussed in chapter 7. Unlike advances celebrated for brilliant design or ingenious ideas, with little attention paid to their broad impact or sustainability, the breadth of the pandemic meant that any innovation's ability to scale became a critical criterion. One of the first questions asked by any health authority or multinational addressing Covid-19 was, Can this idea scale rapidly, and how? There was also recognition, already learned the hard way through fumbles during the earlier Ebola crisis, that introducing and scaling innovation amid a pandemic is challenging, to put it lightly. In low-resource settings, changing systems or adopting new tools is difficult enough in everyday circumstances, and doubly so during a health emergency. But, as Germany illustrated with its hackathon, rapid scaling is doable. Apple and Google were also able to launch their collaboration regarding contact-tracing technology within two months of conceiving it.[38] As Covid-19 vaccines increasingly become available and governments around the globe take on the unprecedented task of rapidly immunizing much of the world's population, the lessons of rapid scaling could not be more important. Digital health tools and health data management developed during the crisis period, such as India's CoWin solution, are greatly aiding this mass immunization movement and will likely serve as digital platforms for other health services.

Agility

Finally, the agility of the social innovation community during Covid-19 provides hope for the field well beyond this immediate crisis. We have already witnessed purpose-driven initiatives, companies, entrepreneurs, and social sector organizations pivoting to meet demands of the moment. Many foundations, investors, and social sector leaders rapidly redeployed their assets. Digital innovators retooled their products to meet the needs of those suffering, whether through platforms such as HelloBetter, technology such as that devised by Apple and Google, or the Indian company Intelehealth, which connects remote patients with frontline health providers and added a Covid-19 response to its offerings in record time. Dimagi quickly retooled its CommCare platform for Indian community health workers to become a leading option for testing and tracing across US cities and states.

What Didn't Work: Disruptions and Challenges

While all those successes merit celebration, and it is hoped they will be strengths the field can build on, the other side of the scorecard shows how much more work is necessary to realize the potential of social innovation.

While the volume of initiatives and good will was promising, Covid-19 exposed deep challenges within our nascent digital health ecosystem. Many governments, health systems, and users remain overwhelmed by the sheer number of available tools and intriguing ideas. Worse, there is little consistency in standards for privacy, interoperability, and regulation. The end result is a cacophony of good intentions and meaningful contributions that threatens to drown out the best ideas in a din of inefficiency.

Incoherency

Foremost among these challenges is the dearth of mechanisms to link supply and demand in a timely, effective, and financially viable manner. Hence, we repeatedly see innovations fail because of a poor fit between a product and its target market. This manifests in inventions designed without an understanding of the regulatory pathways necessary to gain government approval, initiatives that do not adhere to standards of interoperability, or bilateral deals lacking a usable interface between the health and innovation communities. Frequently, the lack of transparency and visibility contributed to the confusion and incoherency. A paucity of information about particular tools, capabilities, underlying technologies, pricing, and evidence of effectiveness meant that people were relying on word of mouth more than reliable and consistent mechanisms. This generally contributed to the growing digital divide, where those having more resources and capabilities were able to undertake the due diligence and assessments, while lower-resourced systems were often left to sort out many choices without much assistance or direction, frequently to their peril.

Inconsistency in Policies and Governance

Underlying these problems, of course, are the complex political dimensions of digital health and data, which lead to inconsistencies and information vacuums. We lack clear global, or in many cases even national, policies regarding data ownership and governance, or rules about interoperability and data sharing. Until it is addressed comprehensively, this gap between our surging technological capabilities and comparatively weak regulatory muscles will continue to impede social innovation's impact opportunities.

Inequality and Access

Already, there is clear data showing how the Covid-19 pandemic widened inequity across multiple dimensions.[39] Covid-19 disproportionately impacted the health and economies of the poorest, most vulnerable communities, but the digital innovation response—while notable for its frugality—still failed to reach many of those populations. This is a systemic problem; there is no clear mechanism to assess, provide, or fund innovations that could aid many of the world's poorest people. It is also an infrastructure challenge; lack of internet or computers, spotty phone or electrical service, and the need for training all deepen existing divides.

Unsustainable Economics

Finally, the economics of social innovation have become impossible to ignore. Many exciting ideas and offers were put forth during the crisis but with limited understanding of what it would take to sustain those efforts. The challenge of rapid scaling meant that many tools could not be priced for the long term, adding to ongoing struggles regarding the private sector's engagement in public health initiatives. While donors and investors have stepped forward—the WHO reports more than $1 billion in donations—we still lack mechanisms, nationally and globally, to ensure that digital public goods are available and financed for the long term in the same ways we have funded the vaccine for polio or the treatment of malaria.

Lessons for the Future

It may be tempting to view social innovation during the Covid-19 period in a bubble, ignoring its impact beyond this specific moment, but that shortsighted outlook would be a missed opportunity for the field and, most importantly, the people whose lives could be improved by its advances. Even taking a narrow perspective, as the aforementioned CSIS report acknowledges, digital innovation will be critical to our preparedness and response to the next disease outbreak.

Despite the challenges, there are some outstanding examples of Covid-19 digital social innovations that are working, scaling, and reaching the most needed, from which we can gain important insights.

With strong government alignment (or even sponsorship) and deep relations to community organizations working on the ground, solutions such as the Tencent and Apple-Google tracing applications or the Johns Hopkins University Covid-19 Dashboard[40] are already being acknowledged as best of class in their utility, relevance, and reach.[41] In sum, we must apply the lessons of Covid-19 to be well positioned for the future.

Foremost, we need to underscore the role that social innovators can play in times of crisis and ensure that policy makers, investors, and social sector funders understand this field's ability to contribute. In doing so, we should devote as much thought to the innovations as we do to the entrepreneurs and enterprises behind them. This means broadening our aperture to support ideas with long-term social impact that come from a wide range of actors, and it necessitates building mechanisms to source, select, and advance the best of them. This is particularly important as most innovations scale through a series of handoffs (acquisitions, licenses, distribution deals) to other partners, which social enterprises traditionally have been reluctant to undertake. Critically, this selection must include application to health or well-being solutions that will survive the pandemic.

In terms of digital innovation specifically, we have witnessed frustrating pitfalls when products and services that could have significant social impact are not managed through a coherent, policy-driven framework. The upshot is that the best tools may fail to reach those markets that need them, or they wither because the commercial interests of a for-profit innovator have not been properly accounted for. What we need is a global framework to shape and implement these approaches so that innovators, health authorities, investors, and citizens all benefit. We already have models in global health to consult for this, including Gavi, the vaccine alliance, and CEPI, the Coalition for Epidemic Preparedness Innovations. Now we must develop an infrastructure to support similar policies regarding digital public goods.

To be better prepared for the next pandemic, governments, multilateral organizations, and leaders from the private and social sectors must address five areas of weakness that present policy and program opportunities.

First, embrace the concept enshrined in the United Nations Digital Roadmap to approach digital innovation as a global public good while protecting the interests of innovators.

Second, clarify the rules of the road for more consistency on policies regarding information privacy, platform interoperability, data governance, and ethics.

Third, design a means akin to the global vaccine alliance for making qualified digital tools accessible to those in vulnerable communities, so often left behind in health innovation, through a mechanism that provides more funding, screening, advocacy, distribution, and support.

Fourth, develop initiatives, technical assistance, and incentives to scale those innovations with the broadest utility rather than focusing on ideas aimed only at the few.

Finally, ensure substantial and sustainable financing through multisector investment schemes that have clear value propositions and metrics for success.

The good news is that there are groups already engaging on these fronts, from global multilaterals such as the WHO and the UN's Digital Compact to efforts such as the Lancet and Financial Times Commission on Governing Health Futures 2030[42] and Transform Health Coalition.[43] One of the most intriguing opportunities—the Trinity Challenge—comes out of Cambridge's Trinity College and supports policy and data governance initiatives to prepare for the next pandemic.[44] Central to all these efforts is the engagement of industry, government, academics, and social sector organizations, whose contributions and alignment will be critical as we shape the rules for the future. As with most of the world's biggest challenges, multisector models and partnerships will increasingly pave the way for effective and long-lasting solutions.

Conclusion

Could we have developed and deployed better social innovations to tackle the Covid-19 pandemic with more forethought and coordination ahead of the crisis, during a moment of relative global calm? Yes, but the digital innovation challenges revealed by the pandemic are good problems to have. We now possess more potential solutions for fighting health emergencies than we know what to do with, and new social innovations are being invented every day. They promise to help us now and far into the future, provided we choose wisely, listen carefully, explain honestly, and widely share the best of these tools. All the ingenuity in the world will not get us where we need to be without a reliable means for evaluating, regulating, disseminating, and funding innovation, and we need to build that infrastructure now—before the next pandemic.

Covid-19 has demonstrated a counterintuitive proposition for many early-stage social innovators, who often believe that government regulation and engagement impede innovation. As we continue to manage the pandemic response and consider future health crises, however, the lesson from this moment might be that the lack of proper frameworks, rules, and mechanisms hindered the digital health ecosystem's ability to enable the advancement of new innovations, scale them, and make sure they reach the people who need them the most. Indeed, the lack of regulation and rules impeded innovation, rather than the other way around.

In the spirit of "let no crisis go to waste," Covid-19 represents an opportunity to better coordinate strategies ensuring that the lifesaving impact of social innovation can flourish at scale. The pandemic has focused the world's collective attention like nothing since World War II. Our response to that earlier crisis—creation of the United Nations—provided an important framework for international cooperation. Nearly a century later, we need a new arena, this time focused on digital diplomacy. And the stakes have never been higher. To meet them, social innovators must be as innovative on policy as we are with products.

FOR FURTHER READING

We are only beginning to unravel the lessons from the Covid-19 pandemic, but several early summaries and analyses include Francois Bonnici and Pavitra Raja, "Six Ways Social Innovators Are Responding to the COVID-19 Pandemic" (World Economic Forum, May 25, 2020); Ann Mei Chang, "Beyond Survival: Five Keys to Unlock Social Innovation Amidst the COVID-19 Crisis" (Bridgespan, March 25, 2020); Ralph Hamann, Jenny Soderbergh, Annika Surmeier, Christing Fyvie, Thanyani Ramarumo, Mandy Rapson, Nadia Sitas, and Ashley Newell, "Turning Short-Term Crisis Relief into Longer-Term Social Innovation" (*Stanford Social Innovation Review*, November 30, 2020); and Jeff Coughlin and Alana Lever, "COVID-19 and the Digital Health Policy Impact" (Health Information and Management Systems Society, October 19, 2020).

Notes

1. J. Stephen Morrison, "Ending the Cycle of Crisis and Complacency in U.S. Global Health Security," Center for Strategic and International Studies, November 20, 2019, https://www.csis.org/analysis/ending-cycle-crisis-and-complacency-us-global-health-security.

2. Covid-19 Dashboard, Center for Systems Science and Engineering, John Hopkins University, July 31, 2021, https://gisanddata.maps.arcgis.com/apps/opsdashboard/index.html#/bda7594740fd40299423467b48e9ecf6. The WHO also has a scorecard of deaths and cases, all presumed to be undercounted.

3. Numerous reports are emerging regarding the difficulties different governments and multilaterals experienced in responding to the pandemic. See "COVID-19 Pandemic," Center for Strategic and International Studies, https://www.csis.org. The WHO initiated an independent panel to assess its own response in September 2020. See "The Independent Panel for Pandemic Preparedness & Response," https://theindependentpanel.org.

4. Cameron Faulkner, "Amazon Doubled Its Profit during a Pandemic," *The Verge*, July 30, 2020, https://www.theverge.com/2020/7/30/21348368/amazon-q2-2020-earnings-COVID-19-coronavirus-jeff-bezos.

5. Tae Kim, "COVID-19 Supercharged 2020's Tech Winners. What about 2021?," Bloomberg.com, December 31, 2020, https://www.bloomberg.com/opinion/articles/2020-12-31/zoom-shopify-and-nvidia-were-tech-winners-in-2020-what-will-win-in-2021.

6. Hamza Mudassir, "COVID-19 Will Fuel the Next Wave of Innovation," *Entrepreneur*, March 16, 2020, https://www.entrepreneur.com/article/347669.

7. World Health Organization, "WHO Expert Panel on Digital Health Meets for First Time," October 25, 2019, https://www.who.int/news/item/25-10-2019-who-expert-panel-on-digital-health-meets-for-first-time.

8. For the purposes of this chapter, a social innovation is a product or service that is a significant or disruptive change in model or approach; is designed for positive social impact, usually touching vulnerable or low-resource communities; will have enduring and sustained positive impact; and almost always involves some multisector collaboration (across public, private, and social sector organizations).

9. See Bertalan Mesco, Director of the Medical Futurist Institute, "Winners and Losers of 2020 in Digital Health," LinkedIn, November 30, 2020, https://www.linkedin.com/pulse/winners-losers-2020-digital-health-bertalan-mesk%C3%B3-md-phd/.

10. I teach the course Impact: Taking Social Innovation to Scale at the Stanford Graduate School of Business. A framework for it is elaborated in chapter 7 of this volume.

11. Aleem Walji, "Opinion: Innovation Often Fails to Scale—Maybe We Can Fix It," Devex, February 15, 2019, https://www.devex.com/news/opinion-innovation-often-fails-to-scale-maybe-we-can-fix-it-94311.

12. Many new public, private, and social sector digital health innovations emerged during the pandemic. See Lauren Horwitz, "How New Digital Health

Services Emerged from Covid-19 Crisis," *Internet of Things World Today*, July 28, 2021, https://www.iotworldtoday.com/2021/07/28/how-new-digital-health-services-emerged-from-covid-19-crisis/.

13. See Gavi, the vaccine alliance, www.gavi.org.

14. See Consortium of Epidemic Preparedness Innovations (CEPI), www.cepi.net.

15. Andrin Schwere, "These 15 Innovations Are Helping Us Fight COVID-19 and Its Aftermath," *World Economic Forum*, September 15, 2020, https://www.weforum.org/agenda/2020/09/these-15-innovations-are-helping-us-to-fight-COVID-19-and-its-aftermath.

16. HelloBetter Corona Online Course, "Calm through the Crisis," July 31, 2021, https://hellobetter.de/en/online-courses/corona/.

17. Dimagi, "Digital Solutions for Covid-19 Response," July 21, 2021, https://www.dimagi.com/COVID-19/.

18. "Coronavirus: Ten African Innovations to Help Tackle COVID-19," *BBC News*, August 15, 2020, https://www.bbc.com/news/world-africa-53776027.

19. For example, see USAID and Global Innovation Exchange's Covid-19 Innovation Hub, https://covid19innovationhub.org/, or the site https://www.covidinnovations.com/, and the Johns Hopkins University and Bill & Melinda Gates Foundation's (my current employer) report, Brandon Howard and the Johns Hopkins Bloomberg School of Public Health, "Johns Hopkins Researchers Publish Assessment of Digital Solutions for COVID-19 Response in Low- and Middle-Income Countries," July 31, 2020, https://www.jhsph.edu/departments/international-health/news/johns-hopkins-researchers-publish-assessment-of-digital-solutions-for-COVID-19-response-in-low-and-middle-income-countries.html.

20. International Game Developers Association, Tech4Covid Stream-a-thon, October 25, 2020, https://igda.org/event/tech4covid-stream-a-thon/2020-20-25/.

21. Kif Leswing, "States Are Finally Starting to Use the Covid-Tracking Tech Apple and Google Built—Here's Why," *CNBC*, October 4, 2020, https://www.cnbc.com/2020/10/03/covid-app-exposure-notification-apple-google.html.

22. As of December 2020, eighteen US states had incorporated some of the Apple Google software into their early alert apps. See "Apple and Google's COVID Contact Tracing Is Finally Coming to California," *The Verge*, December 7, 2020, https://www.theverge.com/2020/12/7/22159842/apple-google-covid-contact-tracing-tech-california.

23. Tencent, "Tencent Cloud Launches International Anti-Covid-19 Service Package," April 14, 2020, https://www.tencent.com/en-us/articles/2201033.html.

24. CommonPass, July 31, 2021, https://commonpass.org.

25. Miriam Berger, "Airlines Launch Trial of an App that Would Verify Travelers' Coronavirus Test Results," *The Washington Post*, October 7, 2020, https://www.washingtonpost.com/travel/2020/10/07/united-cathay-commonpass-covid/.

26. World Health Organization, "Estonia and WHO to Work Together on Digital Health and Innovation," July 10, 2020, https://www.euro.who.int/en/countries/estonia/news/news/2020/10/estonia-and-who-to-work-together-on-digital-health-and-innovation.

27. Jay Peters, "Microsoft, Salesforce, and Oracle Are Working on Digital Vaccination Records," *The Verge*, January 14, 2021, https://www.theverge.com/2021/1/14/22231187/microsoft-salesforce-oracle-digital-vaccination-records.

28. World Health Organization, "Digital Clearing House," July 31, 2021, https://who-dch.powerappsportals.com/en/help/.

29. Thomas Gegenhuber, "Countering Coronavirus with Open Social Innovation, *Stanford Social Innovation Review*, April 29, 2020, https://ssir.org/articles/entry/countering_coronavirus_with_open_social_innovation#.

30. World Economic Forum, "Covid Response Alliance for Social Entrepreneurs," July 31, 2021, https://www.weforum.org/covid-alliance-for-social-entrepreneurs.

31. Johnny Evans, "17+ Ways Apple Is Responding to Coronavirus," Computerworld, March 23, 2020, https://www.computerworld.com/article/3533361/17-ways-apple-is-responding-to-coronavirus.html.

32. Google, "Covid-19 Response," July 31, 2021, https://www.google.com/intl/en_us/covid19/.

33. Brad Smith, "Microsoft Launches Initiative to Help 25 Million People Worldwide Acquire the Digital Skills Needed in a Covid-19 Economy," Microsoft, July 2, 2020, https://blogs.microsoft.com/blog/2020/06/30/microsoft-launches-initiative-to-help-25-million-people-worldwide-acquire-the-digital-skills-needed-in-a-COVID-19-economy/.

34. Intel, "Intel Commits $50 Million with Pandemic Response Technology Initiative to Combat Coronavirus," April 7, 2020, https://newsroom.intel.com/news/intel-commits-technology-response-combat-coronavirus/#gs.je7i91.

35. Bill & Melinda Gates Foundation, "Bill & Melinda Gates Foundation Expands Commitment to Global Covid-19 Response, Calls for International Collaboration to Protect People Everywhere from the Virus," April 15, 2020, https://www.gatesfoundation.org/Media-Center/Press-Releases/2020/04/Gates-Foundation-Expands-Commitment-to-COVID-19-Response-Calls-for-International-Collaboration. I am a part-time employee of the Gates Foundation.

36. Gegenhuber, "Countering Coronavirus with Open Social Innovation."

37. Press Trust of India, "Govt Starts Contest for Strengthening Digital Network Platform for Covid-19 Vaccine Distribution," YourStory, December 23, 2020, https://yourstory.com/2020/12/govt-starts-contest-strengthening-digital-network-platform-covid19-vaccine/amp.

38. Christina Farr, "How a Handful of Apple and Google Employees Came Together to Help Health Officials Trace Coronavirus," CNBC, April 28, 2020, https://www.cnbc.com/2020/04/28/apple-iphone-contact-tracing-how-it-came-together.html.

39. See Joe Myers, "5 Things COVID-19 Has Taught Us about Inequality," World Economic Forum, August 18, 2020, https://www.weforum.org/agenda/2020/08/5-things-covid-19=has-taught-us-about-inequality/.

40. Covid-19 Dashboard, Center for Systems Science and Engineering, John Hopkins University, July 31, 2021, https://gisanddata.maps.arcgis.com/apps/opsdashboard/index.html#/bda7594740fd40299423467b48e9ecf6.

41. Joel Cornell, "The Best COVID-19 Tracking Apps and Websites," *How-To Geek*, April 20, 2020, https://howtogeek.com/668325/the-best-covid-19-tracking -apps-and-websites.

42. *Governing Health Futures 2030: Growing Up in a Digital World*, The Lancet & Financials Times Commission, July 31, 2021, https://www .governinghealthfutures2030.org/.

43. Transform Health Coalition, https://transformhealthcoalition.org.

44. The Trinity Challenge, www.thetrinitychallenge.org, for which I am a trustee.

14

Human and Planetary Health

Covid-19 and a New Frontier for Social Innovation

Sara J. Singer, Sevda Memet, Suruchi Kothari, and Gordon Bloom

The Covid-19 pandemic presented the world with an unparalleled set of problems, a more detailed account of which is provided by Steve Davis in chapter 13 of this volume. Here, we reiterate that the consequences of this pandemic have been devastating, socially and economically, but have also presented important opportunities for social innovation to address the urgency and scale of the fast-moving crisis. In 2020 alone, over ninety-three million people were infected worldwide, resulting in over two million deaths.[1] Beyond the human tragedy produced by this virus, the pandemic has both short-term and longer-term ramifications. Several countries went into "lockdown," transforming personal lives overnight, and many businesses closed, while others faced vast disruptions to services, supply chains, operations, and cash flow.[2] Layoffs and stock market volatility ensued, and we entered the most extensive global recession since the Great Depression.[3]

The magnitude of the disruption wrought by the pandemic surpassed the capabilities and capacity of governments to address this challenge alone, giving rise to collaborations—by necessity and design—with actors from the private and nonprofit sectors.[4] Notwithstanding the initial governmental response, large gaps remained, exacerbated by leadership failures, including failures to address immediate needs related to treating the disease and stemming its spread. Furthermore, there were gaps in medium- and longer-term needs related not only to the disease itself but also to a vast array of consequences of the pandemic, including

BIOGRAPHIES

SARA J. SINGER is professor of medicine at the Stanford School of Medicine and professor of organizational behavior (by courtesy) at the Stanford Graduate School of Business. At Stanford, she leads the Health Leadership, Innovation, and Organization Labs, is associate director of the Clinical Excellence Research Center, and is a faculty affiliate of Stanford Health Policy (previously the Center for Health Policy/Center for Primary Care and Outcomes Research), the Freeman Spogli Institute for International Studies, the Center for Innovation in Global Health, the Woods Institute for the Environment, and the Stanford Medicine Center for Improvement.

SEVDA MEMET, MD, pursued a joint master's degree in business administration and public policy at the Stanford Graduate School of Business as a Knight-Hennessy Scholar. Prior to Stanford, she worked as a medical doctor in hematology-oncology and rare diseases in the Romanian public healthcare system.

SURUCHI KOTHARI, MD, is a primary care physician who completed her residency training at Imperial College, London, in the United Kingdom. At Touch Surgery, she created the Virtual Residency Program and later, at OssoVR, the Osso Training Network, democratizing access to surgical training by leveraging digital and virtual-reality technologies. These solutions have been adopted in over two hundred US residency programs. Kothari is currently chief of staff to the CEO at Agilon Health.

GORDON BLOOM founded the Social Entrepreneurship Collaboratory (SE Labs) at Stanford, Harvard, and Princeton. At Stanford, he is director of the Social Entrepreneurship and Innovation Lab (SE Lab)-Human & Planetary Health; faculty fellow at the Center for Innovation in Global Health and lecturer in the School of Medicine, Division of Primary Care and Population Health, in the Department of Medicine; and affiliate at Stanford Health Policy (previously Center for Health Policy/Center for Primary Care and Outcomes Research) and the Freeman Spogli Institute for International Studies.

EXECUTIVE SUMMARY

The Covid-19 pandemic has challenged traditional definitions of social entrepreneurship and innovation. In this chapter, we highlight the interconnected problems the pandemic entails, how social innovators from traditional and nontraditional backgrounds responded, and implications for a new frontier for social innovation. Covid-19 raised awareness of interconnections between human and planetary health and the ongoing need to sustain balance between them. To fully address needs created by the pandemic and prevent the next one, social innovation must come from many actors working in concert to address social, economic, and environmental factors for immediate and longer-term challenges of human and planetary health.

economic and social repercussions. The multitude and unprecedented scale of needs increased demand for the social economy and catalyzed a tremendous response.[5] Social entrepreneurs and innovators from the nonprofit and for-profit sectors, including a constellation of nontraditional actors, stepped in at the start of the crisis to fill unaddressed and unresolved gaps.

The global pandemic raises questions about several assumptions underpinning traditional definitions of social entrepreneurship and innovation, including the necessity for social innovators to have only prosocial motivations and access to functioning markets in order to solve social problems.[6] Covid-19 spurred evolution in the source and form of social innovation, engaging large numbers of nontraditional as well as traditional entrepreneurs, often repurposing resources in markets that had become unstable or had ceased to function. As a global crisis, the Covid-19 pandemic required more than ever that social innovators "think globally while acting locally" by customizing strategies and solutions for local conditions. The global need for coordination and communication frequently required that social innovators initiate new arrangements while also serving as connections for cross-sector solutions. The multifaceted and complex challenges brought on by this crisis have led to a transformation of the role of social entrepreneurs.

This chapter reviews the impact of Covid-19, highlighting the interconnected problems it entails, how social innovators responded to them, and the implications for a new frontier for social innovation.

We contend that the Covid-19 pandemic created needs and revealed gaps that spurred innovation. Social innovators assessed comparative advantage and self-authorized bold and rapid action, despite risks. Success factors included their inherent agility and ability to implement solutions. The large-scale response required individual initiatives by traditional and nontraditional actors as well as networked, cross-sector collaborative solutions, where governments and the private and social sectors came together to address unprecedented needs. This pandemic also raised awareness of the interconnections between human and planetary health (that is, how our planet's environmental ecosystem and its disruption impact human health), the delicate balance that exists between human and planetary well-being, and the ongoing need to maintain this balance sustainably.[7] The interconnected nature of the disruption created by the pandemic invites a new frontier for social innovation and collective action. To fully address needs created by the pandemic and prevent the next one, social innovation must come from many actors—a collective "collaboratory" of nonprofit, for-profit, solo, and networked individuals, organizations, and governments—working consciously and unconsciously in concert to address social, economic, and environmental factors as the context for addressing immediate and longer-term challenges of human and planetary health.

Covid-19: A Perfect Storm

An assessment of the causes and consequences of the global pandemic provides insight for rethinking social innovation in this new context. A broader perspective allows us to understand Covid-19 as a globally widespread infectious disease resulting from a perfect storm created and propelled by social, economic, and environmental factors. Viewed in this way, the pandemic demonstrates the importance of the interconnections between human and planetary factors. These connections are apparent in the origin of the pandemic and its repercussions.

Originally, Covid-19 was a zoonotic virus, which means it was transmitted from wild animals to humans. Factors enabling animal-to-human transmission of Covid-19 and other zoonotic viruses include a complex interplay of planetary changes: the destruction of animal ecosystems, global warming, and risky human behavior, including illegal wildlife trading.[8] These linkages demonstrate that human health is dependent on the health of our ecosystems, the availability of natural resources, and the conservation of biological systems. Diminishing biodiversity through deforestation and urban growth is increasing the risk of disease pandemics like Covid-19, and a loss of biodiversity results in fewer animal species, with those remaining tending to be those that carry pathogens to humans.[9] Along with Covid-19, HIV, Ebola, SARS, and rabies, there are other viruses transmitted from animals to humans. The US Centers for Disease Control and Prevention (CDC) estimates three of four emerging infectious diseases in humans have animal origins, and they are becoming increasingly common.[10] The active destruction of natural systems over decades, where our societies' activities and structures have disrupted the fine balance between humans and the natural world, impacts our planet's health and ultimately affects human health.

The repercussions of Covid-19 have been vast and multifaceted and demonstrate—like no other event in recent history—how these human and planetary challenges are interconnected. Not only has the pandemic challenged health systems globally, but its impact also created an economic crisis, exacerbated health and social inequities, and highlighted strengths and weaknesses in different forms of governance.

The response of health-care systems to Covid-19 has been heroic yet inadequate. Health-care systems worldwide increased their intensive care capacity, established testing sites, and developed Covid-19 units to isolate and care for patients.[11] Health delivery organizations sourced personal protective equipment and proactively sought private corporations' support to develop needed supplies. In the United Kingdom, high-end fashion brand Burberry manufactured medical masks and gowns to supply health-care providers.[12] In the United States, health-care systems partnered with Ford, Tesla, and General Motors, among others, to build ventilators.[13] Health-care systems vastly accelerated adoption of telehealth, enacting a large-scale shift in practice patterns, with telehealth visits accounting for 50 percent of patients in 2020 compared to 11 percent in 2019.[14]

However, Covid-19 also thwarted health systems' ability to care for patients. Hospitals canceled nonemergency, elective procedures.[15] Clinics postponed non-Covid-related care and non-Covid vaccinations while focusing on treating Covid-infected patients and preventing the virus's spread.[16] The reallocation of health-care services toward treating patients with Covid-19 disrupted care for patients with chronic diseases such as diabetes, hypertension, and cancer.[17] More than 80 percent of mental health patients saw their condition worsen, and 40 percent of US adults reported adverse effects of mental health or substance abuse because of the pandemic.[18] Hospitals and health-care systems faced catastrophic financial consequences in the wake of this virus.[19]

This health-care crisis engendered a far greater economic crisis. The pandemic response and national lockdown resulted in a considerable financial toll, which the International Monetary Fund has described as the worst global downturn since the Great Depression.[20] In the United States alone, this large-scale economic disruption, when measured in lost output and health reduction, is estimated to have cost over $16 trillion.[21]

The economic downturn widened existing inequalities, with disproportionate job losses for women, Blacks and ethnic minorities, and low-income workers.[22] The sectors hit worst included manufacturing, travel, transport, and retail.[23] Conversely, some sectors, notably Big Tech companies, including Apple, Facebook, Alphabet (Google), and Amazon, experienced substantial gains and an "earnings bonanza" during the Covid era.[24] These Big Tech companies not only weathered this storm but also took advantage of new opportunities and rapidly expanded, consolidating their market dominance.[25] Many predict that economic recovery will be highly variable, even after mass distribution of vaccines to prevent Covid-19 infection, with the hardest-hit sectors, including many small businesses, expected to require more than five years to recover, if they recover at all.[26]

People's vulnerability to Covid-19 also varied greatly based on social factors. Reports on the morbidity and mortality of Covid-19 demonstrated that those most adversely impacted were "racial/ethnic minorities, the elderly, the poor, and people with the lowest educational attainment."[27] Their poor outcomes have been attributed to endemic inequities, including poor housing, crowded and polluted neighborhoods, and inadequate access to affordable and nutritious food, putting a healthy diet out of reach.[28] Populations that experience these factors have increased risk of developing asthma, diabetes, hypertension, obesity, and heart disease, all of which increase the risk of severe illness from Covid-19.[29] Inequities and inadequacies in access to high-quality health care further exacerbated the impact of Covid-19 on these populations, increasing the likelihood of poor outcomes and even death.

Minority populations were also at increased risk of contracting Covid-19.[30] Factors associated with high risk of Covid-19 infection include residing in high-density living conditions in large urban centers. Unequal access to water—over thirty million Americans live in areas where water systems violate safety rules[31]—and poor sanitation reduced the capacity for some even to wash their hands. These minorities are also more likely to work in service industries that require their physical presence, making physical distancing less feasible.[32]

The tremendous death toll in the United States has also been attributed to deficiencies in governance. The US government's response to Covid-19 was considered by many both inconsistent and insufficient.[33] The Trump administration failed to acknowledge the threat of this virus, relayed contradictory messages about its risks, and provided unequal assistance across states.[34] The absence of clear guidance led to delays and a wide variation in responses by states and counties, which suffered delays in funding and supplies, as well as insufficient testing and tracing.[35] Some countries fared better than the United States, mainly because of their centralized leadership, while others owed their success to lessons learned during the SARS epidemic twenty years earlier.[36] For pandemic "first-timers," those who responded rapidly, aggressively, and in a coordinated manner (e.g., New Zealand) proved to be more successful in managing the pandemic.[37]

Notwithstanding the undisputedly enormous toll of Covid-19, some have suggested that the pandemic may present a "golden opportunity."[38] Global efforts to halt the virus's spread and the associated decline in economic activity have reduced air and ground travel as well as industrial activity, causing a corresponding fall in air pollution levels and improved water quality.[39] Covid-19 could force people to recognize that current forms of human behavior are unsustainable. The pandemic has given us an opportunity to build back better, toward a greener economy, by investing in efforts to reduce deforestation, halt the wildlife trade, increase decarbonization, and improve sustainability. We need to continue building toward a digital future, embracing telecommuting as a new norm and curtailing unnecessary travel. We must also acknowledge the importance of mental health as integral for our own individual well-being and that of our societies and economies.

Human and Planetary Health: A New Frontier for Social Innovation

The complex set of challenges that caused, and have resulted from, the pandemic demands attention. This perfect storm of interconnected social, economic, and environmental challenges constitutes a human and planetary crisis, and overcoming it will require social innovation at human and planetary scales. Such innovation must address social and economic determinants of health and the natural systems on which human health depends, as well as the immediate, medium-term, and longer-term needs of the human health and medical care systems.

Three brief examples illustrate the potential for social innovation at the frontier of human and planetary health. First, social innovators stemmed the spread of the Nipah virus, which, like Covid-19, originated with animals.[40] Highly virulent, Nipah kills up to 70 percent of people it infects. In Bangladesh, it spreads from bats through date palm sap to humans when they drink it. By introducing bamboo skirts that prevent the bats from contacting the sap, innovators eliminated the risk of Nipah transmission. Longer term, resolving the challenge will require preservation of natural habitats, biodiversity, and food resources so that wild animals prefer not to invade human settlements. Second, social innovators identified an opportunity to reduce deforestation by improving human health.[41] Investigation of illegal logging in Indonesia's tropical forests, which adversely impacts biodiversity, global temperatures, and human health, found expenses for desperately needed health care were the driving force. To stem deforestation, innovators formed a health clinic for the local community, offering discounts to people from villages that demonstrated community-wide reductions in logging and accepting as payment barter in the form of tree seedlings, handicrafts, and labor. After ten years of operation, the clinic has treated twenty-eight thousand patients, significantly reducing infectious and noncommunicable diseases, and illegal logging has declined by 70 percent compared to control sites. Third, social innovators are controlling mosquito-borne illnesses while improving economic opportunities for young people in Kenya.[42] As plastic and other trash accumulates in low-income urban areas, it becomes a medium for proliferating diseases such as the Dengue and Zika viruses. In Nairobi, a pilot program has created a business incubator to accelerate innovative ideas for sustainability. The first wave of local entrepreneurs and community members is exploring the viability of businesses using plastic trash as planters for flowers or seedlings, to make toys or play structures, and to make building materials for houses, with the aim of decreasing mosquitoes and trash accumulation, and generating income for innovators.

Observed Response to Covid-19: Emergence of a Social Innovation Ecosystem

To understand the potential for social innovation to meet the human and planetary health challenges presented by crises like Covid-19, we examine the actual response to the pandemic. We first take a broad view to understand the cross-sector ecosystem constituting the range of actors contributing social innovations to address the Covid-19 pandemic, how these social innovators emerged, and which challenges they sought to address. We then present examples of three specific types of social innovators in order to identify distinctions and commonalities among them. We then propose a *theory of change* for social innovation that addresses the Covid-19 pandemic in the context of human and planetary health. Our goal is to develop a better understanding of the model of cross-sector collective action, collaboration, and experimentation—the "collaboratory" of social innovation that has emerged to combat the pandemic and continues to develop. We hope that insights will help stakeholders identify opportunities for supporting development of a strong, sustainable ecosystem for social innovation and change and for ensuring attention not only to immediate human needs but also to longer-term environmental factors that will serve to mitigate and prevent future pandemics and protect the people and planet.

Broad View of Social Innovation in the Context of Covid-19

Our broad perspective highlights that the response to the crisis created by the Covid-19 pandemic was unprecedented in its speed and breadth, involving a multitude of innovators from various backgrounds and sectors. The ecosystem that rapidly emerged to address the challenges of Covid-19 includes social innovators from both traditional and nontraditional backgrounds, small and large players, and existing and new collaborations. We provide a brief overview of (1) traditional social innovators, established nonprofit organizations, and incubator programs; (2) less-traditional sources of social innovation, including large for-profit organizations, government agencies, and "mom and pop" innovators; and (3) collaborative efforts, including new collaborative networks of individuals and organizations and accelerator initiatives.

We recognize that these categories are not necessarily mutually exclusive or comprehensive, given the great complexity that characterized the Covid response. With these categories, we seek only to illustrate the range of social innovators that emerged in response to Covid-19 and the innovations they developed to address the crisis, complementing government's response and filling in gaps produced by the lack thereof.

Traditional Social Innovators

Traditional social innovators include established nonprofit organizations and incubator programs.

Established Nonprofit Organizations

From the outset of the pandemic, large national and international organizations, as well as smaller, local nonprofits, were engaged in seeking to contribute solutions to the crisis. These organizations were well positioned to respond efficiently and effectively given on-the-ground expertise, experience acting opportunistically to address social needs, flexibility that comes from not being bound by the need to earn a profit, access to networks that help navigate nonmarket forces (policy obstacles), and existing credit among constituents as a trusted source of social solutions.[43] Grant-making nonprofits committed additional funds for immediate, short-term relief to help particularly hard-hit families and communities. For example, in April 2020, the Robert Wood Johnson Foundation, the nation's largest philanthropy dedicated solely to health, provided $50 million in immediate short-term relief to national and community organizations, including $5 million for relief efforts in its home state of New Jersey, hit particularly hard by the virus.[44] Others (e.g., United Way, Goodwill Industries, Salvation Army, YMCA) sought additional contributions, expanded services in which they were already engaged, and mounted recovery initiatives to address drastic increases in hunger, housing, and health-care needs.

Incubator Programs

Nonprofit incubators come in different types and sizes. Some focus on particular objectives, whereas others are more generalist. They may support only a few or many initiatives. Like established nonprofit organizations, these incubators and the innovators they support were well positioned to act in response to Covid-19. For example, Ashoka, a pioneer of the social entrepreneurship movement, supporting fellows worldwide, reported actions in more than ninety countries in response to the crisis and in preparation for a postpandemic world.[45] Cántaro Azul, a social enterprise working to improve access to water in Mexico's rural communities, responded to Covid-19 by raising awareness, promoting preventive measures, and delivering soap and gel, which are difficult to obtain in these areas. Maldita and Teyit, nonprofit news organizations in Spain and Turkey, respectively, empowered and mobilized citizens as fact-checkers to combat misinformation about the virus. Cycling without Age, a social enterprise that fosters stronger ties between communities and the elderly through biking activities, switched to offering support through food, medicine, and online interactions to fight against social isolation. In example after example, these change makers found opportunities to leverage existing assets to address local needs and mobilized, while supporting and inspiring each other to do the same. Hopelab is another nonprofit incubator, based in San Francisco, that focuses on improving the lives of young people. Like Ashoka, in response to Covid-19, Hopelab supported its social innovators in pivoting toward Covid-related causes. For example, Grit Digital Health, which uses a smartphone app called Nod to address loneliness and build resilience among college students, was well positioned to update its solution using the science of social connection to address the unique challenges brought about by physical distancing and isolation during the pandemic.[46]

Less-Traditional Sources of Social Innovation

Among less-traditional sources of social innovation, we recognize large for-profit organizations, government agencies, and "mom and pop" innovators.

Large For-Profit Organizations

The private sector has been an important contributor to the pandemic response, quickly filling in gaps left by the government. Pharmaceutical and biotechnology companies and pharmacy chains have been involved directly in drug and vaccine development as well as testing and vaccine rollout. Beyond these players in the health-care sector, however, have been a number of for-profit companies having core businesses not related to health care but that have nevertheless responded to the crisis by repurposing existing capabilities and resources. For example, manufacturers repurposed production lines to make plastic shields and ventilators. Distilleries and makers of luxury goods repurposed factories to produce disinfectant gel as a sanitizer.[47] These for-profit companies often distributed products produced in response to the pandemic below cost or for free. More recently, Microsoft, Starbucks, and Amazon have been among the companies assisting the government with logistics and operations for vaccine dissemination.[48] Google also disseminated health information through its search pages.[49] By boosting the company's public image and employee morale, these socially innovative endeavors offered the potential to benefit these for-profit organizations, even if not directly improving their bottom line.

Government Agencies

Governments around the world have struggled to respond quickly and effectively to the virus spread. Yet, some government agencies have promoted innovation in the face of the pandemic, and we recognize these activities as part of the social innovation ecosystem. For example, in the United States, state and local governments partnered with hotel chains to repurpose empty hotel rooms and give people experiencing homelessness or those exposed to or recovering from Covid-19 a place to recuperate and quarantine other than in a hospital.[50] The US Department of Health and Human Services and the CDC awarded emergency grants and supplemental funds to support state, tribal, local, and territorial efforts to conduct research into solutions for Covid-19.[51] Similarly, the National Institutes of Health offered funding and increased flexibility for new and continuing Covid-19-specific research through competition supplements, administrative supplements, and new awards.

"Mom and Pop" Innovators

By "mom and pop" innovators, we mean individuals and small groups innovating independently to address Covid-19. The number of small, local, independent initiatives was strikingly large, with common efforts including sourcing personal protective equipment, organizing volunteers or raising funds for a variety of causes, and gathering and serving meals for the hungry. In many communities, dozens if not hundreds or thousands of innovators spontaneously arose in response to this pandemic. Homemakers made and delivered homemade masks. Restaurants that were closed during the pandemic instead prepared and distributed food for essential workers. Anger over government's handling of the pandemic, as well as social unrest and environmental disasters, also galvanized unprecedented levels of community organizing in conjunction with the 2020 election.[52] In some cases, people whose daily routines had been disrupted—students who could not return to school, workers who could not return to their jobs, business owners who lost their customers—had time and resources and wanted to contribute in what has felt like an epic event. Others, already at home, saw needs and also wanted to give back.

Collaborative Efforts

Collaborative efforts include accelerator initiatives and new collaborative networks.

Accelerator Initiatives

Institutions accustomed to helping entrepreneurs launch businesses through collaborative accelerator programs turned their attention to Covid-19 and applied their winning models to advance initiatives to create a more resilient and equitable post-Covid-19 world. Leading universities were among those that redirected their resources by supporting Covid-19-oriented accelerator programs and hackathons. Examples include Stanford Rebuild, a global innovation accelerator program offered free to anyone globally, the Massachusetts Institute of Technology Covid-19 Challenge, the University of California at San Francisco Covid-19 Hackathon, and the Johns Hopkins "Thinking Fast in a Time of Crisis" initiative. Silicon Valley's famous accelerator program, Y Combinator, similarly supported startups focused on Covid-19 through its programs. The Draper Richards Kaplan Foundation, a global venture philanthropy firm supporting early-stage, high-impact social enterprises, also launched in April 2020 a time-limited special initiative to respond to the growing noncoronavirus needs created by the Covid-19 pandemic.[53] It explored over a thousand initiatives and funded eight projects inside their portfolio and externally, including initiatives to expand broadband access, distribute healthy food, provide a communication platform for schools and students, manage mental wellness of health-care workers, and several international projects. By supporting groups of independent innovators that work through these programs together, these accelerator initiatives fostered wide-ranging solutions addressing challenges associated with developing and distributing tests and diagnostics, treatments and vaccines, and tools for patients and health-care providers facing Covid-19[54] and its consequences.[55]

New Collaborative Networks

New collaborative networks also formed to connect those with needs to others who could address them. Many initiatives connected those who could donate food to those who needed it. Some initiatives provided surgical and N95 masks (and other personal protective equipment and testing supplies) internationally, sometimes in the millions of pieces.[56] Other networks moved badly needed nonhealth-related supplies to those most harmed by the economic impacts of Covid-19.[57] Other companies striving to produce medical supplies were connected with organizations that could provide capital to scale production.[58] Often arising organically when someone identified a need or recognized they had access to resources that could benefit someone else, these networks connected suppliers locally or globally with hospitals, governments, and other institutions suffering from shortages of supplies.

Three Examples of Social Innovation

A deeper look into selected case examples—first, an established nonprofit organization; second, a large for-profit organization; and third, a new collaborative network—illustrates some of the achievements of social innovators in response to Covid-19 and allows us to explore how specific social innovations emerged. This closer look reveals distinctions and commonalities among cases, furthering our understanding of the emergence of a "collaboratory" of social innovation in response to crisis.

Partners in Health (PIH) is a well-known and highly regarded social justice organization that views providing high-quality health care globally to those who need it as a moral imperative.[59] Their work since 1987 in tackling—in collaboration with local public health and government entities—global pandemics, including HIV, Ebola, tuberculosis, and cholera, positioned PIH to innovate quickly in response to Covid-19. During the pandemic, it established a US Public Health Accompaniment Unit to bring its global knowledge to US states and community partners.[60] By leveraging its previous experience, PIH rapidly trained an expansive network of contact tracers, case investigators, and care coordinators to help stem the spread of the coronavirus. In partnership with the Commonwealth of Massachusetts, PIH deployed the first large-scale contact-tracing initiative in the United States, the Covid-19 Community Tracing Collaborative (CTC). Its teams provided health education, test results, and access to support services, and initiated follow-up with contacts of individuals who had become infected. Owing to its early success, the CTC program was adopted widely, including in North Carolina, Illinois, Ohio, and the city of Newark, New Jersey, and its network continues to grow. Additionally, PIH leveraged its global network, including seventeen thousand health workers, two hundred public health facilities, and logistics, laboratory, and supply chain systems in eleven countries, to roll out comprehensive preventive responses to Covid-19.[61] It also led operational research with academic partners such as Harvard Medical School to accelerate data availability and inform evidence-based responses, using global data sets to locate disease hot spots (syndromic surveillance), understand herd immunity (serosurveillance), and identify risk factors leading to severe disease in lower- and middle-income countries (LMICs).[62] Partners in Health drew from its experience in LMICs and applied lessons to the United States while also deepening its efforts in LIMCs and disseminating to them key knowledge. Through these efforts, which they were well positioned and mission driven to undertake, PIH filled gaps, deployed interventions at scale, and contributed to reducing the spread of the virus.

General Motors (GM), the largest US automaker, was one private sector company that forsook the pure pursuit of profit in response to this global crisis. Like a nontrivial number of other for-profit companies, GM pivoted amid the pandemic to create "solutions benefiting public good."[63] It stepped up to manufacture ventilators to meet an urgent need for life-saving equipment by establishing a cross-industry partnership with Ventec Life Systems, a medical technology company specializing in portable ventilators, which was also supported by the Trump administration's invocation of the Defense Production Act on March 27, 2020.[64] General Motors provided the resources and purchasing power of a large corporate entity, expertise in "high-scale" manufacturing, and, according to an attendee of an initial face-to-face meeting on March 20, 2020, the "intensity and the intention to make a huge dent in this problem."[65] The company converted an entire manufacturing plant in Indiana to commit it to the task. Obstacles included workers who had never built ventilators before, suppliers that had never built the needed components, and parts that were in short supply. Yet, working with its much smaller medtech and system testing partners and its suppliers, GM redesigned where needed, learned from failures, and persisted to deliver thirty thousand ventilators by September 2020.[66] This achievement can be attributed to their intention, especially that of progressive CEO Mary Barra, the first female CEO of a major automaker, to respond to an urgent social need and to challenge GM to innovate and to adopt a more agile mindset. This pandemic-facilitated social innovation has also found parallel expression in a much broader corporate strategy for environmental sustainability and economic survival. Two elements include (1) a GM product partnership resulting in the joint development with SAIC Motor, a Chinese state-owned automotive company, of a Mini EV car selling for less than $5,000 with a battery range of over a hundred miles, successfully launched in 2020,[67] and (2) the announcement in January 2021 that GM would end the sale of all gasoline and diesel-powered passenger cars and sport utility vehicles by 2035 in order to embrace a future of all electric cars.[68]

New Global Government-Business-Nonprofit Collaboration to Develop Covid-19 Vaccines

The race to develop effective Covid-19 vaccines is an extreme example of new, global, cross-sector, networked collaboration. On April 13, 2020, the World Health Organization published the "Public Statement for Collaboration on COVID-19 Vaccine Development," stating, "We are scientists, physicians, funders and manufacturers who have come together as part of an international collaboration, coordinated by the World Health Organization (WHO), to help speed the availability of a vaccine against COVID-19," with signatories from around the globe.[69]

Global cooperation to develop a vaccine has taken many forms. Scientists worldwide created extensive open networks, sharing knowledge to advance Covid-19 vaccine development. In January 2020, a Chinese scientist quickly made the viral genome sequence of SARS-COV2 available to other experts around the world for vaccine engineering.[70] The

University of Oxford used animal-testing results shared by the National Institutes of Health's Rocky Mountain Laboratory in Montana to develop its vaccine.[71] Collaborations emerged among research centers, university laboratories, hospitals, and vaccine manufacturers in different parts of the world. As a result of cross-sector partnerships, investigators launched more than four hundred clinical trials.[72] Within a year, sixty-eight vaccines were in clinical trials in humans, twenty in the final stages of testing, and more than ninety in preclinical investigation in animals.[73] These global knowledge-sharing efforts and cross-sector partnerships, often benefiting from significant government financial and regulatory support, combined with unprecedented urgency to combat the pandemic. The US Food and Drug Administration (FDA), the European Medicines Agency, and governments around the world have given vaccines emergency approval. As a result, Moderna took forty-two days from getting access to the viral genome to develop an mRNA vaccine and less than one year to receive emergency approval from the FDA. Previously, the fastest time to develop a vaccine was four years, for the mumps.[74] The nonprofit nongovernment sector, including the Bill & Melinda Gates Foundation, Clinton Health Access Initiative, Oxford and many university partners, Partners in Health, and others, has provided financing, advocacy, and distribution mechanisms.[75] Global health mechanisms are being put in place to address equitable vaccine distribution; examples include the COVAX-ACT (access to Covid-19 tools) accelerator; Gavi, the vaccine alliance; and the Coalition for Epidemic Preparedness Innovations (CEPI).[76] There is international commitment to make the Covid-19 vaccine a global public good.[77]

Other collaborations in the field of vaccine development were government initiated. One example is Operation Warp Speed (OWS), an interagency public and multifirm private partnership initiated by the US government to facilitate and accelerate the development, manufacture, and distribution of vaccines, therapeutics, and diagnostics for Covid-19. To accelerate vaccine development, OWS identified and selected the most promising candidates and offered governmental support and funding.[78] To allow trials to "proceed more quickly," the federal government directly supervised protocols for clinical trials rather than taking a more traditional approach that would leave full control of the process to pharmaceutical companies.[79] Partners also pursued steps toward vaccine development simultaneously. On May 15, 2020, OWS announced the selection of fourteen promising candidates from more than a hundred vaccine candidates then in development. They later narrowed these four-teen to the seven most promising candidates. These seven proceeded to early-stage clinical trials followed by large-scale randomized trials for safety and efficacy demonstration. The intention was to deliver 300 million vaccines by January 2021. To achieve this, the government sup-ported development and agreed to pay Johnson & Johnson $1 billion for 100 million doses, Moderna $3.2 billion for 200 million doses, Oxford/ AstraZeneca $1.2 billion for 300 million doses, Novavax $1.6 billion for 100 million doses, and Sanofi-GlaxoSmithKline $2 billion for 100 million doses. Additionally, though it did not support Pfizer's vaccine de-velopment, the government agreed to pay the company $1.95 billion for 100 million doses to manufacture and distribute its vaccine once ap-proved by the FDA.[80] In total, OWS awarded more than $12 billion in vaccine-related contracts and deployed an overall budget of an estimated $18 billion.[81]

In addition to extensive levels of cooperation, multiple simultaneous trials, and redundant contracting, another characteristic of vaccine de-velopment for Covid-19 was the emergence of multiple vaccine platforms, including traditional recombinant protein, replicating and nonreplicat-ing viral vectors, and nucleic acid DNA and mRNA technologies. Like the vaccines they produced, each of these platforms had benefits and lim-itations, and no platform could meet the global need for vaccine. Thus, a strategy of pursuing all available technologies was crucial.[82] Partner-ships like the one between Pfizer and BioNTech, which focused on using the mRNA technology, blossomed based on prior collaboration between the two companies.[83]

Conclusion: A Framework for Social Innovation in a Crisis and Implications for a New Frontier

The enormous need for services, research, and mobilization of resources as a result of the pandemic, and left unfulfilled through government ac-tion alone, spurred unprecedented levels, forms, and the rapid pace of social innovation. The specific case study examples we explored in this chapter resembled the broad array of traditional social innovators, less-traditional sources of social innovation, and collaborative efforts that re-sponded to the needs created by the Covid-19 pandemic. Their breadth demonstrated the ability and willingness of all forms of social innova-tors to contribute within the context of a crisis. It is uncertain whether

FIGURE 14-1

Model of social innovation in a crisis

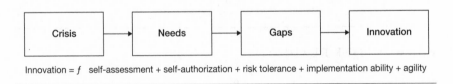

Innovation = f self-assessment + self-authorization + risk tolerance + implementation ability + agility

engagement of nontraditional social innovators in prosocial activities will continue beyond the pandemic. The future participation of for-profit businesses in particular will likely depend on their recognition of benefits to their public image and employee morale and their experience of cross-sector partnership associated with their contributions to the Covid response. Increased pressure from consumers, investors, regulators, and employees for companies to balance purpose and profit would also enhance the likelihood that for-profit businesses would orient toward future stakeholders rather than just pursuing shareholder value.

As depicted in figure 14-1, these social innovators shared common traits, including that they assessed the needs they could observe; considered their available resources, relationships, and comparative advantage; and self-authorized despite the risks of waste or failure. Additional success factors included having inherent agility and ability to implement and scale. Social innovators, including solo and networked individuals, nonprofit and for-profit organizations, and governments, worked consciously and unconsciously in concert to address immediate and medium-term needs during the pandemic.

Resulting from a perfect storm of social, economic, and environmental factors, the Covid-19 pandemic also laid bare the important interconnections between human and planetary factors. Since the main goal after responding to the pandemic remains preventing another similar event,[84] to avail ourselves of the golden opportunity presented by the pandemic, the social innovation ecosystem must urgently embrace and encourage contributions from traditional nonprofit as well as nontraditional individual, corporate, government, and cross-sector collaborative sources of social innovation. Efforts across this ecosystem are required to address the longer-term social, economic, and environmental factors, including social inequalities and planetary health, that will mitigate and prevent future pandemics as well as immediate human needs. Such sustainability efforts will make organizations and nations more resilient.

FOR FURTHER READING

For readers wishing to dive deeper into human and planetary health, we recommend *Accountable: The Rise of Citizen Capitalism* by Michael O'Leary and Warren Valdmanis (Harper Business, 2020), which provides insights on how the pursuit of sustained financial success and the exercise of social responsibility to employees, consumers, and society are essential for our future. Jeff Tollefson's "Why Deforestation and Extinctions Make Pandemics More Likely" (*Nature*, 2020) provides insights into the nexus between the loss of biodiversity and emerging diseases. Lissy Romanow's "Grassroots Organizing and Preparing for the Unprecedented" (*Stanford Social Innovation Review*, 2020) emphasizes how individuals and small groups innovated independently to address the challenges of Covid-19. Finally, "Rediscovering Social Innovation" by James A. Phills Jr., Kriss Deiglmeier, and Dale T. Miller (*Stanford Social Innovation Review*, 2008) is a seminal article defining social innovation.

Notes

1. K. K. Rebecca Lai, Jin Wu, Richard Harris, Allison McCann, Derek Watkins, and Jugal K. Patel, "Coronavirus Map: Tracking the Spread of the Outbreak," *New York Times*, December 1, 2020, sec. World, https://www.nytimes.com/interactive/2020/world/coronavirus-maps.html.

2. Stanford University, "Stanford Scholars, Researchers Tackle COVID-19 Crisis," *Stanford News*, April 8, 2020, https://news.stanford.edu/2020/04/08/stanford-scholars-researchers-lend-expertise.

3. McKinsey & Company, "Innovation in a Crisis: Why It Is More Critical than Ever," n.d., https://www.mckinsey.com/business-functions/strategy-and-corporate-finance/our-insights/innovation-in-a-crisis-why-it-is-more-critical-than-ever.

4. Selam Gebrekidan and Matt Apuzzo, "Covid Response Was a Global Series of Failures, W.H.O.-Established Panel Says," *New York Times*, January 18, 2021, sec. World, https://www.nytimes.com/2021/01/18/world/europe/virus-WHO-report-failures.html.

5. Organisation for Economic Cooperation and Development (OECD), "Social Economy and the COVID-19 Crisis: Current and Future Roles," OECD.org, July 30, 2020, http://www.oecd.org/coronavirus/policy-responses/social-economy-and-the-covid-19-crisis-current-and-future-roles-f904b89f/.

6. Sophie Bacq and G. T. Lumpkin, "Social Entrepreneurship and COVID-19," *Journal of Management Studies* 58, no. 1 (October 17, 2020): 285–288, https://doi.org/10.1111/joms.12641.

7. C. B. Bhattacharya, "How the Great COVID-19 Reset Can Help Firms Build a More Sustainable Future," World Economic Forum, May 15, 2020, https://www.weforum.org/agenda/2020/05/the-covid-19-reset-sustainability/.

8. Inger Andersen and Johan Rockstrom, "COVID-19 Is a Symptom of a Bigger Problem: Our Planet's Ailing Health," *Time*, June 5, 2020, https://time.com /5848681/covid-19-world-environment-day.

9. Jeff Tollefson, "Why Deforestation and Extinctions Make Pandemics More Likely," *Nature* 584, no. 7820 (August 7, 2020): 175–176, https://doi.org/10.1038 /d41586-020-02341-1.

10. Centers for Disease Control and Prevention (CDC), "Zoonotic Diseases," Centers for Disease Control and Prevention, 2018, https://www.cdc.gov/onehealth /basics/zoonotic-diseases.html.

11. American Hospital Association, "Hospitals and Health Systems Face Unprecedented Financial Pressures Due to COVID-19," American Hospital Association, May 5, 2020, https://www.aha.org/guidesreports/2020-05-05-hospitals -and-health-systems-face-unprecedented-financial-pressures-due.

12. Olivia Petter, "Burberry Given £500,000 to Make PPE Equipment for the NHS," *The Independent*, September 4, 2020, https://www.independent.co.uk/life -style/fashion/burberry-ppe-nhs-500-000-nhs-government-a9704571.html.

13. Kirsten Korosec, "Ford, GM, Tesla Given the 'Go Ahead' to Produce Ventilators, Trump Says," *TechCrunch*, March 22, 2020, https://techcrunch.com /2020/03/22/ford-gm-tesla-given-the-go-ahead-to-produce-ventilators-trump -says/.

14. Oleg Bestsennyy, Greg Gilbert, Alex Harris, and Jennifer Rost, "Telehealth: A Post-COVID-19 Reality?," McKinsey & Company, 2020, https://www.mckinsey .com/industries/healthcare-systems-and-services/our-insights/telehealth-a-quarter -trillion-dollar-post-covid-19-reality.

15. McKinsey & Company, "Innovation in a Crisis."

16. Tollefson, "Why Deforestation and Extinctions Make Pandemics More Likely."

17. Yogini V. Chudasama, Clare L. Gillies, Francesco Zaccardi, Briana Coles, Melanie J. Davies, Samuel Seidu, and Kamlesh Khunti, "Impact of COVID-19 on Routine Care for Chronic Diseases: A Global Survey of Views from Healthcare Professionals," *Diabetes & Metabolic Syndrome: Clinical Research & Reviews* 14, no. 5 (2020): 965–967, https://doi.org/10.1016/j.dsx.2020.06.042.

18. Korosec, "Ford, GM, Tesla Given the 'Go Ahead' to Produce Ventilators, Trump Says"; Mark É. Czeisler et al., "Mental Health, Substance Use, and Suicidal Ideation during the COVID-19 Pandemic—United States, June 24–30, 2020," *Morbidity and Mortality Weekly Report* 69, no. 32 (2020): 1049–1057, https://www.cdc .gov/mmwr/volumes/69/wr/pdfs/mm6932a1-H.pdf.

19. David Cutler, "How Will COVID-19 Affect the Health Care Economy?," *Journal of the American Medical Association* 323, no. 22 (2020): 2237–2238, https://doi.org/10.1001/jama.2020.7308.

20. Gita Gopinath, "The Great Lockdown: Worst Economic Downturn since the Great Depression," International Monetary Fund (blog), April 14, 2020,

https://blogs.imf.org/2020/04/14/the-great-lockdown-worst-economic-downturn
-since-the-great-depression/.

21. David M. Cutler and Lawrence H. Summers, "The COVID-19 Pandemic
and the $16 Trillion Virus," *Journal of the American Medical Association* 324, no. 15
(2020): 1495–1496, https://doi.org/10.1001/jama.2020.19759.

22. Catalyst, "The Detrimental Impact of Covid-19 on Gender and Racial
Equality: Quick Take," Catalyst, December 8, 2020, https://www.catalyst.org
/research/covid-effect-gender-racial-equality.

23. Statista, "Coronavirus Impact Index by Industry 2020," Statista, January 22,
2021, https://www.statista.com/statistics/1106302/coronavirus-impact-index-by
-industry-2020.

24. McKinsey & Company, "Innovation in a Crisis."

25. Richard Waters, "Big Tech Has the Cash to Expand after Crisis," ft.com,
March 19, 2020, https://www.ft.com/content/27fdaf5c-f4ab-4a0f-ba9e
-038911b49fe8.

26. McKinsey & Company, "COVID-19 Recovery in Hardest-Hit Sectors
Could Take More than 5 Years," mckinsey.com, July 29, 2020, https://www
.mckinsey.com/featured-insights/coronavirus-leading-through-the-crisis/charting
-the-path-to-the-next-normal/covid-19-recovery-in-hardest-hit-sectors-could-take
-more-than-5-years.

27. Ibraheem M. Karaye and Jennifer A. Horney, "The Impact of Social
Vulnerability on COVID-19 in the U.S.: An Analysis of Spatially Varying Relationships," *American Journal of Preventive Medicine* 59, no. 3 (2020): 317–325,
https://doi.org/10.1016/j.amepre.2020.06.006.

28. Ibid.

29. Ibid.

30. Ibid.

31. Justin Worland, "America's Clean Water Crisis Goes Far beyond Flint.
There's No Relief in Sight," *Time*, February 20, 2020, https://time.com/longform
/clean-water-access-united-states.

32. Karaye and Horney, "The Impact of Social Vulnerability on COVID-19 in
the U.S."

33. Daniel M. Gerstein, "Assessing the US Government Response to the
Coronavirus," *Bulletin of the Atomic Scientists* 76, no. 4 (2020): 166–174, https://doi
.org/10.1080/00963402.2020.1778356.

34. Nicole Huberfeld, Sarah H. Gordon, and David K. Jones, "Federalism
Complicates the Response to the COVID-19 Health and Economic Crisis: What
Can Be Done?," *Journal of Health Politics, Policy and Law* 45, no. 6 (2020): 951–965,
https://doi.org/10.1215/03616878-8641493; Gavin Yamey and Clare Wenham,
"The U.S. and U.K. Were the Two Best Prepared Nations to Tackle a Pandemic—
What Went Wrong?," *Time*, July 1, 2020, https://time.com/5861697/us-uk-failed
-coronavirus-response; Peter Beaumont and Julian Borger, "WHO Warned of
Transmission Risk in January, Despite Trump Claims," *The Guardian*, April 9,
2020, sec. World News, https://www.theguardian.com/world/2020/apr/09/who
-cited-human-transmission-risk-in-january-despite-trump-claims.

35. Huberfeld, Gordon, and Jones, "Federalism Complicates the Response to the COVID-19 Health and Economic Crisis."

36. Ian Bremmer, "The Best Global Responses to the COVID-19 Pandemic," *Time*, June 12, 2020, https://time.com/5851633/best-global-responses-covid-19.

37. Ibid.

38. Rachel Kyte, "No Silver Lining to Coronavirus, but a Golden Opportunity," *Climate Change News*, May 1, 2020, https://www.climatechangenews.com /2020/05/01/no-silver-lining-golden-opportunity-build-back-better/.

39. Organisation for Economic Cooperation and Development (OECD), "Making the Green Recovery Work for Jobs, Income and Growth," OECD.org, October 6, 2020, https://www.oecd.org/coronavirus/policy-responses/making-the -green-recovery-work-for-jobs-income-and-growth-a505f3e7/.

40. Jonathan H. Epstein et al., "Nipah Virus Dynamics in Bats and Implications for Spillover to Humans," *Proceedings of the National Academy of Sciences* 117, no. 46 (2020): 29190–29201, https://doi.org/10.1073/pnas.2000429117.

41. Isabel J. Jones et al., "Improving Rural Health Care Reduces Illegal Logging and Conserves Carbon in a Tropical Forest," *Proceedings of the National Academy of Sciences* 117, no. 45 (2020): 28515–28524, https://doi.org/10.1073/pnas.2009240117.

42. Angelle Desiree and Amy Krystosik, "Trash to Treasure," Disease Ecology, Health and the Environment, ecohealthsolutions.stanford.edu, accessed February 1, 2021, https://ecohealthsolutions.stanford.edu/research/trash-treasure.

43. James Austin, Howard Stevenson, and Jane Wei-Skillern, "Social and Commercial Entrepreneurship: Same, Different, or Both?," *Entrepreneurship Theory and Practice* 30, no. 1 (January 2006): 1–22, https://doi.org/10.1111/j.1540-6520 .2006.00107.x.

44. Robert Wood Johnson Foundation, "RWJF Support for Those Facing Greatest Strain under the COVID-19 Pandemic," Robert Wood Johnson Foundation, April 7, 2020, https://www.rwjf.org/en/library/articles-and-news/2020/04/rwjf -provides-50-million-in-relief-for-people-facing-the-greatest-strain-under-the -covid-19-pandemic.html.

45. Ashoka and Changemakers, "Changemakers Respond to COVID-19," *Ashoka Insight*, March 25, 2020, https://medium.com/change-maker/changemakers -respond-to-covid-19-3ff47494d575.

46. Julianne Holt-Lunstad, "Why Universities Need to Address Loneliness in COVID Plans," thriveglobal.com, August 14, 2020, https://thriveglobal.com/stories /why-universities-need-to-address-loneliness-in-covid-plans/?utm_source =Newsletter_Transaction&utm_medium=Thrive&utm_campaign=Published.

47. Richard Kestenbaum, "LVMH Converting Its Perfume Factories to Make Hand Sanitizer," *Forbes*, March 15, 2020, https://www.forbes.com/sites/richard kestenbaum/2020/03/15/lvmh-converting-its-perfume-factories-to-make-hand -sanitizer/?sh=2dc6e8254a9a.

48. Gillian Friedman and Lauren Hirsch, "Help with Vaccination Push Comes from Unexpected Businesses," *New York Times*, January 23, 2021, sec. Business, https://www.nytimes.com/2021/01/23/business/vaccines-microsoft-amazon -starbucks.html?smid=em-share.

49. Ibid.

50. California Department of Social Services, "Project Roomkey/Housing and Homelessness COVID Response," 2021, accessed August 3, 2021, https://www.cdss.ca.gov/inforesources/cdss-programs/housing-programs/project-roomkey.

51. US Department of the Treasury, "The CARES Act Works for All Americans," US Department of the Treasury, 2020, https://home.treasury.gov/policy-issues/cares; Centers for Disease Control and Prevention (CDC), "Coronavirus Disease 2019," Centers for Disease Control and Prevention, 2021, https://www.cdc.gov/media/releases/2021/p0107-covid-19-funding.html.

52. Lissy Romanow, "Grassroots Organizing and Preparing for the Unprecedented," *Stanford Social Innovation Review*, November 19, 2020, https://ssir.org/articles/entry/grassroots_organizing_and_preparing_for_the_unprecedented.

53. DRK Foundation, "Respond," DRK Foundation, accessed February 1, 2021, https://www.drkfoundation.org/respond.

54. Y Combinator, "YC Startups Helping with the COVID-19 Crisis," Y Combinator, 2020, https://www.ycombinator.com/covid; Stanford Rebuild, "Showcase Team Gallery," Stanford Rebuild, 2020, https://rebuildsprint.stanford.edu/showcase-teams.

55. Stanford Rebuild, "Showcase Team Gallery"; CoachMe Health, "CoachMe Health," CoachMe Health, 2020, https://www.coachmehealth.org.

56. Coronavirusmatch, "Coronavirusmatch," Coronavirusmatch, 2020, https://www.coronavirusmatch.org/.

57. Essential Supply, "Grocery Delivery," Essential Supply, 2020, https://www.essentialsupply.org.

58. Ibid.

59. Partners in Health, accessed January 31, 2021, www.pih.org.

60. Partners in Health, "Mobilizing against COVID-19 and Ensuring a Healthier Future for All," Partners in Health, 2020, https://www.pih.org/sites/default/files/2020-05/Partners_In_Health_COVID19_Global_Project_Concept_May_2020.pdf.

61. Ibid.

62. Ibid.

63. Efrat Shadmi et al., "Health Equity and COVID-19: Global Perspectives," *International Journal for Equity in Health* 19, no. 1 (2020), https://doi.org/10.1186/s12939-020-01218-z.

64. Greg Slabodkin, "An Insider's Look at How GM, Ventec Ramped Up Ventilator Production amid COVID-19," medtechdive.com, July 13, 2020, https://www.medtechdive.com/news/an-insiders-look-at-how-gm-ventec-ramped-up-ventilator-production-amid-co/581461/.

65. Shadmi et al., "Health Equity and COVID-19."

66. Reuters Staff, "GM, Ventec Life Systems Deliver 30,000 Ventilators to U.S. Government," Reuters, September 1, 2020, https://www.reuters.com/article/us-health-coronavirus-autos-ventilators/gm-ventec-life-systems-deliver-30000-ventilators-to-u-s-government-idUSKBN25S4Z1.

67. Bloomberg, "Tesla's Nemesis in China Is a Tiny $5,000 Electric Car from GM," *Bloomberg News*, September 25, 2020, https://www.bloomberg.com/amp/news

/articles/2020-09-25/tesla-s-nemesis-in-china-is-a-tiny-5-000-electric-car
-from-gm.

68. Steven Mufson, "General Motors to Eliminate Gasoline and Diesel
Light-Duty Cars and SUVs by 2035," *Washington Post*, January 28, 2021, https://
www.washingtonpost.com/climate-environment/2021/01/28/general-motors
-electric/.

69. World Health Organisation (WHO), "Public Statement for Collaboration
on COVID-19 Vaccine Development," April 13, 2020, https://www.who.int/news
/item/13-04-2020-public-statement-for-collaboration-on-covid-19-vaccine
-development.

70. Charlie Campbell, "Exclusive: Chinese Scientist Who First Sequenced
COVID-19 Genome Speaks about Controversies Surrounding His Work," *Time*,
August 24, 2020, https://time.com/5882918/zhang-yongzhen-interview-china
-coronavirus-genome/.

71. Matt Apuzzo and David D. Kirkpatrick, "Covid-19 Changed How the
World Does Science, Together," *New York Times*, April 1, 2020, www.nytimes.com
/2020/04/01/world/europe/coronavirus-science-research-cooperation.html.

72. Gonzalo Rivas and Claudia Suaznabar, eds., *Responding to COVID-19 with
Science, Innovation, and Productive Development* (Washington, DC: Inter-American
Development Bank, April 25, 2020), https://publications.iadb.org/publications
/english/document/Responding-to-COVID-19-with-Science-Innovation-and
-Productive-Development.pdf.

73. Carl Zimmer, Jonathan Corum, and Sui-Lee Wee, "Coronavirus Vaccine
Tracker," *New York Times*, June 10, 2020, sec. Science, https://www.nytimes.com
/interactive/2020/science/coronavirus-vaccine-tracker.html?auth=login
-email&login=email.

74. Jocelyn Solis-Moreira, "COVID-19 Vaccine: How Was It Developed so
Fast?," medicalnewstoday.com, December 15, 2020, https://www.medicalnewstoday
.com/articles/how-did-we-develop-a-covid-19-vaccine-so-quickly.

75. World Health Organisation (WHO), "172 Countries and Multiple Candi-
date Vaccines Engaged in COVID-19 Vaccine Global Access Facility," WHO,
August 24, 2020, https://www.who.int/news/item/24-08-2020-172-countries-and
-multiple-candidate-vaccines-engaged-in-covid-19-vaccine-global-access-facility.

76. Ibid.

77. Gavi, "Are Vaccines a Global Public Good?," Gavi, September 11, 2020,
https://www.gavi.org/vaccineswork/are-vaccines-global-public-good.

78. US Department of Health and Human Services, "COVID-19 Vaccines,"
HHS.gov, December 12, 2020, https://www.hhs.gov/coronavirus/covid-19-vaccines
/index.html; US Department of Health and Human Services, "HHS Announces
$22 Billion in Funding to Support Expanded Testing, Vaccination Distribution," HHS
.gov, January 6, 2021, https://www.hhs.gov/about/news/2021/01/06/hhs-announces
-22-billion-in-funding-to-support-expanded-testing-vaccination-distribution.html.

79. US Department of Health and Human Services, "COVID-19 Vaccines."

80. Emily Barone, "The Trump Administration's 'Operation Warp Speed' Has
Spent $12.4 Billion on Vaccines. How Much Is That Really?," *Time*, December 14,
2020, https://time.com/5921360/operation-warp-speed-vaccine-spending/.

81. U.S. Department of Health and Human Services, "HHS Announces $22 Billion in Funding to Support Expanded Testing, Vaccination Distribution."

82. Lawrence Corey, John R. Mascola, Anthony S. Fauci, and Francis S. Collins, "A Strategic Approach to COVID-19 Vaccine R&D," *Science* 368, no. 6494 (May 11, 2020): 948–950, science.sciencemag.org/content/368/6494/948?utm _campaign=fr_sci_2020-05-14&et_rid=143961329&et_cid=3326744, 10.1126/ science.abc5312.

83. Bojan Pancevski and Jared S. Hopkins, "How Pfizer Partner BioNTech Became a Leader in Coronavirus Vaccine Race," *Wall Street Journal*, October 22, 2020, www.wsj.com/articles/how-pfizer-partner-biontech-became-a-leader-in -coronavirus-vaccine-race-11603359015.

84. Neal Myrick, "Green Leadership Will Be More in Demand Than Ever after COVID-19," World Economic Forum, June 15, 2020, https://www.weforum.org /agenda/2020/06/environmental-leadership-will-be-more-in-demand-than-ever -after-covid-19.

15

Corporate Carbon Reduction Pledges

An Effective Tool to Mitigate Climate Change?

Stephen Comello, Julia Reichelstein, and Stefan Reichelstein

With the quest for rapid decarbonization gaining global momentum, a sizable number of major corporations since 2019 have begun to report more granular information regarding their own carbon emissions. For the most part, these disclosures have been voluntary and forward looking, pertaining to both current and anticipated future emissions of carbon dioxide (CO_2) and other greenhouse gases into the atmosphere. The disclosing firms frequently "pledge" to achieve a net-zero carbon position by a particular date several decades into the future, most commonly the year 2050. Individual corporate goals complement the carbon reduction targets set by national governments in the form of Nationally Determined Contributions (NDCs) in international climate treaties, such as the 2015 Paris agreement. The number of firms with net-zero targets more than doubled in 2020, increasing from 500 in 2019 to 1,000 in 2020.[1]

In this chapter, we first summarize the specific plans articulated by seven major corporations for reducing their corporate carbon footprint (CCF). Our sample is not intended to be representative of the entire population of firms that have become active in this regard. Instead, our selection aims to cover a broad range of industries, including manufacturers and distributors of consumer products, energy companies, and internet technology firms. We then compare and discuss key features of the decarbonization plans put forth by these seven firms to highlight substantial differences regarding the specificity and measurement of the articulated goals. Our discussion points to considerable variation in the use of so-called carbon offsets. We also discuss alternatives for making CCF disclosures more transparent and credible in the future, including the possibility of such disclosures becoming mandatory rather than voluntary.

Information on the carbon reduction plans disclosed by individual firms has been collected by multiple analysts, including Bloomberg New Energy Finance (BNEF), the Carbon Disclosure Project, and Science-Based Targets. Figure 15-1 replicates a graph taken from BNEF, illustrating the CCF reduction plans of five global oil and gas companies.[2] A common feature of these projections is that firms plan to achieve a "net-zero" position by a certain year—that is, their carbon footprint, measured as Scope 1 plus Scope 2 emissions, is projected to go to zero

BIOGRAPHIES

STEPHEN COMELLO is a lecturer in management and codirector of the Energy Business Innovations focus area at the Stanford Graduate School of Business. He is also a senior research fellow at the Steyer-Taylor Center for Energy Policy and Finance. He holds a PhD in civil and environmental engineering from Stanford University.

JULIA REICHELSTEIN is an investor with Piva Capital, a venture capital fund focused on the future of industry and energy. Before joining Piva, she led digital expansion for Entrepreneurial Finance Lab (EFL), a global financial technology firm that increases access to credit in emerging markets through alternative data credit scoring. She holds a BA in economics and an MBA from Stanford University.

STEFAN REICHELSTEIN is the director of the Mannheim Institute for Sustainable Energy at the University of Mannheim (Germany).[3] As the William R. Timken Professor Emeritus at Stanford, he also serves as the faculty research director of the Steyer-Taylor Center for Energy Policy and Finance and as a senior fellow of the Precourt Institute for Energy.

EXECUTIVE SUMMARY

In the intensifying public debate about limiting the harmful effects of climate change, many global corporations have articulated "net-zero" goals for reducing and ultimately eliminating their own greenhouse gas emissions. We first examine the details of the carbon reduction goals articulated by seven large firms in different industries. The individual reduction goals are shown to vary substantially in terms of specificity and scope, largely because of variations in the measurement of carbon footprints. Particular sources of variation arise from how "gross emissions" are determined and from firms' willingness to recognize carbon credits that offset their own emissions.

FIGURE 15-1

CO$_2$ reduction goals of five oil and gas firms in terms of their Scope 1 and Scope 2 emissions

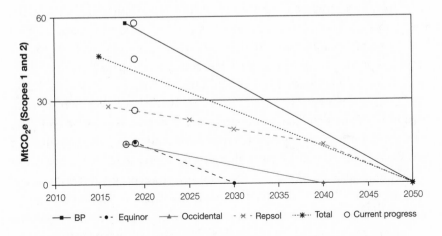

Source: Based on data from Kyle Harrison et al., "Corporate Net Zero Targets," Bloomberg New Energy Finance, January 2021, https://www.bnef.com/core/themes/305.

at some point within the next thirty years.[4] As we will discuss in detail, the net-zero goal frequently allows credits to be subtracted from the firm's emissions to obtain a measure of net emissions. As shown in figure 15-1, companies such as Repsol also set "milestones" that project their net carbon footprint at one or several intermediate points between the present and 2050. We note that in drawing this graph,

BNEF apparently makes the implicit, and ultimately central, assumption that a firm's carbon footprint decreases linearly between any two milestones.

Corporate carbon footprint reduction plans have gained considerable attention in the public discussion about limiting the damaging effects of climate change. This interest reflects the growing concern that despite all protestations about the threat posed by climate change, the world's economies have failed to collectively bend the overall curve of annual CO_2 emissions, at least before the arrival of the Covid-19 pandemic in 2020. In the absence of effective policies such as direct emission regulations and/or carbon pricing, corporate pledges to reduce emissions are seen as a potentially significant commitment and coordination mechanism for enabling the world to limit the overall global temperature increase on earth to a range of 1.5 to 2°C higher than pre-industrial levels.

The projected paths of direct (Scope 1) emissions of all economic entities (i.e., firms, households, governmental agencies) can, at least in principle, be aggregated into a forecast for the carbon emission path for the global economy. Such aggregate carbon emission trajectories have been forecast by numerous analysts and observers. Figure 15-2, for example, reproduces a graph from a McKinsey white paper.

Climate scientists for the United Nations' Intergovernmental Panel on Climate Change (IPCC) projected in 2018 that in order to have at least a two-thirds chance of limiting the temperature increase to 1.5°C, total cumulative anthropogenic emissions would have to stay within a 420 Gt carbon budget. That budget would increase to 570 Gt in order to maintain at least a one-half probability of keeping the temperature increase to 1.5°C and 840 Gt to have a one-third probability.[5] Aggregate carbon emission paths like the one shown in figure 15-2 suggest the analogy of the atmosphere as a "bathtub" for anthropogenic carbon emissions. The carbon budget determines the size of this bathtub, which would overflow if the cumulative future emissions (i.e., the area under the curve) were to exceed the size of the tub.

The shape of the projected emissions curve is clearly crucial, with total cumulative emissions being larger for a concave (delayed reductions) as opposed to a convex (accelerated reductions) shape, holding the endpoints of the curve fixed. This observation illustrates the elementary point that when individual corporations set goals for their own future carbon footprints, not only do the endpoints between today and the projected net-

FIGURE 15-2

A business-as-usual and a 1.5°C pathway for global carbon emissions up to the year 2050

Global carbon dioxide emissions, gigatons (GtCO₂) per year

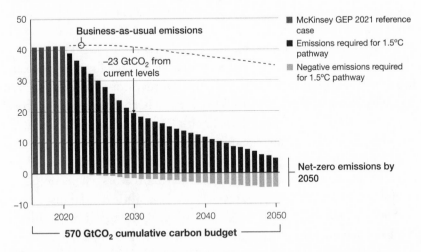

Source: Christopher Blaufelder et al., "A Blueprint for Scaling Voluntary Carbon Markets to Meet the Climate Challenge," McKinsey & Company, January 29, 2021, https://www.mckinsey.com/business-functions /sustainability/our-insights/a-blueprint-for-scaling-voluntary-carbon-markets-to-meet-the-climate -challenge.

zero date matter but equally so does the projected path connecting the endpoints. Milestones effectively trace out the shape of the anticipated individual firm-level trajectories and thereby yield a more precise prediction of the total projected cumulative emissions.

Two central questions in this context are why firms issue voluntary decarbonization pledges and why the set of firms joining this bandwagon has expanded rapidly since 2019. Economists have long pointed to climate change as a prime illustration of the "tragedy of the commons," when individuals do not internalize the full social cost that their actions impose on a commons. In the context of climate change, the terrestrial atmosphere is a commons (bathtub), yet economic agents only internalize a minor fraction of the social cost associated with their own activities that cause the public good to deteriorate.[6] The pace of global carbon emissions and the more frequent occurrence of extreme weather events since the early 2010s have arguably accentuated the prospects of an impending crisis for this public good. The decarbonization goals articulated by large multinational firms quantify their intended contribution to the preservation of the public good. While the stated goals are voluntary at this point, their achievement in the future may be driven at least partly by future carbon regulations.

There is increasing evidence that firms face pressure from multiple stakeholder groups to articulate their contribution toward the public good of an atmosphere in which the concentration of CO_2 remains within acceptable limits. These stakeholder groups potentially include the firm's customers, managers, directors, and, for publicly listed firms, the broader investment community.[7] Some institutional investors, such as the New York City Pension Fund and BlackRock, have become particularly vocal in this regard. For instance, BlackRock's Larry Fink stated in his 2020 letter to CEOs that climate change will be a "defining factor in companies' long-term prospects" and that BlackRock "will be increasingly disposed to vote against management and board directors when companies are not making sufficient progress on sustainability-related disclosures and the business practices and plans underlying them."[8] The 2021 letter to CEOs became more explicit, as it called on all companies in BlackRock's portfolio "to disclose a plan for how their business model will be compatible with the net-zero economy" and added, "We expect you to disclose how this plan is incorporated into your long-term strategy and reviewed by your board of directors."[9]

In the face of growing pressure from both internal and external stakeholders, there appear to be clear benefits from joining the group of firms that have articulated net-zero pledges. At the same time, such pledges may not entail substantial costs in the minds of either the firm's management or its shareholders. Obviously, any commitment to a net-zero goal by the year 2050 is well beyond the personal planning horizon of current corporate officers. Furthermore, as we will argue, stated net-zero pledges at the beginning of the 2020s frequently offer considerable "wiggle room" insofar as there are no restrictions on the types of carbon offsets that are eligible for subtraction from the firm's gross carbon emissions. A 2020 article in *The Economist*[10] points out that the average price for carbon offsets in the voluntary carbon markets was a mere $3 per metric ton of CO_2 in 2018. At these rates, each major oil company represented in figure 15-1 could meet the net-zero target in 2021 by paying somewhere in the range of $60 to $90 million annually while leaving their Scope 1 and Scope 2 emissions unchanged.

Corporate Carbon Reduction Goals: Select Examples

This section describes the carbon reduction goals articulated by seven large firms in multiple industries.

Google

Google LLC is a technology company that specializes in internet-related services and products, which include online advertising technologies, a leading internet search engine, cloud computing, software, and some hardware products. The firm's nineteen operational campuses across twenty-one locations for its data centers in the United States, Europe, South America, and Asia achieved $161 billion in sales revenue in 2019. The firm defines its operational emissions as including all Scope 1 and Scope 2 emissions. Regarding Scope 3, the company includes emissions related to business travel, candidate travel, and employee commuting.[11] Google has articulated its carbon neutrality commitment for these operational emissions[12] and has pronounced itself carbon neutral since 2007 because its annual carbon footprint, measured according to its own methodology, has been less than or equal to zero.

Google's primary approach to reducing emissions is through energy efficiency improvements (at its data centers), generating on-site solar power, and investing in renewable power generation plants in various locations. For off-site renewable power plants (mostly wind and solar photovoltaic), Google will typically enter into long-term contracts with entities willing to purchase the generated electricity, allowing Google to match 100 percent of its annual electricity consumption with renewable energy generation. By the end of 2019, Google had 5.5 GW of renewable power generation capacity under contract, the majority of which was in the same grid locations as its data centers. Nonetheless, a significant share of the energy generated by Google's renewable energy facilities is sold to third parties, such as utilities. To bring its remaining corporate carbon footprint (CCF) to zero, Google purchases carbon offsets it deems to be of "high quality." Typical carbon offset projects include landfill gas capture, agricultural methane capture, and deforestation avoidance credits.

In September 2020, Google announced new decarbonization targets, the primary one being carbon-free energy on a "24-by-7" basis for its direct operations by 2030.[13] To calibrate the size of this goal, in 2020 only 61 percent of all electricity used by the firm was matched with regional, carbon-free resources on an hourly basis, with high and low examples being Oklahoma and Singapore, at 96 percent and 3 percent, respectively.[14] The firm has acknowledged the challenge of achieving its 24/7 goal and has outlined potential enabling technologies. These include demand response mechanisms and demand matching for its data centers and the use of clean dispatchable power generation (e.g., advanced nuclear, enhanced geothermal, low-impact hydro, long-duration storage, green hydrogen, and carbon capture and sequestration).

An additional major goal—which the company pronounced as having been achieved on the day of the announcement in September 2020—was to eliminate all legacy carbon emissions via purchased carbon offsets, effectively making the sum of Google's past CCFs zero.

Xcel

Xcel Energy, Inc. (Xcel), is an investor-owned electricity and natural gas company that operates through four regulated utility subsidiaries in eight states across the Midwest and Western United States. The firm serves 3.7 million electricity customers and 2.1 million natural gas customers, and in 2019 it achieved revenues of $11.5 billion. In December 2018, Xcel set the goal of providing its retail and wholesale customers with 100 percent carbon-free electricity by 2050, with an intermediate goal of an 80 percent CO_2 reduction for all electrical energy delivered by the year 2030 compared to 2005 baseline levels.[15] This pledge pertains to emissions from Xcel-owned generating plants (Scope 1) and electricity purchased from other producers that is ultimately supplied to the firm's customers (Scope 3).

Xcel follows the common practice of reporting *CO_2 equivalents* to aggregate the emissions of all greenhouse gases (GHG), such as methane, nitrous oxide, and several fluorocarbons in a composite emission measure usually termed CO_2e.[16] For Xcel, the combustion of fossil fuels comprises 99 percent of CO_2e emissions from generated electricity, while the remaining 1 percent is attributable to methane emissions.[17] By the end of 2020, Xcel had already achieved a 50 percent emission reduction from its 2005 baseline,[18] which in absolute terms expressed in megatons amounted to about 40 $MtCO_2e$.[19]

The company has outlined investment and operational changes that are intended to enable its net-zero trajectory.[20] Primarily, this entails investing in solar and wind generation, with a projected 2030 energy mix of 60 percent renewables, 15 percent natural gas, 15 percent coal, and 10 percent nuclear. Xcel's strategy broadly entails a mix of natural gas, wind, solar, and "advanced technologies" while maintaining existing nuclear generation facilities and reducing the operation of existing coal plants. From an electricity demand perspective, the firm plans to undertake end-customer energy efficiency programs and strategic electrification, including the buildout of electric vehicle infrastructure. Notably, carbon offsets are not considered an instrument for achieving Xcel's carbon commitments. To meet its 2050 goals beyond 2030, the company advocates for research and development to enable the final 20 percent emission reductions, as the current suite of technology options are not viewed as commercially viable for "providing customers reliable, affordable clean energy."[21]

REI

Recreational Equipment, Inc. (REI) is an American retail and outdoor recreation services corporation with 168 locations, thirteen thousand employees, and about $3 billion in net sales in 2019. It has declared that it will become "carbon neutral" in emissions with respect to its operations and products sold under its own brand beginning in 2020. The supply chain tied to products sold under the REI brand accounts for approximately one-quarter of the company's about 1 $MtCO_2e$ total CCF.[22] In addition, the firm has committed to reducing its total CCF (Scopes 1–3) by 55 percent by 2030 compared to a 2019 baseline.[23] This will entail reducing the emissions associated with the nearly one thousand product items carried by the retailer, constituting approximately at least 42 percent of its total footprint.

REI first achieved carbon neutrality in its direct operations in September 2020, through a combination of ongoing capital investments in buildings, changes in energy purchasing, and carbon offsets.[24] Since 2006, the firm has embarked on upgrades to its retail, distribution, and administrative buildings, including HVAC replacements that eliminated the use of Freon and the installation of energy efficiency measures such as LED lighting. Since 2014, REI's operations have been powered by 100 percent renewable energy, achieved through a combination of on-site generation, utility green tariffs, and renewable-energy credits. Finally, to eliminate the remaining CO_2 from direct operations, in late

2020 REI joined Climate Neutral, an organization that measures the corporate CO_2 footprint of brands and then facilitates the purchase of carbon offsets through its project pool.[25]

Unilever

Unilever plc is a multinational consumer goods company organized into three main divisions—foods and refreshments, home care, and beauty and personal care. From the sale of its four hundred products in 190 countries, the firm earned revenue in 2019 of approximately $60 billion. Unilever has publicized its Sustainable Living Plan (USLP) since 2010, which sets time-bound goals for achieving, among other things, reductions in carbon emissions. In 2019, Unilever reported a GHG footprint of about 60 $MtCO_2e$, 98 percent of which was attributable to Scope 3 emissions.[26] The USLP sets two marquee commitments, the first pertaining to no carbon emissions from Unilever's operations (Scopes 1 and 2) by 2030. The second goal, set relative to a 2010 baseline, is to reduce the firm's GHG footprint across the entire value chain by 50 percent on a "per consumer use basis" by the year 2030.[27] This carbon intensity measure is based on the quantity of CO_2e allocated per single portion, use, or serving of a Unilever product for one person.[28] It is based on the amount of product sold to the consumer in combination with the recommended dose, use, or habits data.[29] In 2019, this intensity measure was set at 45.5 g of CO_2 per use. Importantly, this figure includes the emissions attributed to the consumer use of products sold by Unilever (one of the categories among the Scope 3 emissions), accounting for about 66 percent of Unilever's CCF in 2019.

To meet its climate goals, Unilever intends to use 100 percent renewable energy to power all firm-controlled operations. The company also plans to rely increasingly on sustainable sourcing of commodities such as palm oil, soy, and paper and pulp, and reformulating products with the objective of using fewer input ingredients.[30]

In June 2020, the firm released an additional statement to "fight climate change and protect nature as part of a new integrated business strategy." Specifically, Unilever additionally forecasts achieving net-zero emissions from all products by 2039, covering all associated emissions from the sourcing of the materials to the point of sale.[31] However, this new goal does not include the consumer use stage. One key pillar for achieving the 2039 goal is for the firm to attain a "deforestation-free" supply chain by 2023 through investment in a combination of restricted supplier contracting and investing in satellite imaging and data processes for monitoring and verification. Finally, Unilever has stated that it intends to balance any residual emissions in the supply chain by 2039 through carbon offsets that are either purchased or self-generated.

United Airlines

United Airlines, Inc., operates about 1,400 aircraft, with 4,900 daily flights to 361 airports across the world. Total operating revenue in 2019 was about $43 billion. In December 2020, United pledged to reduce its CO_2e emissions by 100 percent by 2050 on an absolute basis.[32] The firm's climate strategy is focused primarily on mitigating its aircraft emissions related to fuel combustion, as about 81 percent of United's annual CCF (42 $MtCO_2e$) results from jet fuel consumed by its own aircraft (Scope 1). United also provides regional transportation service under the brand United Express, within which six separately owned airlines operate short and medium feeder flights.[33] The jet fuel emissions from these flights (Scope 3) account for about 17 percent of United's CCF. Accordingly, a total of about 98 percent of the firm's corporate emissions stem from jet fuel combustion.[34]

United has outlined three broad approaches to achieve its climate pledge: increasing fuel efficiency, reducing the carbon intensity of fuels, and removing carbon dioxide from the atmosphere. Aircraft body upgrades support fuel efficiency. For example, United reported that the implementation of Boeing's split scimitar winglets reduced fuel consumption by 2 percent. Regarding the carbon intensity of fuel, the firm has entered into long-term contracts to purchase sustainable aviation fuel, which can reduce life cycle emissions by 60 percent. In particular, United has made a $30 million equity investment in Fulcrum BioEnergy and has entered into a long-term supply agreement for ninety million gallons per year for ten years.[35]

United Airlines is also bound by the Carbon Offsetting and Reduction Scheme for International Aviation (CORSIA) of the International Civil Aviation Organization, the United Nations agency for aviation. Starting in 2027, for US domiciled air carriers, CORSIA calls for international aviation to offset part of its CO_2 emissions through the reduction of emissions outside the international aviation sector, essentially through carbon offsets. Examples of offset projects mentioned there include those that reduce emissions from electricity generation, industrial processes, and agriculture. CORSIA's goal is to keep global net CO_2 emissions from international aviation at 2019 levels going forward. This goal has been labeled "carbon neutral growth."[36]

United Airlines has indicated that the CORSIA offsets will ultimately be insufficient[37] and therefore the company will seek to remove all its carbon permanently using direct air capture technology.[38] In late 2020, United made a multimillion-dollar investment in 1point5, a development company formed by Oxy Low Carbon Ventures and Rusheen Capital Management to finance and deploy Carbon Engineering's large-scale direct air capture technology.[39] As a first demonstration, 1point5 is to deliver a facility located in the Permian Basin of Texas that will capture and permanently sequester 1 $MtCO_2$ per year when operational, which is expected sometime in 2022 or 2023.[40]

BP

The British multinational oil and gas company BP plc operates in all segments of the oil and gas industry, with investments in renewable energy increasing since 2015. In 2019, BP achieved about $277 billion in revenue based on operations in over eighty countries. That year, the company produced 2.6 million barrels of oil per day.[41] Because of the sheer volume of its fossil fuel production, the firm reported a sizable carbon footprint of about 55 $MtCO_2e$ from direct operations in 2019. The combustion of oil and gas sold by the company accounts for an additional 360 $MtCO_2e$ in Scope 3 emissions. This number reflects BP's equity share in joint ventures. In February 2020, BP articulated a net-zero goal to be achieved no later than 2050.[42] This goal is seen as part of a new strategy to transform BP from an international oil company to an integrated energy company.[43]

Known as the "Net Zero Ambition,"[44] BP's 2020 targets can be divided into direct operations, upstream production activities, and downstream product use. It seeks to achieve net-zero emissions from its direct operations (Scopes 1 and 2) and from its upstream production of oil and gas (Scope 3)[45] on an absolute basis by 2050, with a 20 percent reduction by 2025. Regarding its other Scope 3 emissions, BP has pledged to reduce the carbon intensity of the products it sells by 50 percent by 2050, with a goal of 5 percent reduction by 2025.[46] The carbon intensity measure is calculated on a per unit of energy basis (e.g., tCO_2 per MJ of energy) and pertains to the estimated life cycle emissions associated with the production, processing, transportation, and use of all marketed products. These products include fuels, natural gas, and electric power supplied to customers. The general expectation expressed by BP is that the absolute level of emissions associated with marketed products will grow until 2030, even as the carbon intensity falls. Beyond 2030, the firm projects that its total emissions will fall, in part because of the company's intention to limit its engagement in the oil and gas sector.[47]

To meet its targets, BP aims to increase the capacity of its renewable energy projects. For instance, by the end of 2020, it had deployed 3.3 GW of renewable energy projects and amassed an approximately 11 GW development pipeline (20 percent solar, 80 percent offshore wind). The firm has also stated that it will increase low-carbon investments to $5 billion per year by 2030, up from current levels of $0.5 billion. These funds will be used to scale up deployment in mobility electrification, sustainable fuels, hydrogen energy, and carbon capture, utilization, and sequestration technologies. The company will seek divestments to lower its CCF and to develop technology that reduces its carbon footprint from refining operations. To achieve the company's aims beyond 2030, natural climate solutions will be eligible as carbon offsets.

Through its Target Neutral activities, BP already purchases carbon offsets for its own operations and on behalf of its customers to help them achieve their carbon targets. For its own operations, some offsets are used to comply with obligations under mandatory emissions schemes, such as the California Cap-and-Trade Program.[48] For example, a BP subsidiary with operations in California purchased offsets for 1.7 $MtCO_2e$ as part of its requirement to meet the state's cap-and-trade emissions trading scheme for the 2015–2017 compliance period.[49] Beyond compliance markets, BP sees carbon offsets as a growing industry. In December 2020, the firm acquired a majority stake in Finite Carbon, at the time the largest developer of forest carbon offsets in the United States (70 $MtCO_2e$ registered offsets).[50]

Microsoft

The integrated technology company Microsoft Corporation had $143 billion in sales revenue in 2020. Microsoft's cloud operations were distributed across more than one hundred data centers in fifty-four regions, delivering computing services in 140 countries. In 2020, the firm accounted for a CCF of about 11 $MtCO_2$, including Scope 1 to 3 emissions.[51] In January 2020, the firm announced it would be carbon negative by 2030 and by 2050 remove all the CO_2 it had cumulatively emitted since its founding.[52] Broadly, the firm has identified four ways to achieve this goal: (1) an internal carbon fee; (2) data center energy efficiency and exclusive reliance on renewable energy; (3) supply chain partnering and coordination; and (4) the use of CO_2 removal technologies.

Microsoft has been charging an internal carbon fee since 2012 on Scope 1 and 2 emissions and business air travel (Scope 3). In 2020, the fee was increased to $15 per tCO_2 for all business groups and now also applies to all Scope 3 emissions, though initially at a lower rate.[53] The company has provided the following quantitative reduction goals for the coming decades: reduce Scope 1 and Scope 2 emissions by 2025 through energy efficiency and 100 percent renewable energy, eliminate diesel generators as a backup power source for data centers by 2030 and replace them with batteries or hydrogen fuel cells, and electrify the more than 1,800 campus operations vehicle fleet. By 2030, the firm also aims to reduce its Scope 3 emissions by 55 percent through an updated supplier code of conduct, requiring disclosure of GHG emissions, and implementation of an audit management system to track progress on the emission goals by its suppliers. Starting in 2021, supplier emissions will become an evaluation criterion for the purchasing departments at Microsoft.[54]

To zero out residual emissions and become carbon negative on an annual basis by 2030, Microsoft is investing in carbon removal solutions rather than so-called avoidance offsets. In this context, the company commented:

> As we shifted our focus from carbon offsets to carbon removals, we entered a relatively new landscape. We could no longer rely as heavily on carbon registries to validate project quality, because their standards were designed almost exclusively to measure and verify the claims of projects that avoid or reduce emissions, and we experienced a lack of consistency in how the standards address key criteria. We are eager for standards to address these issues in their crediting systems. For now, although we did look to existing standards for some guidance, we largely needed to set our own course.[55]

In July 2020, Microsoft issued a request for proposals to source carbon removal projects, with an initial focus on nature-based climate solutions given pricing and availability.[56] Microsoft secured removal of

1.3 $MtCO_2e$ for 2021 from fifteen projects, with 99 percent of ear-marked CO_2 to be removed via natural solutions with a durability (permanence) of less than a hundred years.

Measurement Issues

A common feature of the corporate decarbonization plans discussed in the preceding section is that firms operationalize their CO_2 reduction goals in terms of an annual flow variable, which we represent as $CCF_t = E_t - O_t$. Here, E_t represents gross emissions in year t and O_t represents offsets in that year. We refer to CCF_t interchangeably as the firm's corporate carbon footprint or its net emissions in year t. Firms with "net-zero" pledges project that their adopted measure of CCF_t will go to zero by a target date, frequently the year 2050. As argued in the previous section, the goals Microsoft and Google have articulated are far more ambitious, to the extent that they seek to eliminate all legacy emissions from the firm's past. For Microsoft, this will require that the sum of all CCF_t starting in 1985 and ending in 2030 not exceed zero. This more demanding criterion, also put forth by Google, refers to *climate neutrality*.

There are a host of measurement issues pertaining to both gross emissions and offsets.[57] As illustrated in the conceptual framework shown in figure 15-3, the purchase of offsets frequently relies on a marketplace in which suppliers make projects available that corporate emitters then claim as offsets. In the current environment, buyers of these offsets have wide latitude in determining the eligibility of particular offset projects.

Gross Emissions

There appears to be general agreement that all direct (Scope 1) CO_2 emissions from flue gases and tailpipes emanating from a firm's production and transportation activities are to be included in E_t. Our sample of corporate carbon pledges also suggests that it is common practice to include Scope 2 (indirect) emissions based on the production of energy, meaning electricity, heating, and cooling that is consumed by the firm. In service industries such as internet technology or financial services, this second component of E_t is frequently the dominant part of a firm's CCF_t. The main argument for including these indirect emissions in E_t is that, depending on the jurisdiction, businesses have some control over the energy mix they buy and the choice of their energy suppliers. At the

FIGURE 15-3

Conceptual framework for determining a firm's corporate carbon footprint

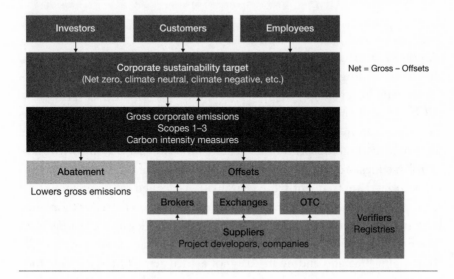

same time, though, there is the obvious issue of double counting in the overall economy: a firm's Scope 2 emissions are also included in the Scope 1 emissions of its energy suppliers. As a consequence, any year-over-year reduction in direct emissions by the energy supplier will also be counted as an improvement in E_t by the party buying the energy.

Issues of double counting become even more prevalent in connection with Scope 3 emissions.[58] Not surprisingly, the supply chain report of the Carbon Disclosure Project estimates that the ratio of indirect supply chain emissions to direct emissions is 10.9 for firms in the retail industry, yet this ratio is only 0.4 for firms in the fossil fuel industry.

For the sample of firms covered in the previous section, we note that there was considerable variation as to which of the many categories among the Scope 3 emissions firms are willing to include in their measure of E_t. While Excel, BP, or Unilever include multiple Scope 3 emission categories, companies such as Google only recognize employee travel and commuting.[59] Similarly, as noted earlier, the utility Xcel excludes from its CCF the emissions associated with the combustion of the natural gas that the firm sells to its customers.

For manufacturing industries in which firms assemble multiple complex components in their products, the boundaries of the Scope 3 emissions become inherently fuzzy as one moves up the value chain across the different tiers of suppliers, which in turn supply multiple customers. The issues associated with the inclusion of Scope 3 emissions are well illustrated in connection with an automotive company such as Toyota.[60] According to the GHG protocol (Corporate Value Chain, Scope 3, Accounting and Reporting Standard), Toyota should estimate the carbon content of all components going into its vehicles by including an "appropriate allocation" for the use of capital goods, upstream transportation, and distribution.[61] Clearly, this is a task of daunting complexity for an automobile consisting of approximately thirty thousand individual parts. Consistent with these concerns, a recent white paper by the Rocky Mountain Institute concludes that "Scope 3 emissions are not well defined for individual industries."[62]

On the product use side, the GHG protocol suggests that Toyota estimate the CO_2 emissions from combusting the fuel used by the vehicles sold over their lifetime and recognize these lifetime emissions in the year of sale. On this last prescription, the GHG protocol appears to conflate stock and flow variables. For instance, when the company acquires a car for use in its own operations, it would presumably recognize the attendant (Scope 1) tailpipe emissions on an ongoing annual basis rather than upfront in the year of acquisition.

As noted at the outset of this chapter, some firms not only set net-zero targets but also specify milestones for partial reductions at intermediate points in time. To account for growth (or contraction) of the business over multiple decades, a meaningful criterion for achieving the milestone goal must put the CCF measure in relation to a suitable activity measure, such as output or sales. The absolute CCF_t metric is then replaced by a *carbon intensity ratio* that includes in the denominator the activity variable to be chosen. For companies with a relatively homogeneous product line, physical measures of output may be suitable, but even then, the reporting entity will retain considerable flexibility in choosing a favorable measure for the denominator of its carbon intensity metric.[63] As described in the previous section, Unilever addresses this issue by imputing a standard quantity of CO_2 per individual portion (use). This quantity is the same for Unilever's entire range of consumer products. To measure reductions in the carbon intensity of diversified industrial conglomerates, it seems that only a financial aggregator, such as sales or cost of goods sold, will be practical as the activity measure in the denominator.

Carbon Offsets

We refer to a carbon offset as one metric ton of CO_2 either not emitted into, or removed from, the atmosphere. Somewhat like indulgences sold by the Catholic Church in past centuries, firms reduce their reported carbon footprint through the purchase of offsets. It is widely acknowledged that there are significant differences in the types of offsets currently traded in voluntary carbon markets. These differences are reflected in the wide range of transaction prices, ranging from $0.10 to $780 per ton, with an average of $3 per metric ton in 2020. The carbon offset supplier NCX, for instance, works with timber farmers, who are paid to delay cutting down trees for one year. In contrast, other offsets involve removing CO_2 from the ambient air (direct air capture) and then sequestering it in geological formations for long periods of time, say a thousand years.

The offsets traded in current voluntary credit markets can be grouped into avoidance and removal offsets. *Avoidance offsets* are generated from projects that lead to a reduction in emissions from current emission sources. They account for tons of CO_2 that would have been emitted (compared to a projected baseline) but were avoided in that year because of an intervention. Avoidance offsets typically involve contractual agreements with another party. These offsets can originate in nature or through reliance on a technology-based intervention. Nature-based avoidance offsets can be generated, for instance, if a forest, which from a carbon storage perspective is in a steady state, is preserved rather than logged. Large-scale project developers such as the Nature Conservancy and GreenTrees pay landowners who have a stated intention, and plausible economic motive, to cut down forests not to do so—thus avoiding the emissions of deforestation. Technology-based avoidance offsets hinge on the use of a production process that reduces the amount of emissions compared to the status quo. Applicable examples here include renewable energy projects, green cement, or clean cook stoves.

Our earlier discussion touched on Google's approach of relying on technology-based avoidance offsets, for instance by financing renewable power plants that supply clean energy to the grid. As a consequence, the emissions from fossil fuel energy in that location are displaced by a renewable power plant owned or financed by Google. Even though

Google will frequently not consume the clean energy generated by the plant, the company performs an effective "electron swap" for accounting purposes and recognizes offsets from clean power production based on the carbon intensity of the grid in the location of the renewable power facility. Issues of double counting across the economy will again arise in this context if the company that buys the energy from Google's renewable plant, say a utility such as Xcel, also takes credit under its own CCF measure for the clean electrons sold to its customers.

In contrast, *removal offsets* are generated by projects that actively remove carbon dioxide from the atmosphere and then store it for a period of time. Removal offsets also comprise nature- and technology-based solutions. Nature-based removal offsets sequester additional carbon in the biosphere, for instance through reforestation, advanced weathering, biochar, ocean capture, and soil carbon sequestration. Project Vesta provides an illustration of deploying advanced weathering techniques. Their process distributes volcanic olivine, a natural mineral, on beaches. Ocean waves then grind the mineral to the size of sand particles, which, in turn, absorb atmospheric CO_2 and store it permanently.

Technology-based removal offsets involve the capture of CO_2 followed by storage outside the biosphere. Swiss company Climeworks is a prime example in this context, as it captures CO_2 directly from the ambient air and then permanently sequesters it underground in basaltic rock formations.[64] Figure 15-4 illustrates both nature-based (storage inside the biosphere) and technology-based (storage outside the biosphere) carbon removal mechanisms.

In voluntary carbon markets, buyers who seek to offset their emissions are matched with suppliers who have projects that either avoid CO_2 emissions or remove them. A growing ecosystem is developing to facilitate trades on these voluntary carbon markets—consisting of brokers, exchanges, registries, and verification bodies. The brokers are frequently boutique firms that buy offsets and bundle them to the specific needs of buyers. The exchanges, in contrast, are marketplaces that list a wide range of offsets available for sale. Brokers such as South Pole and BlueSource have built reputations for listing offsets of all types, while a firm such as Puro.Earth offers only removal offsets.

Buyers can also purchase offsets directly from suppliers ("over the counter" purchases).[65] Since 2019, there has been an increased trend toward over-the-counter purchases, especially from larger firms, such as Stripe and United Airlines, that seek direct interactions with specific

FIGURE 15-4

Alternative carbon-removal mechanisms that subsequently store the carbon dioxide either within the biosphere (e.g., forests) or outside it (e.g., geologic formations)

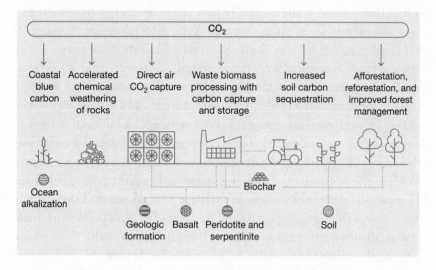

Source: Andrew Bergman and Anatoly Rinberg, "Harms and Co-benefits of Large-Scale CDR Deployment," in *Carbon Dioxide Removal Primer* (CDR Primer, 2021), https://cdrprimer.org/read/chapter-1#sec-1-6.

suppliers deemed to be of high quality. Once an offset is purchased, it is retired to avoid the possibility of multiple parties receiving credit.

Carbon markets first came to prominence in 1997, when the Kyoto Protocol established carbon credits as a mechanism for countries and firms to offset their emissions. The volume of offsets supplied (issued) and bought (retired) has seen rapid growth in the late 2010s. As shown in figure 15-5, volume supply doubled between 2018 and 2019 (to 138 million)[66] and then grew again by one-third from 2019 to 2020 (to 181 million).[67] At the time of writing, the vast majority of these offsets are avoidance offsets, which tend to be cheaper than removal offsets. In 2019, just over half of all offsets (53 percent) were nature-based.[68]

The average price of an offset has been declining, from an average of $7 per metric ton of CO_2 in 2008 to around $3 per metric ton in 2019.[69] Overall, transaction prices vary dramatically based on the degree of verification and the geographic location of the offset project. The graphic in figure 15-6 illustrates the wide range of offset prices observed in the

FIGURE 15-5

Volume of carbon offsets issued and volume purchased and later retired

Voluntary carbon market, millions of metric tons of carbon dioxide equivalent

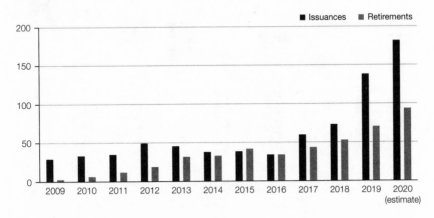

Source: Christopher Blaufelder et al., "A Blueprint for Scaling Voluntary Carbon Markets to Meet the Climate Challenge," McKinsey & Company, January 29, 2020, https://www.mckinsey.com/business-functions /sustainability/our-insights/a-blueprint-for-scaling-voluntary-carbon-markets-to-meet-the-climate -challenge.

voluntary carbon markets. As noted, the prices of offsets can approach $800 per ton for select over-the-counter transactions.

In light of figure 15-6, it is instructive to estimate the cost of the technology-based avoidance offsets that a company such as Google incurs when it builds (finances) a renewable power plant in some off-site location. As described earlier, the renewable energy is frequently sold to third parties, and Google claims the carbon offsets by effectively swapping the carbon-free energy produced for "gray" grid power consumed by its data centers.

The unit economics of a renewable power plant is proportional to the difference between the price per MWh under the power purchasing agreement (PPA; negotiated between the investor and the purchasing entity known as the "off-taker") and the life cycle cost of generating 1 MWh of electricity, the so-called levelized cost of electricity (LCOE).[70] For a solar photovoltaic installation in California, for example, a reasonable value in 2021 would be PPA = 30 dollars per MWh and LCOE = 32 dollars per MWh. The facility would then be unprofitable (negative net

FIGURE 15-6

Voluntary carbon offset prices by sector

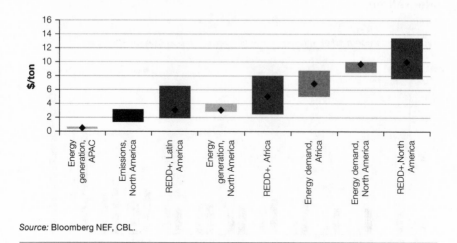

Source: Bloomberg NEF, CBL.

present value) at the rate of $2 per MWh for the investor (Google), but each megawatt hour of clean electricity will generate carbon offsets. The magnitude and cost of the resulting offsets depend on the carbon intensity of the grid in which the solar facility operates. For the California grid in 2020, the average amount of CO_2 emitted was 0.2 tons per MWh. The cost of offsetting one metric ton of CO_2 for the investor was therefore $10 (i.e., $2/0.2 = 10$). This cost would shrink to one-third ($3.33 per ton of CO_2) if the solar facility were to operate in the state of Colorado, where the grid emitted on average 0.6 tons per MWh. In effect, these types of avoidance offsets become cheaper for the investor if the same "clean" electrons are counted as displacing "gray" electrons with a higher CO_2 emissions basis.

The wide range of carbon offset prices observed in voluntary carbon markets suggests significant quality variances. While the Taskforce on Scaling Voluntary Carbon Markets (TSVCM) reports that 90 percent of credits do adhere to verification through certification bodies such as Verified Carbon Standard or American Carbon Registry, such verification arguably represents only a minimum standard. There does not appear to be a bright-line standard for what constitutes a "high-quality" carbon offset. Certain qualitative criteria mentioned repeatedly can be summarized under the acronym PLAN: permanence, leakage, additionality, and negativity.

Permanence, or durability, of an offset refers to the amount of time that the CO_2 is expected to be stored rather than released into the atmosphere. A company such as NCX deliberately focuses on short-term durability when it offers one-year contracts to landowners that pay them to delay cutting down a tree for at least one more year. Such contracts can obviously be renewed and have the advantage of avoiding the long lead times required to verify and accrue credits in connection with some nature-based offsets.[71] Typically, technology-based removal offsets have longer permanence, as carbon is stored outside the biosphere, with relatively low risk of being released in the foreseeable future. Some buyers, such as Stripe, have set permanence thresholds of at least a thousand years for the offsets they purchase. CarbonPlan, a nonprofit focused on improving the functioning of voluntary carbon markets, seeks to quantify the trade-off between permanence and the cost of different types of carbon removal offsets (see figure 15-7).[72]

Leakage in connection with avoidance offsets would occur if credits were issued because the supplier agrees to preserve a particular forest or natural habitat, including the carbon stored there, yet the supplier released the same amount of CO_2 by taking down another natural habitat in another location. Leakage is closely related to the criterion of *additionality*. The requirement here is that the carbon reduction would not have happened without the intervention generating the offset (for a discussion of additionality, see also Matt Bannick's chapter 6 in this volume). Additionality is harder to establish with avoidance offsets, as, by definition, the offset hinges on a counterfactual claim: without the intervention, a specific amount of carbon dioxide would have been emitted from this source. There has been increased press coverage of the additionality issues with nature-based solutions. Bloomberg Green reported that a number of nature-based avoidance credits were issued by GreenTrees and the Nature Conservancy on forests that were never under threat of being cut down.[73] For removal credits, especially technology-driven ones, additionality will frequently be easier to establish. It appears implausible that the suppliers of these offsets would extract CO_2 from the ambient air or the flue gases from an industrial facility and then sequester the CO_2 geologically without the monetary incentive of selling the corresponding offsets. In 2020, Microsoft announced a shift from buying nature-based avoidance offsets to buying only removal offsets, specifically because additionality was difficult to establish for the avoidance offsets the company had historically purchased.

FIGURE 15-7

Logarithmic scale of the association between the permanence (duration) and the cost (price) of carbon offsets

Each point shows the cost and permanence for an individual project. Shapes represent project categories: forests (triangle), soil (square), biomass (diamond), direct air capture (inverted triangle), mineralization (cross), and ocean (circle).

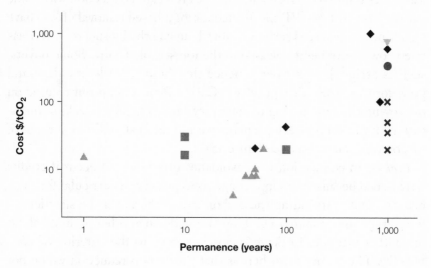

Source: CarbonPlan.

Finally, the *negativity* criterion postulates that the emissions generated by implementing an offset project are properly subtracted from the total emissions claimed by the offset. In connection with a direct air capture plant, this would require that the project generate credits in the amount of CO_2 directly removed from the atmosphere minus the CO_2 that was emitted to generate the energy required to power the capture plant.

Carbon offset buyers such as Stripe and Microsoft have articulated their own criteria for what constitutes a high-quality offset. Stripe has committed to spending $1 million annually on removal offsets. In 2020, the company led a transparent procurement process to buy offsets directly from suppliers only from projects that could remove and store carbon outside the biosphere for at least a thousand years. The first year's purchases went to just four projects, with Stripe paying $75 to $775 per ton of carbon removed, up to 258 times the 2020 average price of offsets.

Beyond the immediate offsets generated, Stripe's impact concept emphasizes the idea of bringing the price of removal technologies down the cost learning curve. As mentioned earlier, Microsoft will for now only acquire removal offsets, but it does not exclude nature-based removal offsets with a shorter durability. Numerous other firms with net-zero commitments are taking a similar path, shunning avoidance credits in the short run and instead investing directly in removal technologies for the long run.[74] As discussed, United Airlines is a company in that group.

Not everyone agrees that the best way forward is to focus exclusively on removal offsets. The TSVCM calls for reliance on avoidance credits in the short term, as they are currently the most cost-efficient way to reduce overall emissions subject to appropriate verification. Only when the cost of removal offsets has been brought down sufficiently and there has been sufficient focus on abatement of new emissions does the TSVCM call for a shift toward removal technologies that would offset the remaining "hard to abate" emissions. The TSVCM also estimates that demand for carbon credits would need to increase by a factor of fifteen by 2030 and a factor of a hundred by 2050 to achieve the 1.5°C global warming limit.

At this stage, it remains an open question as to what extent voluntary carbon markets will also grow because of firms' mandatory carbon compliance obligations, such as the European Union's Emission Trading Scheme (ETS) or the California Cap-and-Trade system. Under both regulatory schemes, the obligated firms must generally obtain allowances for their local Scope 1 emissions. The California Cap-and-Trade system allows firms to substitute allowances with carbon offsets obtained from approved supply sources up to an 8 percent ceiling of the emissions regulated by the state of California. Companies such as BP are taking advantage of this alternative compliance option. The recent acquisition of a majority stake in Finite Carbon, a nature-based offset project developer, will presumably enable BP to secure offsets at favorable spot and future prices.[75] The offsets purchased in this manner therefore satisfy both BP's regulatory requirement and the achievement of its voluntary CCF reduction goals.

Improving the Transparency and Accountability of CCF Disclosures

The late 2010s have witnessed a surge of firms making the kinds of carbon reduction pledges summarized here. Since these voluntary disclosures

FIGURE 15-8

Illustration of a hypothetical time-consistent emission trajectory

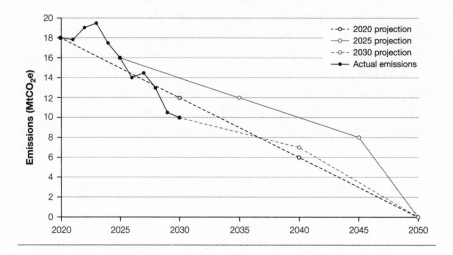

thus far exhibit considerable variation in terms of specificity and scope, the immediate question going forward is what reporting format would make the disclosures more credible and allow the public to hold firms accountable for their earlier projections. Put differently, in the current disclosure environment, there do not seem to be any meaningful trade-offs for firms to join the "net-zero by 2050 club," assuming they do not anticipate having to issue progress reports in the foreseeable future.[76]

It is well established that the internal management control systems of major corporations revolve around a comprehensive system of standard setting combined with subsequent comparisons of the standards with actual results achieved.[77] In the context of corporate carbon reporting, the initial disclosure, say in 2019, regarding a firm's anticipated CCF_t trajectory can be viewed as the initial standard. The credibility of this initial disclosure would be enhanced considerably if it were accompanied by a commitment to provide updated trajectories that relate actual results to the earlier projections. Figure 15-8 illustrates the idea of time-consistent carbon trajectories for a hypothetical setting in which the firm commits to updates on actual emissions annually and updated forecast trajectories every five years. Another assumption maintained in this illustration is that the initial and the updated trajectories all have a 2050 net-zero goal as well as milestones that are ten years apart.[78] The dashed lines reflect the assumption of linear interpolation between any two milestones.

In the hypothetical scenario considered in figure 15-8, the firm would commit to issuing a total of six carbon footprint trajectories over the next thirty years, commencing in 2020. Beginning in 2025, each trajectory would splice together the actual results since 2020 with a forecast segment (dashed line), each one five years shorter than the previous one. Thus, subsequent disclosures would take the actual carbon footprint in that year as the initial baseline value, allowing dynamic performance assessments that compare multiple standard values, issued at five-year intervals in the past, to the actual result achieved in a given year. As illustrated in figure 15-8, the trajectory forecast every five years is likely to change over time. Furthermore, actual values need not be consistent with any of the previous forecasts for that particular year.[79]

As discussed earlier, any measure of CCF_t that includes indirect emissions (Scopes 2 and 3) as part of gross emissions is subject to economy-wide double counting. Such measures will also be muddled by the subjective choice individual companies make in including different categories of their Scope 3 emissions. Similarly, as argued in the previous section, there is currently considerable variation in the quality of offsets, particularly avoidance offsets, that companies are willing to include in their measure of O_t. It would therefore be more informative to the general public if, beyond their current carbon footprint disclosures, firms were to report their Scope 1 net emissions, which we denote as $CCF_{1t} = E_{1t} - O_{1t}$. This measure takes a firm's direct emissions and subtracts only removal offsets with a certified high sequestration duration (e.g., carbon capture combined with geological sequestration). As such, the two components of the metric allow an apples-to-apples comparison of tons of CO_2 "permanently" released into and removed from the atmosphere in a particular year.

Our advocacy for this "core" carbon footprint measure is based on the observation that it is ultimately the sum of all CCF_{1t}, added up across all economic entities and years up to some horizon date T, that determines the concentration of greenhouse gases in the atmosphere at the horizon date T.[80] Put differently, the concentration of CO_2 equivalents in the atmosphere and therefore the global temperature increase relative to pre-industrial levels hinges on the cumulative value of all CCF_{1t} when added up across all economic entities and years up to the planning horizon.[81]

A standardized measurement of carbon footprints would, of course, have to be in place if reporting were to become mandatory. To that end, US companies have an obligation to report their Scope 1 emissions to the US Environmental Protection Agency.[82] For a wide range of industrial sectors, European installations are obligated to report their annual Scope 1 emissions to the European Union Transaction Log under the ETS.[83]

Since 2013 publicly listed firms in the United Kingdom have also been mandated to disclose their annual direct (Scope 1) and indirect (Scope 2) GHG emissions as part of their annual financial reports.[84] Corporate GHG emissions are to be reported in tons of CO_2 equivalents, with the conversion factors for gases other than CO_2 published annually by the British government. The disclosure mandate does not prescribe a specific method for calculating GHG emissions, but it requires the use of "robust and accepted methods" and recommends a "widely recognized independent standard."

Several academic studies have examined whether the UK reporting mandate had a *real effect* insofar as the reporting obligation induced firms to reduce their emissions more quickly than other firms not subject to the regulation.[85] Benedikt Downar and his colleagues hypothesize the emergence of such a real effect resulting from stakeholder pressure.[86] Essentially, the carbon footprint figures publicized in a firm's annual report would create a "pillory" for showing subsequent improvements, yet the UK mandate may not actually have entailed the reporting of substantial additional public information, because many of the treated firms were already engaged in voluntary carbon reporting to the CDP.[87] Furthermore, as noted, all European installations covered by the EU ETS scheme already had to report their Scope 1 emissions to the European Union Transaction Log, and that information has always been in the public domain.

Using a difference-in-differences empirical design, Downar and colleagues estimate that UK firms subject to the carbon reporting mandate under the 2013 act subsequently decreased their Scope 1 emissions by an additional 8 percent compared to a control group of European firms not subject to the British regulation.[88] The authors interpret their finding as evidence that reporting on current emissions leads to additional transparency beyond the information already available through other channels. In anticipation of having to disclose their carbon footprint in subsequent years, firms apparently did feel additional pressure to show ongoing improvements.[89]

Conclusion

As part of the public debate about mitigating the damaging effects of climate change, a growing coalition of global corporations has issued voluntary forecasts regarding their intended contributions toward driving overall global CO_2 emissions to zero. At the same time, an increasing number of national governments have articulated net-zero targets, as illustrated in figure 15-9. While for some companies, such as REI, these efforts have always been part of their mission (even their corporate DNA), many global players in carbon-intensive industries have joined this group in the late 2010s, resulting in a surge of new pledges. Increased stakeholder pressure appears to be a major motivation for firms to make these emission reduction pledges. At the same time, our assessment is that the various existing pledges leave substantial "wiggle room," largely because of scope, horizon, and measurement issues. This may allow some firms to wear the "green mantle" without having to make significant efforts beyond those that will emerge anyhow from more stringent carbon regulations in the future.

FIGURE 15-9

Growing share of emissions for which national governments have set net-zero targets

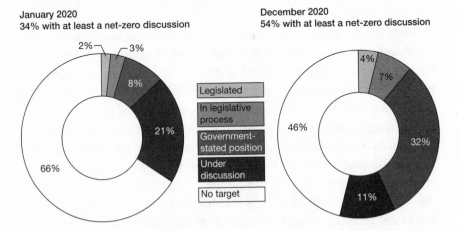

Source: Kyle Harrison et al., "Corporate Net Zero Assessment Tool," Bloomberg New Energy Finance, March 2021, https://www.bnef.com/insights/25987?query=eyJxdWVyeSI6Imt5bGUgaGFycmlzb24iLCJwYW dlIjoxLCJvcmRlciI6InJlbGV2YW5jZSJ9.

Our analysis has focused on how corporate carbon footprints are measured. In that context, the selective inclusion of indirect emissions that fall into the bucket of Scope 3 emissions under the international GHG protocol creates the most significant variation in corporate CO_2 reporting. Further latitude with these pledges arises because firms in different industries will adopt different metrics for the carbon intensity of their products and operations. Yet carbon intensity measures are essential in order to quantify decarbonization progress at intermediate milestones, before firms arrive at their net-zero goal several decades into the future.

Avoidance offsets are another variable that creates substantial variation and latitude in comparing the carbon footprint reductions actually achieved.[90] As the set of firms embracing the "net-zero by 2050" goal has rapidly expanded, the supply of avoidance offset providers appears to have grown correspondingly, leading to a situation where avoidance offsets trade on average at extremely low prices per metric ton of CO_2. Unless firms either declare that avoidance offsets are excluded from their CCF measures or restrict attention to removal offsets, subject to carefully defined durability standards, carbon reduction pledges will be achievable at negligible expense. In that sense, we fully agree with the sentiment expressed by Microsoft's Brad Smith when he stated that "we need to get real on carbon math. The current methods used for carbon accounting are ambiguous and too discretionary. We need clear protocols to ensure that progress reported on an accounting statement is truly progress in the real world."[91]

Aside from carbon footprint measurement issues, we argue that the informativeness and accountability of corporate carbon pledges would be enhanced if companies were to update these projections at regular intervals. The resulting collection of emission reduction curves would allow the public to examine not only how forecasts of future emissions have changed over time but also to what extent intermediate goals at milestones have been met or missed. Firms could self-commit to such time-consistent carbon emission projections. The existing mandate to report concurrent Scope 1 and Scope 2 emissions for listed firms in the United Kingdom also suggests that extended reporting on time-consistent emission trajectories could be made mandatory information in firms' annual reports.

FOR FURTHER READING

Chapter 2 of the 2018 *IPCC Special Report*[92] outlines the changes required to limit overall global temperature increases to 1.5°C compared to preindustrial levels. The *CDR Primer* by Jennifer Wilcox, Ben Kolosz, and Jeremy Freeman covers the science, technology, and opportunities for natural, engineered, and hybrid carbon removal solutions.[93] Data-Driven EnviroLab (datadrivenlab.org) and the NewClimate Institute (newclimate.org) offer an overview of net-zero carbon pledges put forth by companies, regions, and cities. Finally, suggestions for improving corporate carbon-reduction pledges can be found in "The Future of ESG Is . . . Accounting?" (*Harvard Business Review*, 2020) by Richard Barker, Robert G. Eccles, and George Serafeim, and "Three Ways to Improve Net-Zero Emission Targets" (*Nature*, 2021) by Joeri Rogelj, Oliver Geden, Annette Cowie, and Andy Reisinger.

Notes

1. Data-Driven EnviroLab & NewClimate Institute, "Accelerating Net Zero: Exploring Cities, Regions, and Companies' Pledges to Decarbonize," Data-Driven EnviroLab & NewClimate Institute, September 2020, https://newclimate.org/wp-content/uploads/2020/09/NewClimate_Accelerating_Net_Zero_Sept2020.pdf.

2. We note in passing that the major US oil companies ExxonMobil and Chevron are not represented on this chart.

3. Stefan Reichelstein acknowledges financial support from the Deutsche Forschungsgemeinschaft under grant TRR 266.

4. According to the International Greenhouse Gas Protocol, Scope 1 emissions are direct greenhouse gas emissions from flue gases and tailpipes, while Scope 2 includes the emissions associated with electric power, heat, and cooling produced by external suppliers. Finally, Scope 3 captures the indirect emissions in connection with the use of a firm's products as well as the emissions associated with the production of inputs supplied to the firm by its supply chain. The GHG protocol classifies these emissions into multiple categories on both the firm's upstream and downstream sides. See https://ghgprotocol.org/sites/default/files/standards/Corporate-Value-Chain-Accounting-Reporing-Standard_041613_2.pdf.

5. The corresponding estimates increase to 1,170 Gt of CO_2 in order to have a two-thirds chance of keeping the global temperature increase to 2°C and 2,030 Gt of CO_2 for a one-third chance. See Valérie Masson-Delmotte et al., eds., *Global Warming of 1.5°C: An IPCC Special Report on the Impacts of Global Warming of 1.5°C above Pre-industrial Levels and Related Global Greenhouse Gas Emission Pathways, in the Context of Strengthening the Global Response to the Threat of Climate Change, Sustainable Development, and Efforts to Eradicate Poverty* (IPCC, 2018), https://www.ipcc.ch/site/assets/uploads/sites/2/2019/06/SR15_Full_Report_Low_Res.pdf.

6. The Stern Review refers to "the greatest market failure ever seen" in connection with climate change. See Nicholas Stern, *The Economics of Climate Change: The Stern Review* (Cambridge: Cambridge University Press, 2006).

7. A survey published by Barclays Private Bank found that 87 percent of the world's wealthiest individuals, families, family offices, and foundations reported that the effects of climate change played a part in their investment choices. See Matthew Vincent, "The Problem with Zero Carbon Pledges," *Financial Times*, November 29, 2020.

8. William Sprouse, "BlackRock CEO: Climate Change Is Causing a Fundamental Reshape of Finance," *CFO Magazine*, January 2020.

9. Andrew Sorkin, "BlackRock Chief Pushes a Big New Climate Goal for the Corporate World," *New York Times*, January 27, 2021.

10. "Cheap Cheats: Why Are Carbon Offsets so Cheap?," *The Economist*, September 19–25, 2020.

11. *Alphabet's 2020 CDP Climate Change Response* (Mountain View: Google, August 2020), https://www.gstatic.com/gumdrop/sustainability/alphabet-2020-cdp-climate-change-response.pdf.

12. *Google Environmental Report 2019* (Mountain View: Google, 2020), https://www.gstatic.com/gumdrop/sustainability/google-2019-environmental-report.pdf.

13. S. Pichai, *Realizing a Carbon-Free Future: Google's Third Decade of Climate Action* (Mountain View: Google, September 2020), https://www.gstatic.com/gumdrop/sustainability/carbon-free-by-2030.pdf.

14. *24/7 by 2030: Realizing a Carbon-free Future* (Mountain View: Google, September 2020), https://www.gstatic.com/gumdrop/sustainability/247-carbon-free-energy.pdf.

15. Xcel Energy, Inc., *2019 CDP Disclosure*, https://www.xcelenergy.com/staticfiles/xe-responsive/Environment/Xcel%20Energy%20CDP%20Climate%20Change%20Questionnaire%202019.pdf.

16. The IPCC has issued guidelines for setting the relative weights attached to greenhouse gases other than CO_2 in order to reflect their potency and longevity in the atmosphere.

17. Methane is being addressed through voluntary programs such as the US Environmental Protection Agency's Natural Gas STAR program, which provides a framework to implement methane-reducing technologies and practices and document voluntary emission-reduction activities.

18. Catherine Morehouse, "Xcel Cuts Carbon Emissions 50% by 2021, Eyes Colorado Transmission, Plants to Reach 2030 Goal," *Utility Dive*, January 29, 2021, https://www.utilitydive.com/news/xcel-cuts-carbon-emissions-50-by-2021-eyes-colorado-transmission-coal-pl/594179/.

19. Base year emissions ~80 $MtCO_2e$.

20. Xcel Energy, *Carbon Report 2019*, https://www.xcelenergy.com/staticfiles/xe/PDF/Xcel%20Energy%20Carbon%20Report%20-%20Feb%202019.pdf.

21. Ibid.

22. Recreational Equipment, Inc., "REI Co-op Achieves 14-Year Carbon Neutrality Commitment, Announces Ambitious New Climate Platform," September 24, 2020, https://www.rei.com/newsroom/article/rei-co-op-achieves-14-year-carbon-neutrality-commitment-announces-ambitious-new-climate-platform.

23. Sarah Grothjan, "REI's New Climate Commitment Includes Pledge to Halve Its Carbon Footprint by 2030," REI Co-op, September 24, 2020, https://www.rei.com/blog/news/reis-climate-commitment-halve-carbon-footprint-by-2030.

24. REI Co-op, "Climate Change & Our Environmental Impact," REI Co-op, May 2021, https://www.rei.com/stewardship/climate-change.

25. Climate Neutral, "Climate Neutral Certified," Climate Neutral, May 2021, https://www.climateneutral.org/.

26. Unilever includes upstream ingredients and packaging use and downstream distribution, retail, and consumer use. Consumer use accounts for nearly 66% of the firm's total CCF.

27. Unilever, "Unilever Sets Out New Actions to Fight Climate Change, and Protect and Regenerate Nature, to Preserve Resources for Future Generations," press release, June 15, 2020, https://www.unilever.com/news/press-releases/2020/unilever-sets-out-new-actions-to-fight-climate-change-and-protect-and-regenerate-nature-to-preserve-resources-for-future-generations.html.

28. "Purpose led, future fit," slogan in Unilever annual report on form 20-F, 2019, https://www.unilever.com/Images/unilever-annual-report-and-accounts-2019-20f_tcm244-547894_en.pdf.

29. Based on projections for changes in the number of consumer uses of products, this equates to a 5% decrease in absolute emissions by the 2030 target. Also, the target does not include production for which Unilever does not have full control over the finished product sold, "products developed and manufactured through our joint venture operations, products distributed to professional markets via Food Solutions, bulk items and export items that are sold to third parties as unfinished products, promotional items and complex packs, and tools and devices."

30. Unilever, "Decarbonising Our Business" May 2021, https://www.unilever.com/sustainable-living/reducing-environmental-impact/greenhouse-gases/.

31. Unilever, *CDP Climate Change Questionnaire 2020*, https://www.unilever.com/Images/unilever-cdp-climate-2020_tcm244-558529_en.pdf.

32. United Airlines, Inc., "United Makes Bold Environmental Commitment Unmatched by Any Airline; Pledges 100% Green by Reducing Greenhouse Gas Emissions 100% by 2050," December 10, 2020, https://hub.united.com/united-pledges-100-green-2050-2649438060.html.

33. Ibid.

34. United Airlines, Inc., "Fuel Efficiency and Emissions Reductions," 2019, https://www.united.com/ual/en/us/fly/company/global-citizenship/environment/fuel-efficiency-and-emissions-reduction.html.

35. United Airlines, Inc., "United Airlines Pledges $40 Million to Further Decarbonize Commercial Air Travel," October 25, 2019, https://hub.united.com/united-pledges-to-further-decarbonize-commercial-air-travel-2641103060.html. For reference, United consumed 4.3 billion gallons in 2019. See United Airlines Fourth Quarter and Full-Year 2020 Results, https://hub.united.com/2021-01-20-united-announces-2020-financial-results-2021-will-focus-on-transition-to

-recovery-expects-to-exceed-2019-adjusted-ebitda-margin-by-2023-2650045521
.html.

36. International Civil Aviation Organization, *Carbon Offsetting and Reduction Scheme for International Aviation (CORSIA) Frequently Asked Questions*, updated December 30, 2020, https://www.icao.int/environmental- protection/CORSIA /Documents/CORSIA_FAQs_December%202020_final.pdf.

37. "While they may offer customers some peace of mind, traditional carbon offsets do almost nothing to tackle the emissions from flying," Scott Kirby, chief executive of United Airlines, said in an interview. "And, more importantly, they simply don't meet the scale of this global challenge." See Steven Mufson, "United Airlines Aims to Suck Carbon Dioxide from the Friendly Skies," *Washington Post*, January 12, 2021.

38. Robinson Meyer, "The Weekly Planet: The Only Way to Achieve Carbon-Neutral Flight, According to an Airline," *The Atlantic*, December 15, 2020, https:// www.theatlantic.com/science/archive/2020/12/united-airlines-wants-have-its -carbon-and-eat-it-too/617399/.

39. 1PointFive, "Oxy Low Carbon Ventures, Rusheen Capital Management Create Development Company 1PointFive to Deploy Carbon Engineering's Direct Air Capture Technology," launch press release, August 19, 2020, https://www .1pointfive.com/launch-release.

40. Oxy Low Carbon Ventures, "1PointFive Selects Worley for FEED on Milestone Direct Air Capture Facility," Oxy Low Carbon Ventures, February 22, 2021, https://www.oxylowcarbon.com/news/1pointfive-selects-worley-for-feed.

41. Bernard Looney, Murray Achincloss, and Craig Marshall, "BP Fourth Quarter and Full Year 2020 Financial Results Presentation," BP, February 2021, https://www.bp.com/content/dam/bp/business-sites/en/global/corporate/pdfs /investors/bp-fourth-quarter-2020-results-presentation-slides-and-script.pdf.

42. BP, *Energy with Purpose: BP Sustainability Report 2019*, https://www.bp.com /content/dam/bp/business-sites/en/global/corporate/pdfs/sustainability/group -reports/bp-sustainability-report-2019.pdf.

43. Giulia Chierchia, "Reimaging Energy," BP, September 14, 2020, https:// www.bp.com/content/dam/bp/business-sites/en/global/corporate/pdfs/investors /bpweek/bpweek-reimagining-energy-slides-and-script.pdf.

44. BP, *Energy with Purpose*; all targets are relative to a 2015 baseline.

45. This goal is set on an equity share basis based on the company's net share of production, thus excluding production by its partner Rosneft. Furthermore, this aim includes the emissions from the combustion of upstream production of crude oil, natural gas, and natural gas liquids. For further details, see BP, *Energy with Purpose*, 24.

46. Chierchia, "Reimaging Energy," 14.

47. Marshall et al., "BP Fourth Quarter and Full Year 2020 Financial Results Presentation."

48. California Air Resources Board, "Cap-and-Trade Program Data," https://ww2.arb.ca.gov/our-work/programs/cap-and-trade-program/cap-and-trade -program-data.

49. BP Products North America, Inc., purchased credits from offset projects approved by the California Air Resources Board for projects located in various states in the United States. The types of projects for which activities provided the carbon offsets were forests (75% of credits), mine methane capture (12%), and ozone-depleting substances (13%). The 1.7 $MtCO_2e$ represents 8% of the BP subsidiary's total obligation during the compliance period, which was the maximum allowable during that period. This "offset usage limit" drops to 4% for the 2021–2025 period. See California Air Resources Board, "Cap-and-Trade Program Data."

50. BP, "BP Acquires Majority Stake in Largest US Forest Carbon Offset Developer Finite Carbon," press release, December 16, 2020, https://www.bp.com /en/global/corporate/news-and-insights/press-releases/bp-acquires-majority-stake -in-largest-us-forest-carbon-offset-developer-finite-carbon.html.

51. Scope 3 emissions include six upstream categories (purchased goods and services, capital goods, fuel and energy-related activities, upstream transportation, waste, and employee commuting) and four downstream categories (downstream transportation, use of sold products, end of life of sold products, and downstream leased assets).

52. Microsoft, *2020 Microsoft Environmental Sustainability Report—a Year of Action*, https://query.prod.cms.rt.microsoft.com/cms/api/am/binary/RWyG1q.

53. Ibid. This fee will increase over time so that there is a single fee across the entire emission portfolio.

54. This is only a sample from the most recent updates. For other targets, see Microsoft Corporation, *CDP Climate Change Questionnaire 2020* (Redmond, WA: Microsoft, 2020), https://query.prod.cms.rt.microsoft.com/cms/api/am/binary /RE2EWBx.

55. Ibid.

56. B. Smith, "Microsoft Will Be Carbon Negative by 2030," https://blogs .microsoft.com/blog/2020/01/16/microsoft-will-be-carbon-negative-by-2030/.

57. We use the terms "credit" and "offset" interchangeably.

58. Steve Milloy reports that Exxon Mobil will be reporting Scope 3 emissions related to the sale of oil. He argues that such reporting not only leads to undesirable double counting but is also redundant because it is known that every barrel of oil ultimately results in about 0.42 tons of CO_2 emissions. See Steve Milloy, "Scope 3 Emissions: A Climate Accounting Absurdity," Real Clear Energy, December 16, 2020, https://www.realclearenergy.org/articles/2020/12/16/scope_3_emissions_a _climate_accounting_absurdity_653453.html.

59. Similarly, aircraft manufacturer Boeing currently only recognizes emissions from business travel in its Scope 3 calculations. See Boeing, *Global Environment Report 2020 Companion Summary* (Chicago: Boeing, 2021), http://www.boeing.com /resources/boeingdotcom/principles/environment/pdf/er-companion-summary -092820.pdf.

60. Scope 3 accounted for more than 98% of emissions associated with vehicle production in 2020. See Toyota Industries Corporation, "Scope 3 Emissions," https://www.toyota-industries.com/csr/environment/process/scope3/.

61. *GHG Protocol: Corporate Value Chain (Scope 3) Accounting and Reporting Standard, Supplement to the GHG Protocol Corporate Accounting and Reporting Standard* (World Resources Institute and World Business Council for Sustainable Development, September 2011).

62. Rocky Mountain Institute, *The Next Frontier of Carbon Accounting: A Unified Approach for Unlocking Systemic Change* (Boulder, CO: Rocky Mountain Institute, 2020), https://rmi.org/insight/the-next-frontier-ofcarbon-accounting/.

63. According to its CEO Martin Brudermüller, German chemical company BASF intends to measure its carbon intensity by using "tons of chemical product" as the denominator. See video produced on February 9, 2021, https://www.youtube.com/watch?v=umVk2cKwTM8. BASF produces a wide range of chemical products that differ significantly in terms of their individual carbon content. Thus, a mere change in the product mix could result in a substantial reduction in the firm's carbon intensity metric, even though the emissions per ton of each individual product remain unchanged.

64. Ryan Orbuch, "Stripe's First Carbon Removal Purchases," Stripe, May 18, 2020, https://stripe.com/blog/first-negative-emissions-purchases#recognition-footer.

65. Kyle Harrison, "Voluntary Carbon Offsets: A Shortcut for Heavy Emitters," Bloomberg New Energy Finance, April 22, 2020, https://www.bnef.com/insights/22881.

66. Ibid.

67. Taskforce on Scaling Voluntary Carbon Markets, *TSVCM Final Report* (Washington, DC: Taskforce on Scaling Voluntary Carbon Markets, 2021), https://www.iif.com/Portals/1/Files/TSVCM_Report.pdf.

68. McKinsey & Company, *How the Voluntary Carbon Market Can Help Address Climate Change* (San Francisco: McKinsey & Company, December 17, 2020), https://www.mckinsey.com/business-functions/sustainability/our-insights/how-the-voluntary-carbon-market-can-help-address-climate-change.

69. Ibid.

70. See Gunther Glenk and Stefan Reichelstein, "Intermittent versus Dispatchable Power Sources: An Integrated Competitive Assessment," working paper, University of Mannheim, July 2021.

71. Taskforce on Scaling Voluntary Carbon Markets, *TSVCM Final Report*.

72. Danny Cullenward, Joseph Hamman, and Jeremy Freeman, "Insights from Our First Project Reports," CarbonPlan, 2020, https://carbonplan.org/research/stripe-reports-insights.

73. Eric Roston, "United Will Suck Carbon from the Air Instead of Buying Offsets," Bloomberg, December 10, 2020, https://www.bloomberg.com/news/articles/2020-12-10/united-will-suck-carbon-from-the-air-instead-of-buying-offsets?sref=qfKj5WRL.

74. Ibid.

75. Michael Holder, "BP Invests and Gets Majority Stake in US Forest Offset Firm Finite Carbon," GreenBiz, December 22, 2020, https://www

.greenbiz.com/article/bp-invests-and-gets-majority-stake-us-forest-offset-firm
-finite-carbon.

76. In the literature on voluntary disclosure, such an outcome is referred to as a pooling equilibrium. The literature has also established conditions when such pooling equilibria will either be impossible or at least improbable because some players will be able to credibly differentiate themselves from the pool.

77. See Srikant Datar and Madhav Rajan, *Horngren's Cost Accounting* (Upper Saddle River, NJ: Prentice Hall, 2019).

78. This aligns with SBTi's best practice recommendation of setting climate ambitions with target dates five to fifteen years in the future. See Science Based Targets, *SBTi Progress Report 2020* (Washington, DC: Science Based Targets, 2021), https://sciencebasedtargets.org/resources/files/SBTiProgressReport2020.pdf.

79. Forthcoming measurement, reporting, and verification guidelines from the Science Based Targets Initiative will likely suggest the ongoing communication of annual and historic results as part of a firm's climate disclosures. See Science Based Targets, "From Ambition to Impact: How Companies Are Reducing Emissions at Scale with Science-Based Targets," in *SBTi Progress Report 2020*.

80. This consideration is precisely the basis for the IPCC when it calculates (probabilistic) carbon budgets for keeping the global temperature increase below specific ceiling values.

81. The GHG Protocol observes that compliance regimes like the Kyoto Protocol focus on direct emissions as part of top-down country-level inventory development. These calculations would be complemented by an aggregation of bottom-up company data as long as the metric is unambiguous, verifiable, and avoids double counting. The core carbon footprint metric CCF_{It} meets these criteria.

82. Sorabh Tomar examines whether this reporting requirement vis-á-vis the EPA had by itself a real effect in terms of the firms subsequently lowering their emissions. See Sorabh Tomar, "CSR Disclosure and Benchmarking-Learning: Emissions Responses to Mandatory Greenhouse Gas Disclosure," SMU Cox School of Business, September 6, 2019, https://ssrn.com/abstract=3448904.

83. See Benedikt Downar, Juergen Ernstberger, Stefan Reichelstein, Sebastian Schwenen, and Alexander Zaklan, "The Impact of Mandatory Carbon Reporting on Emissions and Financial Operating Performance," presented at the annual *Review of Accounting Studies Conference*, December 2020.

84. The 2013 Regulations of the Companies Act 2006 makes "listed companies" obligated parties in this regard. Section 385 (2) of the act defines a listed company as a UK-incorporated company whose equity shares are either listed on the Main Market of the London Stock Exchange, an exchange in a European Economic Area state, the New York Stock Exchange, or Nasdaq. The act applies to all fiscal years ending on or after September 30, 2013.

85. See Valentin Jouvenot and Philipp Krueger, "Mandatory Corporate Carbon Disclosure: Evidence from a Natural Experiment," University of Geneva, Geneva Finance Research Institute, August 8, 2019, https://ssrn.com/abstract=3434490.

86. Benedikt Downar, Juergen Ernstberger, Stefan Reichelstein, Sebastian Schwenen, and Alexander Zaklan, "The Impact of Mandatory Carbon Reporting on Emissions and Financial Operating Performance," *Review of Accounting Studies*, August 5, 2021.

87. See Jody Grewal, "Real Effects of Disclosure Regulation on Voluntary Disclosers," *Journal of Accounting and Economics*, February 18, 2021, https://doi.org/10.1016/j.jacceco.2021.101390.

88. Downar et al., "The Impact of Mandatory Carbon Reporting on Emissions and Financial Operating Performance," 2021.

89. The 2013 UK mandate also requires that firms disclose a carbon intensity variable. Downar et al. estimate the effect of the disclosure mandate on firms' carbon intensity by considering both sales and cost of goods sold as the activity variable in the denominator. They find that the firms in the treatment group exhibited a significant incremental reduction in carbon intensity of approximately 13 percent when the denominator in the carbon intensity ratio is cost of goods sold and 10 percent when it is Sales. See ibid.

90. Carbon offsets are also controversial in the accounting for carbon reduction pledges by national governments. To illustrate, in April 2021, the European Union passed a law requiring a 55% reduction in emissions relative to 1990 levels by 2030. Critics pointed out that this reduction goal is stated net of CO_2 removals through forests and soil within Europe, yet this natural carbon offset, amounting to around 260 million tons of CO_2 per year, was not included in the calculation of the 1990 status quo emission level.

91. Brad Smith, "One Year Later: The Path to Carbon Negative—a Progress Report on Our Climate Moonshot," Official Microsoft Blog, January 28, 2021, https://blogs.microsoft.com/blog/2021/01/28/one-year-later-the-path-to-carbon-negative-a-progress-report-on-our-climate-moonshot/.

92. Masson-Delmotte et al., *Global Warming of 1.5°C*.

93. Wilcox, Kolosz, and Freeman, *CDR Primer*, 2021.

Acknowledgments

This book was inspired by the change makers, those who harness the power of organizations and management principles to make the world a better place for all humanity. It is not only a celebration of their efforts but also a guide for the next generation to follow in their footsteps and achieve even greater things.

To produce a book like this truly takes a village. Although I cannot properly acknowledge the dozens of people who contributed to this effort, I wanted to highlight a few. First, many thanks to Bernadette Clavier, my partner at Stanford's Center for Social Innovation, who provided tremendous support and encouragement throughout the writing process. I thank my colleague Jennifer Aaker for her helpful advice and guidance during the conceptualization phase of this project. I am grateful to all the authors, from whom I learned a great deal about the exciting field of social innovation. I greatly appreciate the heroic efforts of Russ Siegelman, who took the time to provide cogent feedback on all the chapters. I am also grateful to my colleagues who attended the conference to work on this book, including Anat Admati, Paul Pfleiderer, and Ken Shotts. In particular, Paul did amazing work in helping to develop Bill Meehan's chapter. Finally, Liz Peintner did a terrific job in leading the effort to put together the glossary.

Scott Berinato was a fantastic editor, providing not only helpful feedback on the chapters but also being a tireless advocate for this endeavor. I appreciate his pushing us to balance rigor, relevance, and clarity.

Glossary

The coauthors have compiled a glossary of terms frequently used in this volume, using both their own definitions and those of other sources they frequently cite in their teaching and practitioner roles. Liz Peintner organized the effort to compile this glossary.

achievement gap

According to *The Glossary of Education Reform* by the Great Schools Partnership, the *achievement gap* refers to "any significant and persistent disparity in academic performance or educational attainment between different groups of students, such as white students and minorities, for example, or students from higher-income and lower-income households. . . . The most commonly discussed achievement gap in the United States is the persistent disparity in national standardized-test scores between white and Asian-American students, two groups that score higher on average, and African-American and Hispanic students, two groups that score lower on average." See https://www.edglossary.org/achievement-gap/.

additionality

According to Paul Brest and Kelly Born, *additionality* means that "the investment must increase the quantity or quality of the social or environmental outcome beyond what would otherwise have occurred. The counterfactual is that ordinary, socially neutral investors would have provided the same capital in any event." See https://ssir.org/up _for_debate/article/impact_investing#.

carbon emission scopes / Scope 1, 2, and 3 emissions

The US Environmental Protection Agency defines *carbon emission scopes* as follows: "Scope 1 emissions are direct greenhouse (GHG) emissions that occur from sources that are controlled or owned by an organization (e.g., emissions associated with fuel combustion in boilers, furnaces, vehicles). Scope 2 emissions are indirect GHG emissions associated with the purchase of electricity, steam, heat, or cooling. . . . Scope 3 emissions are the result of activities from assets not owned or controlled by the reporting organization, but that the organization indirectly impacts in its value chain. Scope 3 emissions include all sources not within an organization's scope 1 and 2 boundary." See https://www.epa.gov/climateleadership/scope-1-and-scope-2 -inventory-guidance and https://www.epa.gov/climateleadership /scope-3-inventory-guidance.

carbon offset
The *CDR Primer* defines *carbon offsets* as "programs or policy regimes in which companies or individuals pay for activities that result in emissions reductions or carbon dioxide removal (CDR). In voluntary offset programs, individuals or companies pay project developers (or similar) directly to implement some activity that results in emissions reductions or CDR. In compliance offset programs, such as cap-and-trade programs, companies that are responsible for large amounts of emissions are allowed to continue to emit above a certain cap in exchange for projects taking place elsewhere that reduce emissions or remove carbon." See https://cdrprimer.org/read /concepts.

collective impact
John Kania and Mark Kramer define *collective impact* as "the commitment of a group of important actors from different sectors to a common agenda for solving a specific social problem . . . [which] involves a centralized infrastructure, a dedicated staff, and a structured process that leads to a common agenda, shared measurement, continuous communication, and mutually reinforcing activities among all participants." See https://ssir.org/articles/entry/collective_impact#.

corporate carbon footprint (CCF) / carbon footprint
A *carbon footprint* represents the total annual direct and indirect emissions of greenhouse gases—measured in carbon dioxide equivalents (CO_2e)—attributable to an organization, based on an accepted carbon accounting and reporting standard (e.g., GHG protocol).

corporate social responsibility (CSR)

The term *corporate social responsibility* is often used interchangeably with corporate citizenship or corporate responsibility to describe the social responsibility of business. It is also used more specifically to describe the corporate function having traditional components that include corporate philanthropy and employee volunteering and that is often associated with the branding and marketing functions of the corporation.

decarbonization

Decarbonization is a general term for processes or actions taken to reduce or remove greenhouse gas emissions caused by human activities.

design thinking

Design thinking is a set of abilities for creative problem solving. At its simplest, it uses a designer's mindset to identify problems or opportunities and create viable solutions. It uses a human-centered approach to gain deep empathy for those being designed for and utilizes an iterative process, including rapid prototyping and testing, to develop successful outcomes (see also the definition of human-centered design / user-centered design).

Dodd-Frank Act

The Dodd-Frank Wall Street Reform and Consumer Protection Act was enacted in 2010 and is considered the most significant federal legislation passed in response to the financial crisis of 2008–2009. It was primarily intended to overhaul the US financial system, but it incidentally altered reporting requirements for many public and private entities. See https://www.investopedia.com/terms/d/dodd-frank -financial-regulatory-reform-bill.asp.

earned revenue

Earned revenue is income generated by public benefit corporations and nongovernmental organizations that comes from sources other than donations.

environmental, social, and governance (ESG) criteria
Environmental, social, and governance (ESG) criteria "are a set of standards for a company's operations that socially conscious investors use to screen potential investments. Environmental criteria consider how a company performs as a steward of nature. Social criteria examine how it manages relationships with employees, suppliers, customers, and the communities where it operates. Governance deals with a company's leadership, executive pay, audits, internal controls, and shareholder rights." See https://www.investopedia.com/terms/e/environmental -social-and-governance-esg-criteria.asp.

equity
Equity is a fairness principle that recognizes how differences in access to opportunity, networks, or resources determine outcomes for individuals and that accommodates such differences in order to change the status quo. It is different from equality, which, while also about fairness, assumes similar starting places and involves treating everyone the same regardless of where they start. Other approaches to equity focus on "proportionality," or ensuring that people get what they deserve. In the social sector, the manifestation of equity is often the purposeful allocation of resources (e.g., opportunity, networks, funds, time, support) in a way that eliminates disparities in desired outcomes.

Financial Accounting Standards Board (FASB)
The *Financial Accounting Standards Board (FASB)* is "the independent, private-sector, not-for-profit organization . . . that establishes financial accounting and reporting standards for public and private companies and not-for-profit organizations that follow Generally Accepted Accounting Principles (GAAP). The FASB is recognized by the U.S. Securities and Exchange Commission as the designated accounting standard setter for public companies." See https://www.fasb.org/facts/.

Global Reporting Initiative (GRI)
The *Global Reporting Initiative* (known as GRI) "is an international independent standards organization that helps businesses, government and other organizations understand and communicate their impacts on issues such as climate change, human rights and corruption." See https://www.globalreporting.org/about-gri/.

Greenhouse Gas (GHG) Protocol Corporate Accounting and Reporting Standard
The *Greenhouse Gas (GHG) Protocol Corporate Accounting and Reporting Standard* "provides requirements and guidance for companies and other organizations preparing a corporate-level GHG emissions inventory." See https://ghgprotocol.org/corporate-standard.

human-centered design / user-centered design
Human- or user-centered design is often used interchangeably with design thinking (see the definition of design thinking). When it is distinguished from design thinking, it usually refers to the interactions between designer and end user that occur during the process of defining a problem or opportunity and developing a solution, including user empathy and engagement, solution co-design, prototyping, and testing.

impact investing
The Global Impact Investing Network defines *impact investing* as the act of making investments "with the intention to generate positive, measurable social and environmental impact alongside a financial return." See https://thegiin.org/impact-investing/.

impact measurement
Impact measurement identifies and considers the positive and negative effects that an innovation or organization has on people and the planet (based on a modification of a definition by the Global Impact Investing Network; see https://thegiin.org/imm/).

indirect impact
Indirect impact is impact that is not directly attributable to a firm's operations, including the delivery of its products or services. In the case of an entrepreneurial enterprise, the most significant indirect impact may be the creation of an entirely new market.

opportunity gap
An *opportunity gap* results when there is significant and persistent disparity in conditions, resources, effort, or activities that causes a disparity in outcomes for different groups. In educational improvement efforts, this term is sometimes used instead of "achievement gap"

to implicate the policies, practices, or systems created and enacted by those who shape the student's educational setting, rather than the achievement of the students who are subject to such factors.

philanthropist
A *philanthropist* is anyone who gives anything—time, money, experience, skills, and networks—in any amount to create a better world.

program-related investments (PRI)
The US Internal Revenue Service defines *program-related investments (PRIs)* as "those in which: 1) the primary purpose is to accomplish one or more of the [investing] foundation's exempt purposes, 2) production of income or appreciation of property is not a significant purpose, and 3) influencing legislation or taking part in political campaigns on behalf of candidates is not a purpose." See https://www.irs.gov /charities-non-profits/private-foundations/program-related -investments.

randomized controlled trial (RCT) / randomized evaluation
The Abdul Latif Jameel Poverty Action Lab (J-PAL) defines *randomized evaluation* as "a type of impact evaluation method. Study participants are randomly assigned to one or more groups that receive (different types of) an intervention, known as the 'treatment group' or groups, and a comparison group that does not receive any intervention. Researchers then measure the outcomes of interest in the treatment and comparison groups. Randomized evaluations make it possible to obtain a rigorous and unbiased estimate of the causal impact of an intervention; in other words, what specific changes to participants' lives can be attributed to the program. They also allow researchers and policymakers to tailor their research designs to answer specific questions about the effectiveness of a program and its underlying theory of change." See https://www.povertyactionlab.org/resource/introduction -randomized-evaluations.

scale
Scale is the process of realizing the greatest possible impact of an innovation so that it matches the level of its societal need and maximizes its potential. A variety of strategies may be used to that effect, including growing an organization, replicating a model, partnering

with the government, influencing regulations, or changing cultures and norms.

social enterprise / social venture

Social innovation practitioners use *social enterprise* in one of two ways: either broadly to designate the human pursuit of social progress or more narrowly to describe an organization, either for profit or non-profit, that pursues social and environmental goals. In situations involving trade-offs, the social mission guides decision-making. For-profit social enterprises maximize social impact alongside financial return, whether as a concession to profitability or in addition to market-rate returns.

Social ventures are organizations (for profit, nonprofit, or hybrid) for which the primary purpose is to solve a social or environmental problem to benefit society as a whole. The cost of operations is offset, as much as possible, through income earned by the venture. Social ventures may be structured as nonprofit, for profit, or a hybrid of the two.

social entrepreneur / impact entrepreneur

Impact professionals use the term *social entrepreneur* in one of two ways. The first designates a person who pursues an innovative solution to address a social problem regardless of the form the solution might take. The second describes a person who establishes a social enterprise as a means of addressing social problems or effecting social change. *Impact entrepreneur* can be used interchangeably with social entrepreneur to refer to entrepreneurs concerned with social or environmental issues.

social entrepreneurship

Roger L. Martin and Sally Osberg define *social entrepreneurship* as having "the following three components: (1) identifying a stable but inherently unjust equilibrium that causes the exclusion, marginalization, or suffering of a segment of humanity that lacks the financial means or political clout to achieve any transformative benefit on its own; (2) identifying an opportunity in this unjust equilibrium, developing a social value proposition, and bringing to bear inspiration, creativity, direct action, courage, and fortitude, thereby challenging the stable state's hegemony; and (3) forging a new, stable equilibrium that releases trapped potential or alleviates the suffering of the targeted group, and through imitation and the creation of a stable ecosystem around the new equilibrium ensuring a better future for the targeted group and even society at large." See https://ssir.org/articles/entry/social_entrepreneurship_the_case_for_definition#.

social impact
Social impact is the change (either positive or negative) for people and communities that results from a deliberate activity or service. It is sometimes used to reflect social and environmental outcomes as measurements.

social impact bonds (SIBs) / pay for success bonds
A *social impact bond* "is a contract with the public sector or governing authority, whereby it pays for better social outcomes in certain areas and passes on the part of the savings achieved to investors. A social impact bond is not a bond, per se, since repayment and return on investment are contingent upon the achievement of desired social outcomes. If the objectives are not achieved, investors receive neither a return nor repayment of principal. SIBs derive their name from the fact that their investors are typically those who are interested in not just the financial return on their investment, but also in its social impact." See https://www.investopedia.com/terms/s/social-impact-bond.asp.

social innovation(s) / social innovator
Social innovation is the process of developing and deploying effective solutions to challenging and often systemic social and environmental issues that results in products or services that (a) present a significant or disruptive change in model or approach; (b) provide for the most vulnerable or low-resourced communities; and (c) will have enduring and sustained positive impact. Social innovations often involve some form of multisector collaboration across public, private, and social sector organizations.

social progress
Social progress, as defined by the Social Progress Imperative, "is the capacity of a society to meet the basic human needs of its citizens, establish the building blocks that allow citizens and communities to

enhance and sustain the quality of their lives, and create the conditions for all individuals to reach their full potential." See https://www.socialprogress.org/index/global/methodology.

social sector

When used in contrast to the public and private sectors, the term *social sector* includes those organizations and enterprises for which the primary focus is social impact and that are neither public nor private sector organizations, including but not limited to nonprofits and nongovernmental organizations (NGOs), research and academic institutions, and philanthropic organizations. The term is sometimes used more broadly to designate all organizations created with the intention of producing a societal benefit regardless of sector.

social value

Social value is the value accrued to society (as opposed to a private individual) that results from activities by a variety of actors, such as businesses, social enterprises, philanthropists, government agencies, or nongovernmental organizations (NGOs).

Sustainability Accounting Standards Board (SASB)

The *Sustainability Accounting Standards Board (SASB)* is "an independent nonprofit organization that sets standards to guide the disclosure of financially material sustainability information by companies to their investors. SASB Standards identify the subset of environmental, social, and governance (ESG) issues most relevant to financial performance in [multiple] industries." See https://www.sasb.org/about/.

theory of change

A *theory of change* is a comprehensive, research-based description of how a social innovation will actually achieve the desired impact. It includes a series of cause-and-effect relationships that map the multiple intermediate steps by which a social innovation achieves social impact.

value chain

A *value chain* is an analytical framework that describes the full range of activities needed to create a product or service, usually comprised of defined steps or stages that describe the journey from research and ideation to distribution at scale.

value proposition
The *value proposition* is the value an innovation or enterprise promises to deliver. A social value proposition tells stakeholders how the solution will serve current and unmet needs, what benefits it will provide compared to other solutions, and what impact it will have on a community.

venture capital
Venture capital (VC) is "a form of private equity and a type of financing that investors provide to startup companies and small businesses that are believed to have long-term growth potential." See https://www.investopedia.com/terms/v/venturecapital.asp.

Index

Note: Figures are identified by *f* following the page number. Tables are identified by *t* following the page number. Endnote information is identified by *n* and note number following the page number.

About the Editor

NEIL MALHOTRA is the Edith M. Cornell Professor of Political Economy at the Stanford Graduate School of Business. He has been teaching business ethics at the Stanford Graduate School of Business since 2008. He is also the director of the Center for Social Innovation, where he manages the Certificate in Public Management and Social Innovation. In addition to developing a curriculum focused on social issues, impact measurement, and mission-driven business, he manages cocurricular activities related to impact investing, social entrepreneurship, and nonprofit management. He is the coauthor of *Leading with Values: Strategies for Making Ethical Decisions in Business and Life*. His research has investigated issues such as democratic accountability, political polarization, and the relationship among business, society, and government. Specifically, he has researched corporate self-regulation, the political preferences of business elites, and the economic effects of political polarization. He has published over seventy-five articles in leading journals across the natural and social sciences, including the *American Political Science Review*, the *American Journal of Political Science*, the *Journal of Politics*, *Science*, and the *Proceedings of the National Academy of Sciences*. He received his PhD in political science from Stanford University and his BA in economics from Yale University.